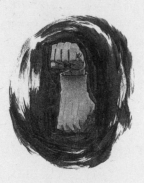

The story's still pretty gloomy in this volume.
When that happens, it usually ends up affecting my
actual life as well. Planning things in your head
is one thing, but putting pen to paper is another.

KOHEI HORIKOSHI

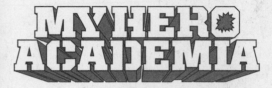

MY HERO ACADEMIA

9

SHONEN JUMP Manga Edition

STORY & ART **KOHEI HORIKOSHI**

TRANSLATION & ENGLISH ADAPTATION **Caleb Cook**
TOUCH-UP ART & LETTERING **John Hunt**
DESIGNER **Shawn Carrico**
SHONEN JUMP SERIES EDITOR **John Bae**
GRAPHIC NOVEL EDITOR **Mike Montesa**

BOKU NO HERO ACADEMIA © 2014 by Kohei Horikoshi
All rights reserved.
First published in Japan in 2014 by SHUEISHA Inc., Tokyo.
English translation rights arranged by SHUEISHA Inc.

The stories, characters and incidents mentioned in this publication are entirely fictional.

Printed in the U.S.A.

Published by VIZ Media, LLC
P.O. Box 77010
San Francisco, CA 94107

10 9 8 7 6 5 4 3
First printing, August 2017
Third printing, August 2018

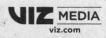
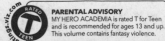

MY HERO ACADEMIA

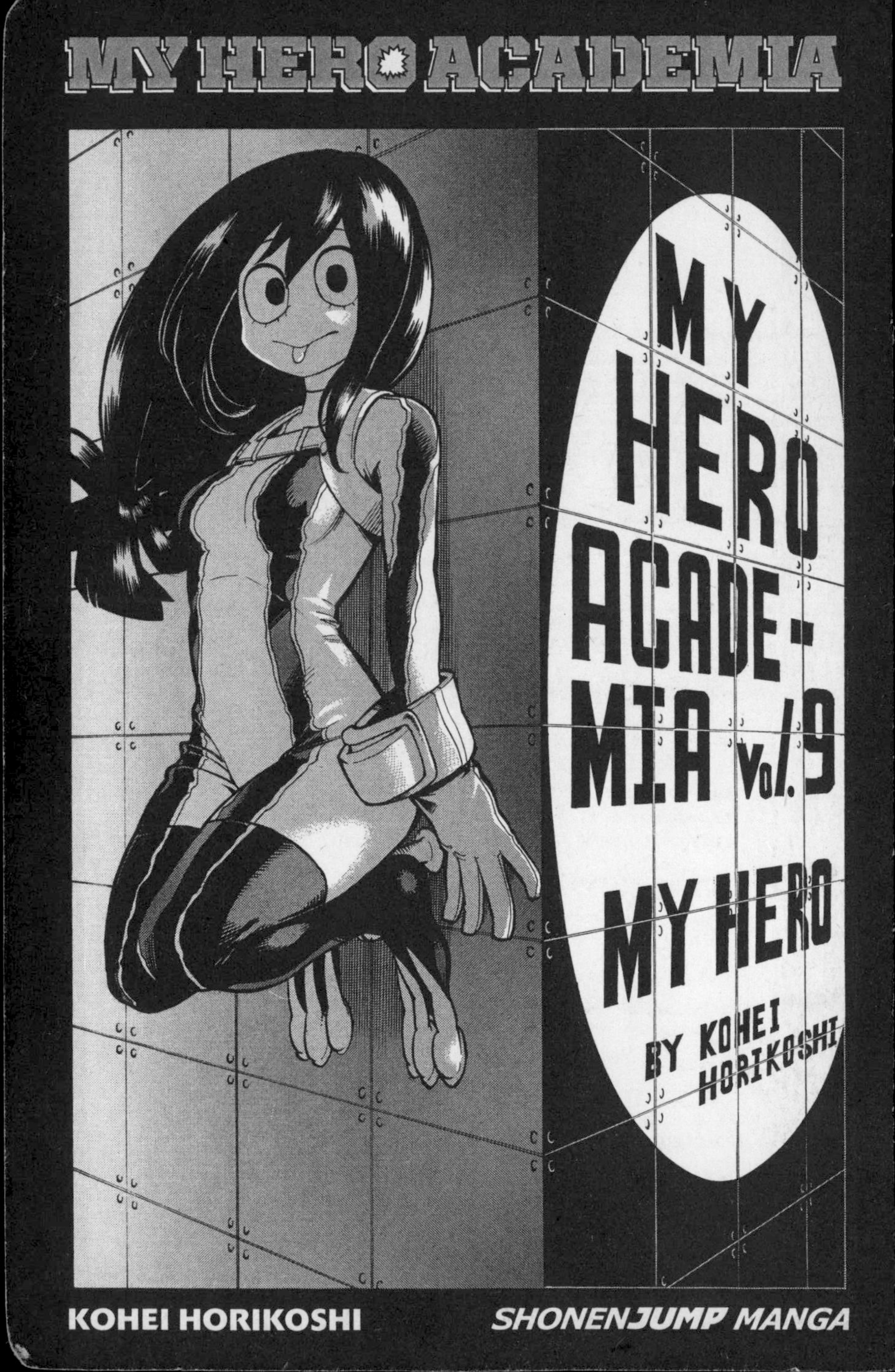
MY HERO ACADE-MIA Vol. 9
MY HERO
BY KOHEI HORIKOSHI

KOHEI HORIKOSHI

SHONEN JUMP MANGA

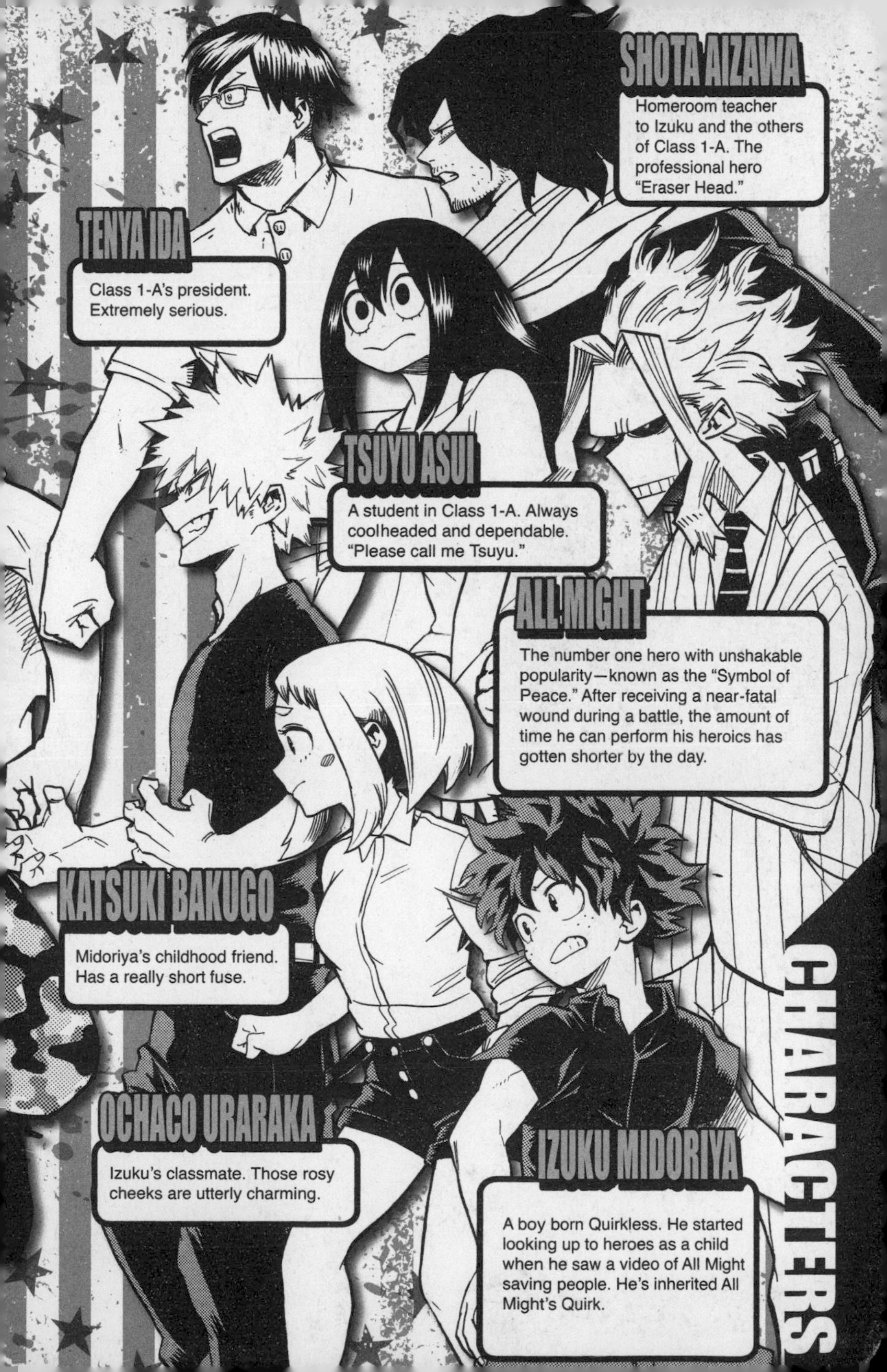

CHARACTERS
SHOTA AIZAWA
Homeroom teacher to Izuku and the others of Class 1-A. The professional hero "Eraser Head."
TENYA IDA
Class 1-A's president. Extremely serious.
TSUYU ASUI
A student in Class 1-A. Always coolheaded and dependable. "Please call me Tsuyu."
ALL MIGHT
The number one hero with unshakable popularity—known as the "Symbol of Peace." After receiving a near-fatal wound during a battle, the amount of time he can perform his heroics has gotten shorter by the day.
KATSUKI BAKUGO
Midoriya's childhood friend. Has a really short fuse.
IZUKU MIDORIYA
A boy born Quirkless. He started looking up to heroes as a child when he saw a video of All Might saving people. He's inherited All Might's Quirk.
OCHACO URARAKA
Izuku's classmate. Those rosy cheeks are utterly charming.

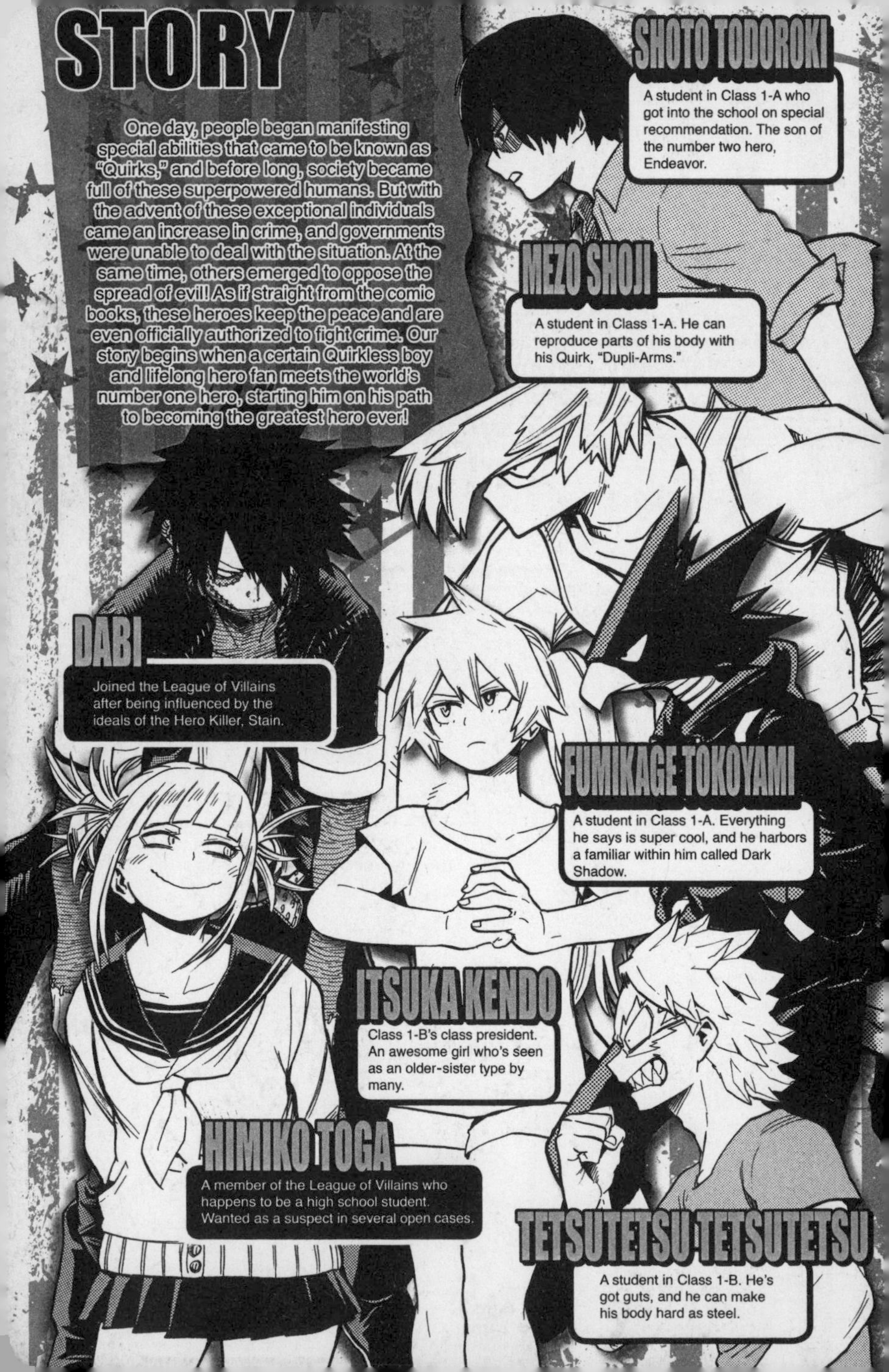

STORY

One day, people began manifesting special abilities that came to be known as "Quirks," and before long, society became full of these superpowered humans. But with the advent of these exceptional individuals came an increase in crime, and governments were unable to deal with the situation. At the same time, others emerged to oppose the spread of evil! As if straight from the comic books, these heroes keep the peace and are even officially authorized to fight crime. Our story begins when a certain Quirkless boy and lifelong hero fan meets the world's number one hero, starting him on his path to becoming the greatest hero ever!

SHOTO TODOROKI

A student in Class 1-A who got into the school on special recommendation. The son of the number two hero, Endeavor.

MEZO SHOJI

A student in Class 1-A. He can reproduce parts of his body with his Quirk, "Dupli-Arms."

DABI

Joined the League of Villains after being influenced by the ideals of the Hero Killer, Stain.

FUMIKAGE TOKOYAMI

A student in Class 1-A. Everything he says is super cool, and he harbors a familiar within him called Dark Shadow.

ITSUKA KENDO

Class 1-B's class president. An awesome girl who's seen as an older-sister type by many.

HIMIKO TOGA

A member of the League of Villains who happens to be a high school student. Wanted as a suspect in several open cases.

TETSUTETSU TETSUTETSU

A student in Class 1-B. He's got guts, and he can make his body hard as steel.

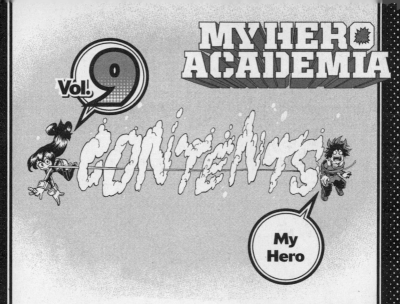

MY HERO ACADEMIA

Vol. 9

CONTENTS

My Hero

No.72	Day Two	7
No.73	Good Evening	27
No.74	Smoke Signal	49
No.75	Stake Your Life, Hero!	69
No.76	My Hero	89
No.77	It's Okay	113
No.78	Whirling Chaos	133
No.79	Drive It Home, Iron Fist!!!	153
No.80	Establishing the Bakugo Bodyguard Brigade	173

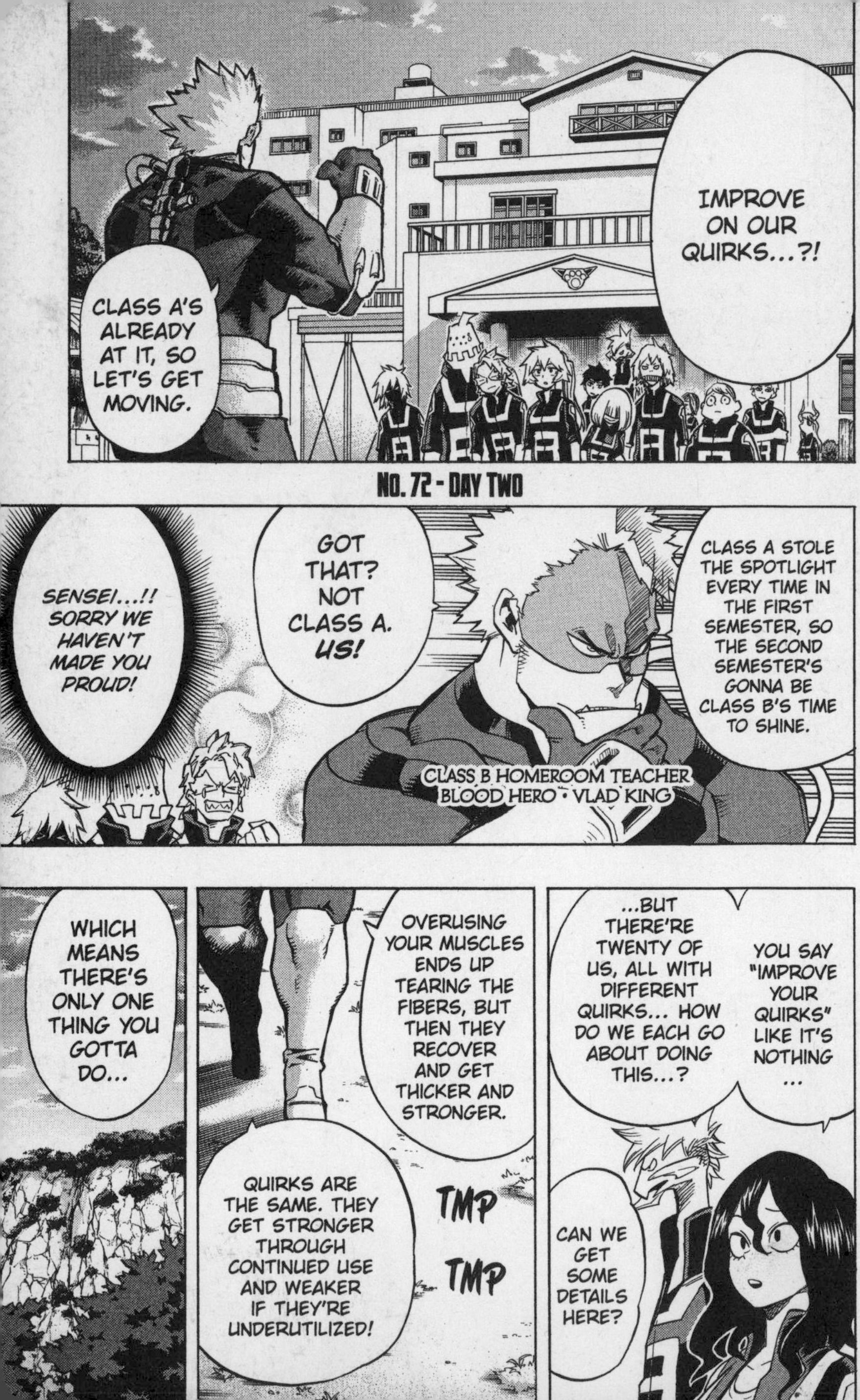
IMPROVE ON OUR QUIRKS...?!
CLASS A'S ALREADY AT IT, SO LET'S GET MOVING.
NO. 72 - DAY TWO
CLASS A STOLE THE SPOTLIGHT EVERY TIME IN THE FIRST SEMESTER, SO THE SECOND SEMESTER'S GONNA BE CLASS B'S TIME TO SHINE.
CLASS B HOMEROOM TEACHER BLOOD HERO • VLAD KING
GOT THAT? NOT CLASS A. US!
SENSEI...!! SORRY WE HAVEN'T MADE YOU PROUD!
YOU SAY "IMPROVE YOUR QUIRKS" LIKE IT'S NOTHING...
...BUT THERE'RE TWENTY OF US, ALL WITH DIFFERENT QUIRKS... HOW DO WE EACH GO ABOUT DOING THIS...?
CAN WE GET SOME DETAILS HERE?
OVERUSING YOUR MUSCLES ENDS UP TEARING THE FIBERS, BUT THEN THEY RECOVER AND GET THICKER AND STRONGER.
QUIRKS ARE THE SAME. THEY GET STRONGER THROUGH CONTINUED USE AND WEAKER IF THEY'RE UNDERUTILIZED!
TMP
TMP
WHICH MEANS THERE'S ONLY ONE THING YOU GOTTA DO...

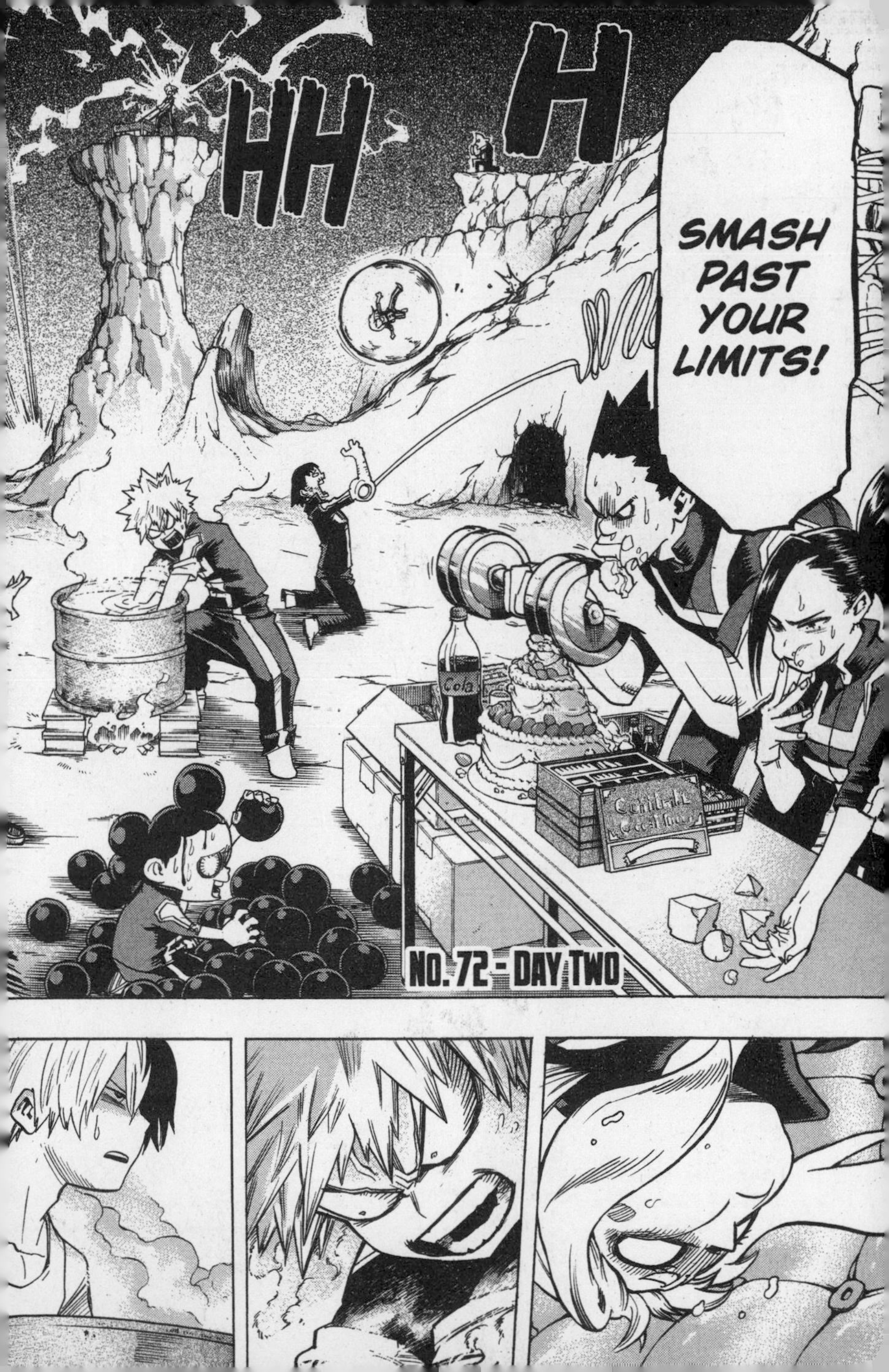
SMASH PAST YOUR LIMITS!
HH H
Cola
No. 72 - DAY TWO

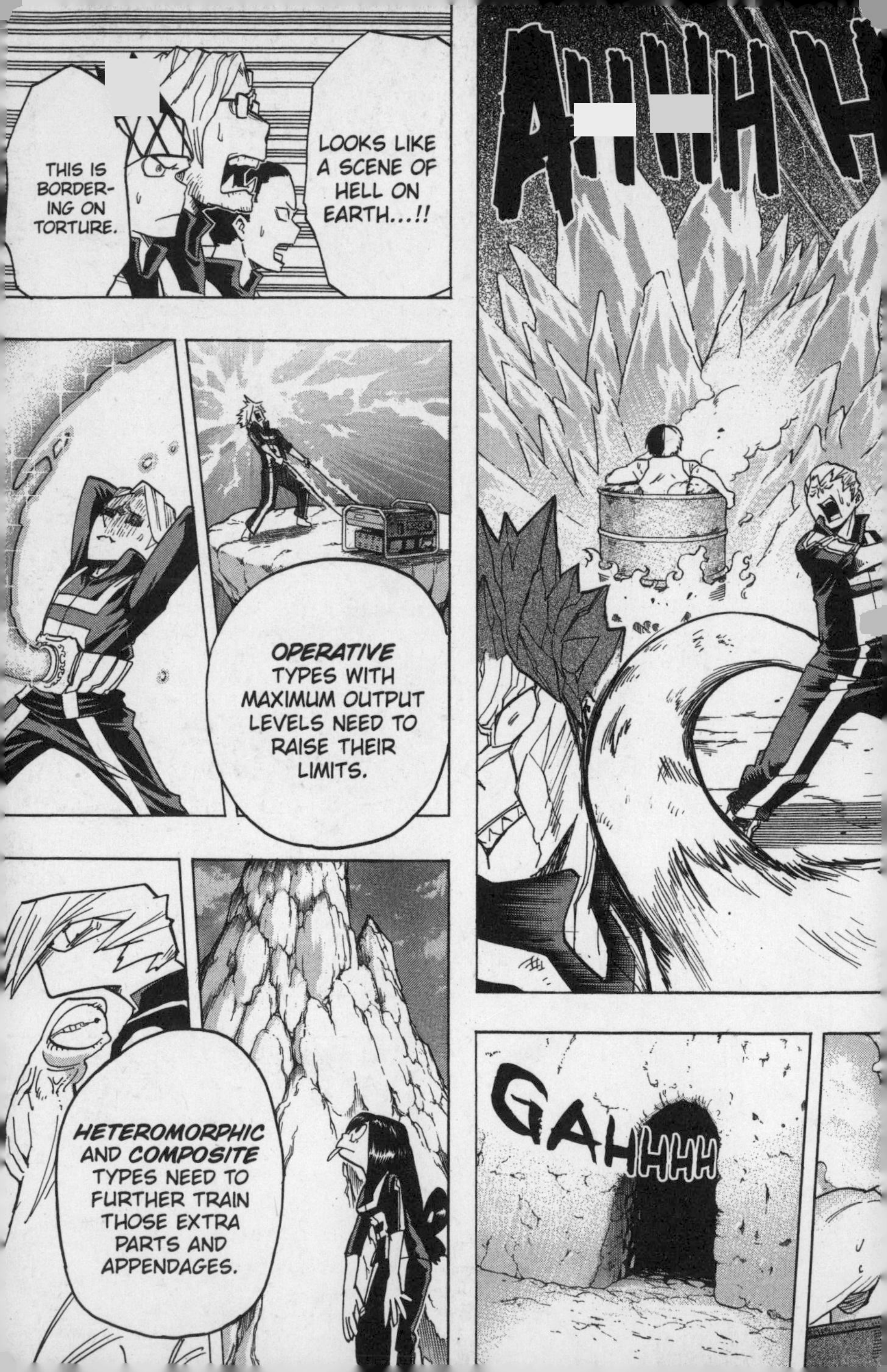
AHHHH
LOOKS LIKE A SCENE OF HELL ON EARTH...!!
THIS IS BORDERING ON TORTURE.
OPERATIVE TYPES WITH MAXIMUM OUTPUT LEVELS NEED TO RAISE THEIR LIMITS.
GAHHHH
HETEROMORPHIC AND *COMPOSITE* TYPES NEED TO FURTHER TRAIN THOSE EXTRA PARTS AND APPENDAGES.

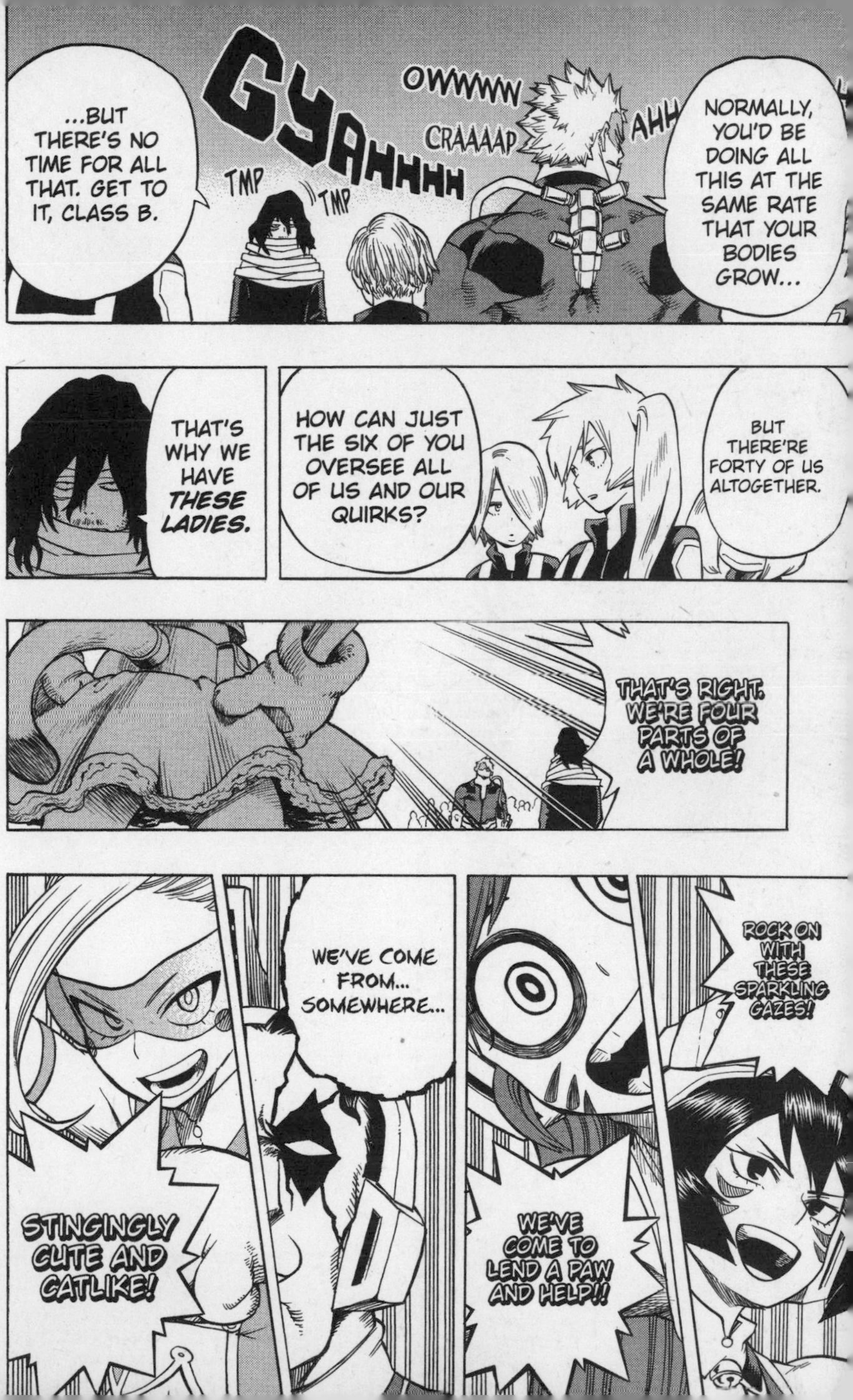
NORMALLY, YOU'D BE DOING ALL THIS AT THE SAME RATE THAT YOUR BODIES GROW...
AHH
CRAAAAP
OWWWWW
GYAHHHHH
TMP
TMP
...BUT THERE'S NO TIME FOR ALL THAT. GET TO IT, CLASS B.
BUT THERE'RE FORTY OF US ALTOGETHER.
HOW CAN JUST THE SIX OF YOU OVERSEE ALL OF US AND OUR QUIRKS?
THAT'S WHY WE HAVE *THESE LADIES.*
THAT'S RIGHT. WE'RE FOUR PARTS OF A WHOLE!
ROCK ON WITH THESE SPARKLING GAZES!
WE'VE COME TO LEND A PAW AND HELP!!
WE'VE COME FROM... SOMEWHERE...
STINGINGLY CUTE AND CATLIKE!

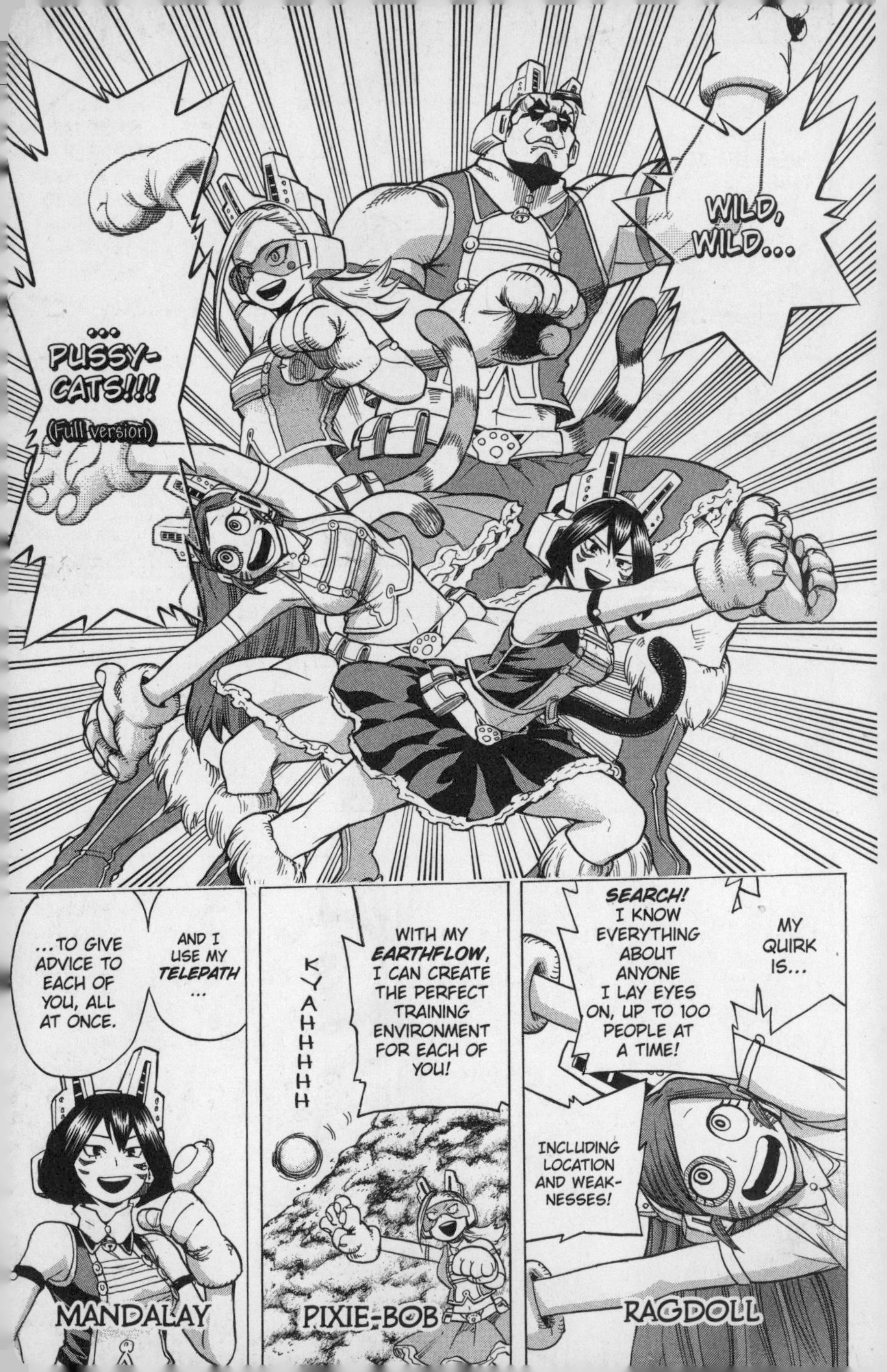
WILD, WILD...
...PUSSY-CATS!!!
(Full version)
MY QUIRK IS...
SEARCH! I KNOW EVERYTHING ABOUT ANYONE I LAY EYES ON, UP TO 100 PEOPLE AT A TIME!
INCLUDING LOCATION AND WEAK-NESSES!
RAGDOLL
WITH MY EARTHFLOW, I CAN CREATE THE PERFECT TRAINING ENVIRONMENT FOR EACH OF YOU!
KYAHHHHH
PIXIE-BOB
AND I USE MY TELEPATH...
...TO GIVE ADVICE TO EACH OF YOU, ALL AT ONCE.
MANDALAY

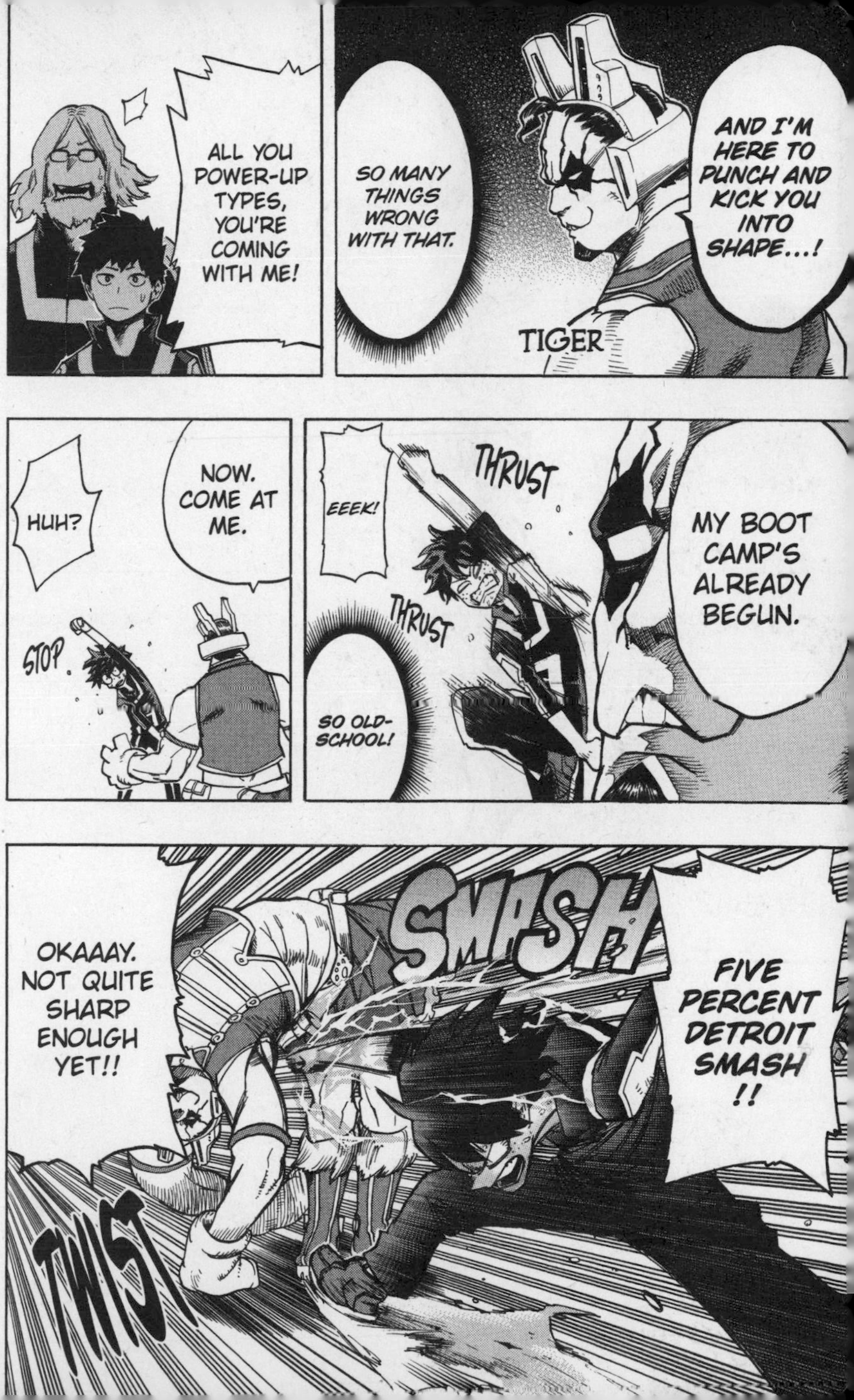
AND I'M HERE TO PUNCH AND KICK YOU INTO SHAPE...!
TIGER
SO MANY THINGS WRONG WITH THAT.
ALL YOU POWER-UP TYPES, YOU'RE COMING WITH ME!
MY BOOT CAMP'S ALREADY BEGUN.
THRUST
EEEK!
THRUST
SO OLD-SCHOOL!
NOW. COME AT ME.
HUH?
STOP
FIVE PERCENT DETROIT SMASH!!
SMASH
OKAAAY. NOT QUITE SHARP ENOUGH YET!!
TWIST

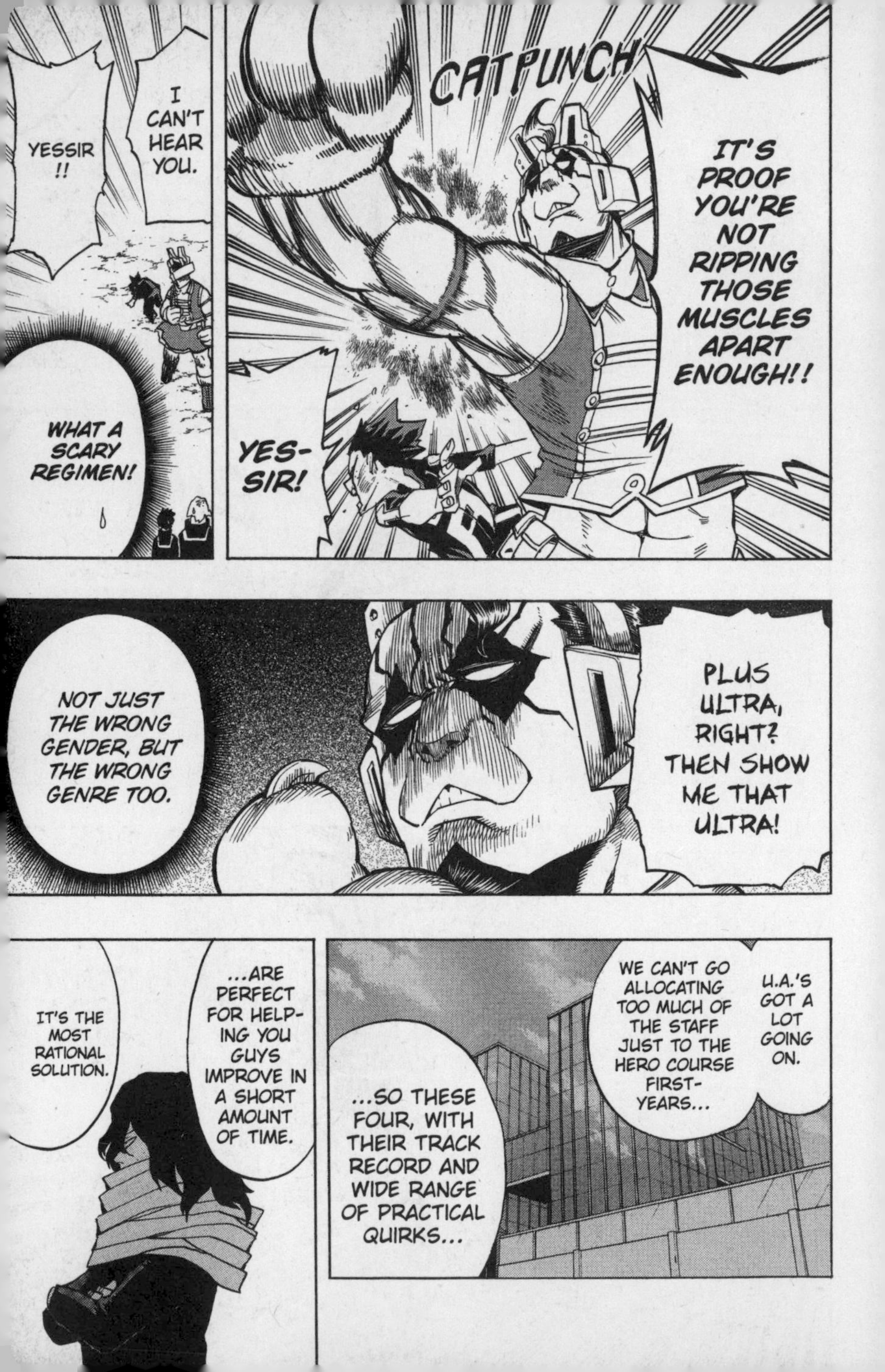
CATPUNCH
IT'S PROOF YOU'RE NOT RIPPING THOSE MUSCLES APART ENOUGH!!
YES-SIR!
I CAN'T HEAR YOU.
YESSIR!!
WHAT A SCARY REGIMEN!
PLUS ULTRA, RIGHT? THEN SHOW ME THAT ULTRA!
NOT JUST THE WRONG GENDER, BUT THE WRONG GENRE TOO.
U.A.'S GOT A LOT GOING ON.
WE CAN'T GO ALLOCATING TOO MUCH OF THE STAFF JUST TO THE HERO COURSE FIRST-YEARS...
...SO THESE FOUR, WITH THEIR TRACK RECORD AND WIDE RANGE OF PRACTICAL QUIRKS...
...ARE PERFECT FOR HELPING YOU GUYS IMPROVE IN A SHORT AMOUNT OF TIME.
IT'S THE MOST RATIONAL SOLUTION.

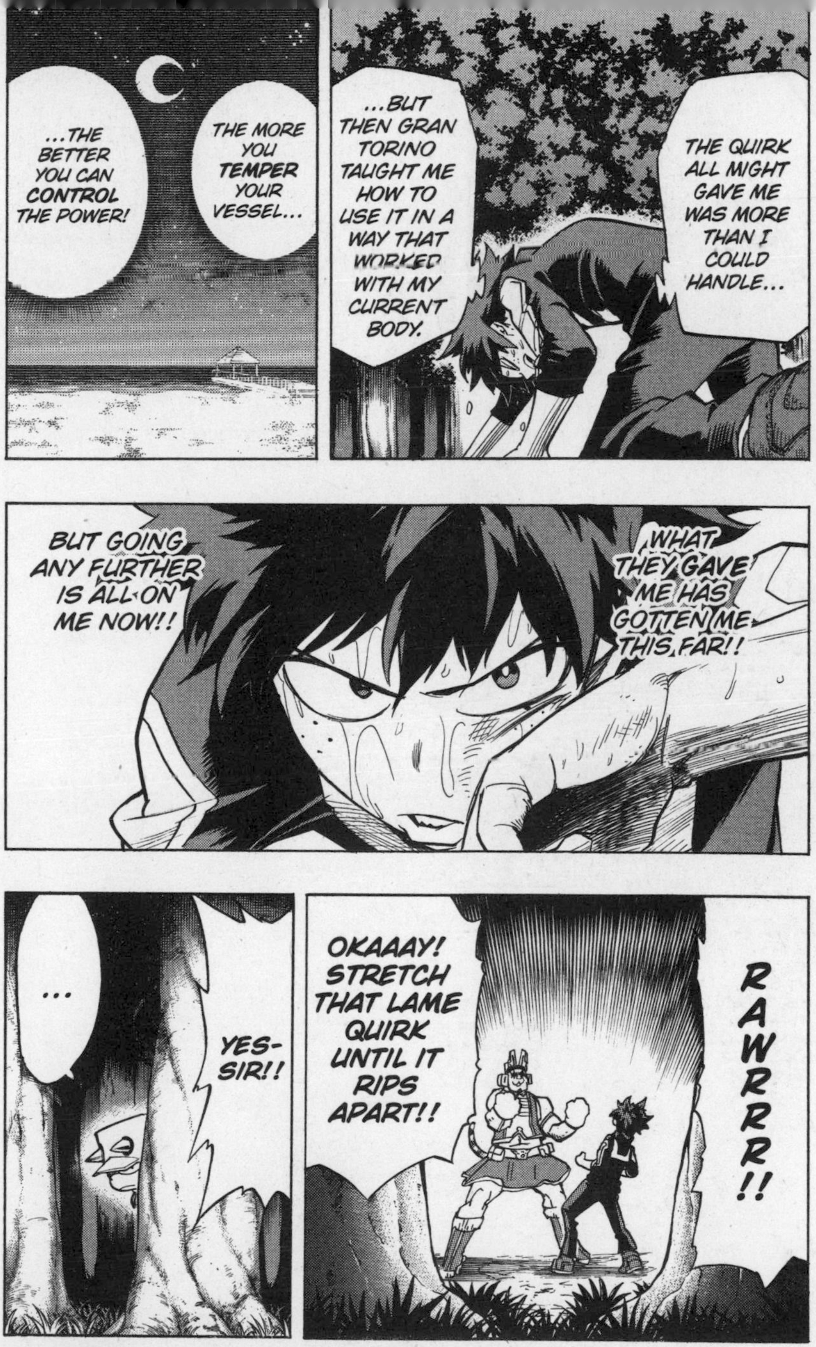
THE QUIRK ALL MIGHT GAVE ME WAS MORE THAN I COULD HANDLE...
...BUT THEN GRAN TORINO TAUGHT ME HOW TO USE IT IN A WAY THAT WORKED WITH MY CURRENT BODY.
THE MORE YOU TEMPER YOUR VESSEL...
...THE BETTER YOU CAN CONTROL THE POWER!
WHAT THEY GAVE ME HAS GOTTEN ME THIS FAR!!
BUT GOING ANY FURTHER IS ALL ON ME NOW!!
RAWRRR!!
OKAAAY! STRETCH THAT LAME QUIRK UNTIL IT RIPS APART!!
YES-SIR!!
...

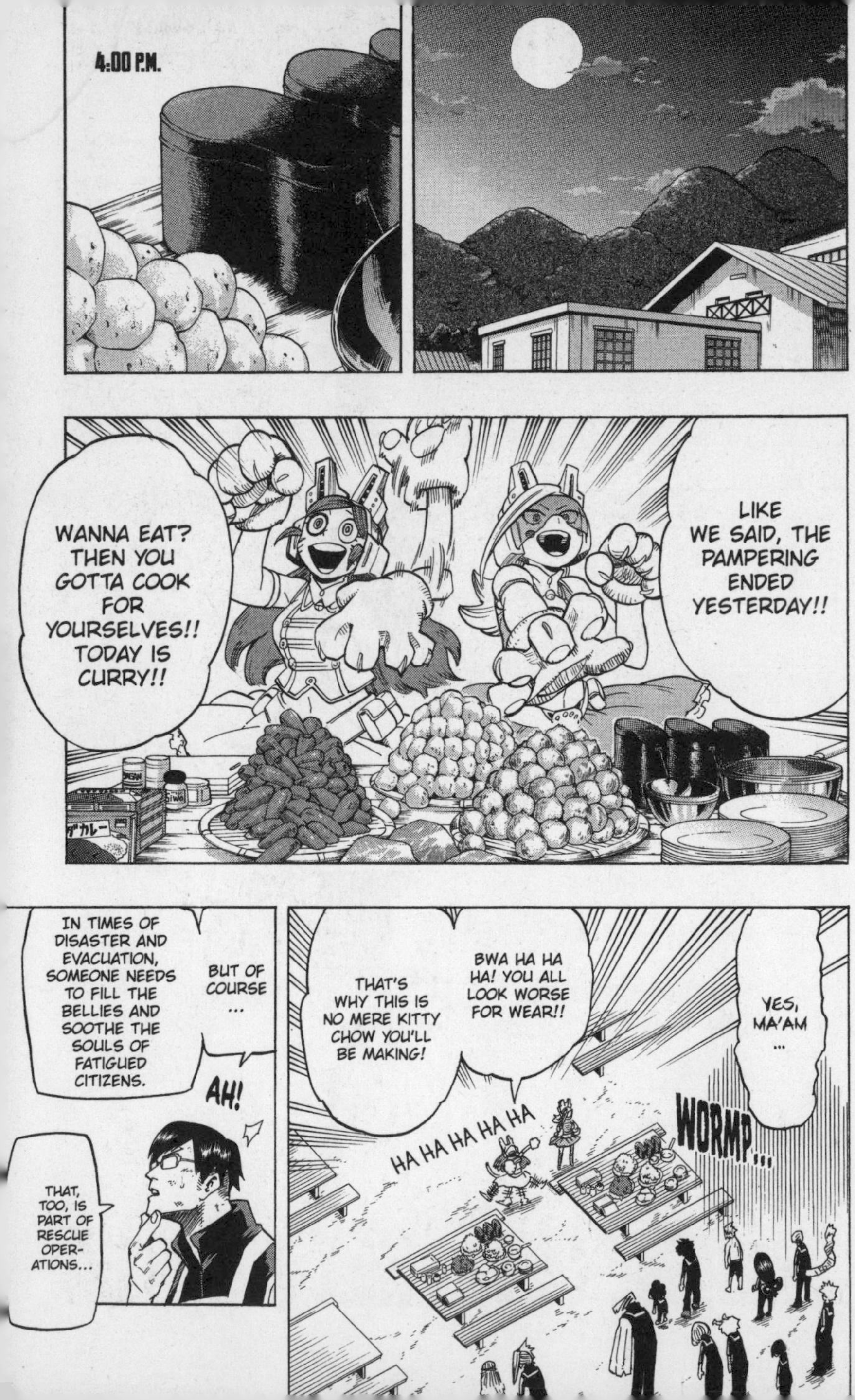
4:00 P.M.
LIKE WE SAID, THE PAMPERING ENDED YESTERDAY!!
WANNA EAT? THEN YOU GOTTA COOK FOR YOURSELVES!! TODAY IS CURRY!!
YES, MA'AM ...
BWA HA HA HA! YOU ALL LOOK WORSE FOR WEAR!!
THAT'S WHY THIS IS NO MERE KITTY CHOW YOU'LL BE MAKING!
WORMP...
HA HA HA HA HA
BUT OF COURSE ...
IN TIMES OF DISASTER AND EVACUATION, SOMEONE NEEDS TO FILL THE BELLIES AND SOOTHE THE SOULS OF FATIGUED CITIZENS.
AH!
THAT, TOO, IS PART OF RESCUE OPERATIONS...

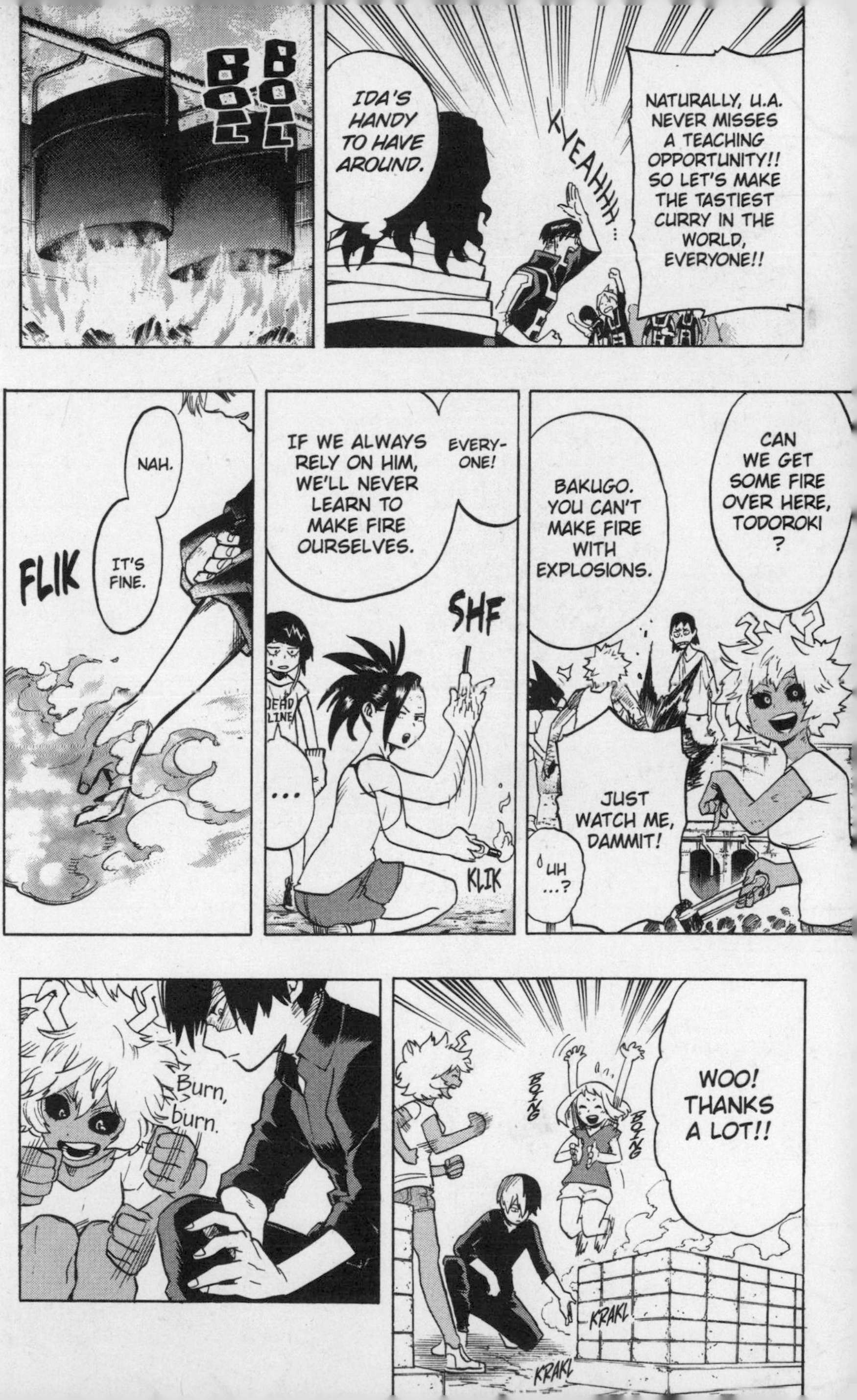
NATURALLY, U.A. NEVER MISSES A TEACHING OPPORTUNITY!! SO LET'S MAKE THE TASTIEST CURRY IN THE WORLD, EVERYONE!!
KYEAHHH...
IDA'S HANDY TO HAVE AROUND.
BOIL
BOIL
CAN WE GET SOME FIRE OVER HERE, TODOROKI?
BAKUGO. YOU CAN'T MAKE FIRE WITH EXPLOSIONS.
JUST WATCH ME, DAMMIT!
UH ...?
EVERYONE!
IF WE ALWAYS RELY ON HIM, WE'LL NEVER LEARN TO MAKE FIRE OURSELVES.
SHF
...
KLIK
NAH.
IT'S FINE.
FLIK
WOO! THANKS A LOT!!
BOING
BOING
KRAKL
KRAKL
Burn, burn.

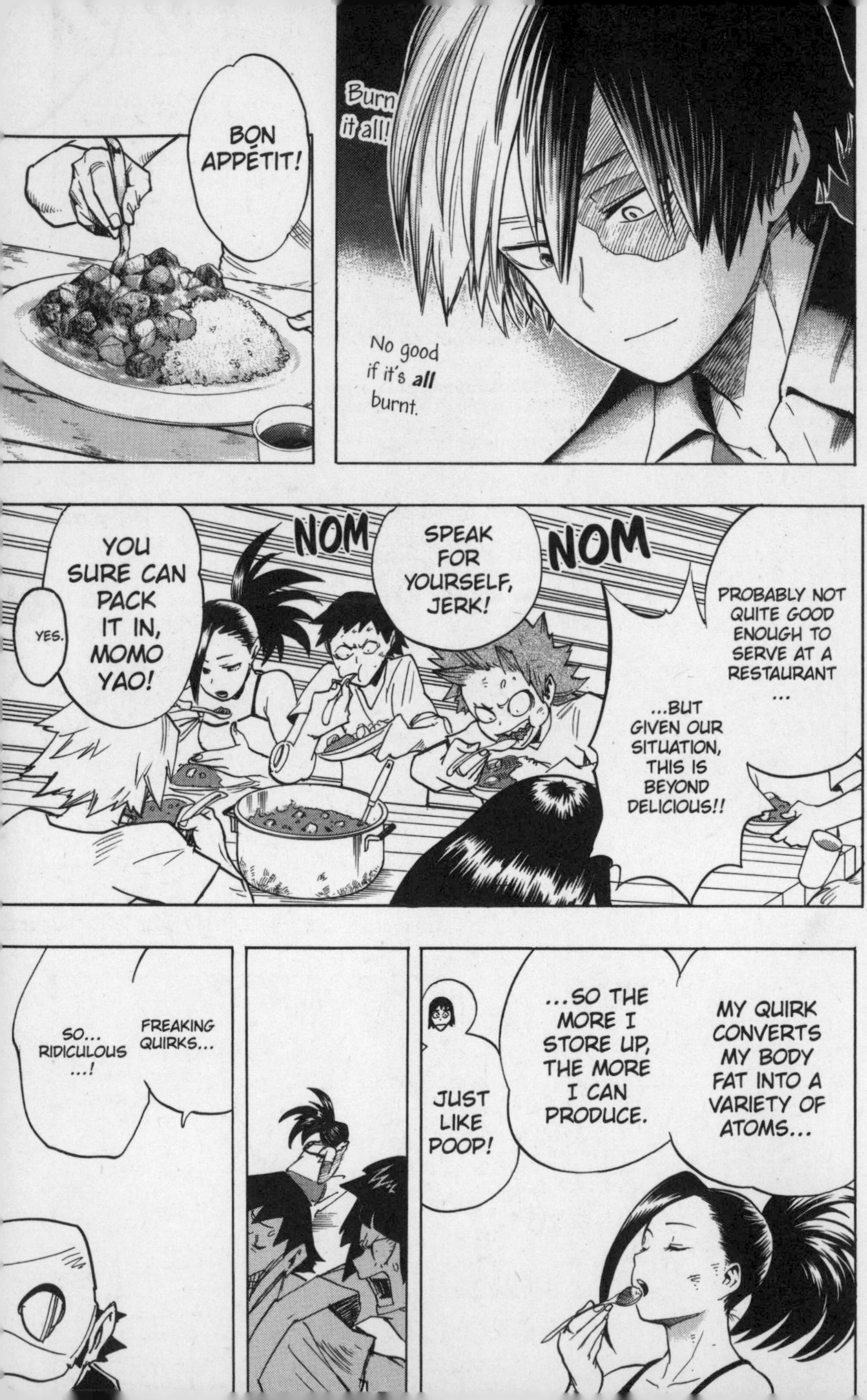
Burn it all!
No good if it's **all** burnt.
BON APPÉTIT!
PROBABLY NOT QUITE GOOD ENOUGH TO SERVE AT A RESTAURANT...
...BUT GIVEN OUR SITUATION, THIS IS BEYOND DELICIOUS!!
NOM
SPEAK FOR YOURSELF, JERK!
NOM
YOU SURE CAN PACK IT IN, MOMO YAO!
YES.
MY QUIRK CONVERTS MY BODY FAT INTO A VARIETY OF ATOMS...
...SO THE MORE I STORE UP, THE MORE I CAN PRODUCE.
JUST LIKE POOP!
FREAKING QUIRKS...
SO... RIDICULOUS ...!

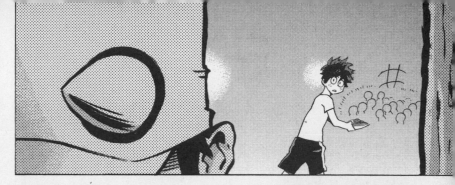

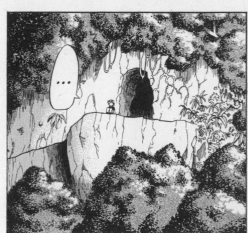

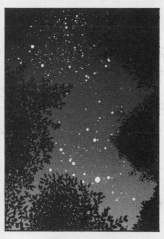

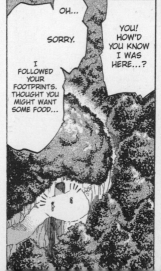

...
GRUMBLE
I BET YOU'RE HUNGRY.
HERE'S A PLATE FOR YOU.
It's curry..
SHOCK
YOU! HOW'D YOU KNOW I WAS HERE...?
OH...
SORRY.
I FOLLOWED YOUR FOOTPRINTS. THOUGHT YOU MIGHT WANT SOME FOOD...

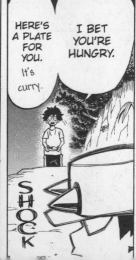

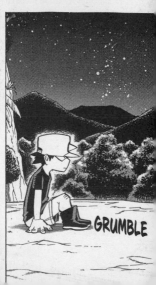

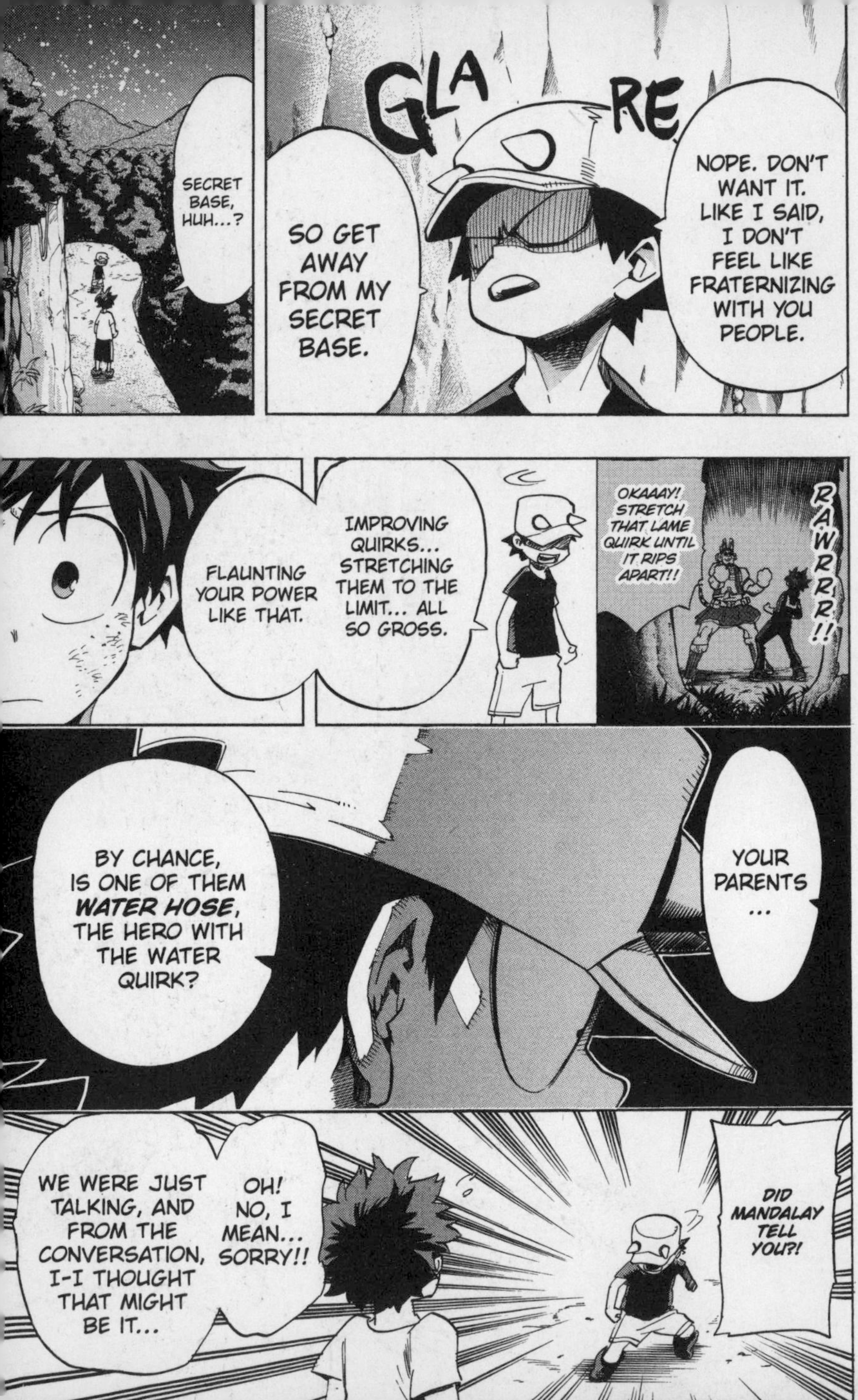
GLARE
NOPE. DON'T WANT IT. LIKE I SAID, I DON'T FEEL LIKE FRATERNIZING WITH YOU PEOPLE.
SO GET AWAY FROM MY SECRET BASE.
SECRET BASE, HUH...?
RAWRRR!!
OKAAAY! STRETCH THAT LAME QUIRK UNTIL IT RIPS APART!!
IMPROVING QUIRKS... STRETCHING THEM TO THE LIMIT... ALL SO GROSS.
FLAUNTING YOUR POWER LIKE THAT.
YOUR PARENTS ...
BY CHANCE, IS ONE OF THEM ***WATER HOSE***, THE HERO WITH THE WATER QUIRK?
DID MANDALAY TELL YOU?!
OH! NO, I MEAN... SORRY!!
WE WERE JUST TALKING, AND FROM THE CONVERSATION, I-I THOUGHT THAT MIGHT BE IT...

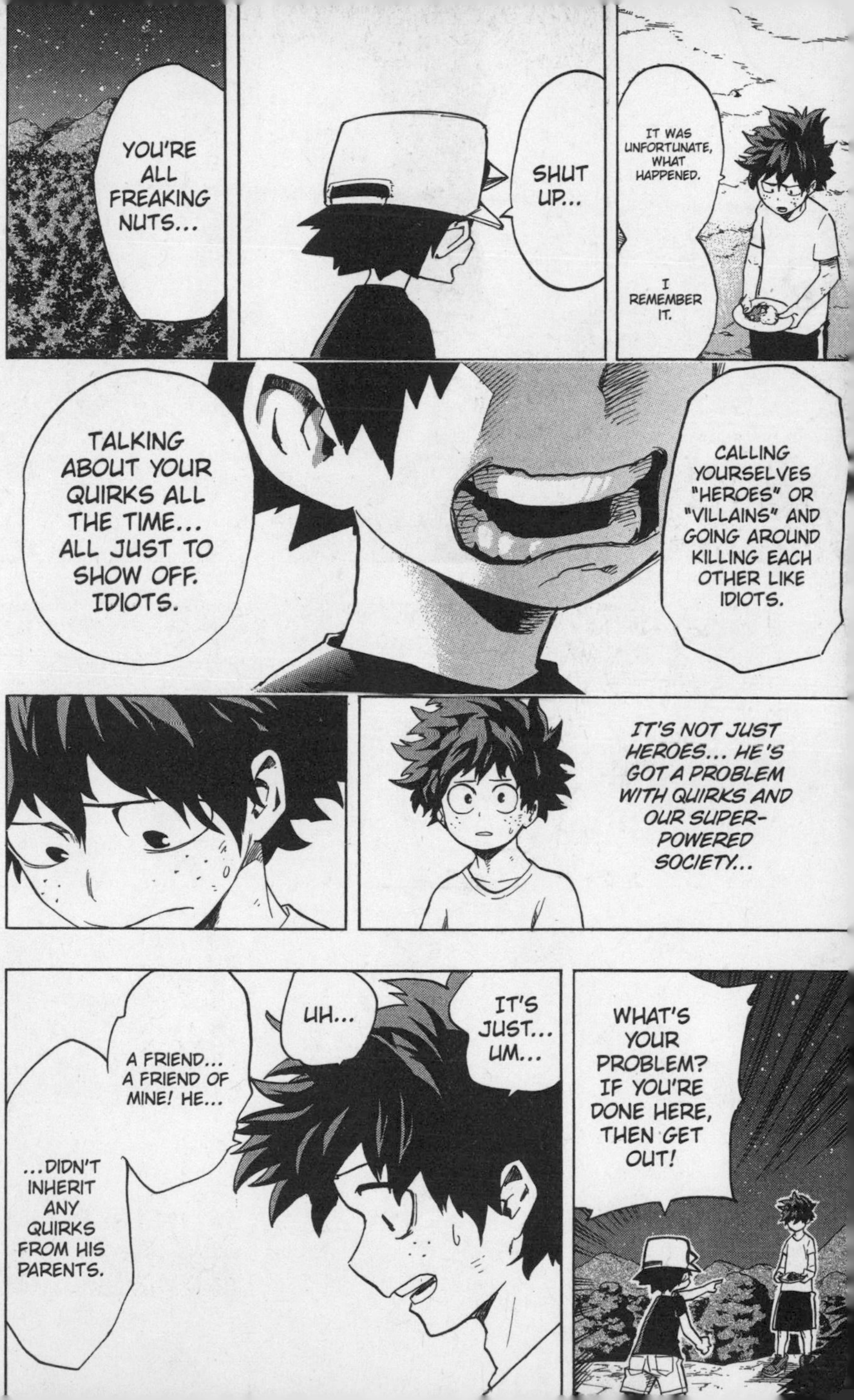

IT WAS UNFORTUNATE, WHAT HAPPENED.
I REMEMBER IT.
SHUT UP...
YOU'RE ALL FREAKING NUTS...
CALLING YOURSELVES "HEROES" OR "VILLAINS" AND GOING AROUND KILLING EACH OTHER LIKE IDIOTS.
TALKING ABOUT YOUR QUIRKS ALL THE TIME... ALL JUST TO SHOW OFF. IDIOTS.
IT'S NOT JUST HEROES... HE'S GOT A PROBLEM WITH QUIRKS AND OUR SUPER-POWERED SOCIETY...
WHAT'S YOUR PROBLEM? IF YOU'RE DONE HERE, THEN GET OUT!
IT'S JUST... UM...
UH...
A FRIEND... A FRIEND OF MINE! HE...
...DIDN'T INHERIT ANY QUIRKS FROM HIS PARENTS.

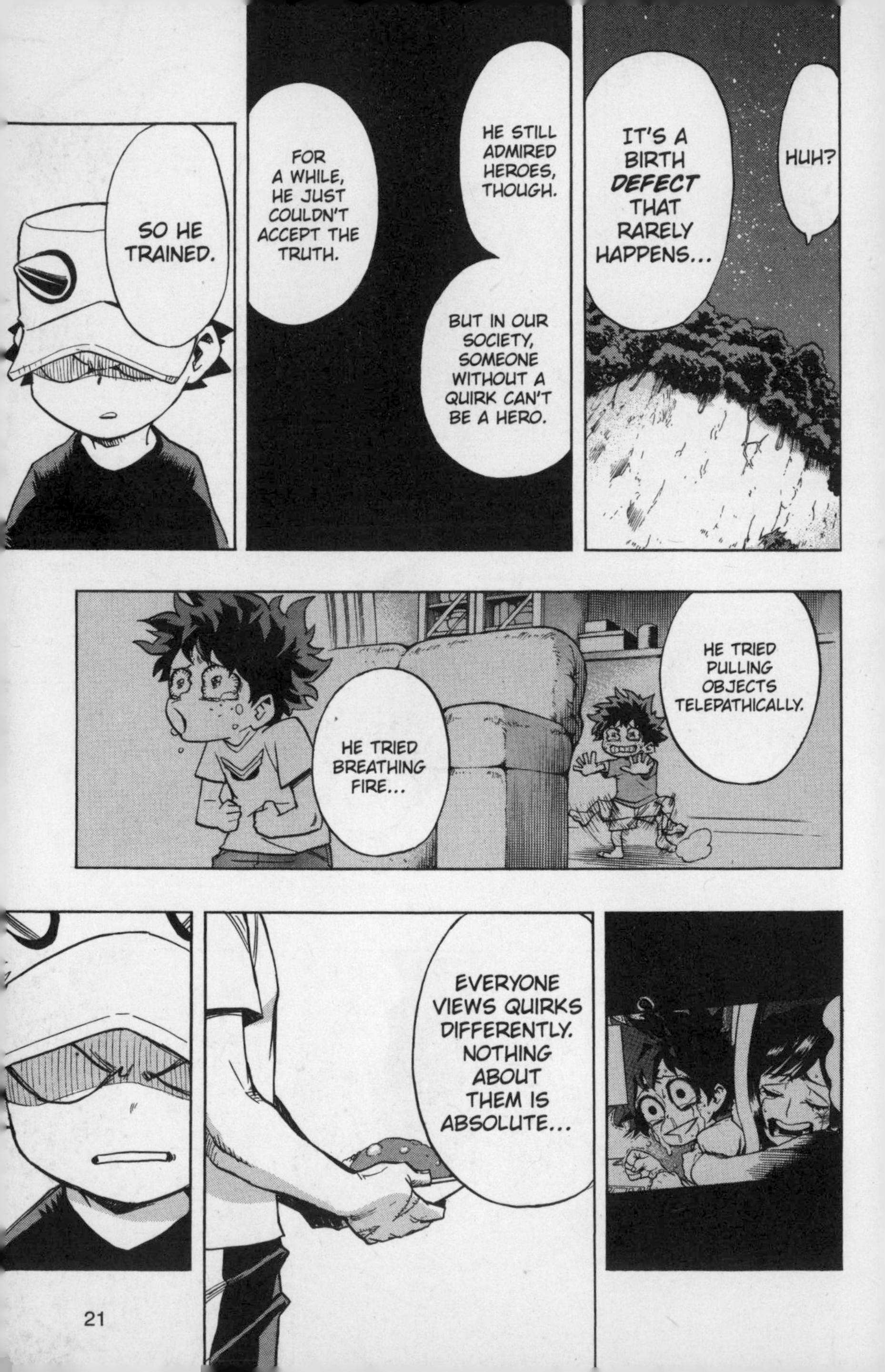
HUH?
IT'S A BIRTH *DEFECT* THAT RARELY HAPPENS...
HE STILL ADMIRED HEROES, THOUGH.
FOR A WHILE, HE JUST COULDN'T ACCEPT THE TRUTH.
BUT IN OUR SOCIETY, SOMEONE WITHOUT A QUIRK CAN'T BE A HERO.
SO HE TRAINED.
HE TRIED PULLING OBJECTS TELEPATHICALLY.
HE TRIED BREATHING FIRE...
EVERYONE VIEWS QUIRKS DIFFERENTLY. NOTHING ABOUT THEM IS ABSOLUTE...

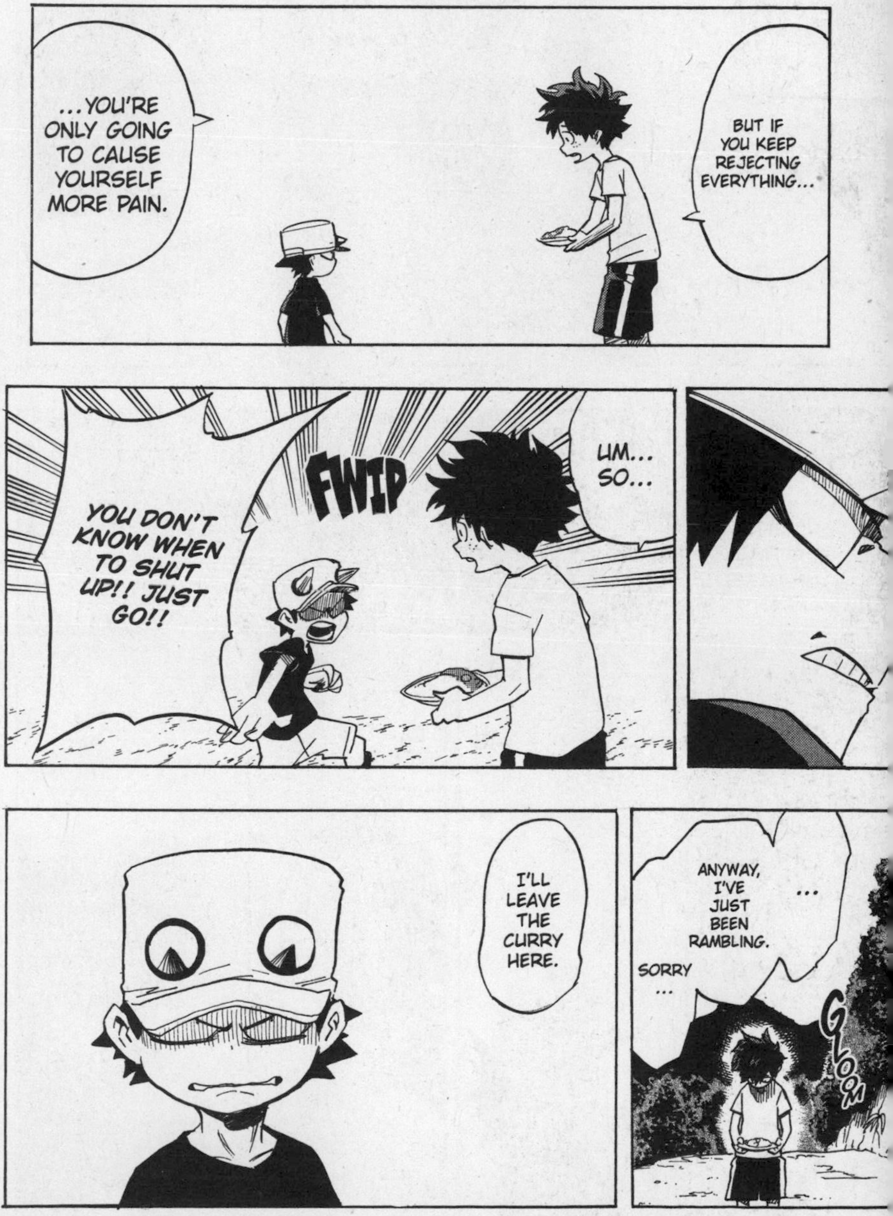
BUT IF YOU KEEP REJECTING EVERYTHING...
...YOU'RE ONLY GOING TO CAUSE YOURSELF MORE PAIN.
UM... SO...
FWIP
YOU DON'T KNOW WHEN TO SHUT UP!! JUST GO!!
...
ANYWAY, I'VE JUST BEEN RAMBLING.
SORRY...
GLOOM
I'LL LEAVE THE CURRY HERE.

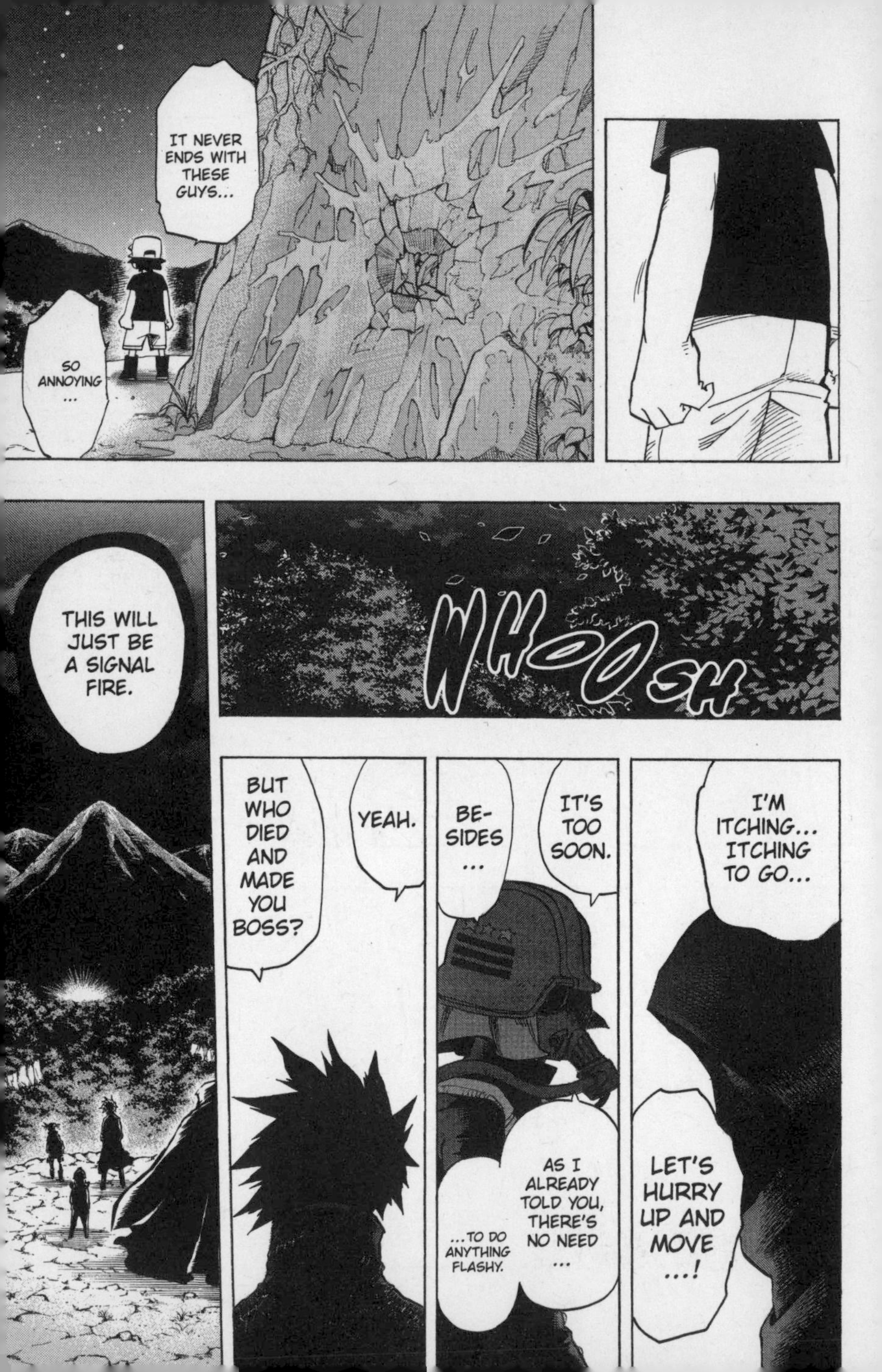
IT NEVER ENDS WITH THESE GUYS...
SO ANNOYING ...
WHOOSH
I'M ITCHING... ITCHING TO GO...
LET'S HURRY UP AND MOVE ...!
IT'S TOO SOON.
BE-SIDES ...
AS I ALREADY TOLD YOU, THERE'S NO NEED ...
...TO DO ANYTHING FLASHY.
YEAH.
BUT WHO DIED AND MADE YOU BOSS?
THIS WILL JUST BE A SIGNAL FIRE.

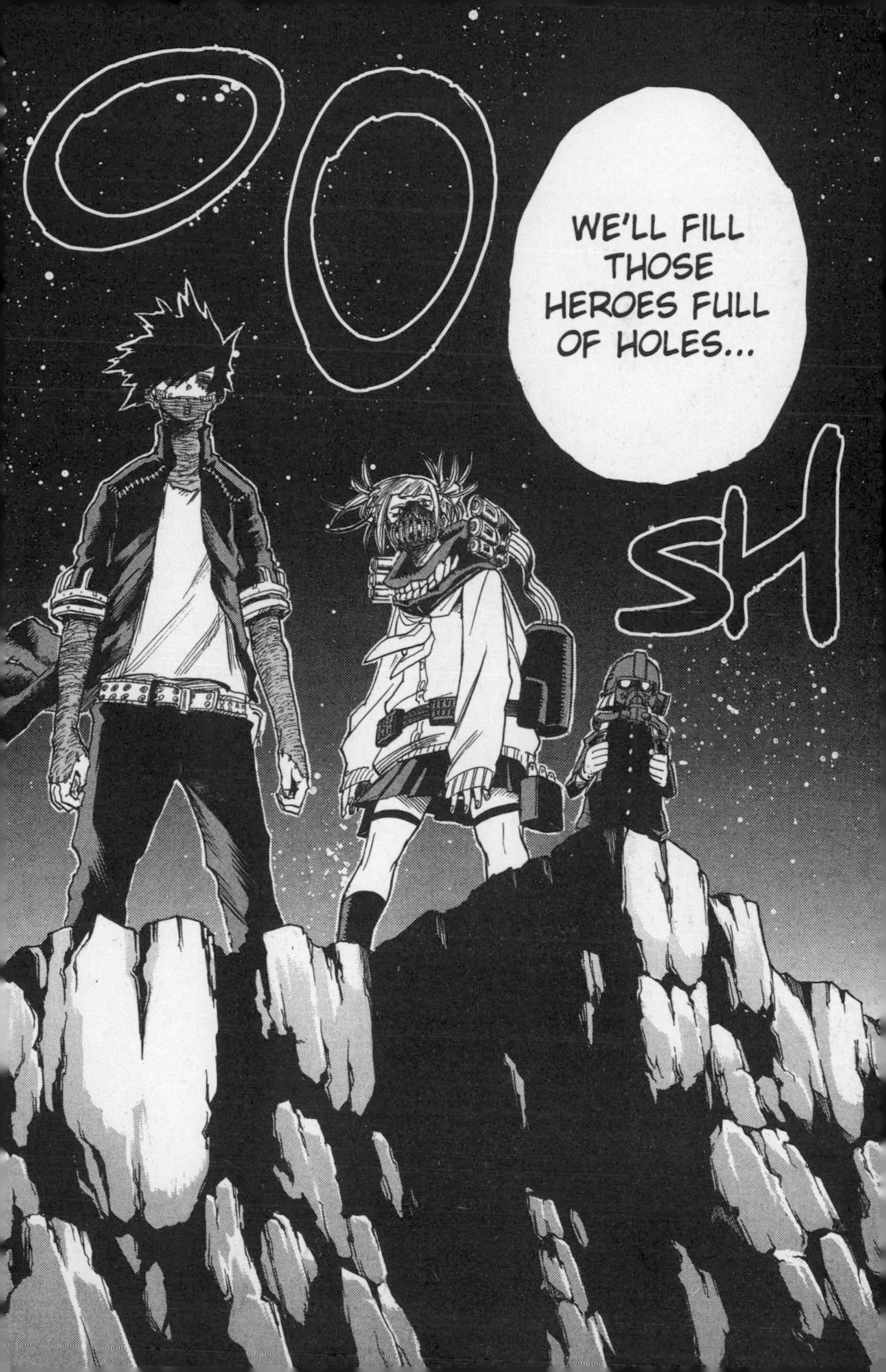
OOSH
WE'LL FILL THOSE HEROES FULL OF HOLES...

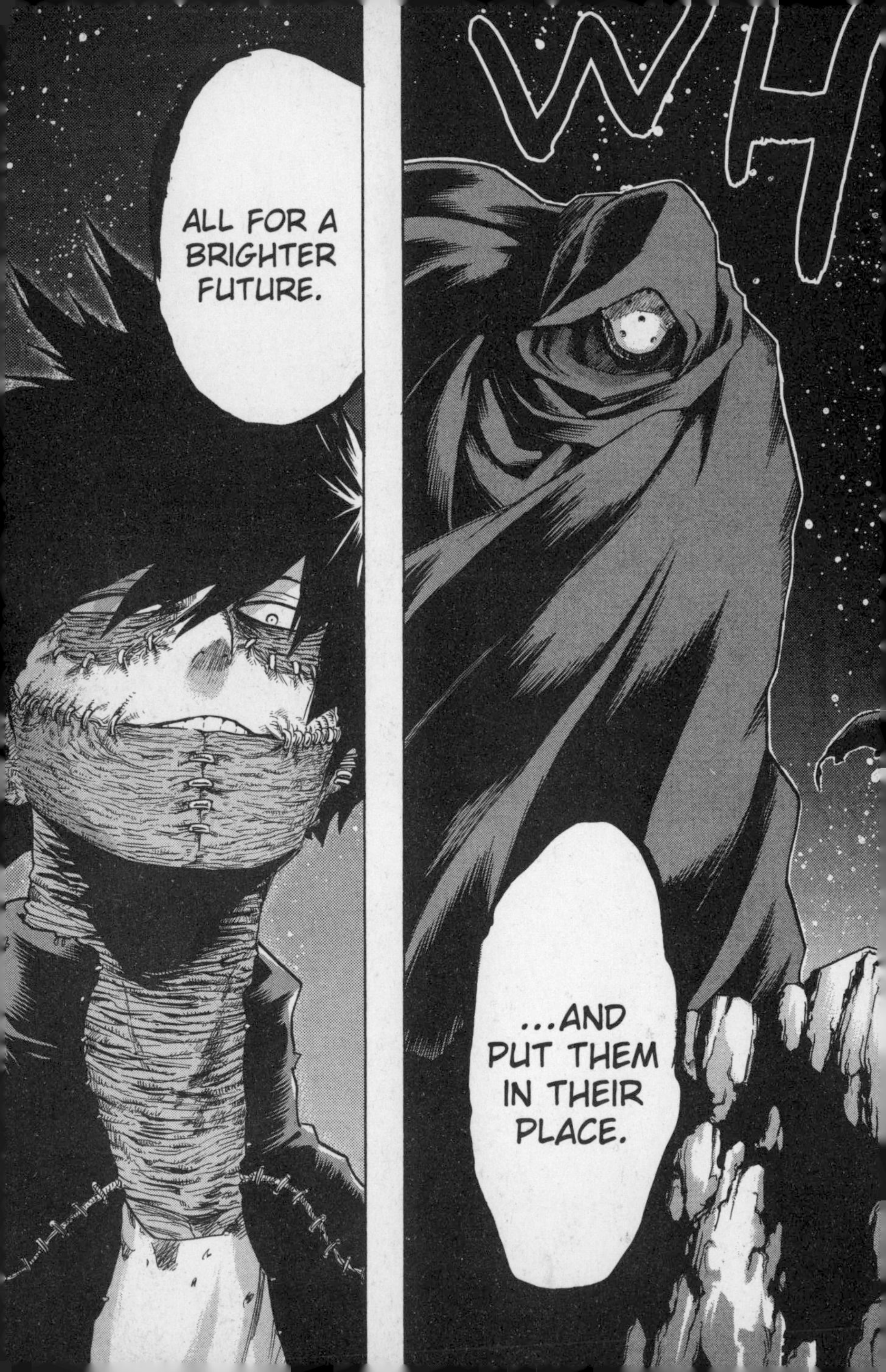
WH
...AND PUT THEM IN THEIR PLACE.
ALL FOR A BRIGHTER FUTURE.

EXTRA INFO ON QUIRK TRAINING

ONE'S QUIRK IS JUST LIKE ANY OTHER PHYSICAL ABILITY, AND JUST LIKE WITH MUSCLES AND BRAINS, THE BODY ADAPTS TO A QUIRK THE MORE IT'S USED.

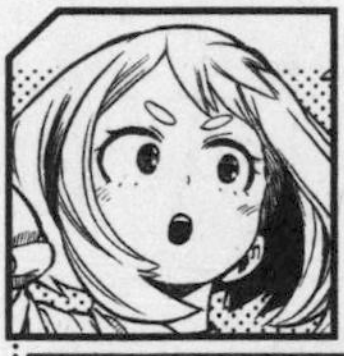

OCHACO URARAKA
ZERO GRAVITY

She trains by repeatedly using her Quirk even when it's already made her queasy. By suppressing her gag reflex and strengthening her inner ear canals, Uraraka can increase the maximum weight limit of what she can float.

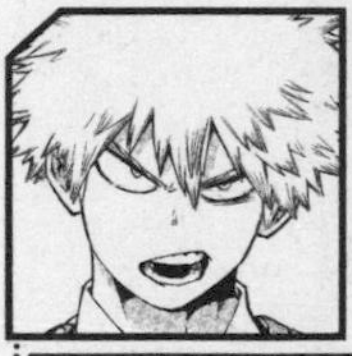

KATSUKI BAKUGO
EXPLOSION

By subjecting his hands to extreme heat, he enlarges his sweat glands. This allows Bakugo to pull off more explosions in succession. He also hopes to create larger-scale explosions.

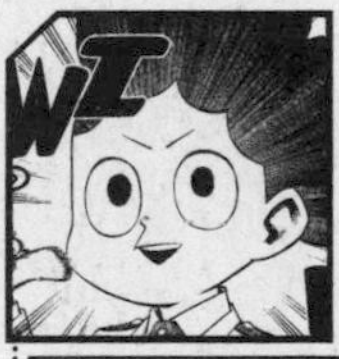

MINORU MINETA
POP OFF

Just as with ordinary muscle training, Mineta's goal is to toughen up his scalp so that he doesn't bleed even with excessive use of his Quirk.

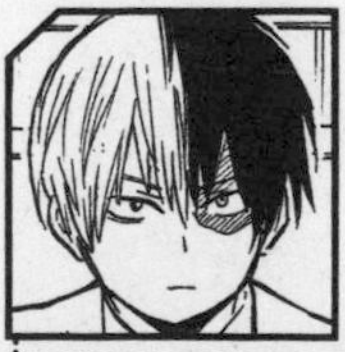

SHOTO TODOROKI
HALF-COLD, HALF-HOT

He attempts to produce ice while submerging himself in hot water. The heat from the water wards off the chills so that his body can grow accustomed to creating ice continuously. Meanwhile, Todoroki also uses his left side to keep the water at a set temperature, an exercise meant to give him control over the temperature of his flames. Through this sort of Quirk training, using fire and ice at the same time might not be just a pipe dream.

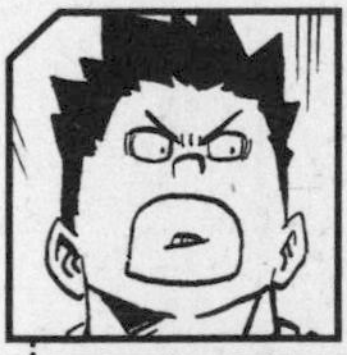

RIKIDO SATO
SUGAR RUSH

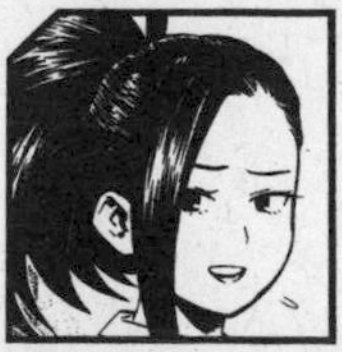

MOMO YAOYOROZU
CREATION

These two continuously use their Quirks while simultaneously taking in the energy they need for activation. This lets their bodies get more used to the effects. Sato's goal is to increase both the effective time period and the degree to which he powers up. Yaoyorozu employs her Quirk while eating food, training herself to produce high-quality objects as an afterthought while doing something else at the same time.

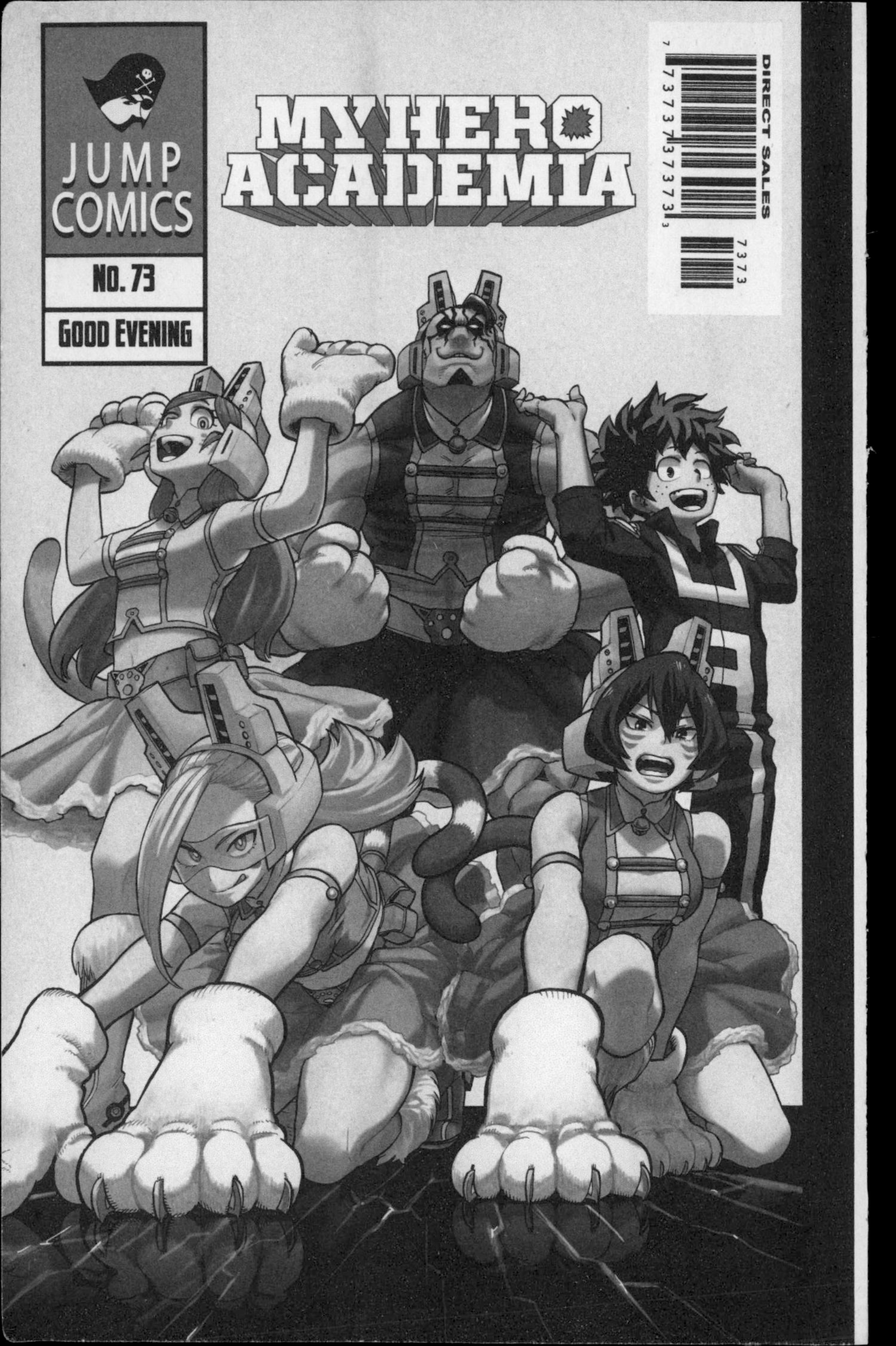
JUMP
COMICS
NO. 73
GOOD EVENING
MY HERO
ACADEMIA
DIRECT SALES
7 73737373737 3
7373

MY HERO ACADEMIA

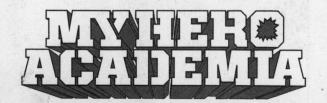

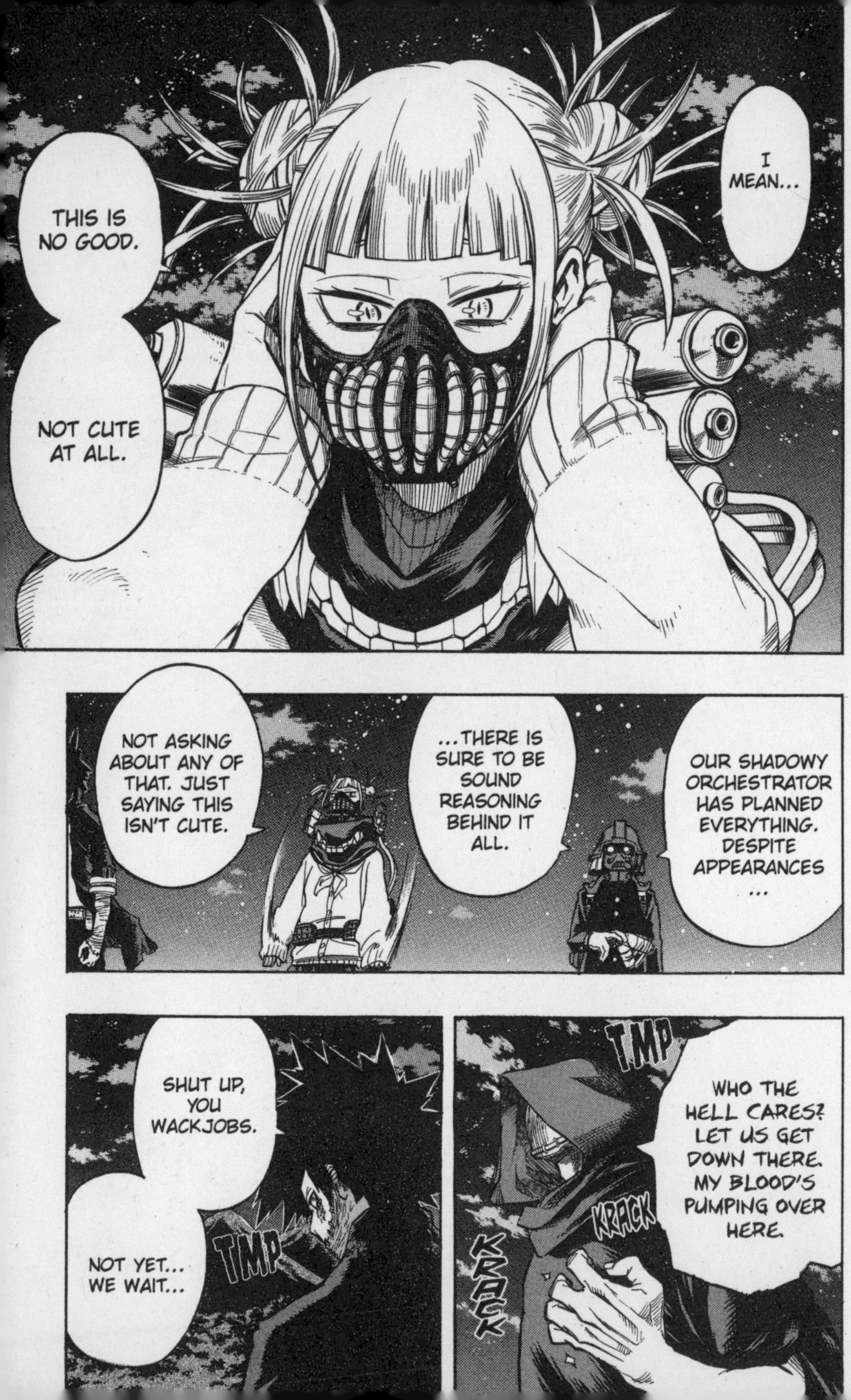
I MEAN...
THIS IS NO GOOD.
NOT CUTE AT ALL.
OUR SHADOWY ORCHESTRATOR HAS PLANNED EVERYTHING. DESPITE APPEARANCES ...
...THERE IS SURE TO BE SOUND REASONING BEHIND IT ALL.
NOT ASKING ABOUT ANY OF THAT. JUST SAYING THIS ISN'T CUTE.
TMP
WHO THE HELL CARES? LET US GET DOWN THERE. MY BLOOD'S PUMPING OVER HERE.
KRACK
KRACK
SHUT UP, YOU WACKJOBS.
TMP
NOT YET... WE WAIT...

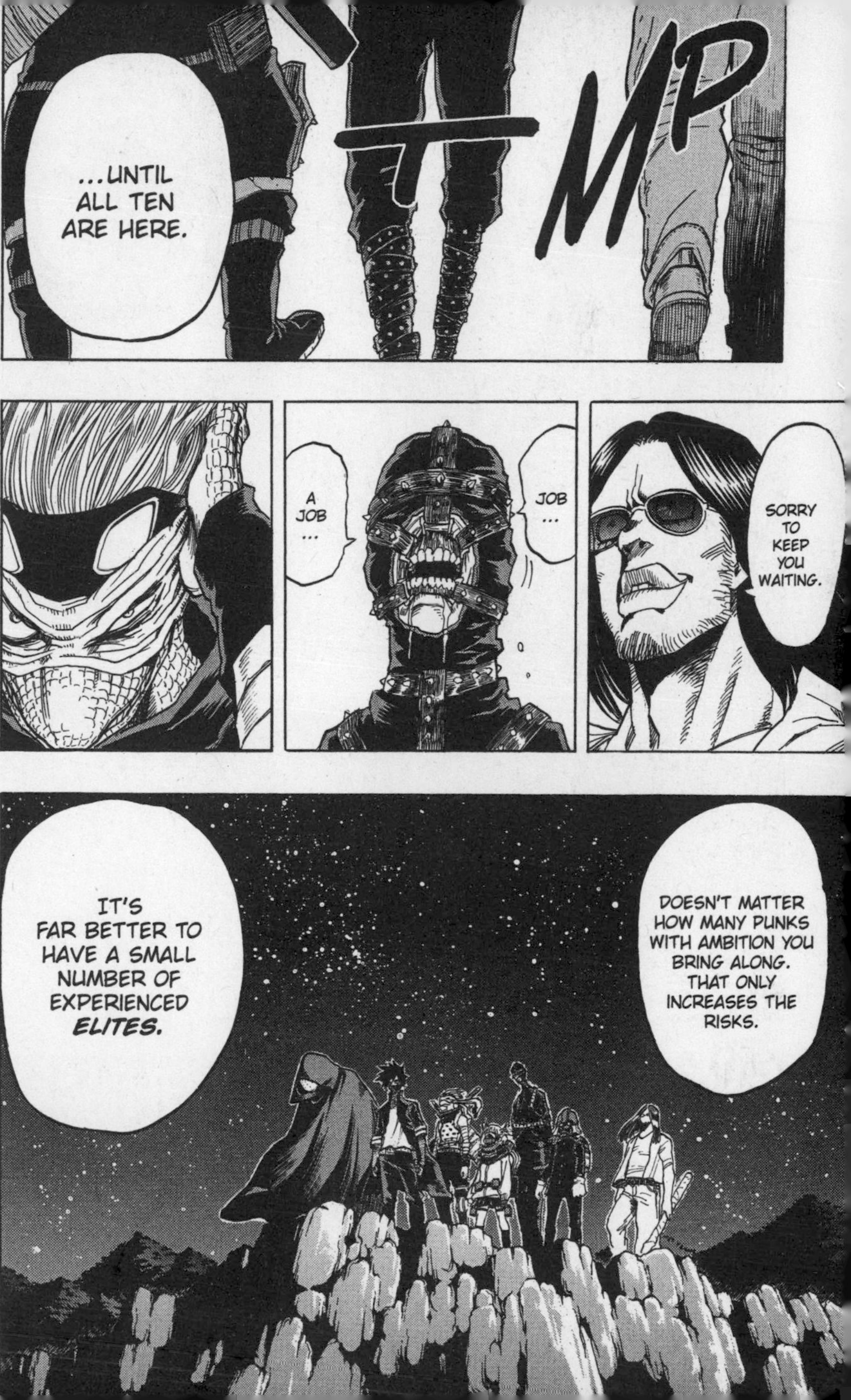
TMP
...UNTIL ALL TEN ARE HERE.
SORRY TO KEEP YOU WAITING.
JOB ...
A JOB ...
DOESN'T MATTER HOW MANY PUNKS WITH AMBITION YOU BRING ALONG. THAT ONLY INCREASES THE RISKS.
IT'S FAR BETTER TO HAVE A SMALL NUMBER OF EXPERIENCED ***ELITES.***

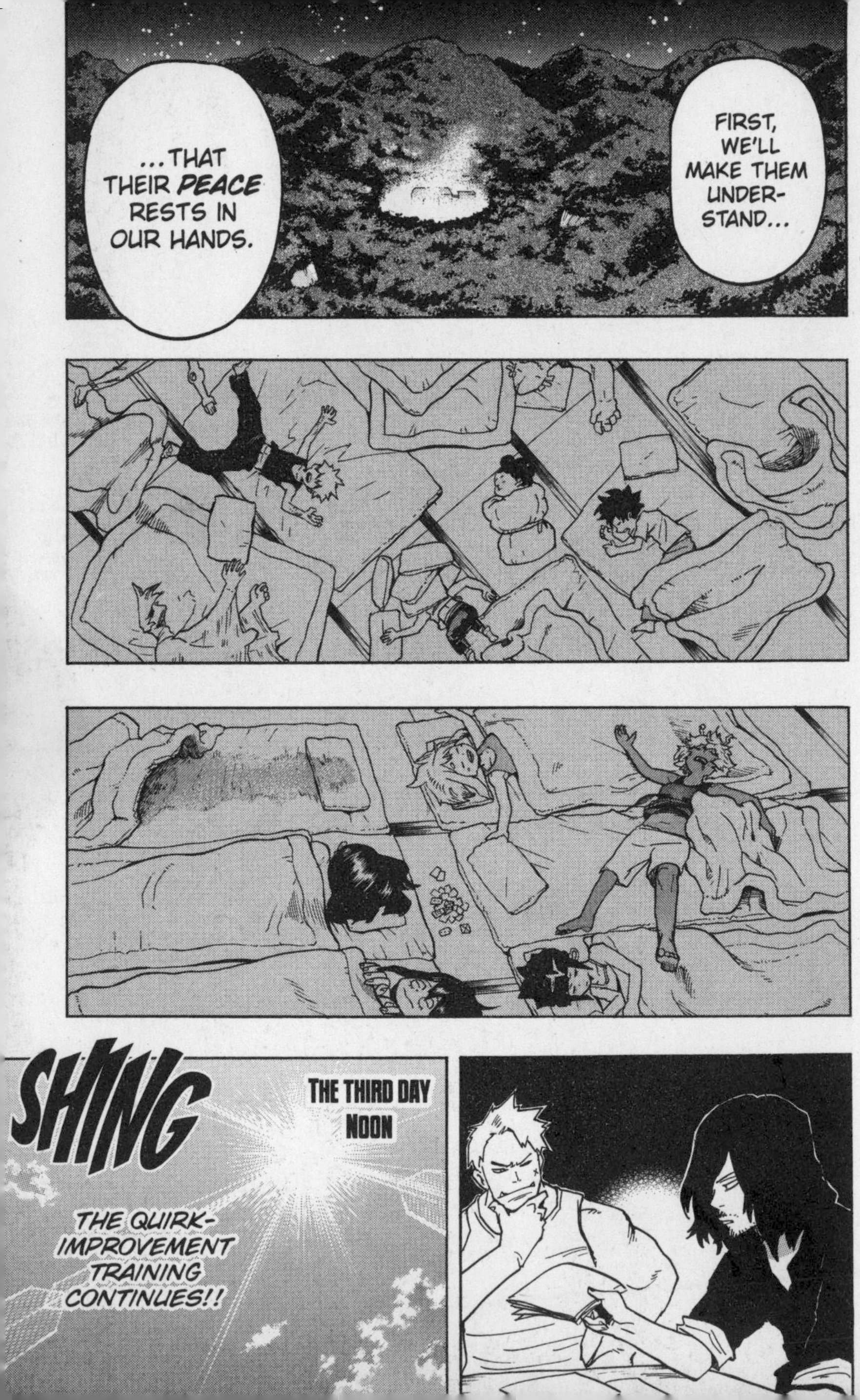
FIRST, WE'LL MAKE THEM UNDER-STAND...
...THAT THEIR PEACE RESTS IN OUR HANDS.
THE THIRD DAY NOON
SHING
THE QUIRK-IMPROVEMENT TRAINING CONTINUES!!

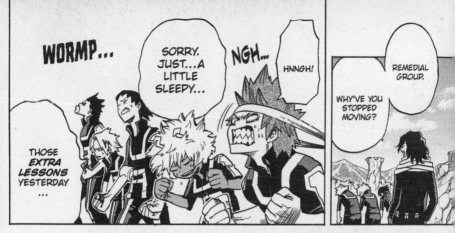

REMEDIAL GROUP.
WHY'VE YOU STOPPED MOVING?
HNNGH!
NGH...
SORRY. JUST...A LITTLE SLEEPY...
WORMP...
THOSE EXTRA LESSONS YESTERDAY ...
I TOLD YOU THIS WOULD BE ROUGH.
ORDINARY BEDTIME
REMEDIAL GROUP BEDTIME
WAKE-UP TIME
SATO AND KAMINARI, REACHING YOUR LIMITS IS A MATTER OF LIFE AND DEATH.
TO INCREASE THAT CAPACITY, REPEATED AND EXTENDED QUIRK USE IS KEY.
Sugar Amount 80%
Electricity Storage
Power Output
Release
SERO... IN ADDITION TO EXTENDING YOUR CAPACITY, YOU NEED TO STRENGTHEN YOUR TAPE AND INCREASE ITS FIRING SPEED.
ASHIDO, YOU NEED TO IMPROVE YOUR SKIN'S RESISTANCE AGAINST YOUR ACID DURING PERIODS OF EXTENDED USE.
AND FINALLY, KIRISHIMA. BUILDING THOSE MUSCLES AND MAKING YOUR BODY EVEN HARDER WILL CREATE A NICE SYNERGY EFFECT.

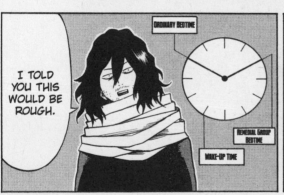

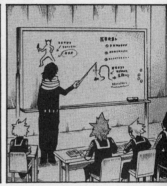

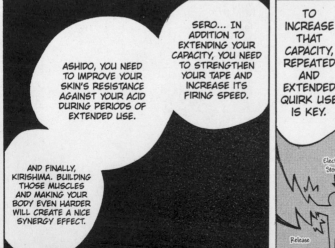

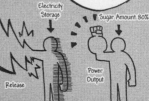

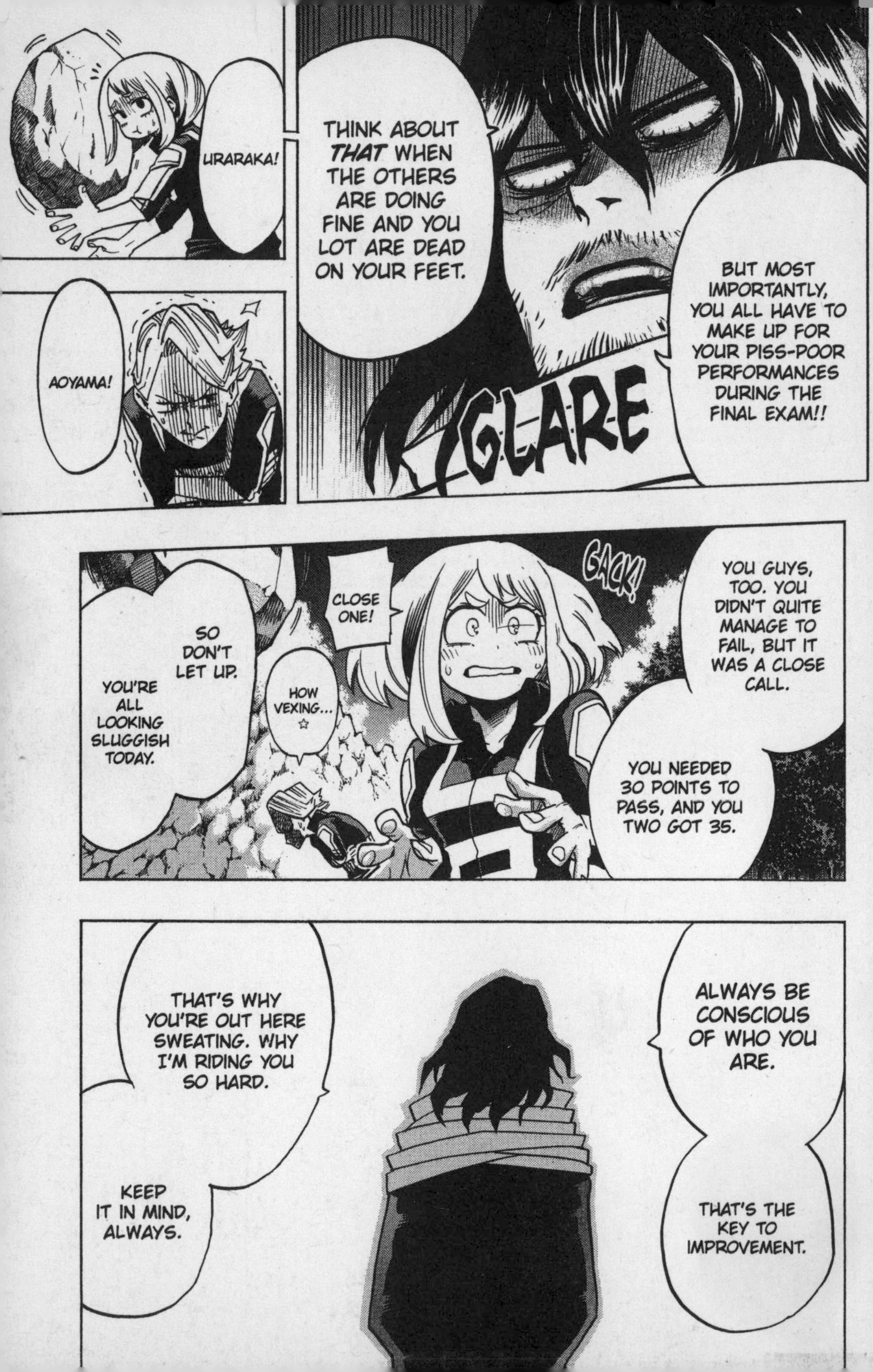
THINK ABOUT *THAT* WHEN THE OTHERS ARE DOING FINE AND YOU LOT ARE DEAD ON YOUR FEET.
BUT MOST IMPORTANTLY, YOU ALL HAVE TO MAKE UP FOR YOUR PISS-POOR PERFORMANCES DURING THE FINAL EXAM!!
GLARE
URARAKA!
AOYAMA!
YOU GUYS, TOO. YOU DIDN'T QUITE MANAGE TO FAIL, BUT IT WAS A CLOSE CALL.
YOU NEEDED 30 POINTS TO PASS, AND YOU TWO GOT 35.
GACK!
CLOSE ONE!
HOW VEXING... ☆
SO DON'T LET UP.
YOU'RE ALL LOOKING SLUGGISH TODAY.
ALWAYS BE CONSCIOUS OF WHO YOU ARE.
THAT'S THE KEY TO IMPROVEMENT.
THAT'S WHY YOU'RE OUT HERE SWEATING. WHY I'M RIDING YOU SO HARD.
KEEP IT IN MIND, ALWAYS.

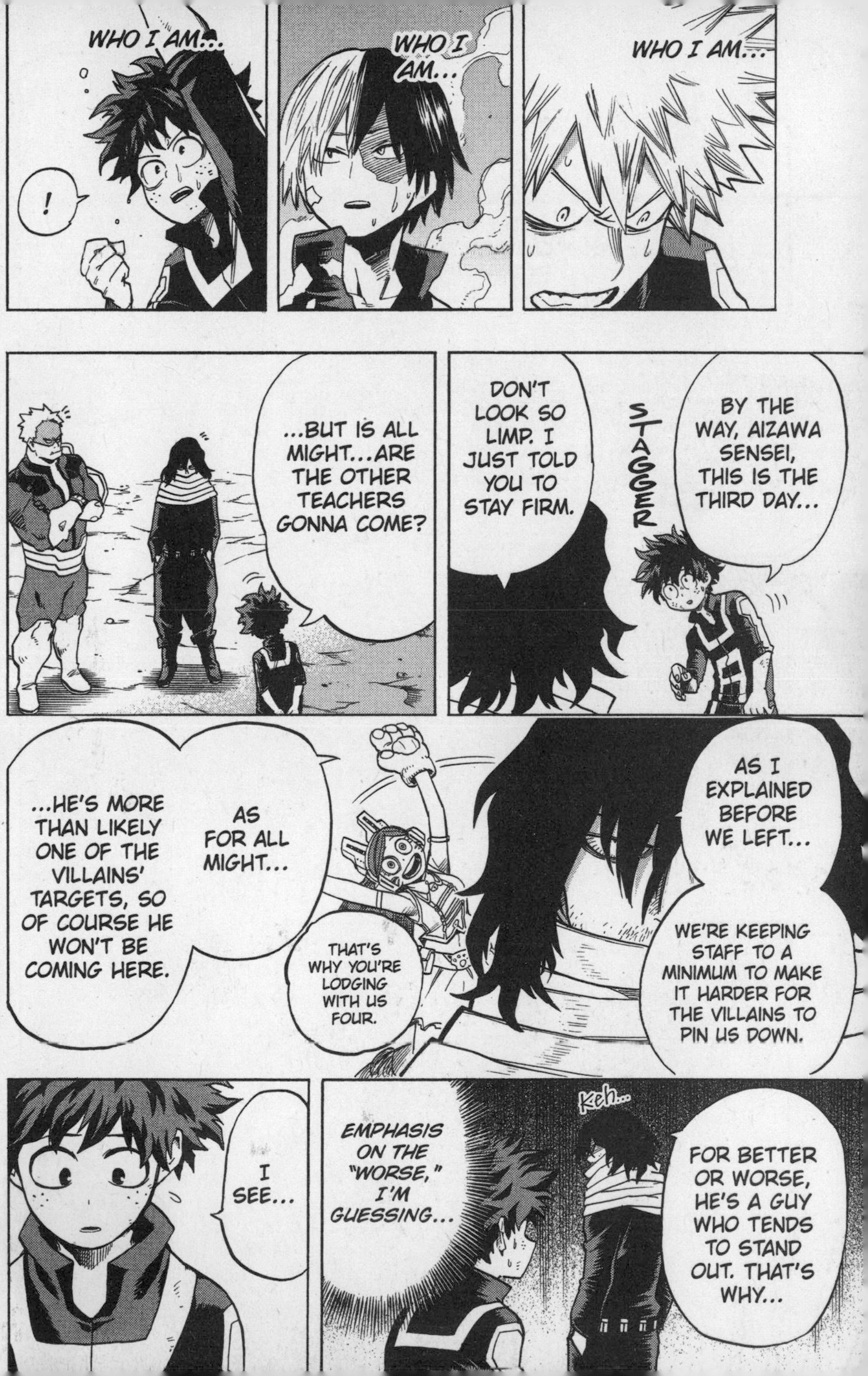
WHO I AM...
WHO I AM...
WHO I AM...
!
BY THE WAY, AIZAWA SENSEI, THIS IS THE THIRD DAY...
STAGGER
DON'T LOOK SO LIMP. I JUST TOLD YOU TO STAY FIRM.
...BUT IS ALL MIGHT...ARE THE OTHER TEACHERS GONNA COME?
AS I EXPLAINED BEFORE WE LEFT...
WE'RE KEEPING STAFF TO A MINIMUM TO MAKE IT HARDER FOR THE VILLAINS TO PIN US DOWN.
THAT'S WHY YOU'RE LODGING WITH US FOUR.
AS FOR ALL MIGHT...
...HE'S MORE THAN LIKELY ONE OF THE VILLAINS' TARGETS, SO OF COURSE HE WON'T BE COMING HERE.
Keh...
FOR BETTER OR WORSE, HE'S A GUY WHO TENDS TO STAND OUT. THAT'S WHY...
EMPHASIS ON THE "WORSE," I'M GUESSING...
I SEE...

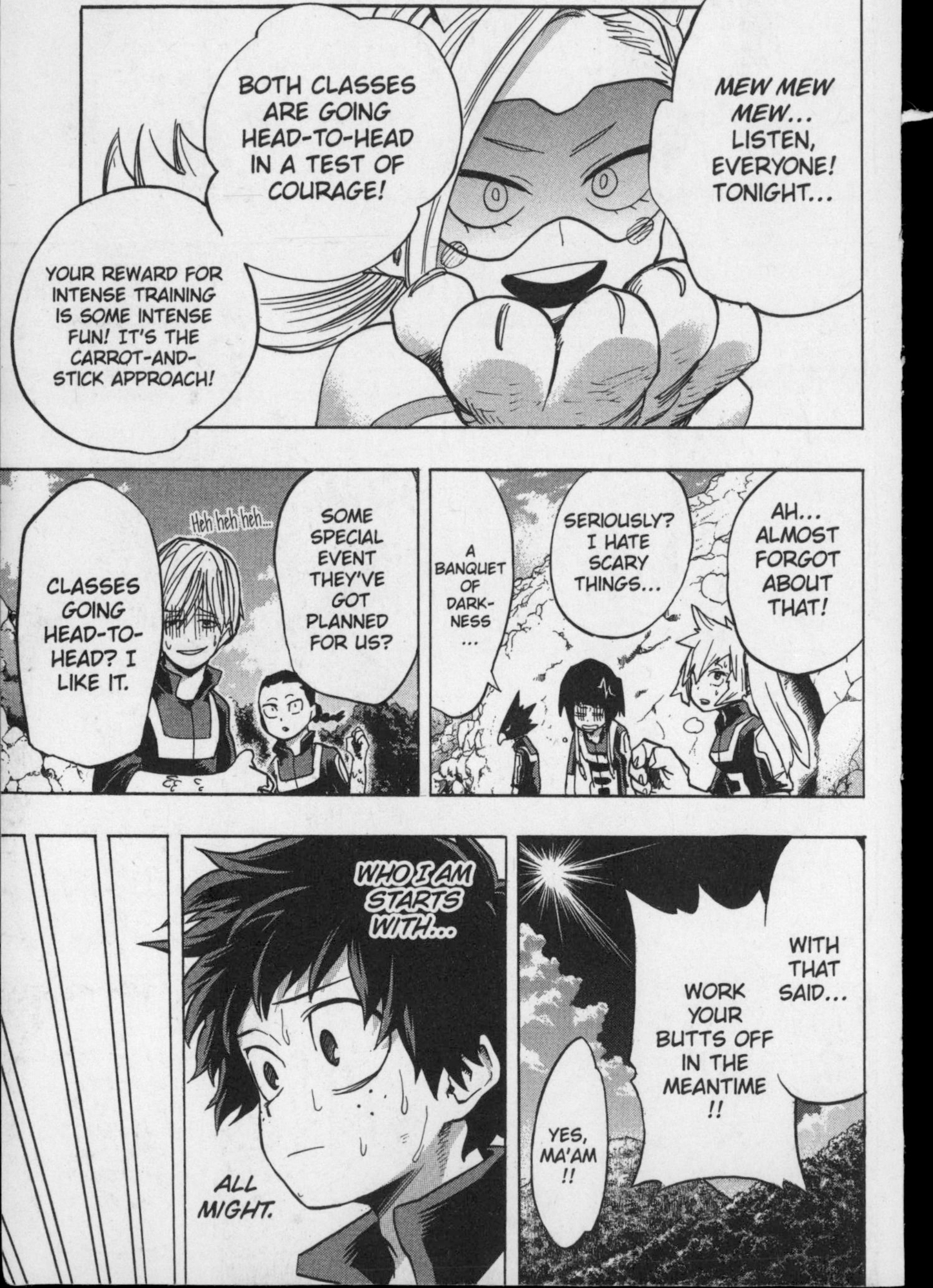
MEW MEW MEW... LISTEN, EVERYONE! TONIGHT...
BOTH CLASSES ARE GOING HEAD-TO-HEAD IN A TEST OF COURAGE!
YOUR REWARD FOR INTENSE TRAINING IS SOME INTENSE FUN! IT'S THE CARROT-AND-STICK APPROACH!
AH... ALMOST FORGOT ABOUT THAT!
SERIOUSLY? I HATE SCARY THINGS...
A BANQUET OF DARKNESS...
SOME SPECIAL EVENT THEY'VE GOT PLANNED FOR US?
Heh heh heh...
CLASSES GOING HEAD-TO-HEAD? I LIKE IT.
WITH THAT SAID...
WORK YOUR BUTTS OFF IN THE MEANTIME!!
YES, MA'AM!!
WHO I AM STARTS WITH...
ALL MIGHT.

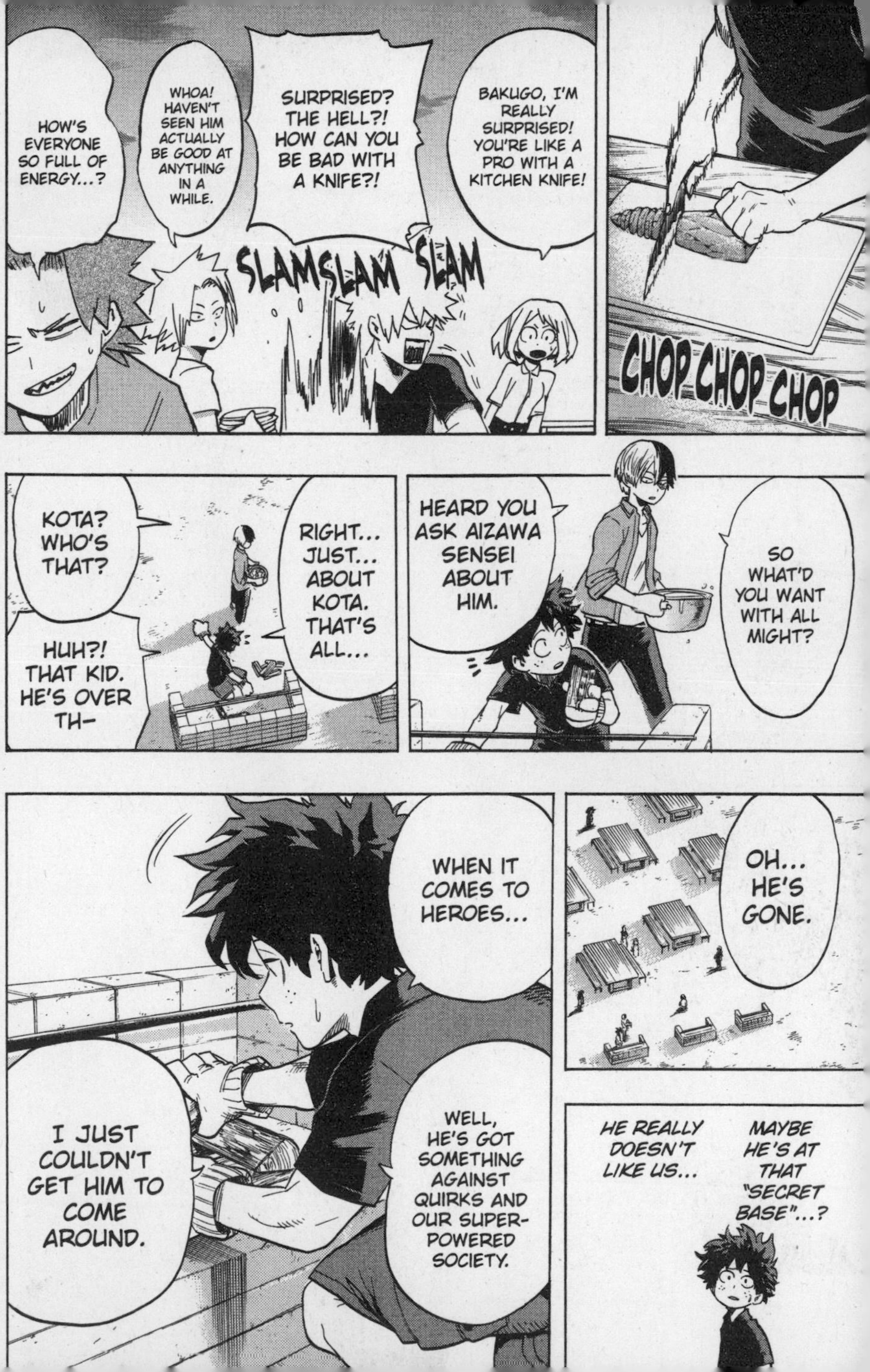
CHOP CHOP CHOP
BAKUGO, I'M REALLY SURPRISED! YOU'RE LIKE A PRO WITH A KITCHEN KNIFE!
SURPRISED? THE HELL?! HOW CAN YOU BE BAD WITH A KNIFE?!
SLAMSLAM SLAM
WHOA! HAVEN'T SEEN HIM ACTUALLY BE GOOD AT ANYTHING IN A WHILE.
HOW'S EVERYONE SO FULL OF ENERGY...?
SO WHAT'D YOU WANT WITH ALL MIGHT?
HEARD YOU ASK AIZAWA SENSEI ABOUT HIM.
RIGHT... JUST... ABOUT KOTA. THAT'S ALL...
KOTA? WHO'S THAT?
HUH?! THAT KID. HE'S OVER TH-
OH... HE'S GONE.
MAYBE HE'S AT THAT "SECRET BASE"...?
HE REALLY DOESN'T LIKE US...
WHEN IT COMES TO HEROES...
WELL, HE'S GOT SOMETHING AGAINST QUIRKS AND OUR SUPER-POWERED SOCIETY.
I JUST COULDN'T GET HIM TO COME AROUND.

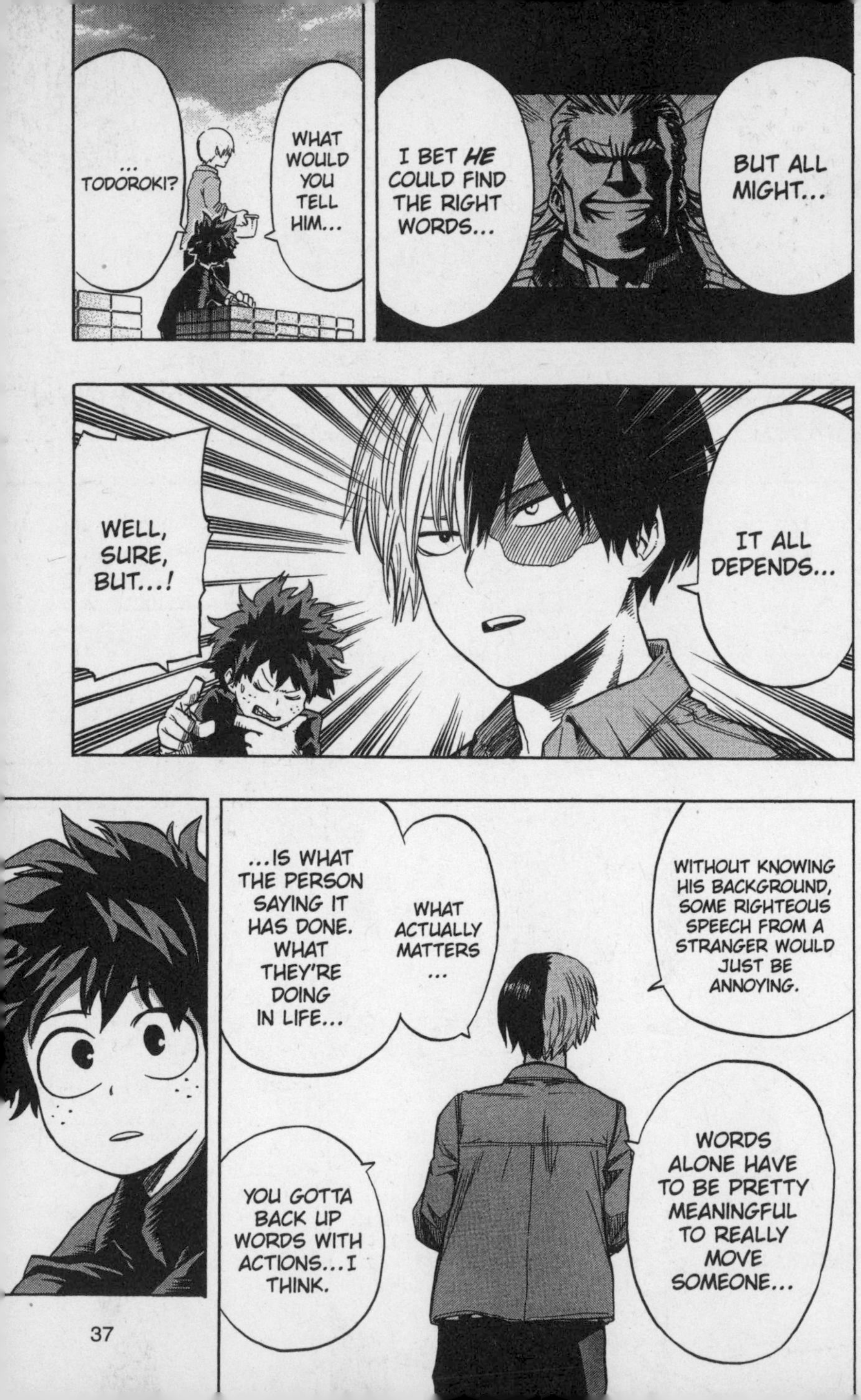
BUT ALL MIGHT...
I BET *HE* COULD FIND THE RIGHT WORDS...
WHAT WOULD YOU TELL HIM...
... TODOROKI?
IT ALL DEPENDS...
WELL, SURE, BUT...!
WITHOUT KNOWING HIS BACKGROUND, SOME RIGHTEOUS SPEECH FROM A STRANGER WOULD JUST BE ANNOYING.
WHAT ACTUALLY MATTERS ...
...IS WHAT THE PERSON SAYING IT HAS DONE. WHAT THEY'RE DOING IN LIFE...
WORDS ALONE HAVE TO BE PRETTY MEANINGFUL TO REALLY MOVE SOMEONE...
YOU GOTTA BACK UP WORDS WITH ACTIONS...I THINK.

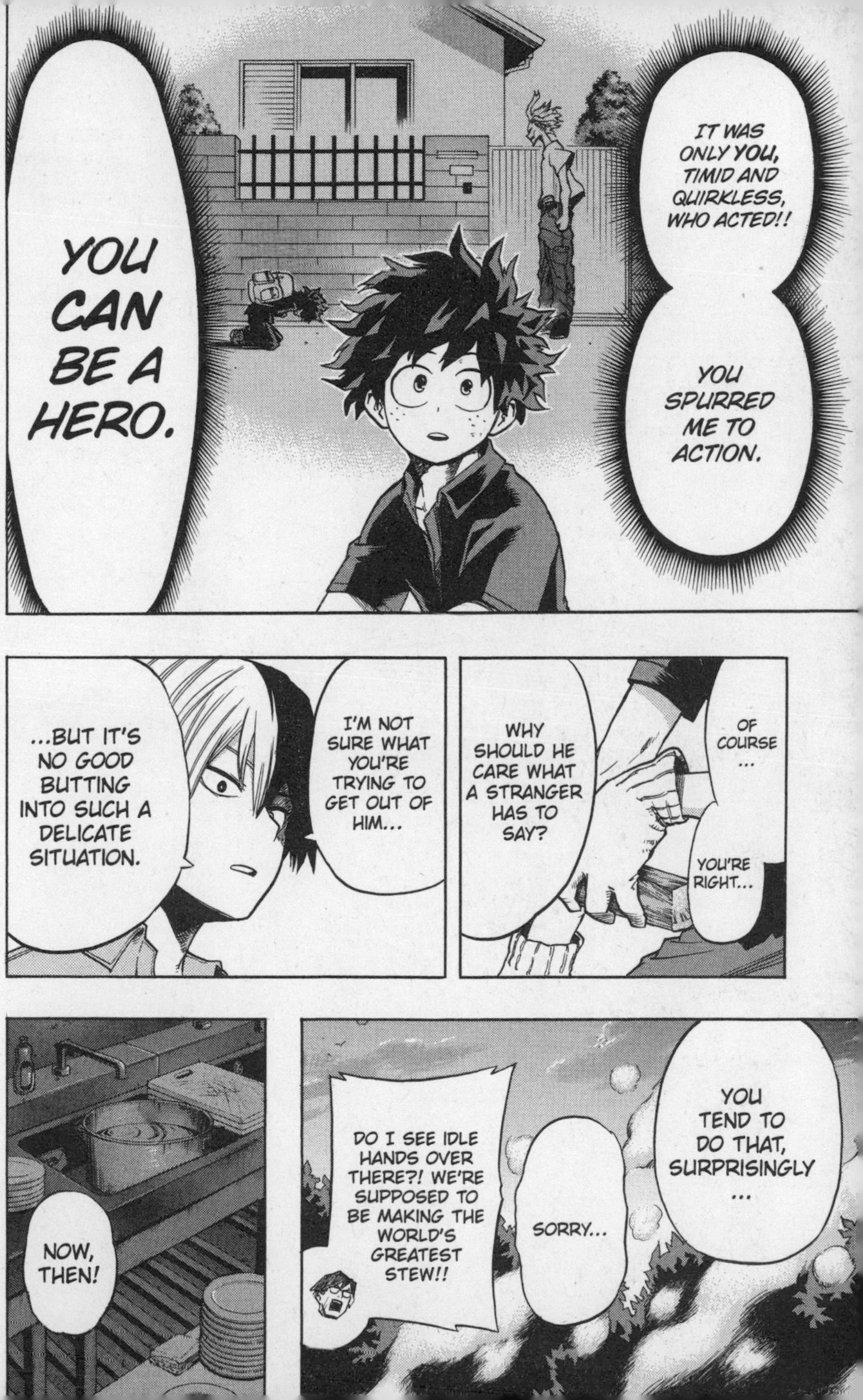
IT WAS ONLY YOU, TIMID AND QUIRKLESS, WHO ACTED!!
YOU SPURRED ME TO ACTION.
YOU CAN BE A HERO.
OF COURSE...
YOU'RE RIGHT...
WHY SHOULD HE CARE WHAT A STRANGER HAS TO SAY?
I'M NOT SURE WHAT YOU'RE TRYING TO GET OUT OF HIM...
...BUT IT'S NO GOOD BUTTING INTO SUCH A DELICATE SITUATION.
YOU TEND TO DO THAT, SURPRISINGLY...
SORRY...
DO I SEE IDLE HANDS OVER THERE?! WE'RE SUPPOSED TO BE MAKING THE WORLD'S GREATEST STEW!!
NOW, THEN!

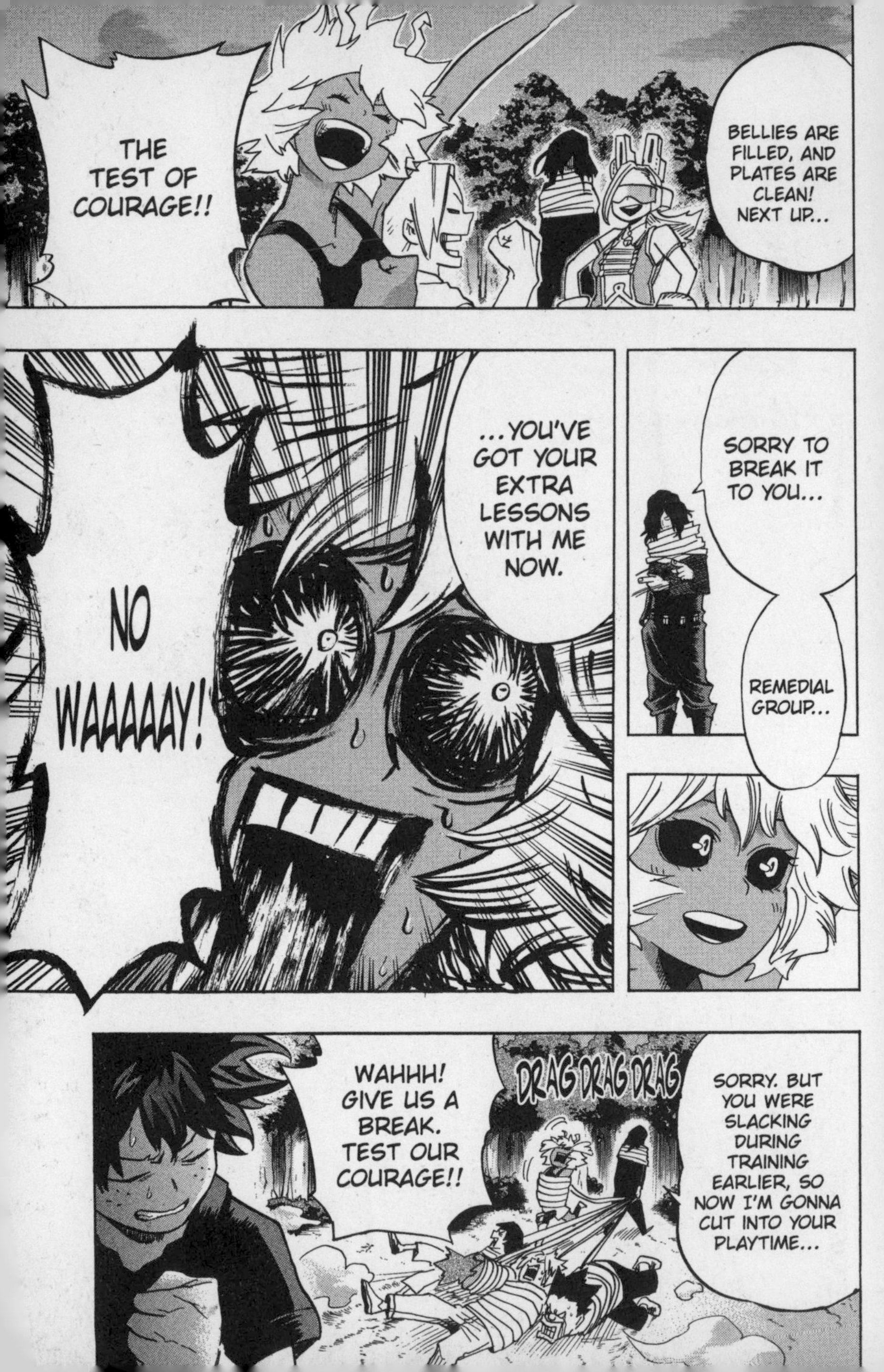
BELLIES ARE FILLED, AND PLATES ARE CLEAN! NEXT UP...
THE TEST OF COURAGE!!
SORRY TO BREAK IT TO YOU...
REMEDIAL GROUP...
...YOU'VE GOT YOUR EXTRA LESSONS WITH ME NOW.
NO WAAAAAY!
SORRY. BUT YOU WERE SLACKING DURING TRAINING EARLIER, SO NOW I'M GONNA CUT INTO YOUR PLAYTIME...
DRAG DRAG DRAG
WAHHH! GIVE US A BREAK. TEST OUR COURAGE!!

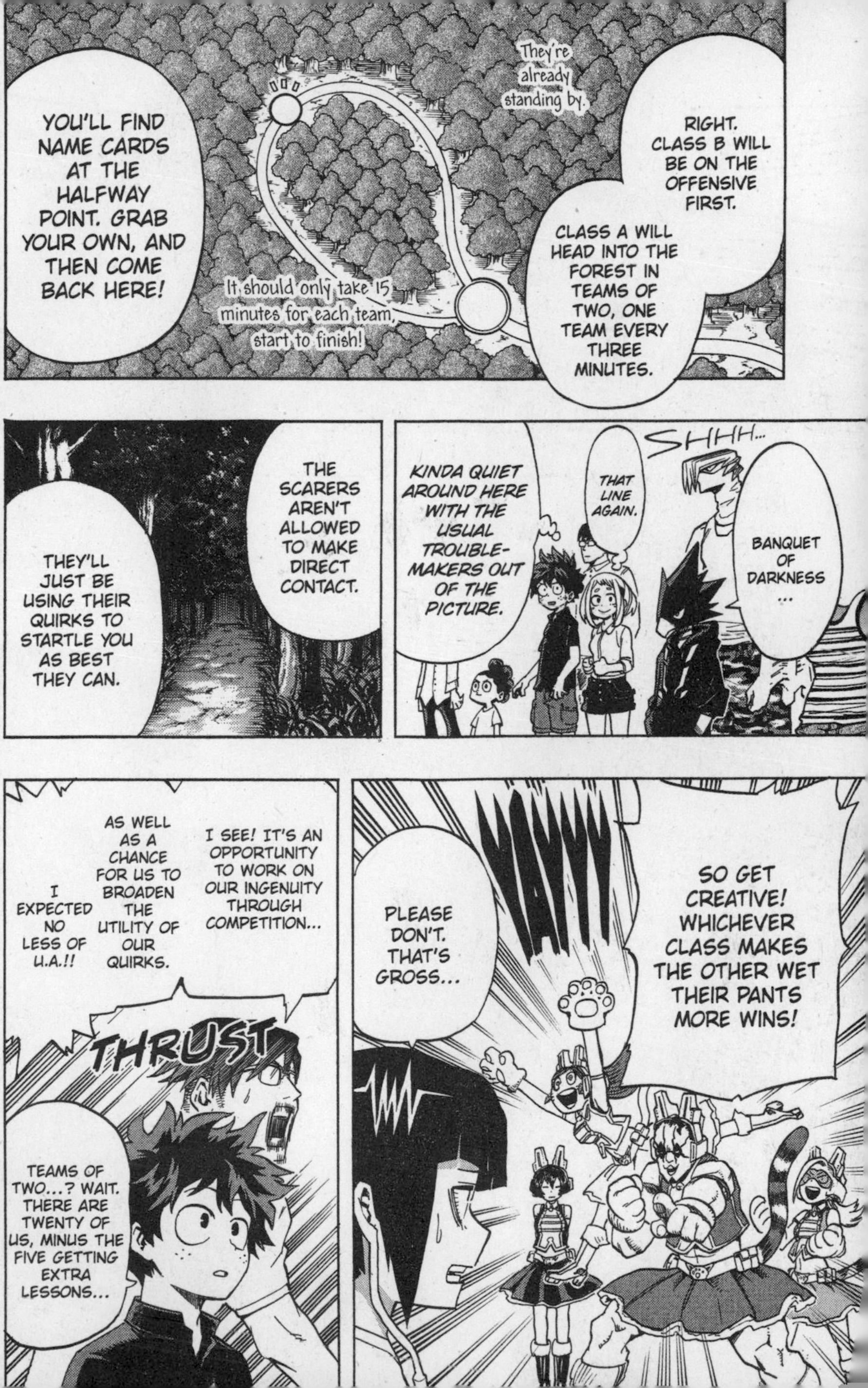
RIGHT. CLASS B WILL BE ON THE OFFENSIVE FIRST.
They're already standing by.
CLASS A WILL HEAD INTO THE FOREST IN TEAMS OF TWO, ONE TEAM EVERY THREE MINUTES.
YOU'LL FIND NAME CARDS AT THE HALFWAY POINT. GRAB YOUR OWN, AND THEN COME BACK HERE!
It should only take 15 minutes for each team, start to finish!
SHHH...
BANQUET OF DARKNESS...
THAT LINE AGAIN.
KINDA QUIET AROUND HERE WITH THE USUAL TROUBLE-MAKERS OUT OF THE PICTURE.
THE SCARERS AREN'T ALLOWED TO MAKE DIRECT CONTACT.
THEY'LL JUST BE USING THEIR QUIRKS TO STARTLE YOU AS BEST THEY CAN.
SO GET CREATIVE! WHICHEVER CLASS MAKES THE OTHER WET THEIR PANTS MORE WINS!
PLEASE DON'T. THAT'S GROSS...
I SEE! IT'S AN OPPORTUNITY TO WORK ON OUR INGENUITY THROUGH COMPETITION...
AS WELL AS A CHANCE FOR US TO BROADEN THE UTILITY OF OUR QUIRKS.
I EXPECTED NO LESS OF U.A.!!
THRUST
TEAMS OF TWO...? WAIT. THERE ARE TWENTY OF US, MINUS THE FIVE GETTING EXTRA LESSONS...

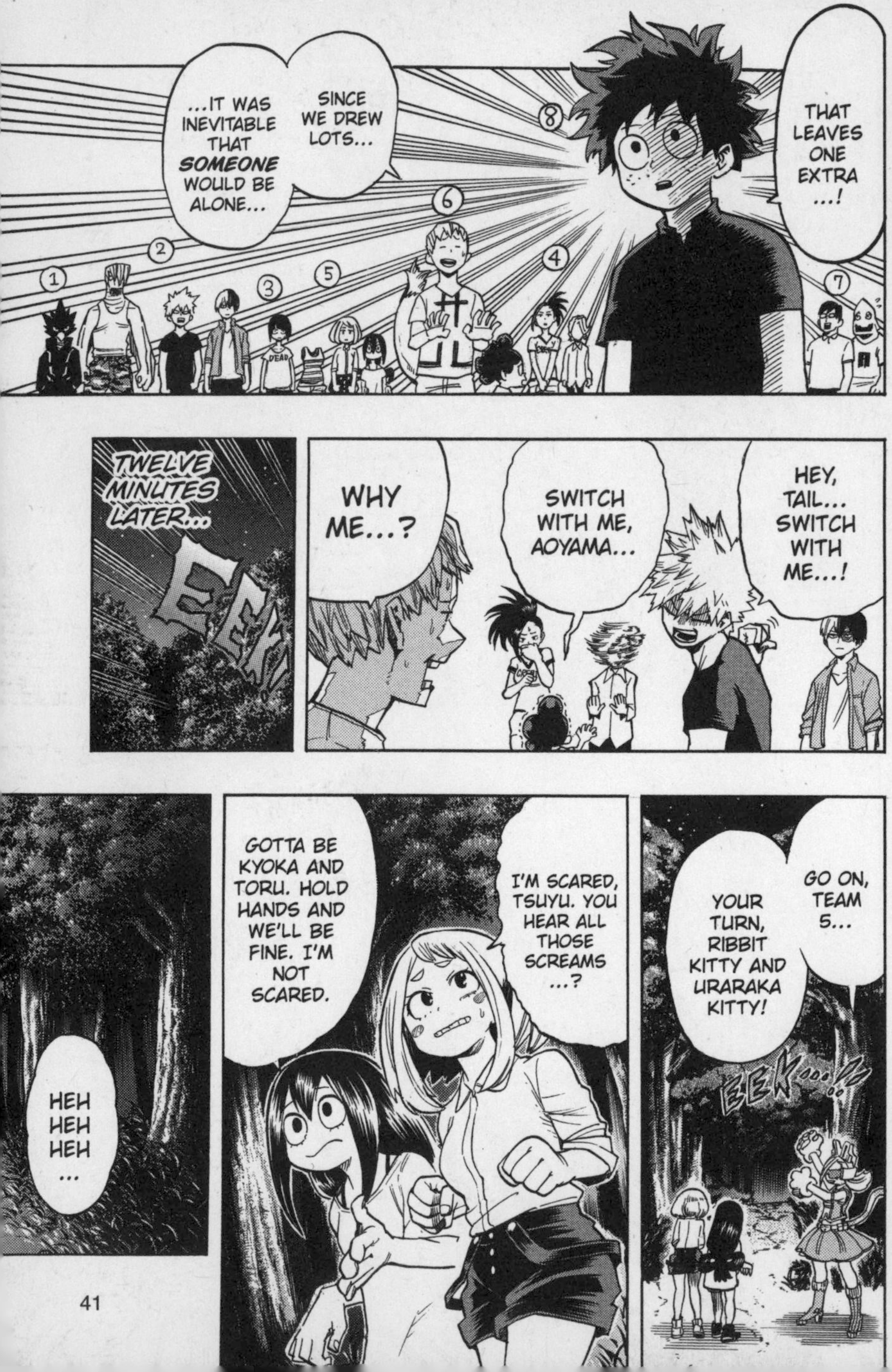
THAT LEAVES ONE EXTRA ...!
SINCE WE DREW LOTS...
...IT WAS INEVITABLE THAT ***SOMEONE*** WOULD BE ALONE...
HEY, TAIL... SWITCH WITH ME...!
SWITCH WITH ME, AOYAMA...
WHY ME...?
TWELVE MINUTES LATER...
EEK
GO ON, TEAM 5...
YOUR TURN, RIBBIT KITTY AND URARAKA KITTY!
EEK...!!
I'M SCARED, TSUYU. YOU HEAR ALL THOSE SCREAMS ...?
GOTTA BE KYOKA AND TORU. HOLD HANDS AND WE'LL BE FINE. I'M NOT SCARED.
HEH HEH HEH ...

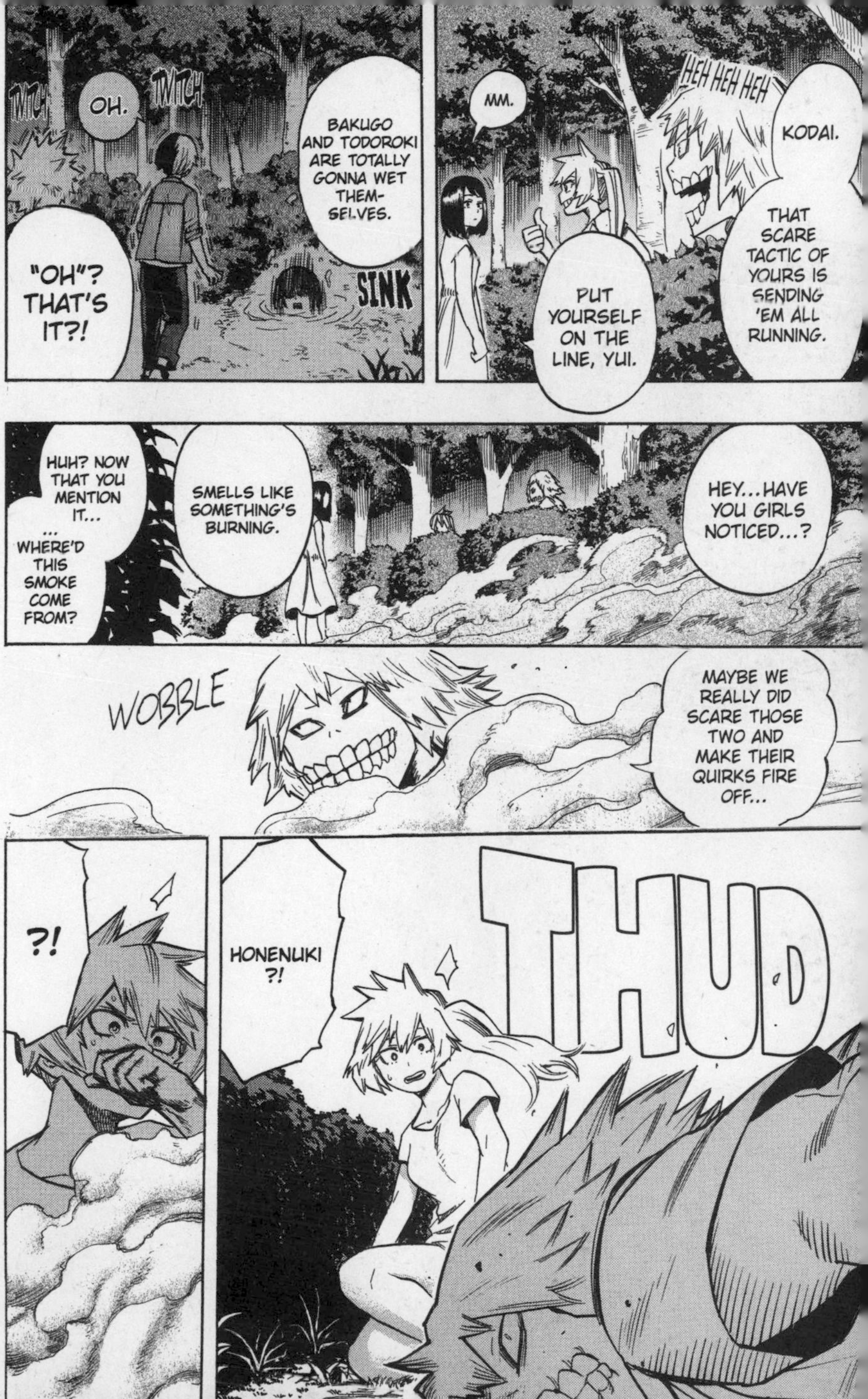
HEH HEH HEH
KODAI.
THAT SCARE TACTIC OF YOURS IS SENDING 'EM ALL RUNNING.
PUT YOURSELF ON THE LINE, YUI.
MM.
BAKUGO AND TODOROKI ARE TOTALLY GONNA WET THEM-SELVES.
TWITCH
OH.
TWITCH
SINK
"OH"? THAT'S IT?!
HEY...HAVE YOU GIRLS NOTICED...?
SMELLS LIKE SOMETHING'S BURNING.
HUH? NOW THAT YOU MENTION IT... ...WHERE'D THIS SMOKE COME FROM?
MAYBE WE REALLY DID SCARE THOSE TWO AND MAKE THEIR QUIRKS FIRE OFF...
WOBBLE
THUD
HONENUKI ?!
?!

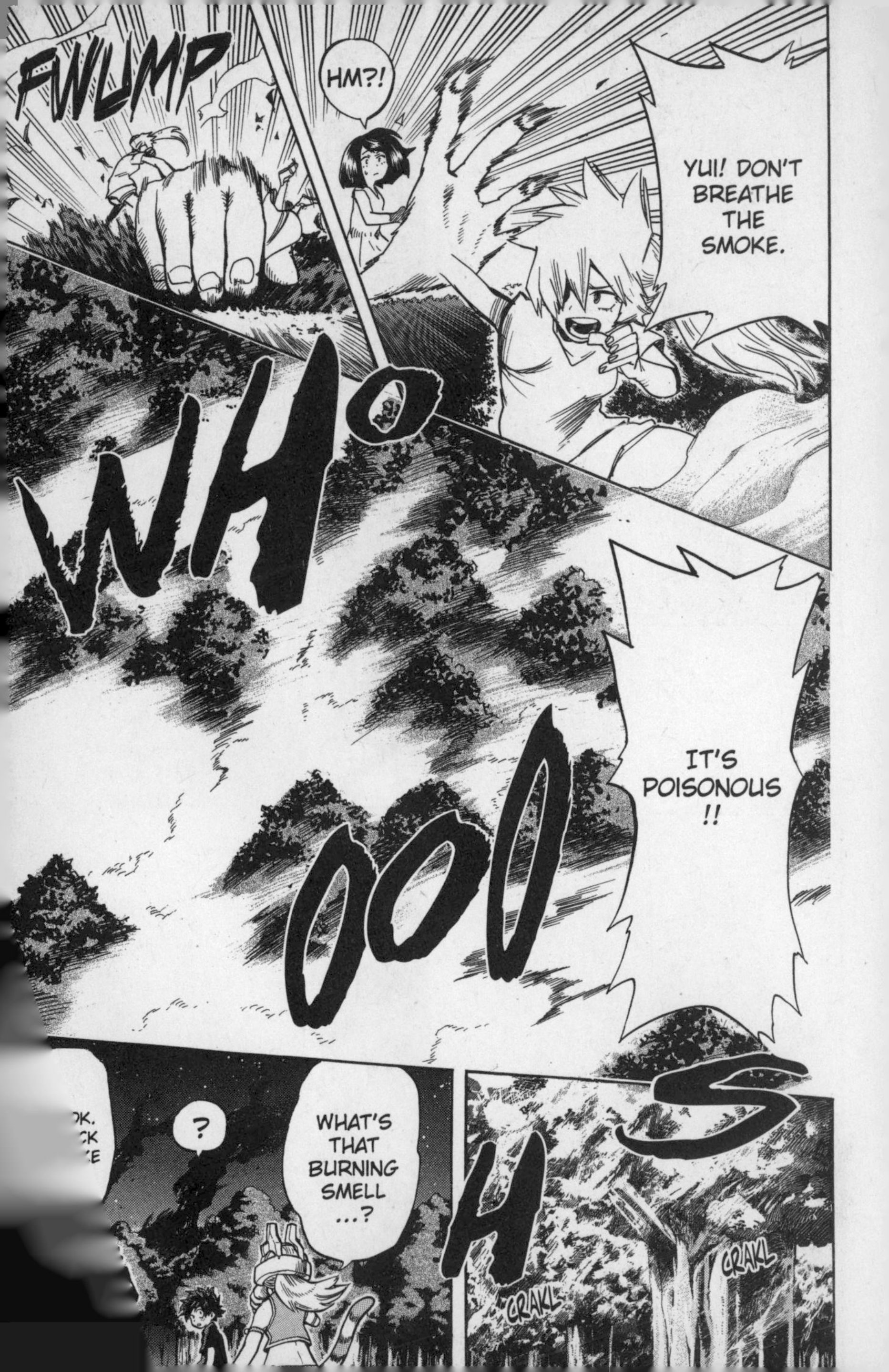
YUI! DON'T BREATHE THE SMOKE.
HM?!
FWUMP
IT'S POISONOUS!!
WHOOOSH
CRAKL
CRAKL
WHAT'S THAT BURNING SMELL ...?
?

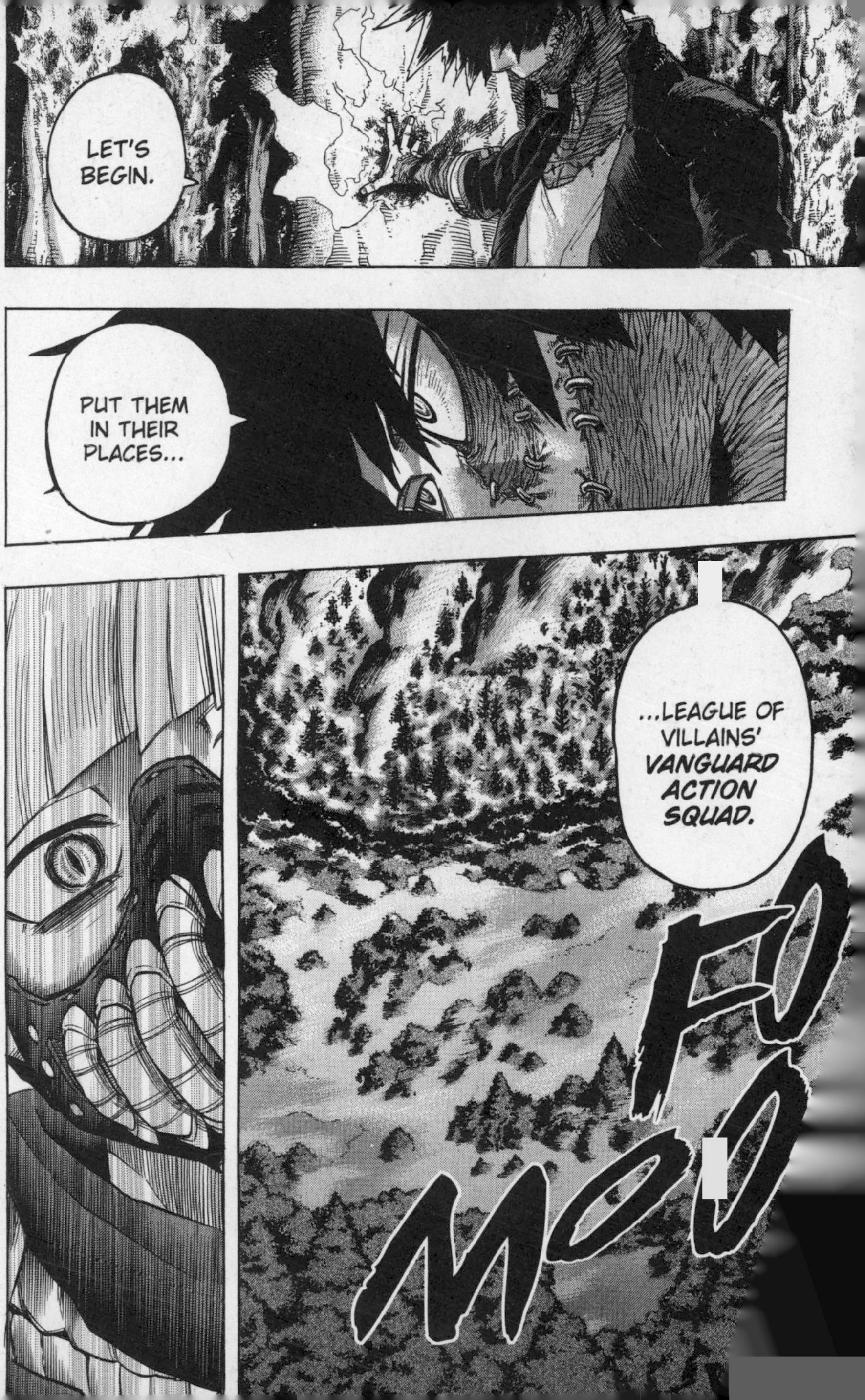
LET'S BEGIN.
PUT THEM IN THEIR PLACES...
...LEAGUE OF VILLAINS' *VANGUARD ACTION SQUAD.*

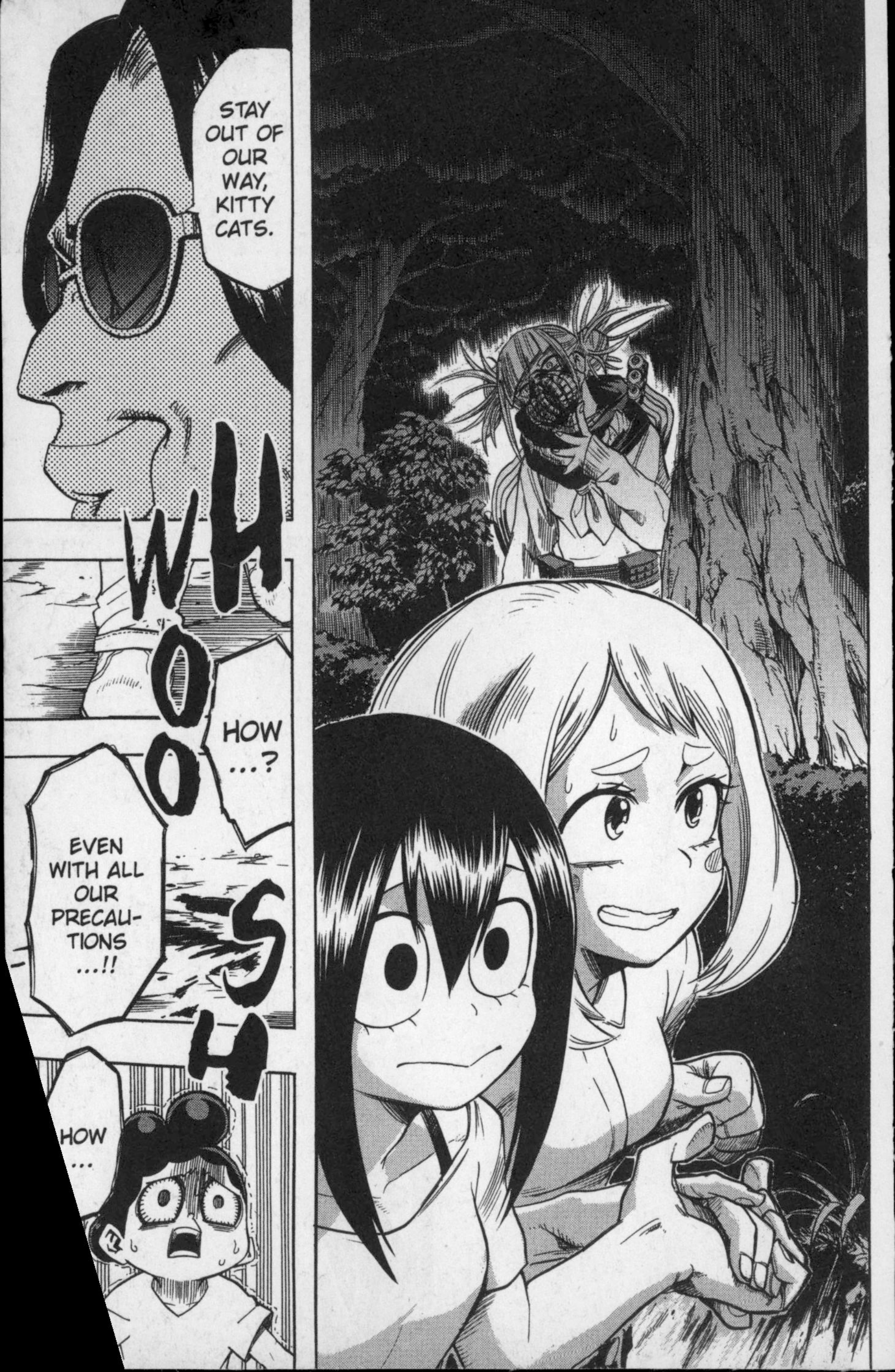
STAY OUT OF OUR WAY, KITTY CATS.
WHOOSH
HOW ...?
EVEN WITH ALL OUR PRECAUTIONS ...!!
HOW ...

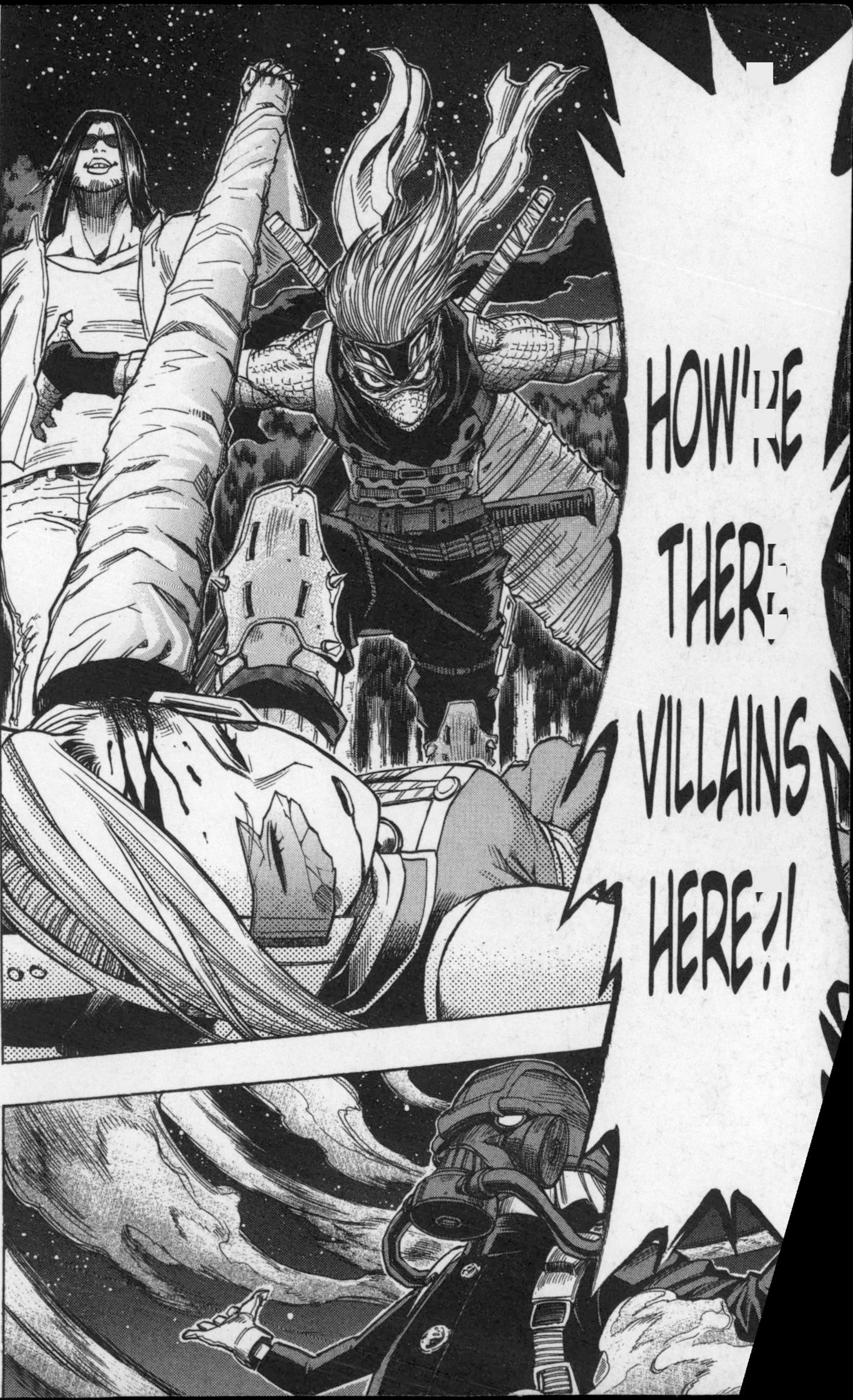
HOW'RE THERE VILLAINS HERE?!

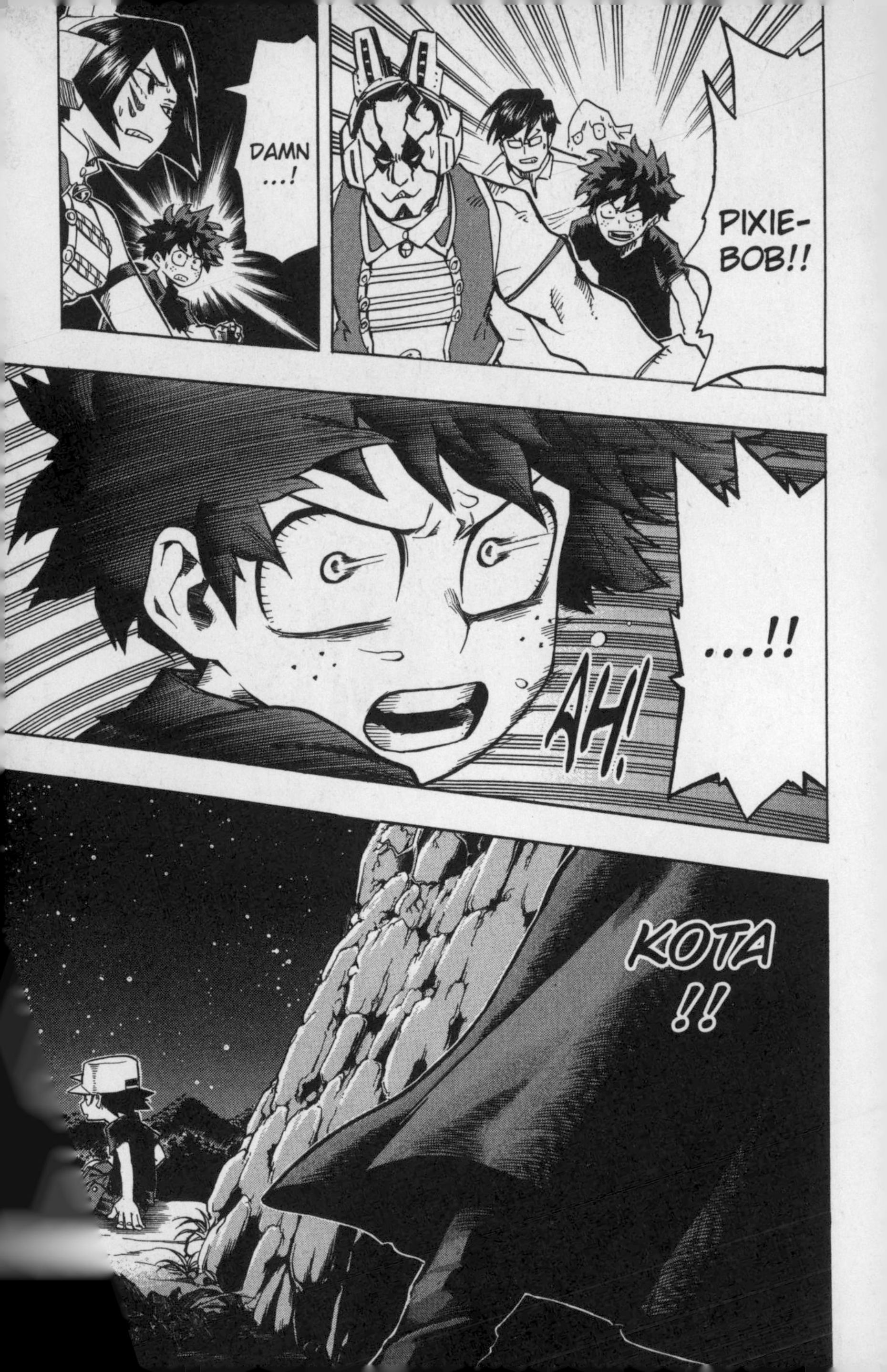
PIXIE-BOB!!
DAMN ...!
...!!
AH!
KOTA !!

EXTRA INFO ON QUIRK TRAINING PART 2

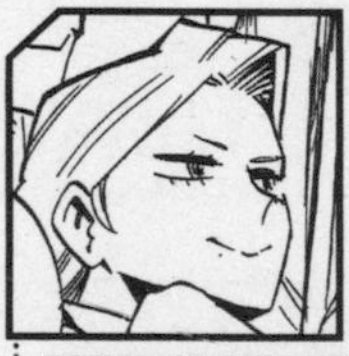

YUGA AOYAMA
NAVEL LASER

By continuing to shoot his laser even when his stomach starts to hurt, Aoyama's body acclimates to the process. This will allow him to fire his laser for longer periods.

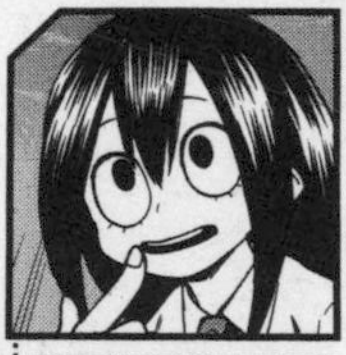

TSUYU ASUI
FROG

By muscle training, Asui is strengthening her jumping capabilities and the power of her tongue.

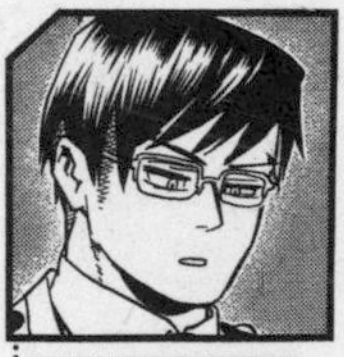

TENYA IDA
ENGINE

I didn't draw him doing this, but Ida's basically just running laps around the camp's perimeter.

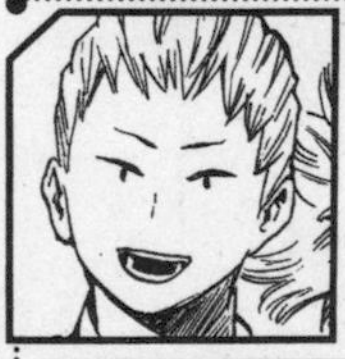

MASHIRAO OJIRO
TAIL

Ojiro strengthens his tail by smashing it against hard objects.

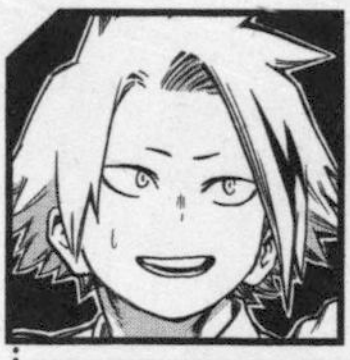

DENKI KAMINARI
ELECTRIFICATION

By continuously releasing electricity, Kaminari hopes to train his body to withstand higher output.

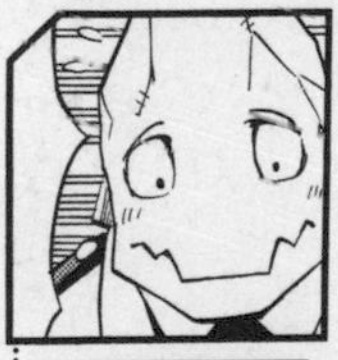

KOJI KODA
DOLITTLE

Koda's training involves shouting so that his voice can reach faraway targets.

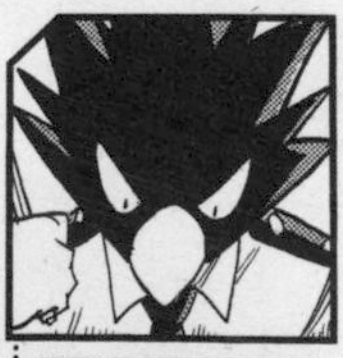

FUMIKAGE TOKOYAMI
DARK SHADOW

He trains by attempting to control Dark Shadow while in complete darkness. You might have noticed a panel with a "Gahhhh" coming from a cave. That's Tokoyami, battling against Dark Shadow.

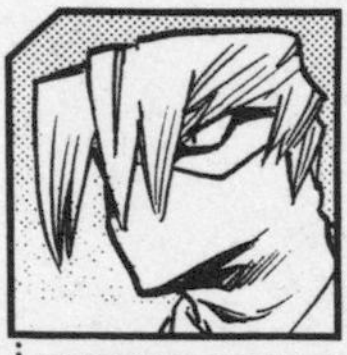

MEZO SHOJI
DUPLI-ARMS

Shoji is working hard at creating his duplicate parts faster and maintaining control over multiple parts at once. This training sounds especially tough.

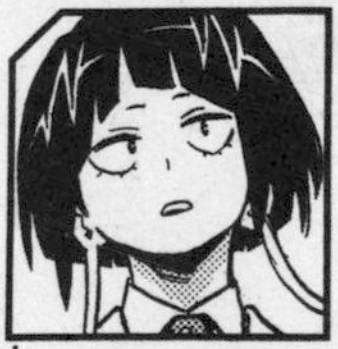

KYOKA JIRO
EARPHONE JACK

Strengthening her jacks will allow for better sound quality, so Jiro is focusing on whipping those ears around. As usual, I didn't draw this happening.

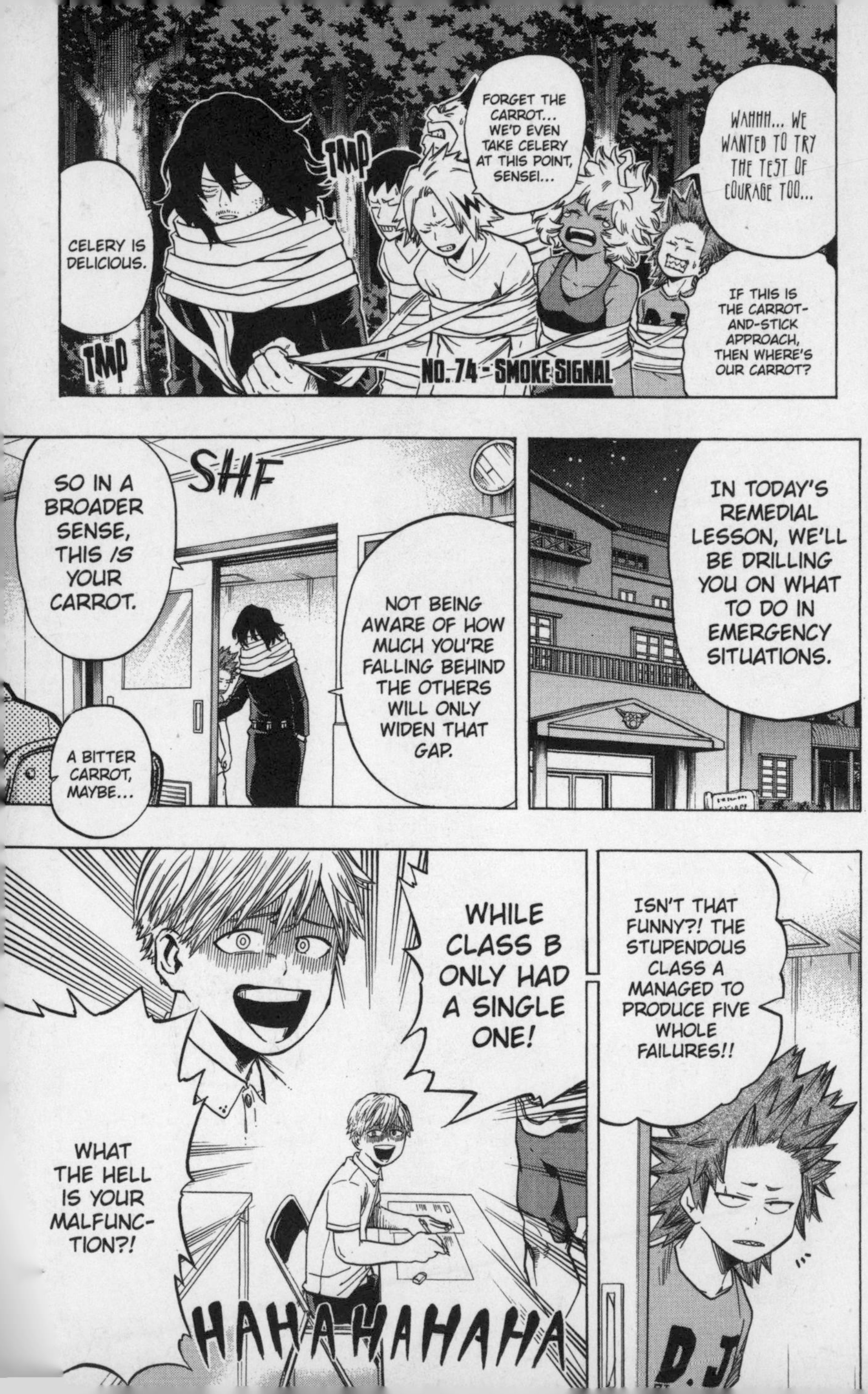
WAHHH... WE WANTED TO TRY THE TEST OF COURAGE TOO...
IF THIS IS THE CARROT-AND-STICK APPROACH, THEN WHERE'S OUR CARROT?
FORGET THE CARROT... WE'D EVEN TAKE CELERY AT THIS POINT, SENSEI...
TMP
CELERY IS DELICIOUS.
TMP
NO. 74 - SMOKE SIGNAL
IN TODAY'S REMEDIAL LESSON, WE'LL BE DRILLING YOU ON WHAT TO DO IN EMERGENCY SITUATIONS.
SHF
NOT BEING AWARE OF HOW MUCH YOU'RE FALLING BEHIND THE OTHERS WILL ONLY WIDEN THAT GAP.
SO IN A BROADER SENSE, THIS *IS* YOUR CARROT.
A BITTER CARROT, MAYBE...
ISN'T THAT FUNNY?! THE STUPENDOUS CLASS A MANAGED TO PRODUCE FIVE WHOLE FAILURES!!
WHILE CLASS B ONLY HAD A SINGLE ONE!
WHAT THE HELL IS YOUR MALFUNCTION?!
HAHAHAHAHAHA

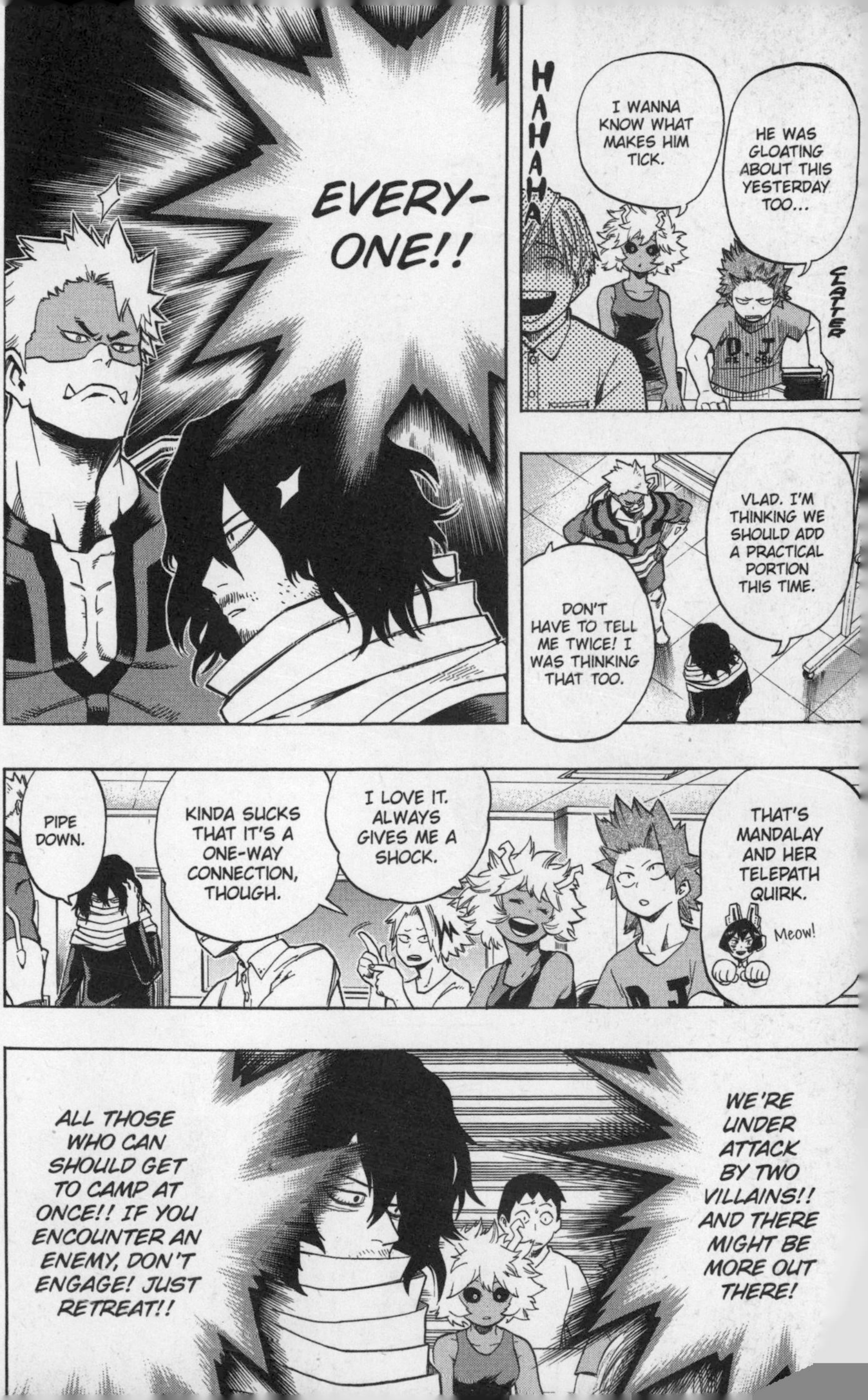
CLATTER
HE WAS GLOATING ABOUT THIS YESTERDAY TOO...
I WANNA KNOW WHAT MAKES HIM TICK.
HAHAHA
VLAD. I'M THINKING WE SHOULD ADD A PRACTICAL PORTION THIS TIME.
DON'T HAVE TO TELL ME TWICE! I WAS THINKING THAT TOO.
EVERY-ONE!!
THAT'S MANDALAY AND HER TELEPATH QUIRK.
Meow!
I LOVE IT. ALWAYS GIVES ME A SHOCK.
KINDA SUCKS THAT IT'S A ONE-WAY CONNECTION, THOUGH.
PIPE DOWN.
WE'RE UNDER ATTACK BY TWO VILLAINS!! AND THERE MIGHT BE MORE OUT THERE!
ALL THOSE WHO CAN SHOULD GET TO CAMP AT ONCE!! IF YOU ENCOUNTER AN ENEMY, DON'T ENGAGE! JUST RETREAT!!

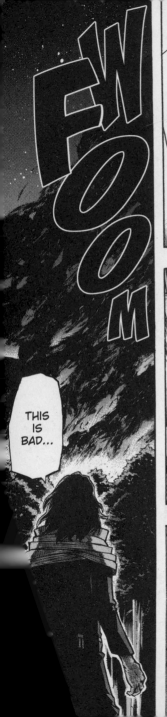

?
HOW'D THE VILLAINS KNOW ...?
VLAD, I'M LEAVING THESE GUYS WITH YOU.
I'M HEADING OUT TO PROTECT THE STUDENTS.
FWIP
HOW DID OUR LOCATION GET LEAKED?!
...
I'D RATHER NOT IMAGINE...!
!
SKF
FWOOOM
THIS IS BAD...

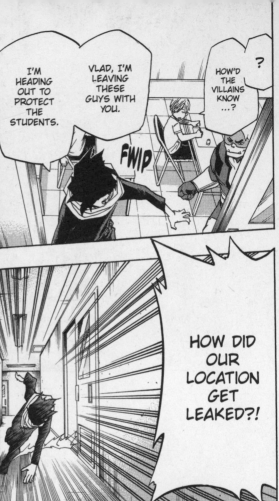

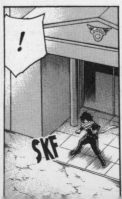

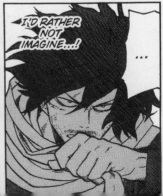

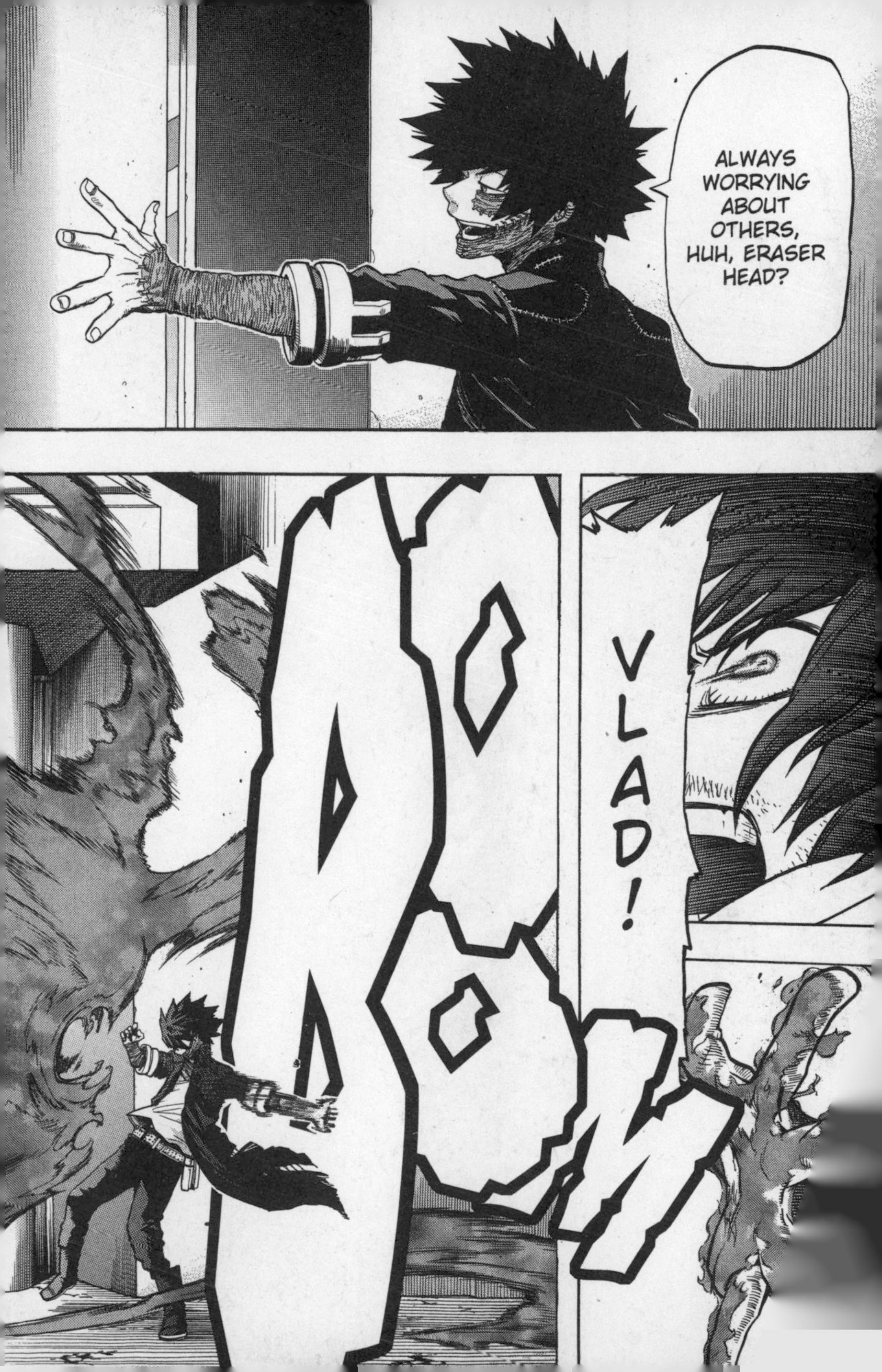
ALWAYS WORRYING ABOUT OTHERS, HUH, ERASER HEAD?
VLAD!

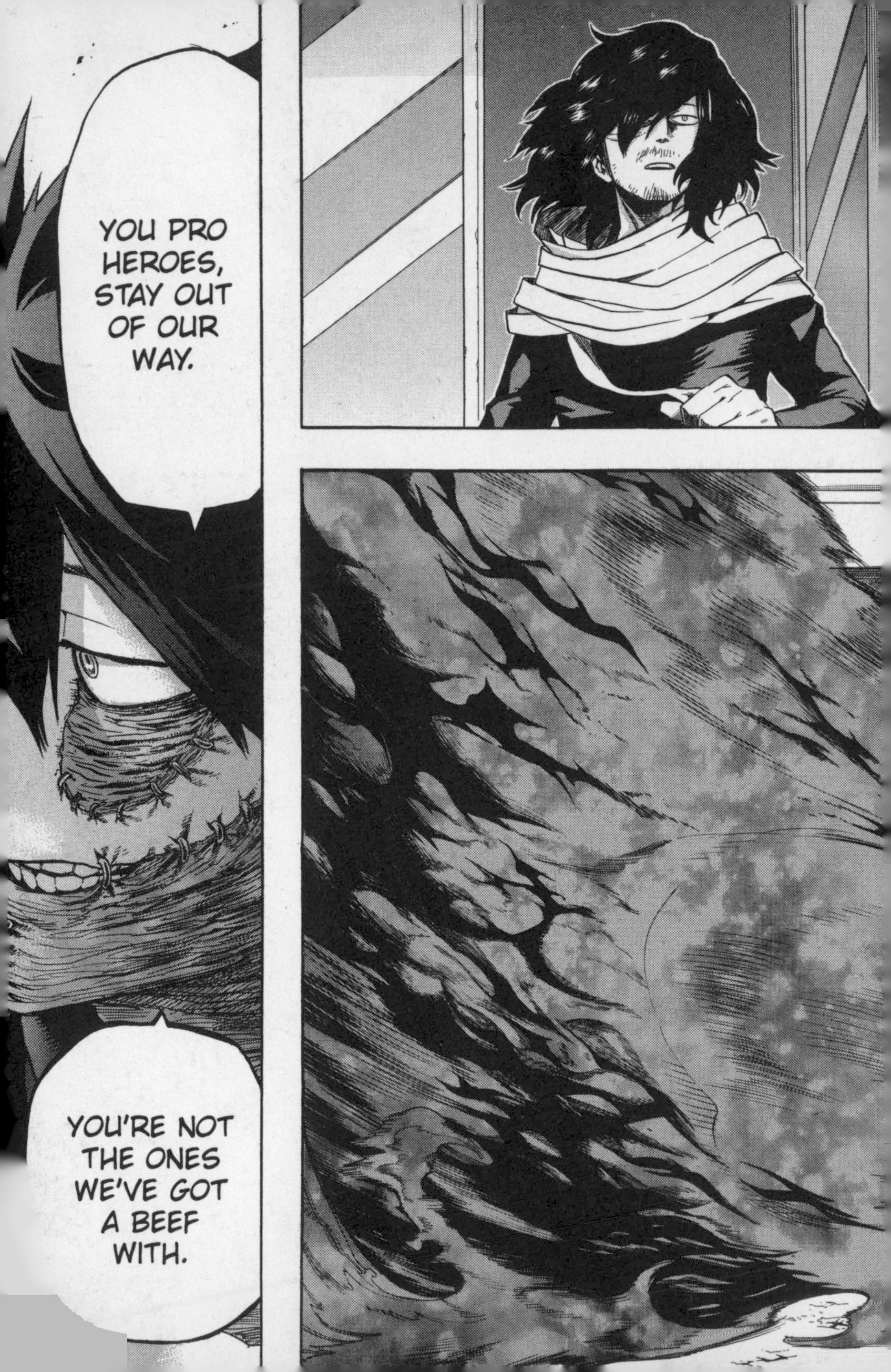
YOU PRO HEROES, STAY OUT OF OUR WAY.
YOU'RE NOT THE ONES WE'VE GOT A BEEF WITH.

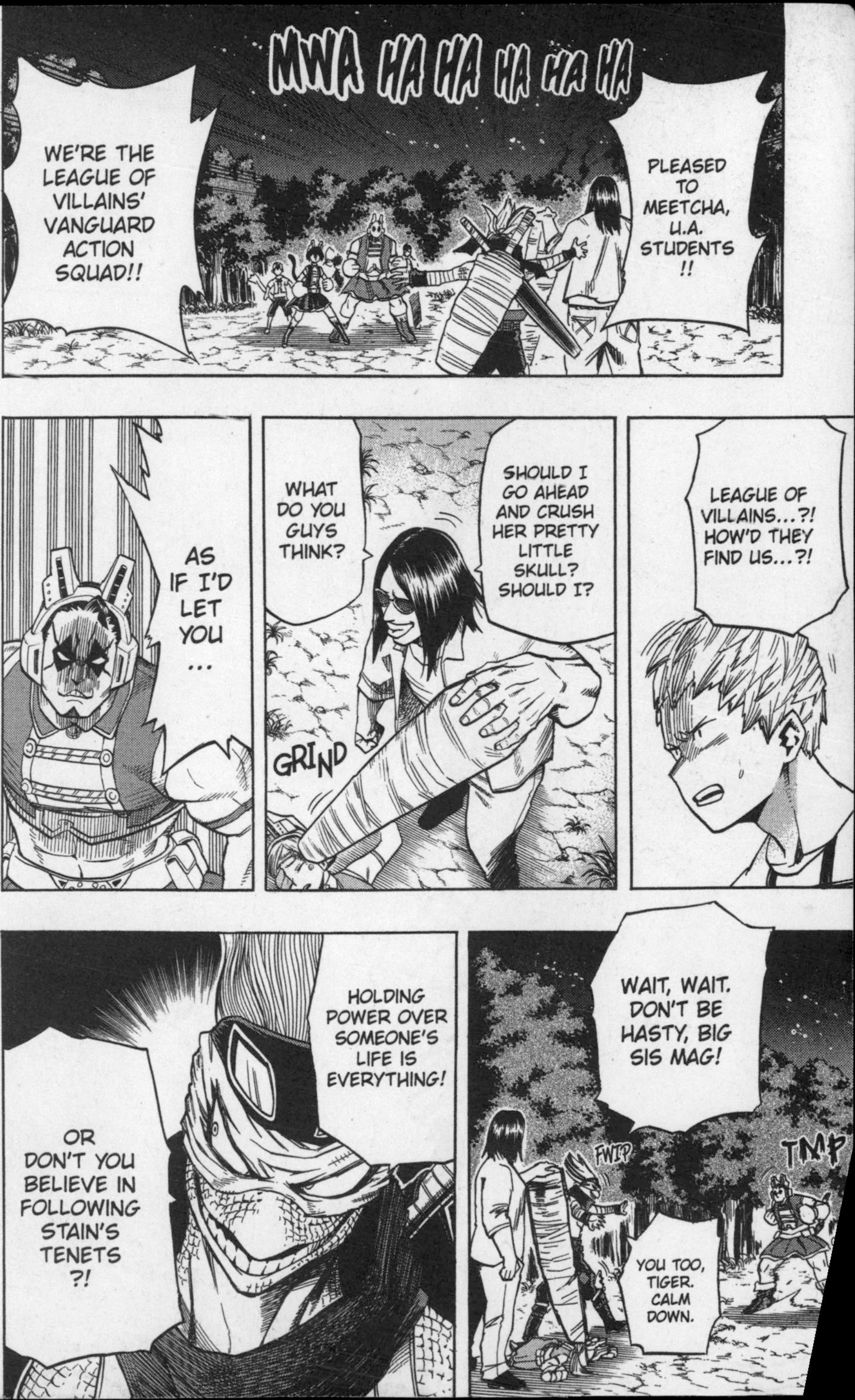
MWA HA HA HA HA HA
PLEASED TO MEETCHA, U.A. STUDENTS!!
WE'RE THE LEAGUE OF VILLAINS' VANGUARD ACTION SQUAD!!
LEAGUE OF VILLAINS...?! HOW'D THEY FIND US...?!
SHOULD I GO AHEAD AND CRUSH HER PRETTY LITTLE SKULL? SHOULD I?
WHAT DO YOU GUYS THINK?
GRIND
AS IF I'D LET YOU ...
WAIT, WAIT. DON'T BE HASTY, BIG SIS MAG!
TMP
FWIP
YOU TOO, TIGER. CALM DOWN.
HOLDING POWER OVER SOMEONE'S LIFE IS EVERYTHING!
OR DON'T YOU BELIEVE IN FOLLOWING STAIN'S TENETS?!

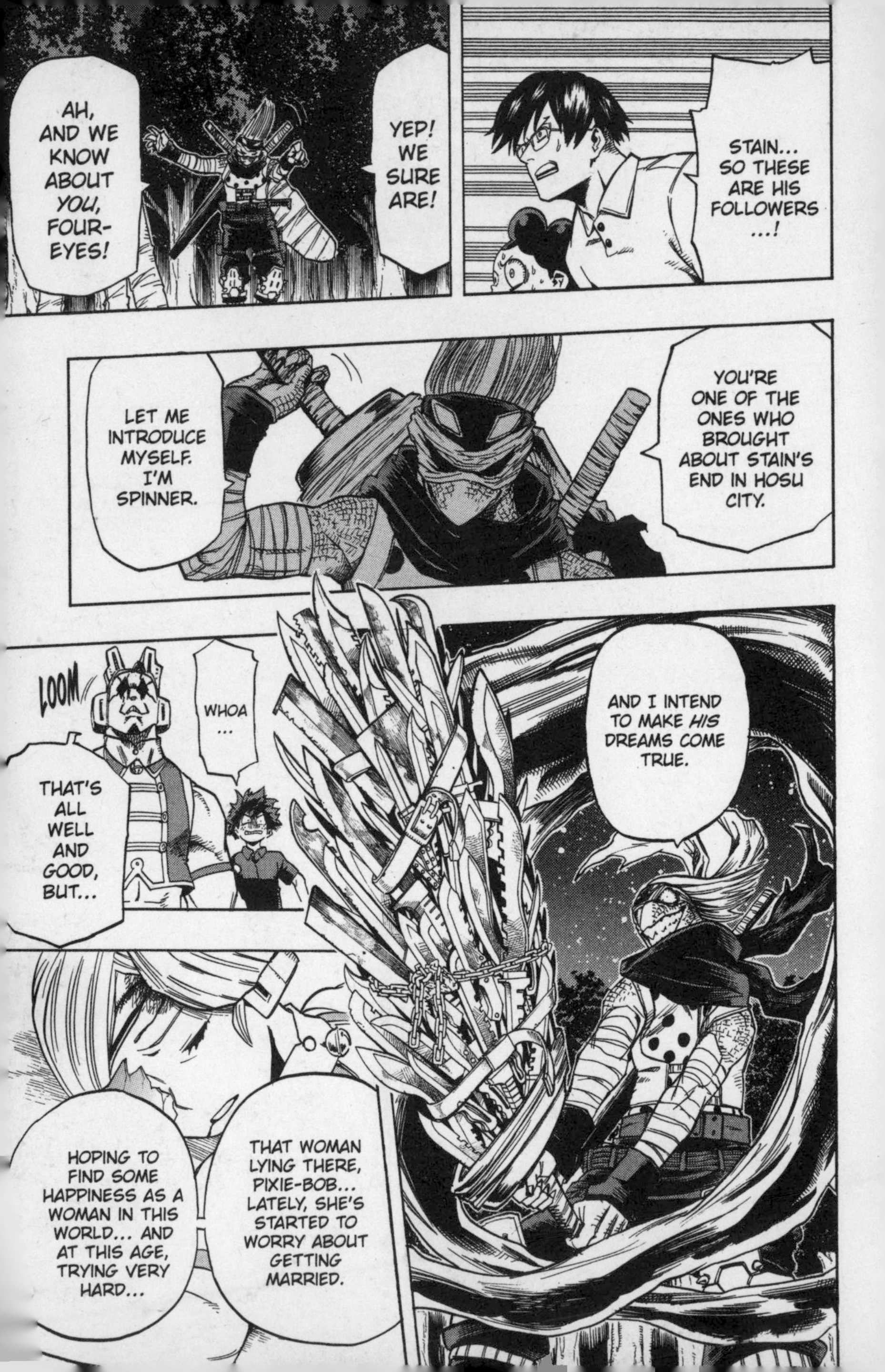
STAIN... SO THESE ARE HIS FOLLOWERS ...!
YEP! WE SURE ARE!
AH, AND WE KNOW ABOUT *YOU*, FOUR-EYES!
YOU'RE ONE OF THE ONES WHO BROUGHT ABOUT STAIN'S END IN HOSU CITY.
LET ME INTRODUCE MYSELF. I'M SPINNER.
AND I INTEND TO MAKE *HIS* DREAMS COME TRUE.
WHOA ...
LOOM
THAT'S ALL WELL AND GOOD, BUT...
THAT WOMAN LYING THERE, PIXIE-BOB... LATELY, SHE'S STARTED TO WORRY ABOUT GETTING MARRIED.
HOPING TO FIND SOME HAPPINESS AS A WOMAN IN THIS WORLD... AND AT THIS AGE, TRYING VERY HARD...

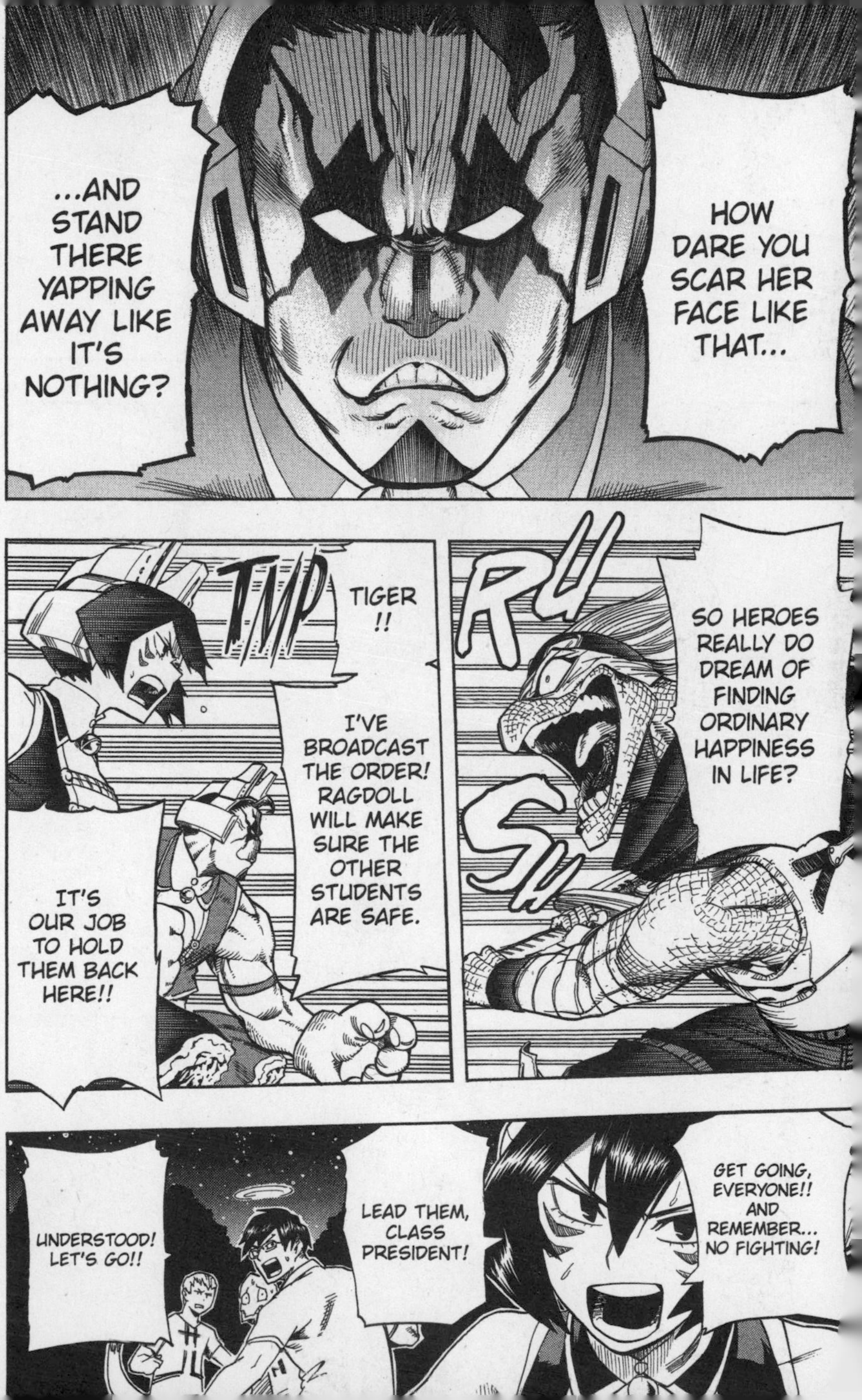
HOW DARE YOU SCAR HER FACE LIKE THAT...
...AND STAND THERE YAPPING AWAY LIKE IT'S NOTHING?
SO HEROES REALLY DO DREAM OF FINDING ORDINARY HAPPINESS IN LIFE?
RU
SH
TIGER !!
TMP
I'VE BROADCAST THE ORDER! RAGDOLL WILL MAKE SURE THE OTHER STUDENTS ARE SAFE.
IT'S OUR JOB TO HOLD THEM BACK HERE!!
GET GOING, EVERYONE!! AND REMEMBER... NO FIGHTING!
LEAD THEM, CLASS PRESIDENT!
UNDERSTOOD! LET'S GO!!

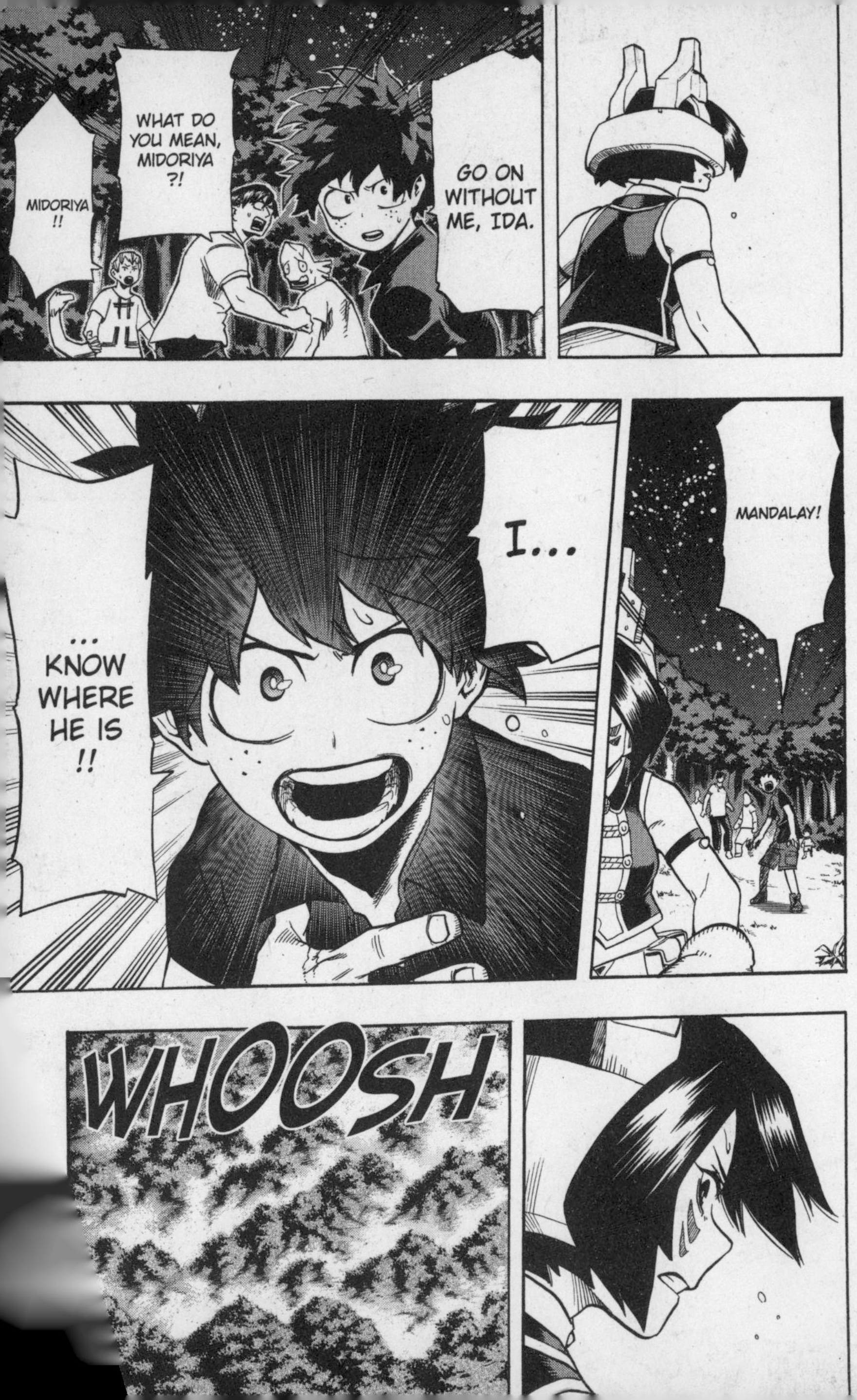
GO ON WITHOUT ME, IDA.
WHAT DO YOU MEAN, MIDORIYA ?!
MIDORIYA !!
MANDALAY!
I...
... KNOW WHERE HE IS !!
WHOOSH

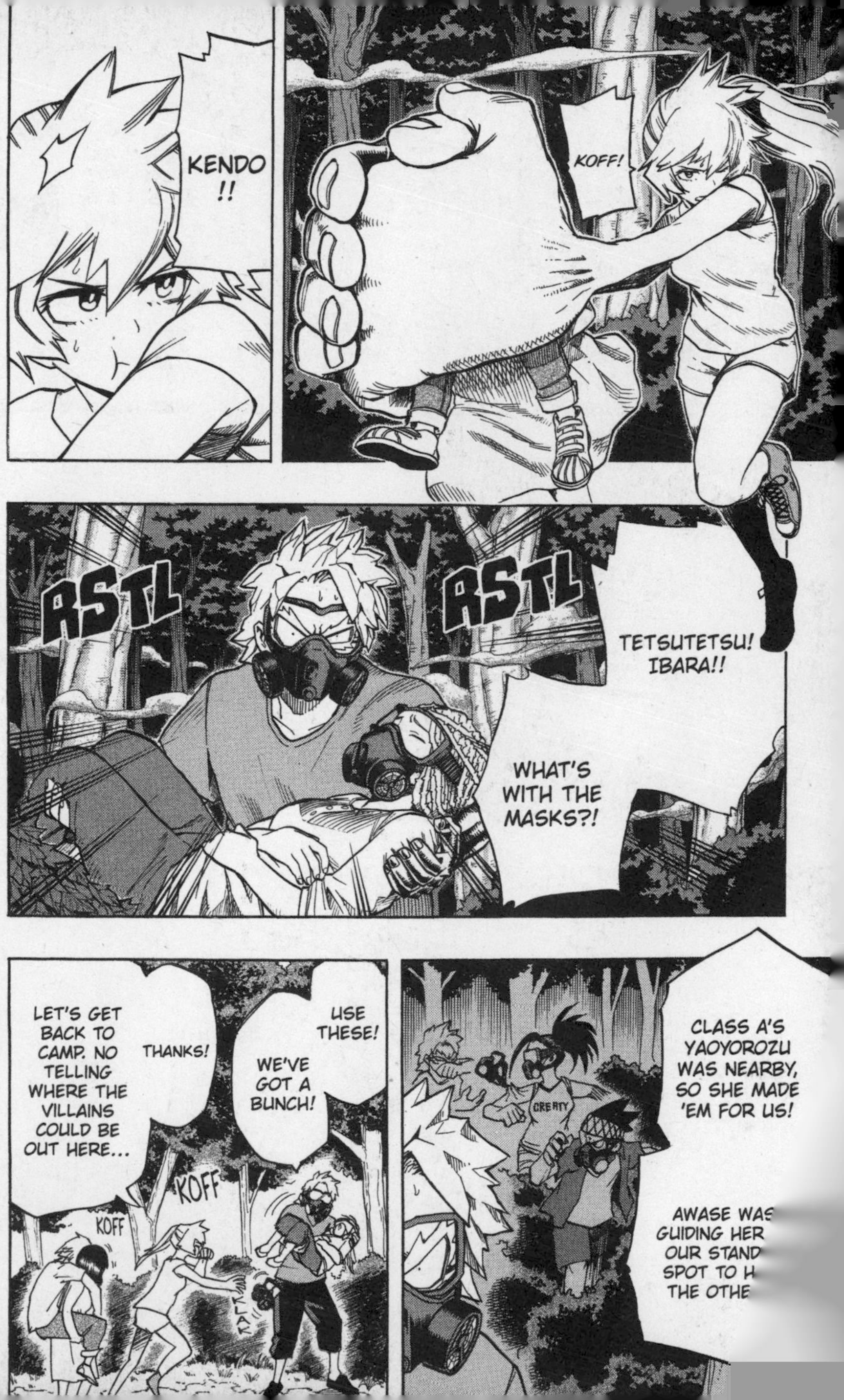
KOFF!
KENDO !!
RSTL
RSTL
TETSUTETSU! IBARA!!
WHAT'S WITH THE MASKS?!
CLASS A'S YAOYOROZU WAS NEARBY, SO SHE MADE 'EM FOR US!
AWASE WAS GUIDING HER OUR STAND SPOT TO H THE OTHE
CREATY
USE THESE!
WE'VE GOT A BUNCH!
THANKS!
LET'S GET BACK TO CAMP. NO TELLING WHERE THE VILLAINS COULD BE OUT HERE...
KOFF
KOFF
KLAK

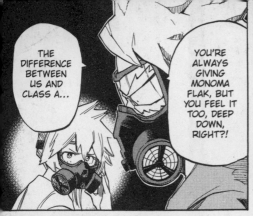

NO!
I'M GONNA FIGHT. YOU TAKE CARE OF SHIOZAKI AND KODAI.
HUH?! BUT WE WERE TOLD NOT TO ENGAGE...
YOU'RE ALWAYS GIVING MONOMA FLAK, BUT YOU FEEL IT TOO, DEEP DOWN, RIGHT?!
THE DIFFERENCE BETWEEN US AND CLASS A...
I KNOW *I* FEEL IT, ANYWAY...!
WE PASSED THE SAME TEST TO GET INTO U.A. WE HAVE THE SAME CURRICULUM.
SO WHAT'S THE DIFFERENCE? IT'S OBVIOUS! WHAT THEY'VE HAD AND WHAT WE DIDN'T...
CRISIS!!
THEY TAKE EVERY CRISIS AND TURN IT INTO AN OPPORTUNITY! GET IT?
HEROES SHOULDN'T BE RUNNING FROM BAD GUYS LIKE THIS!!

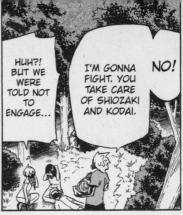

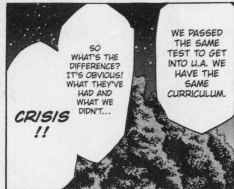

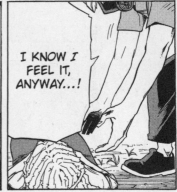

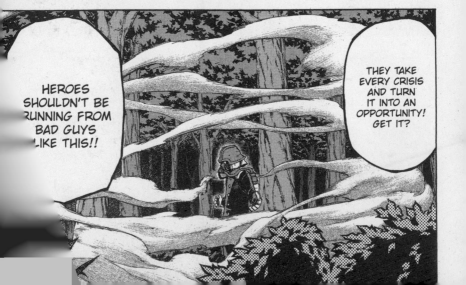

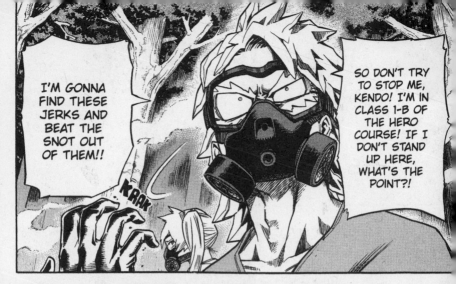

I'M GONNA FIND THESE JERKS AND BEAT THE SNOT OUT OF THEM!!

SO DON'T TRY TO STOP ME, KENDO! I'M IN CLASS 1-B OF THE HERO COURSE! IF I DON'T STAND UP HERE, WHAT'S THE POINT?!

KRAK

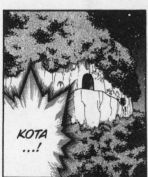

KOTA ...!

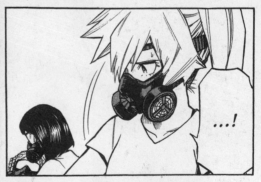

...!

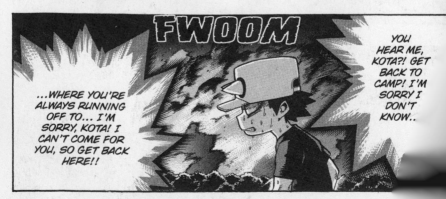

FWOOM

...WHERE YOU'RE ALWAYS RUNNING OFF TO... I'M SORRY, KOTA! I CAN'T COME FOR YOU, SO GET BACK HERE!!

YOU HEAR ME, KOTA?! GET BACK TO CAMP! I'M SORRY I DON'T KNOW..

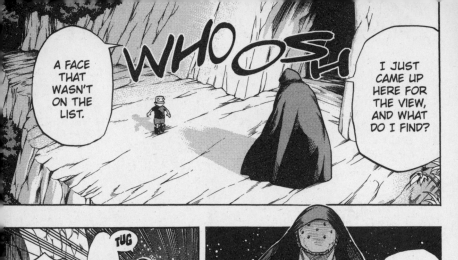

I JUST CAME UP HERE FOR THE VIEW, AND WHAT DO I FIND?
WHOOSH
A FACE THAT WASN'T ON THE LIST.
BY THE WAY, THAT HAT'S PRETTY SLICK, KID.
TUG
HEY!
WAHH...
TOMP
TOMP
WHY DON'TCHA TRADE ME FOR THIS LAME MASK?
I'M A NEWBIE TO THE OPERATION, SO THEY MADE ME WEAR THIS DUMB TOY.
THOM

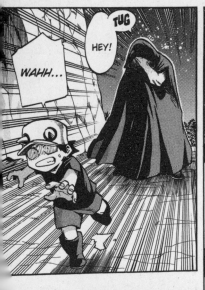

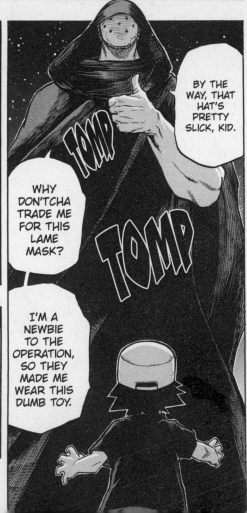

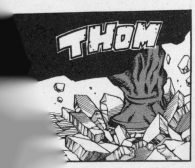

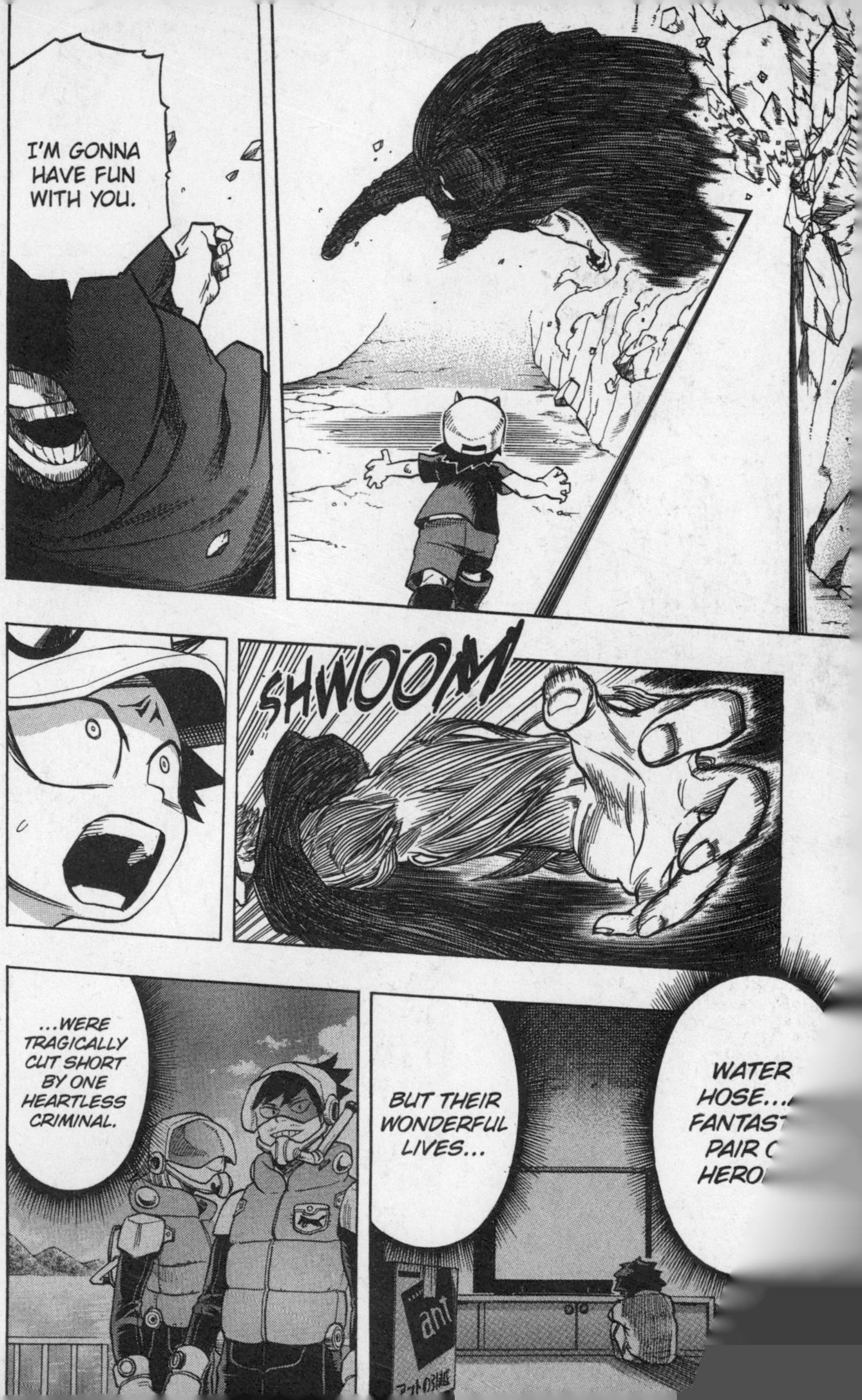
I'M GONNA HAVE FUN WITH YOU.
SHWOOM
WATER HOSE…
BUT THEIR WONDERFUL LIVES…
…WERE TRAGICALLY CUT SHORT BY ONE HEARTLESS CRIMINAL.

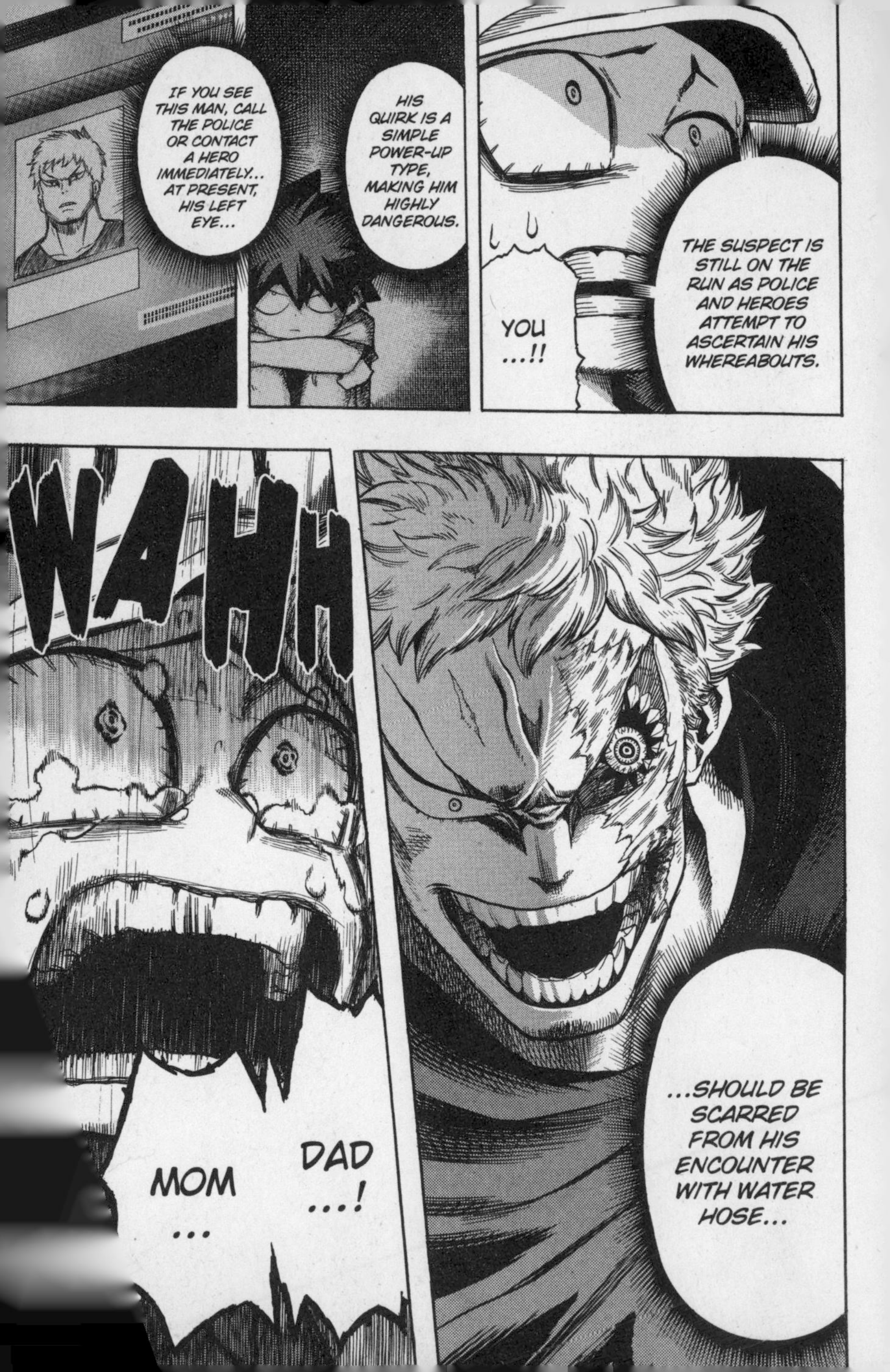
THE SUSPECT IS STILL ON THE RUN AS POLICE AND HEROES ATTEMPT TO ASCERTAIN HIS WHEREABOUTS.
YOU ...!!
HIS QUIRK IS A SIMPLE POWER-UP TYPE, MAKING HIM HIGHLY DANGEROUS.
IF YOU SEE THIS MAN, CALL THE POLICE OR CONTACT A HERO IMMEDIATELY... AT PRESENT, HIS LEFT EYE...
...SHOULD BE SCARRED FROM HIS ENCOUNTER WITH WATER HOSE...
WAHH
DAD ...!
MOM ...

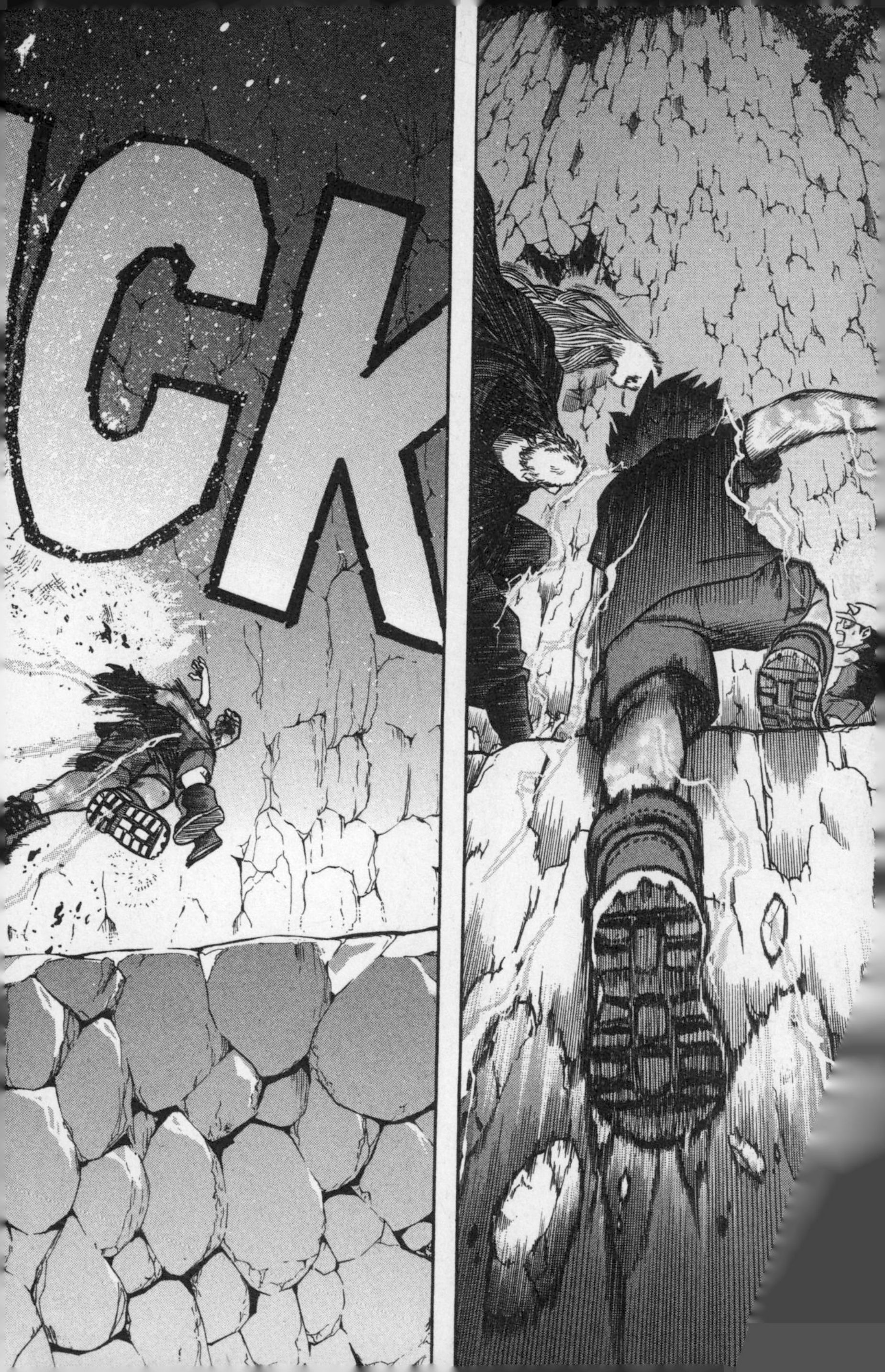
CK

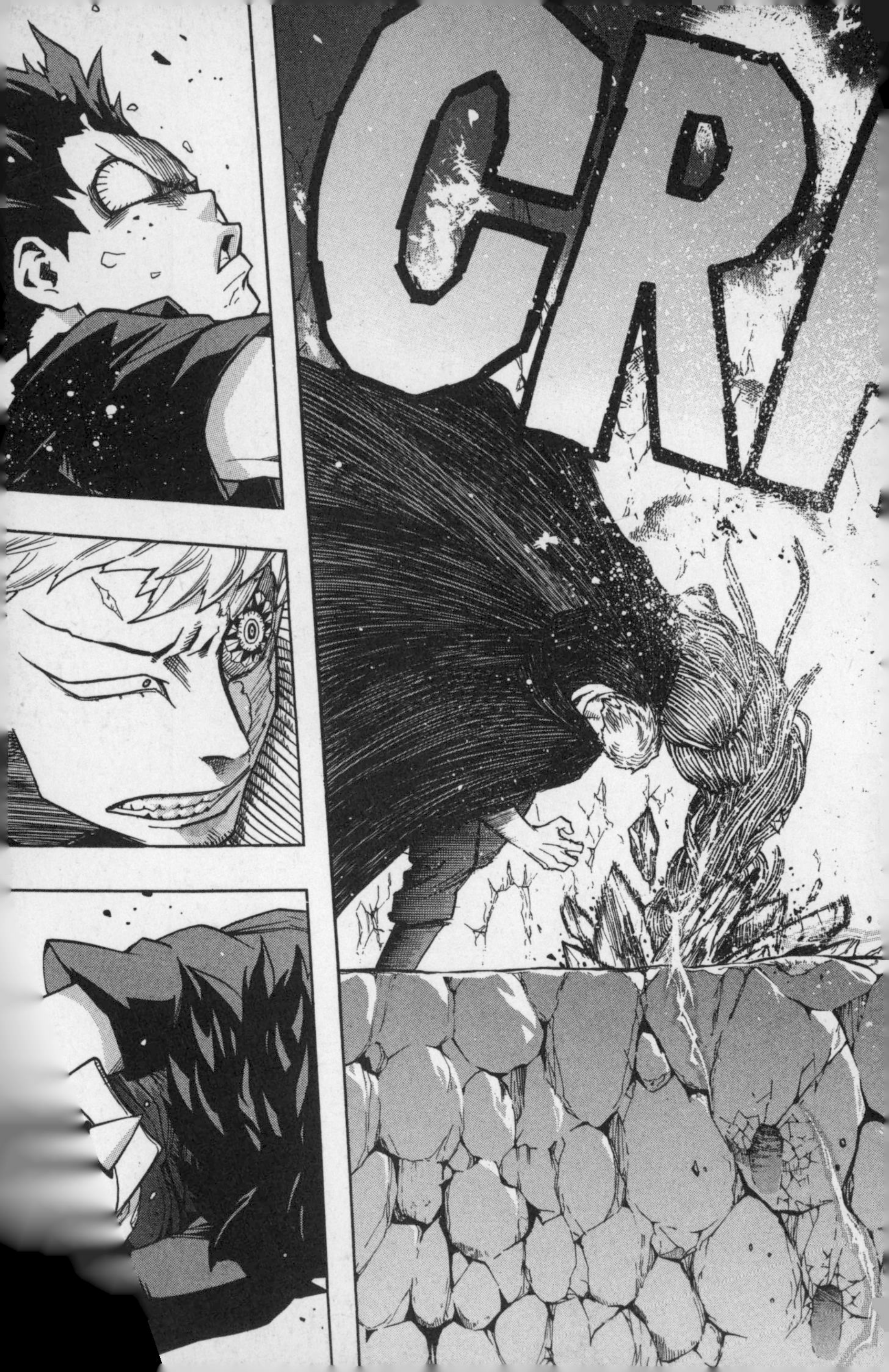
CRA

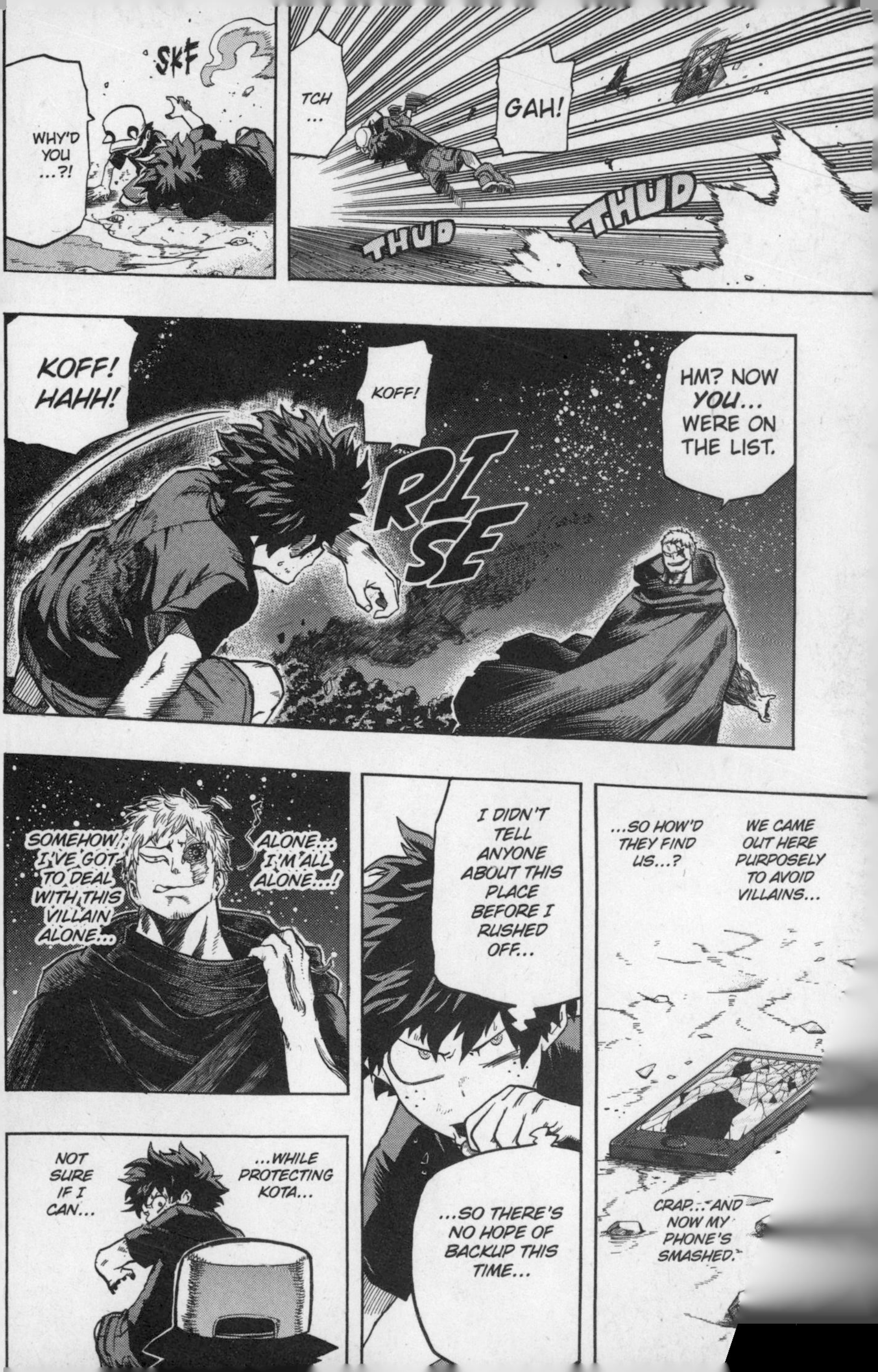
TCH ...
GAH!
THUD
THUD
SKF
WHY'D YOU ...?!
HM? NOW YOU... WERE ON THE LIST.
KOFF!
RISE
KOFF! HAHH!
WE CAME OUT HERE PURPOSELY TO AVOID VILLAINS...
...SO HOW'D THEY FIND US...?
CRAP... AND NOW MY PHONE'S SMASHED.
I DIDN'T TELL ANYONE ABOUT THIS PLACE BEFORE I RUSHED OFF...
...SO THERE'S NO HOPE OF BACKUP THIS TIME...
ALONE... I'M ALL ALONE...!
SOMEHOW I'VE GOT TO DEAL WITH THIS VILLAIN ALONE...
...WHILE PROTECTING KOTA...
NOT SURE IF I CAN...

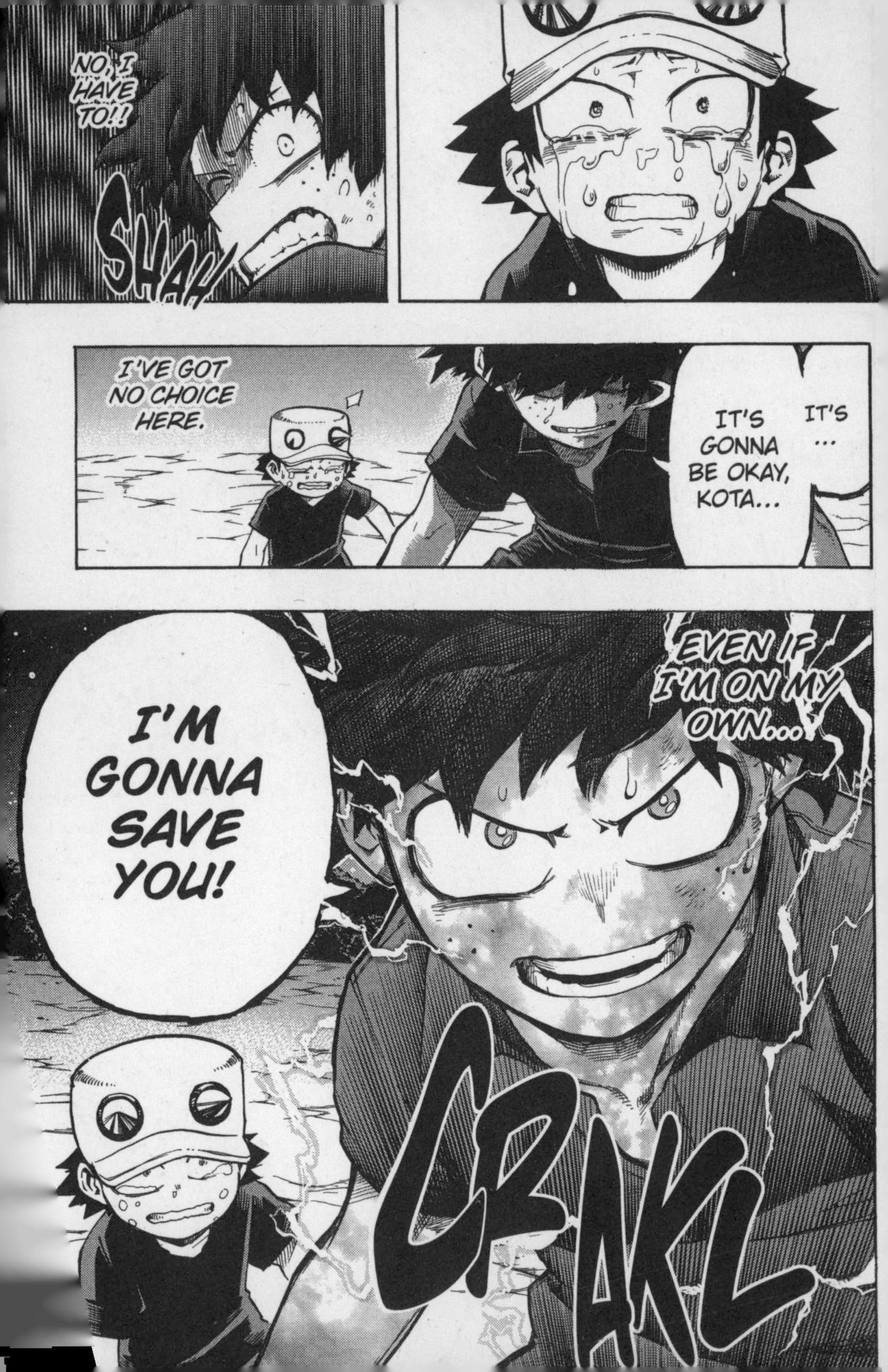
NO, I HAVE TO!!
SHAH
IT'S...
IT'S GONNA BE OKAY, KOTA...
I'VE GOT NO CHOICE HERE.
EVEN IF I'M ON MY OWN...
I'M GONNA SAVE YOU!
CRAKL

HERO

WILD, WILD PUSSYCATS: TIGER (AGE 31) (YAWARA CHATORA)

STREET CLOTHES

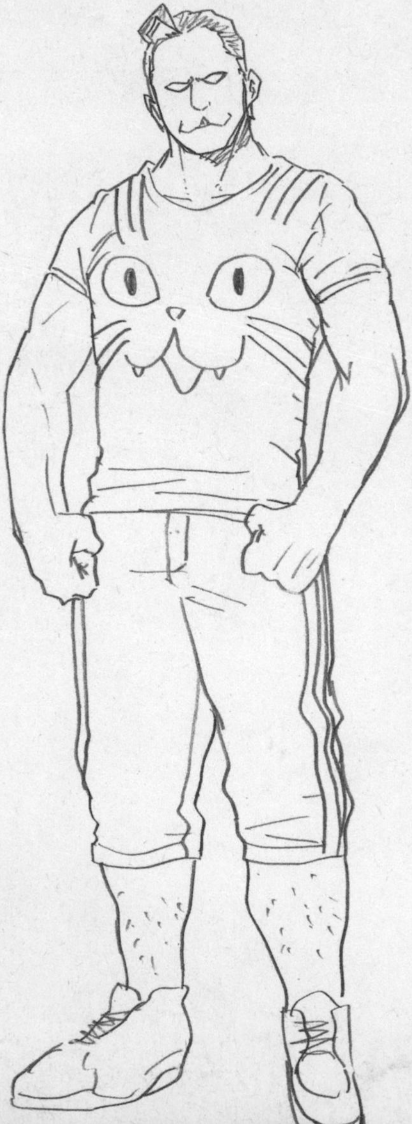

Birthday: 2/29
Height: 190 cm
Favorite Thing: His teammates

BEHIND THE SCENES

Originally a woman. I once visited Thailand.

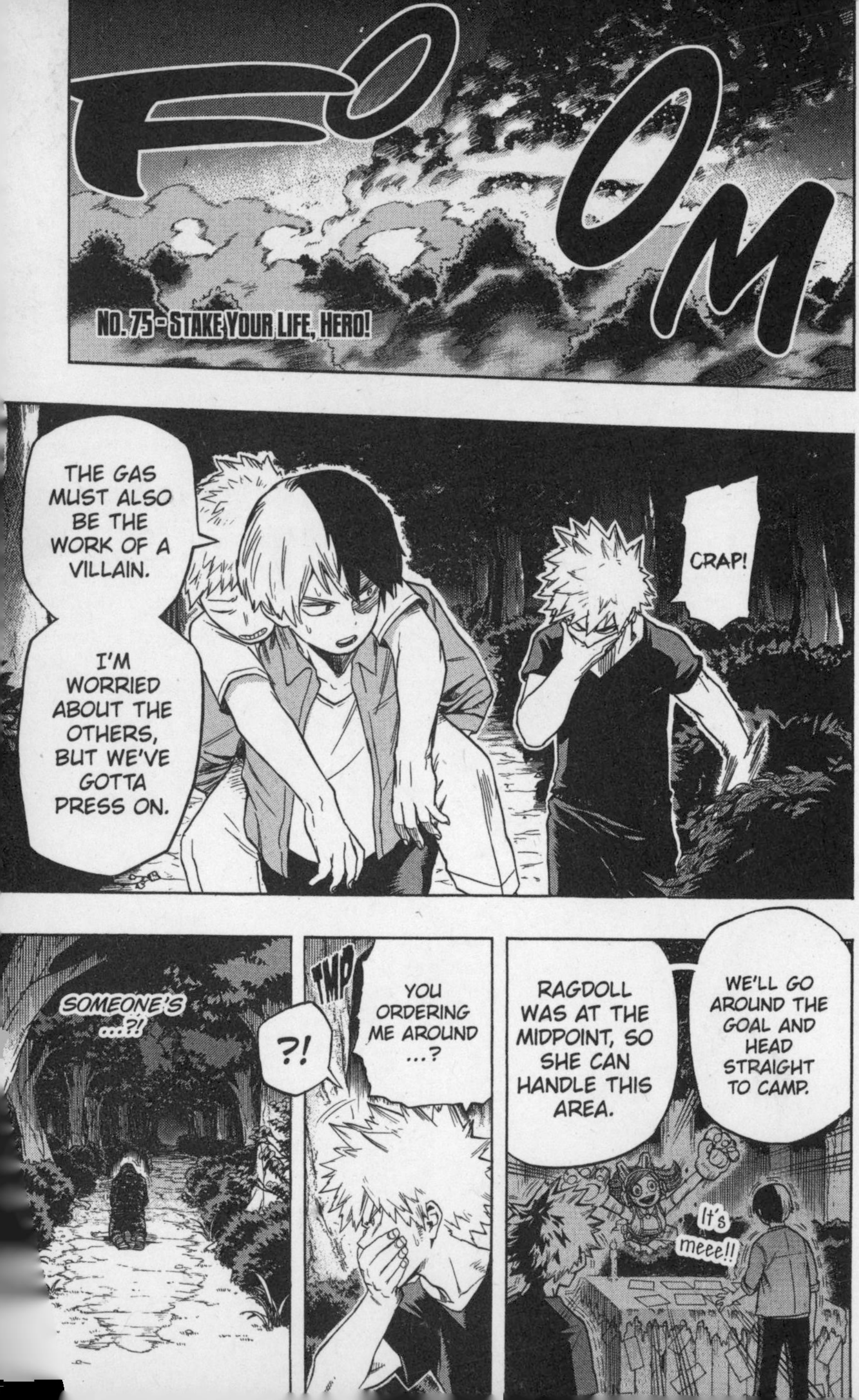
FOOOM
No. 75 - Stake Your Life, Hero!
CRAP!
THE GAS MUST ALSO BE THE WORK OF A VILLAIN.
I'M WORRIED ABOUT THE OTHERS, BUT WE'VE GOTTA PRESS ON.
WE'LL GO AROUND THE GOAL AND HEAD STRAIGHT TO CAMP.
RAGDOLL WAS AT THE MIDPOINT, SO SHE CAN HANDLE THIS AREA.
It's meee!!
TMP
YOU ORDERING ME AROUND ...?
?!
SOMEONE'S ...?!

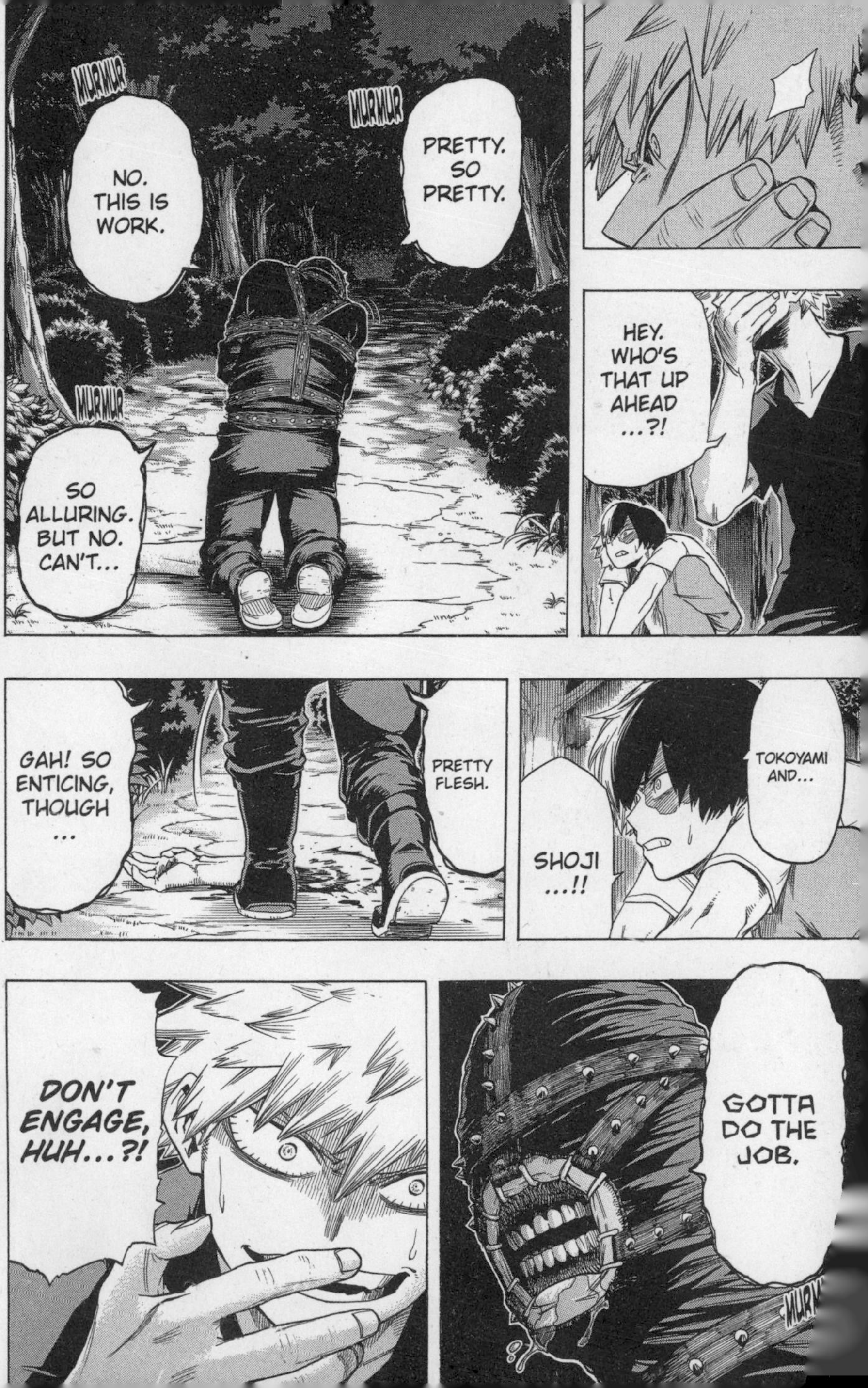
HEY. WHO'S THAT UP AHEAD ...?!
MURMUR
PRETTY. SO PRETTY.
MURMUR
NO. THIS IS WORK.
MURMUR
SO ALLURING. BUT NO. CAN'T...
TOKOYAMI AND...
SHOJI ...!!
PRETTY FLESH.
GAH! SO ENTICING, THOUGH ...
GOTTA DO THE JOB.
DON'T ENGAGE, HUH...?!

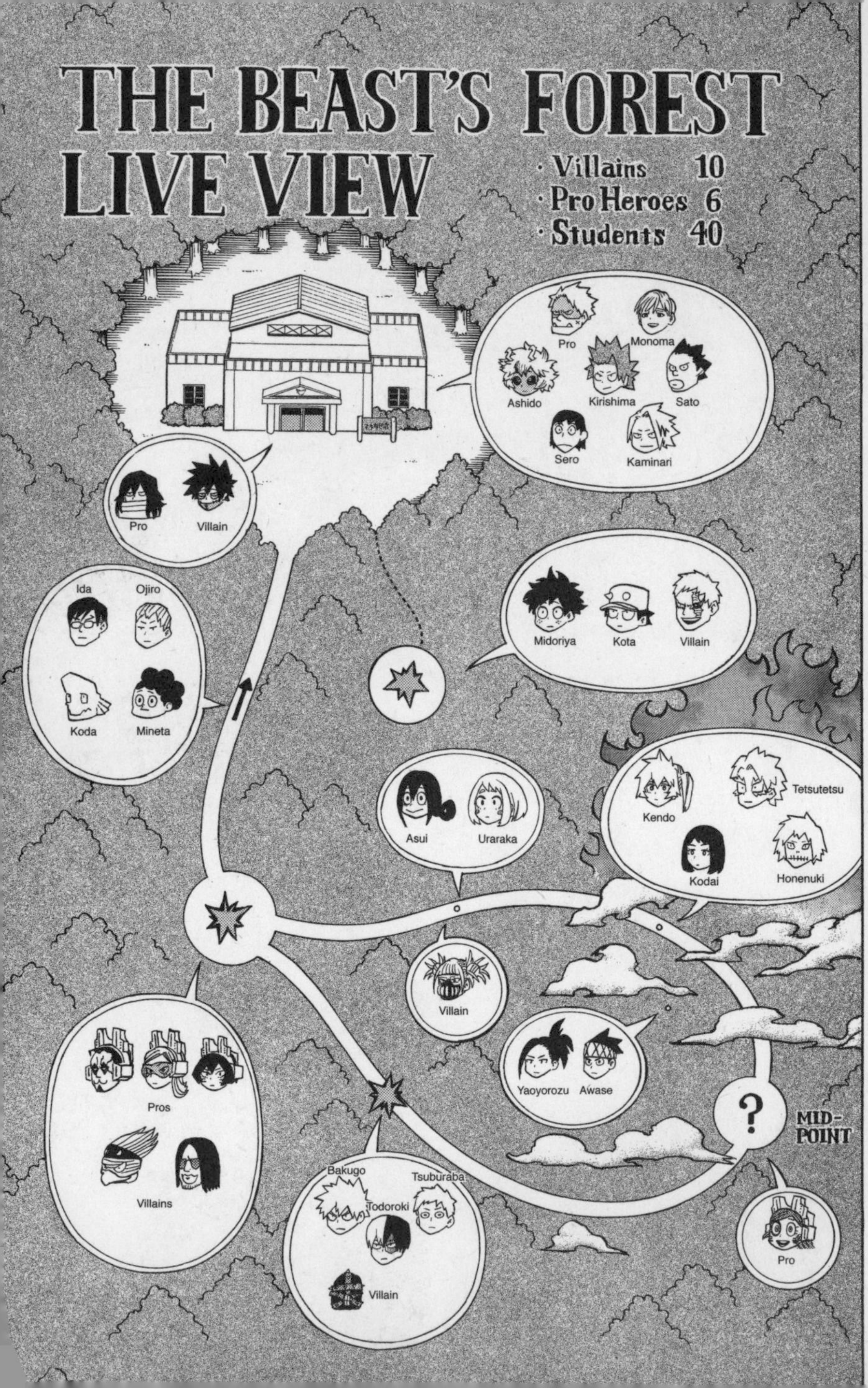
THE BEAST'S FOREST LIVE VIEW
· Villains 10
· Pro Heroes 6
· Students 40
Pro
Monoma
Ashido
Kirishima
Sato
Sero
Kaminari
Pro
Villain
Ida
Ojiro
Koda
Mineta
Midoriya
Kota
Villain
Asui
Uraraka
Kendo
Tetsutetsu
Kodai
Honenuki
Villain
Yaoyorozu
Awase
Pros
Villains
?
MID-POINT
Bakugo
Tsuburaba
Todoroki
Villain
Pro

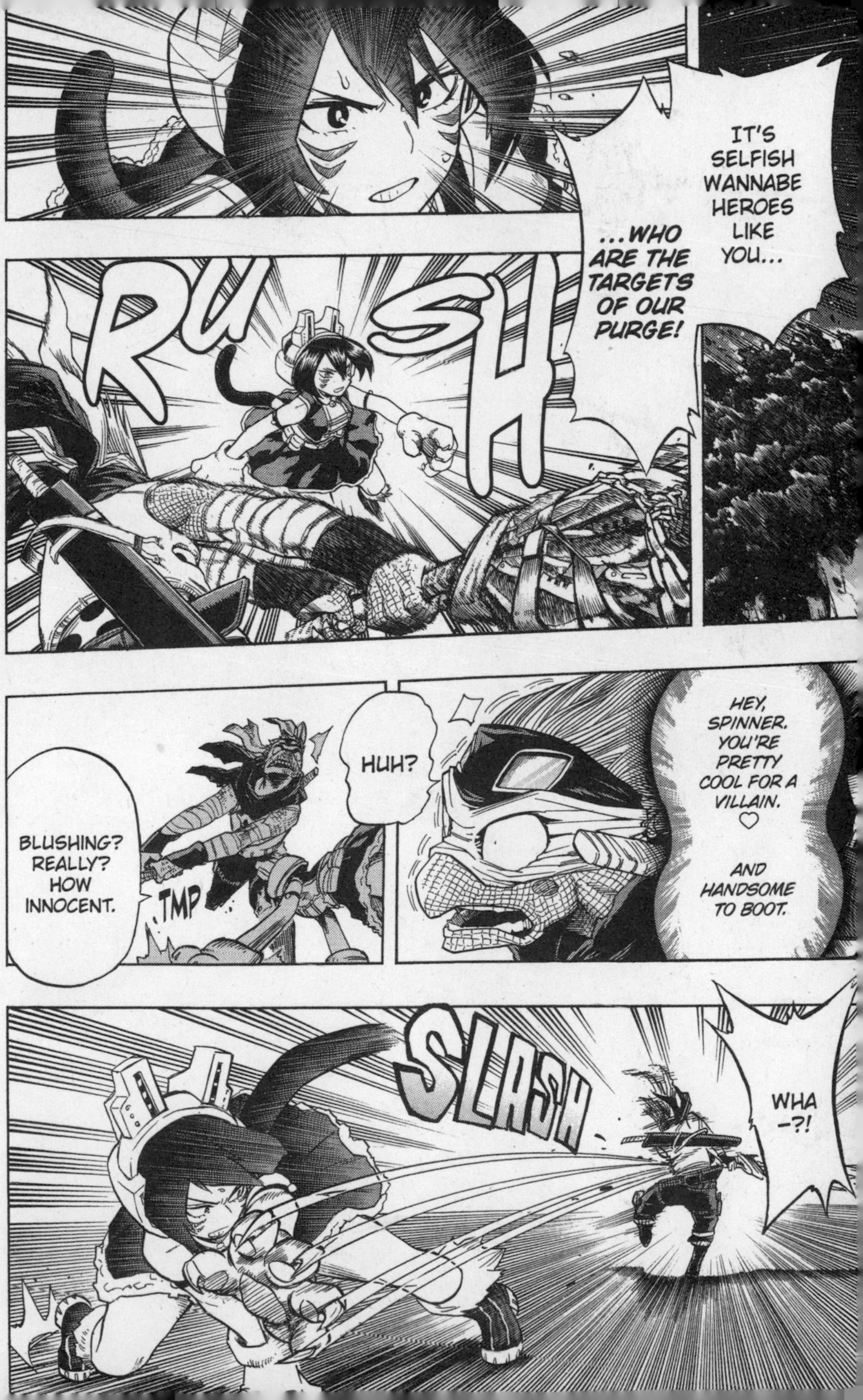
IT'S SELFISH WANNABE HEROES LIKE YOU...
...WHO ARE THE TARGETS OF OUR PURGE!
RUSH
HEY, SPINNER. YOU'RE PRETTY COOL FOR A VILLAIN. ♡
AND HANDSOME TO BOOT.
HUH?
BLUSHING? REALLY? HOW INNOCENT.
TMP
WHA-?!
SLASH

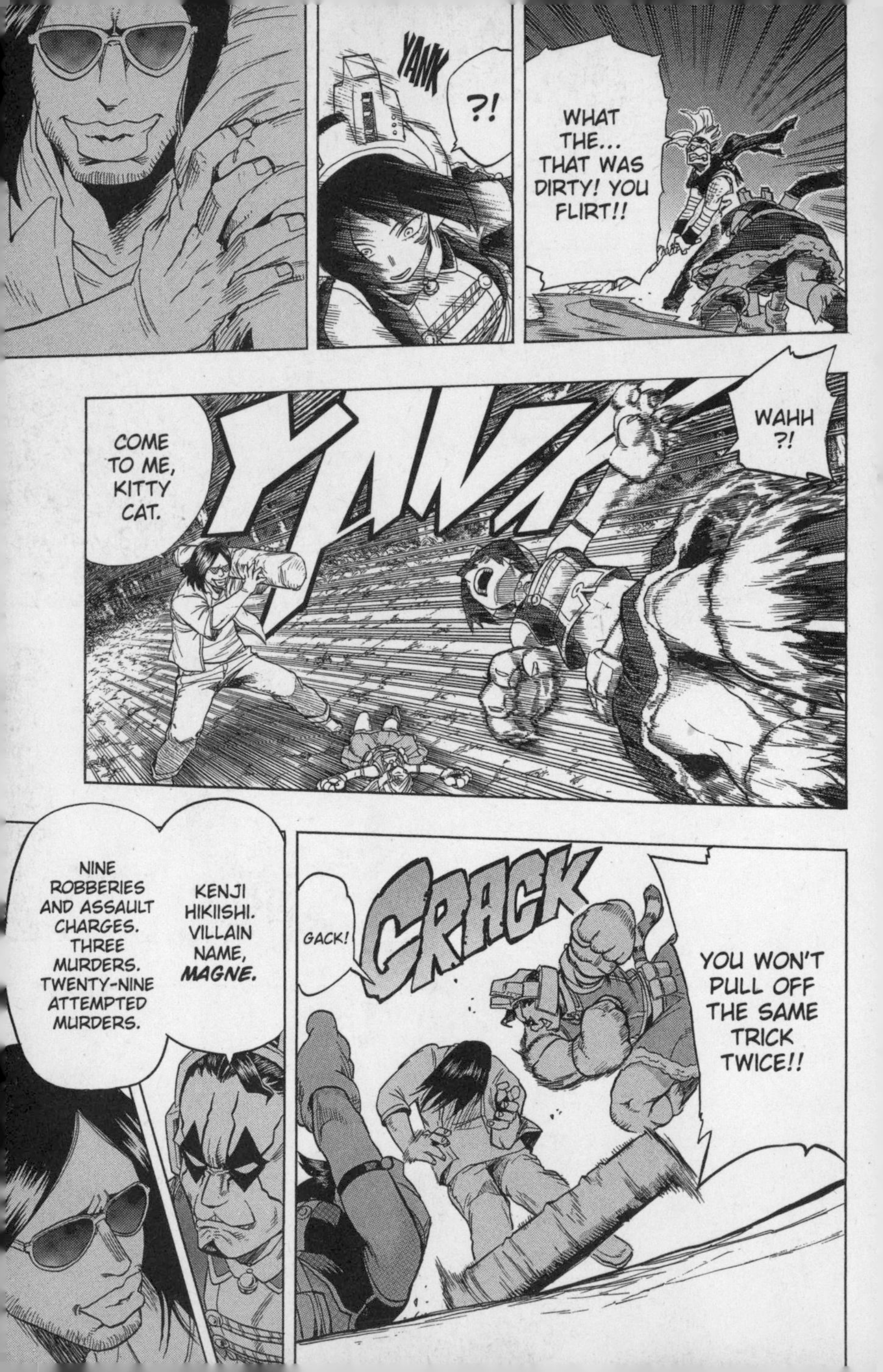
WHAT THE... THAT WAS DIRTY! YOU FLIRT!!
YANK
?!
WAHH ?!
YANK
COME TO ME, KITTY CAT.
YOU WON'T PULL OFF THE SAME TRICK TWICE!!
CRACK
GACK!
KENJI HIKIISHI. VILLAIN NAME, *MAGNE.*
NINE ROBBERIES AND ASSAULT CHARGES. THREE MURDERS. TWENTY-NINE ATTEMPTED MURDERS.

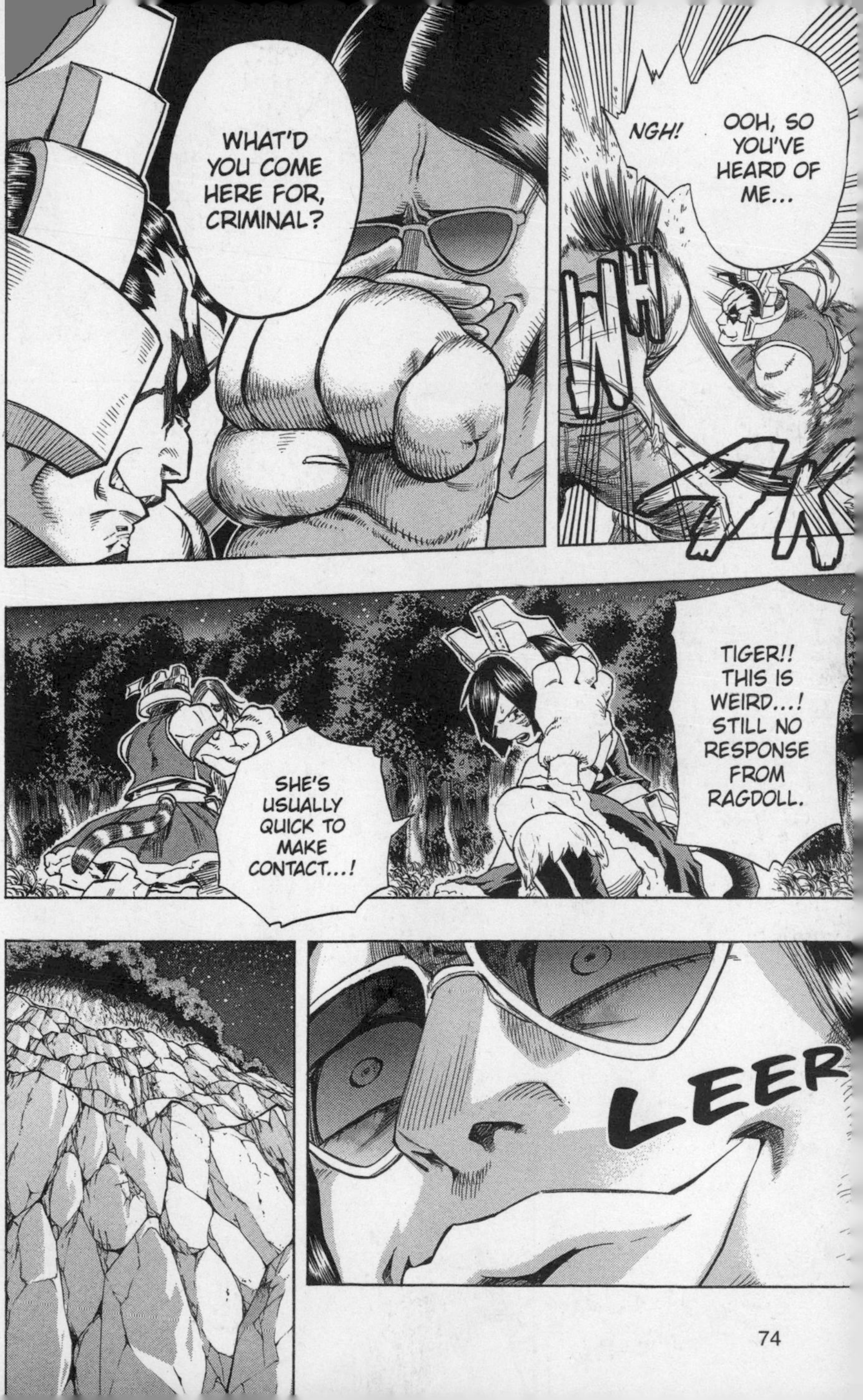
OOH, SO YOU'VE HEARD OF ME...
NGH!
WHAT'D YOU COME HERE FOR, CRIMINAL?
TIGER!! THIS IS WEIRD...! STILL NO RESPONSE FROM RAGDOLL.
SHE'S USUALLY QUICK TO MAKE CONTACT...!
LEER

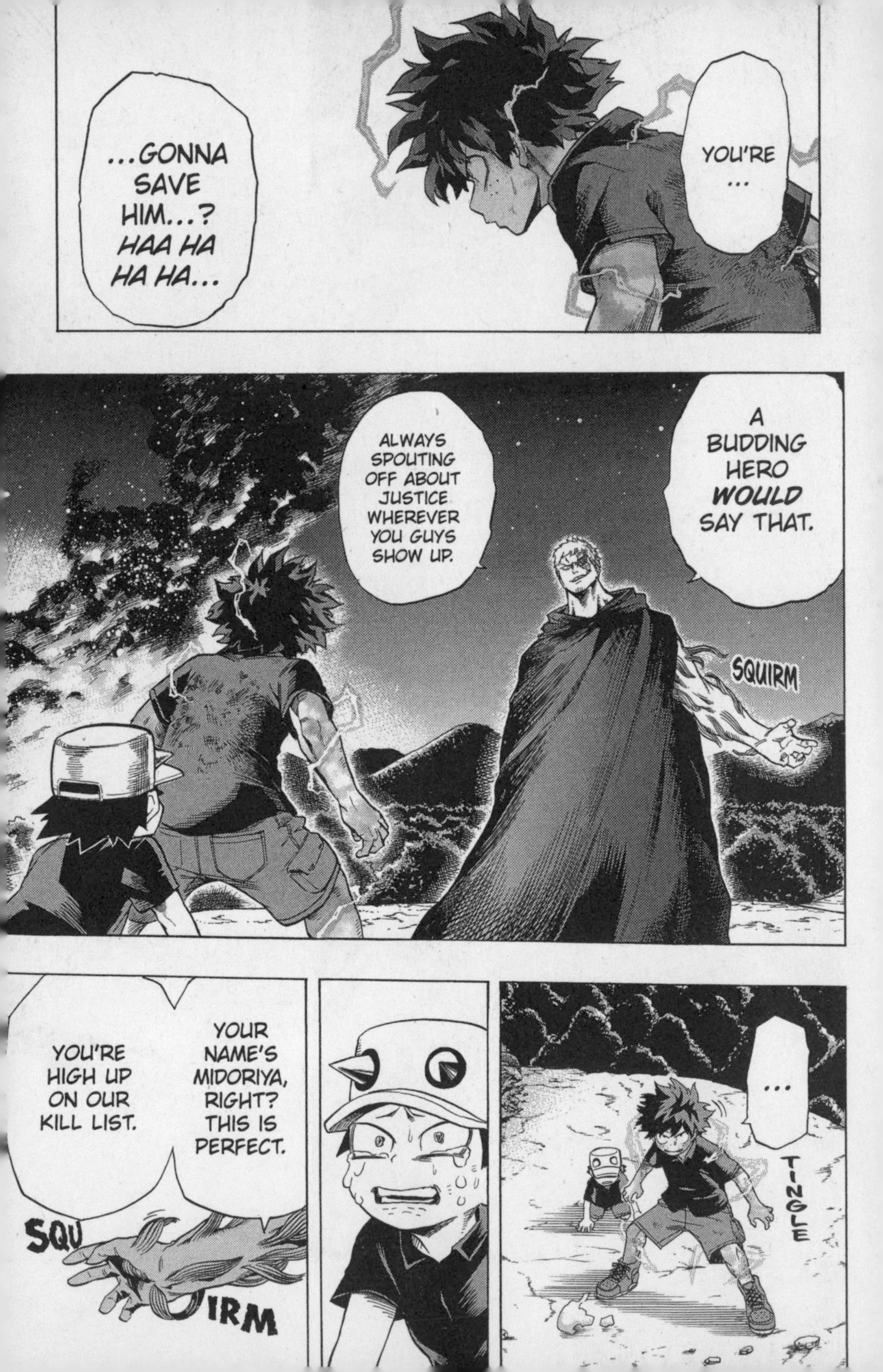
YOU'RE ...
...GONNA SAVE HIM...? *HAA HA HA HA...*
A BUDDING HERO **WOULD** SAY THAT.
ALWAYS SPOUTING OFF ABOUT JUSTICE WHEREVER YOU GUYS SHOW UP.
SQUIRM
...
TINGLE
YOUR NAME'S MIDORIYA, RIGHT? THIS IS PERFECT.
YOU'RE HIGH UP ON OUR KILL LIST.
SQUIRM

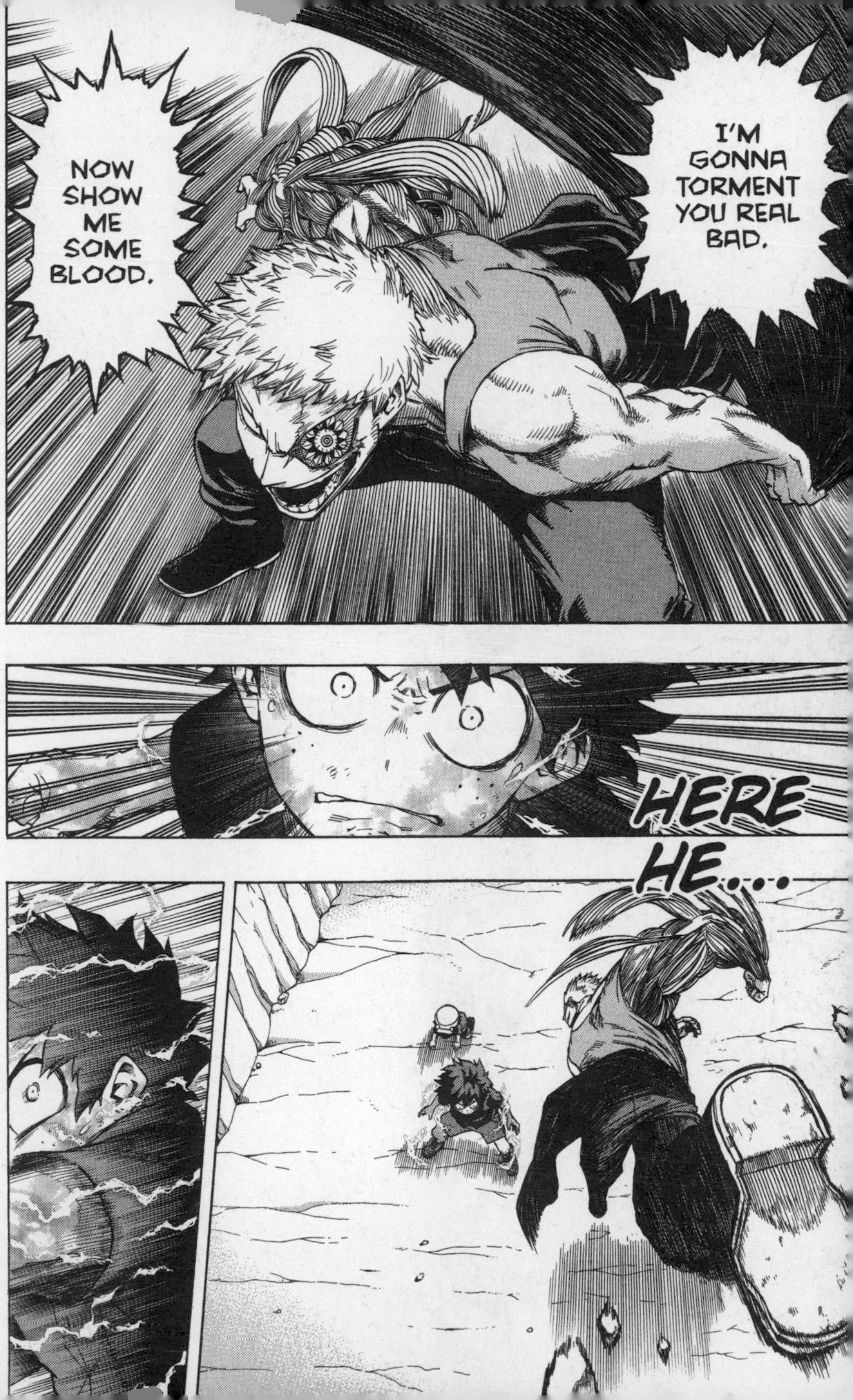
I'M GONNA TORMENT YOU REAL BAD.
NOW SHOW ME SOME BLOOD.
HERE HE...

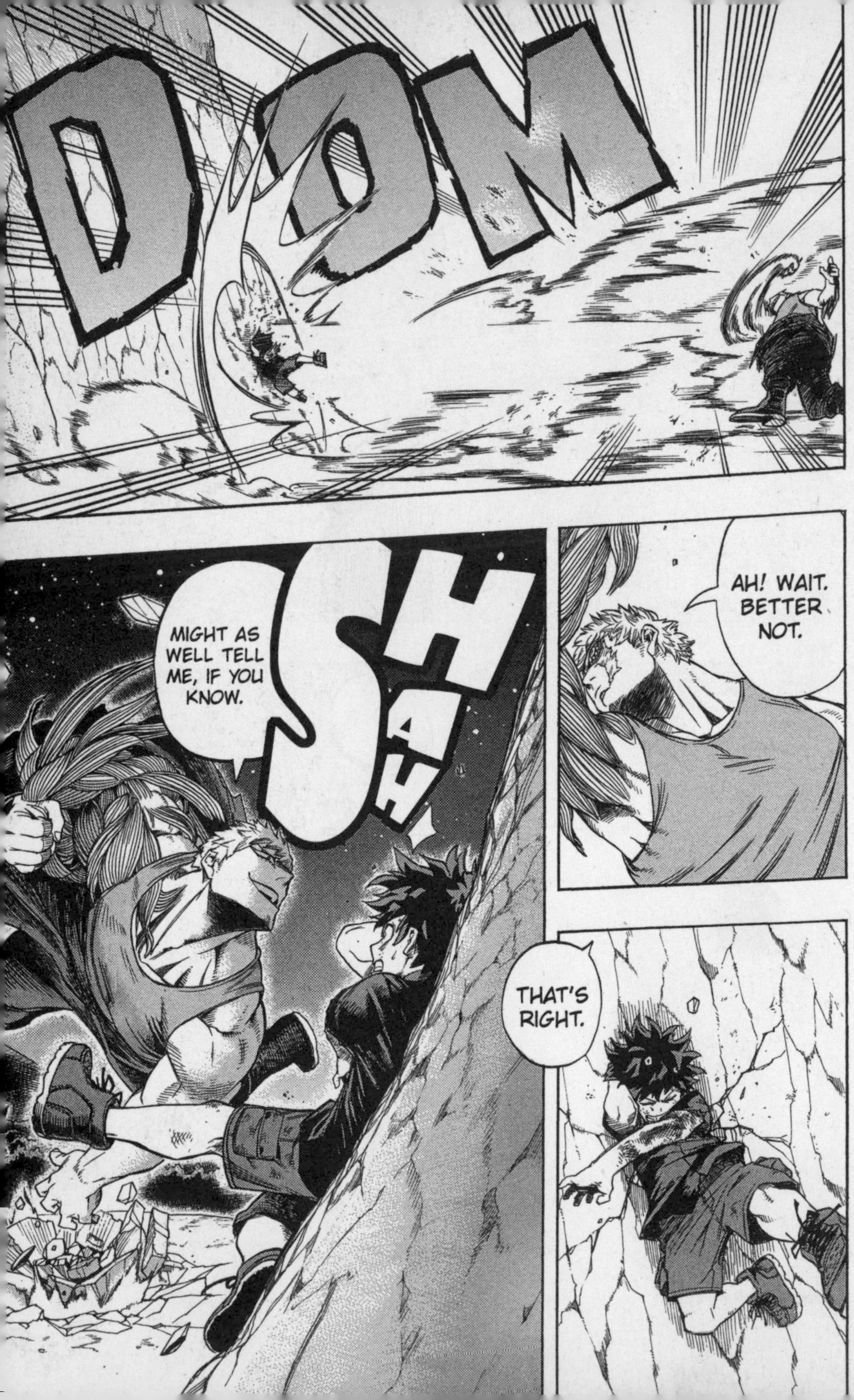
DOOM
AH! WAIT. BETTER NOT.
THAT'S RIGHT.
MIGHT AS WELL TELL ME, IF YOU KNOW.
SHAH!

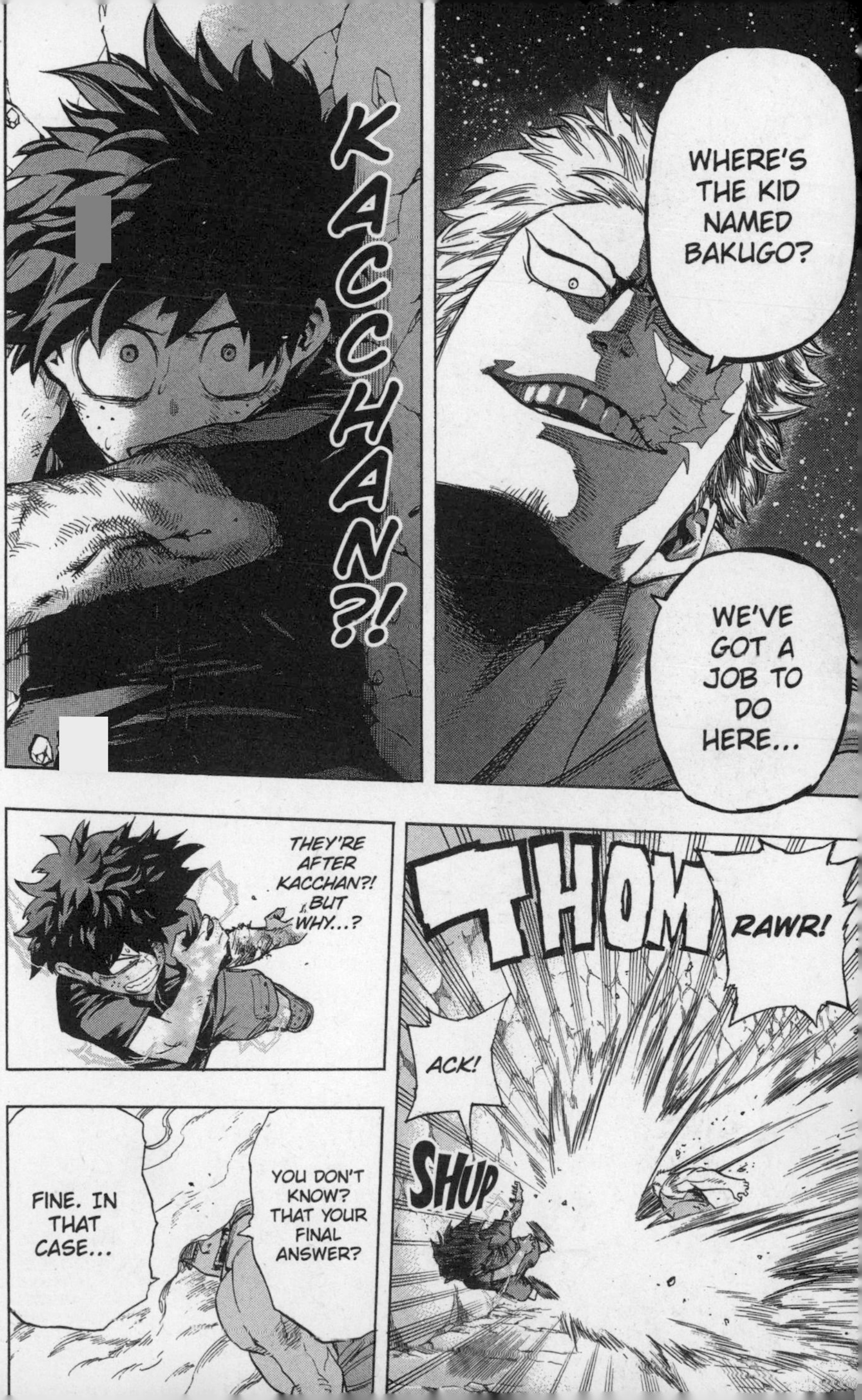
WHERE'S THE KID NAMED BAKUGO?
WE'VE GOT A JOB TO DO HERE...
KACCHAN?!
THOM
RAWR!
ACK!
SHUP
THEY'RE AFTER KACCHAN?! BUT WHY...?
YOU DON'T KNOW? THAT YOUR FINAL ANSWER?
FINE. IN THAT CASE...

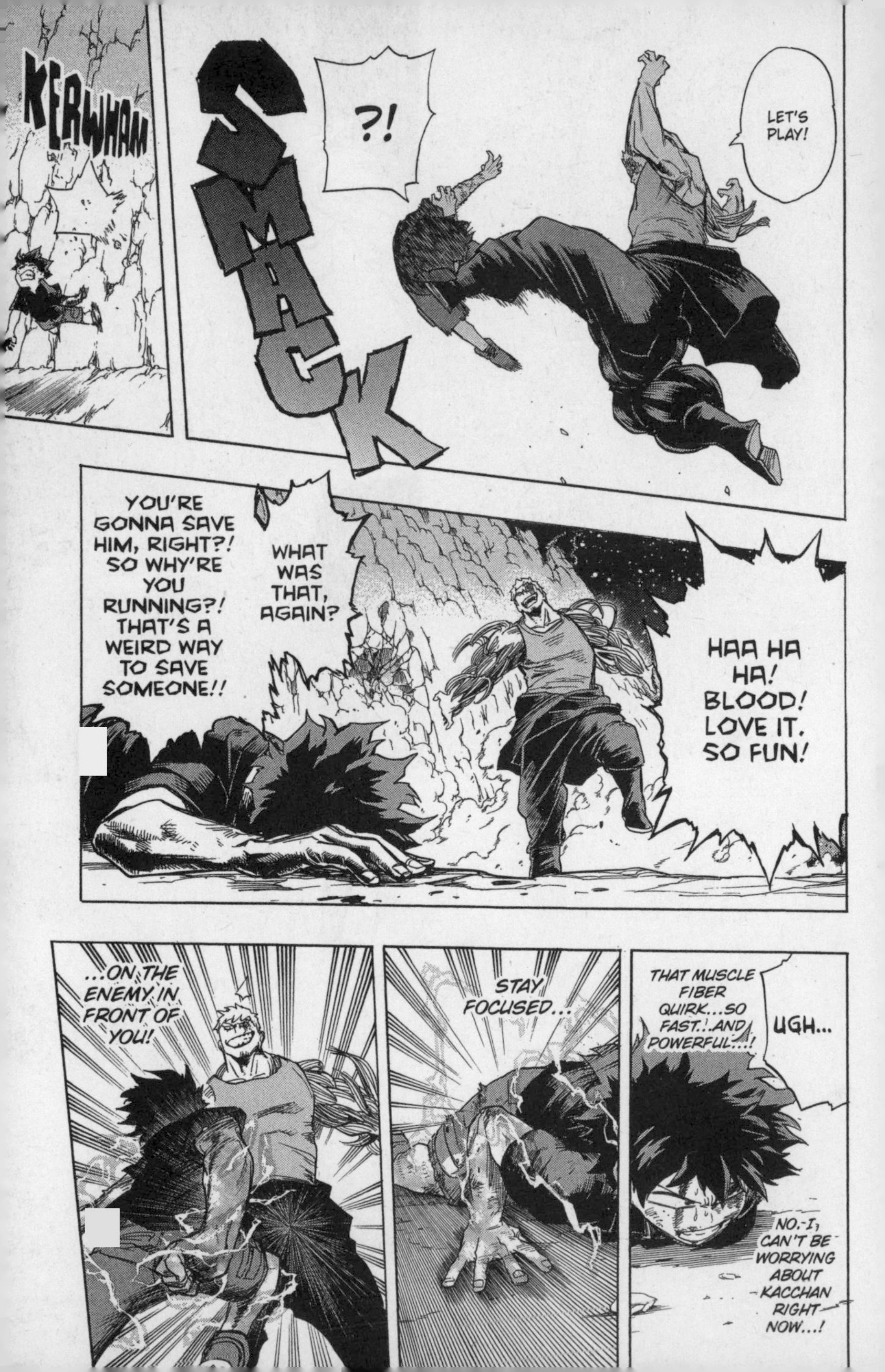
LET'S PLAY!
?!
SMACK
KERWHAM
HAA HA HA! BLOOD! LOVE IT. SO FUN!
WHAT WAS THAT, AGAIN?
YOU'RE GONNA SAVE HIM, RIGHT?! SO WHY'RE YOU RUNNING?! THAT'S A WEIRD WAY TO SAVE SOMEONE!!
UGH...
THAT MUSCLE FIBER QUIRK...SO FAST...AND POWERFUL...!
NO. I, CAN'T BE WORRYING ABOUT KACCHAN RIGHT NOW...!
STAY FOCUSED...
...ON THE ENEMY IN FRONT OF YOU!

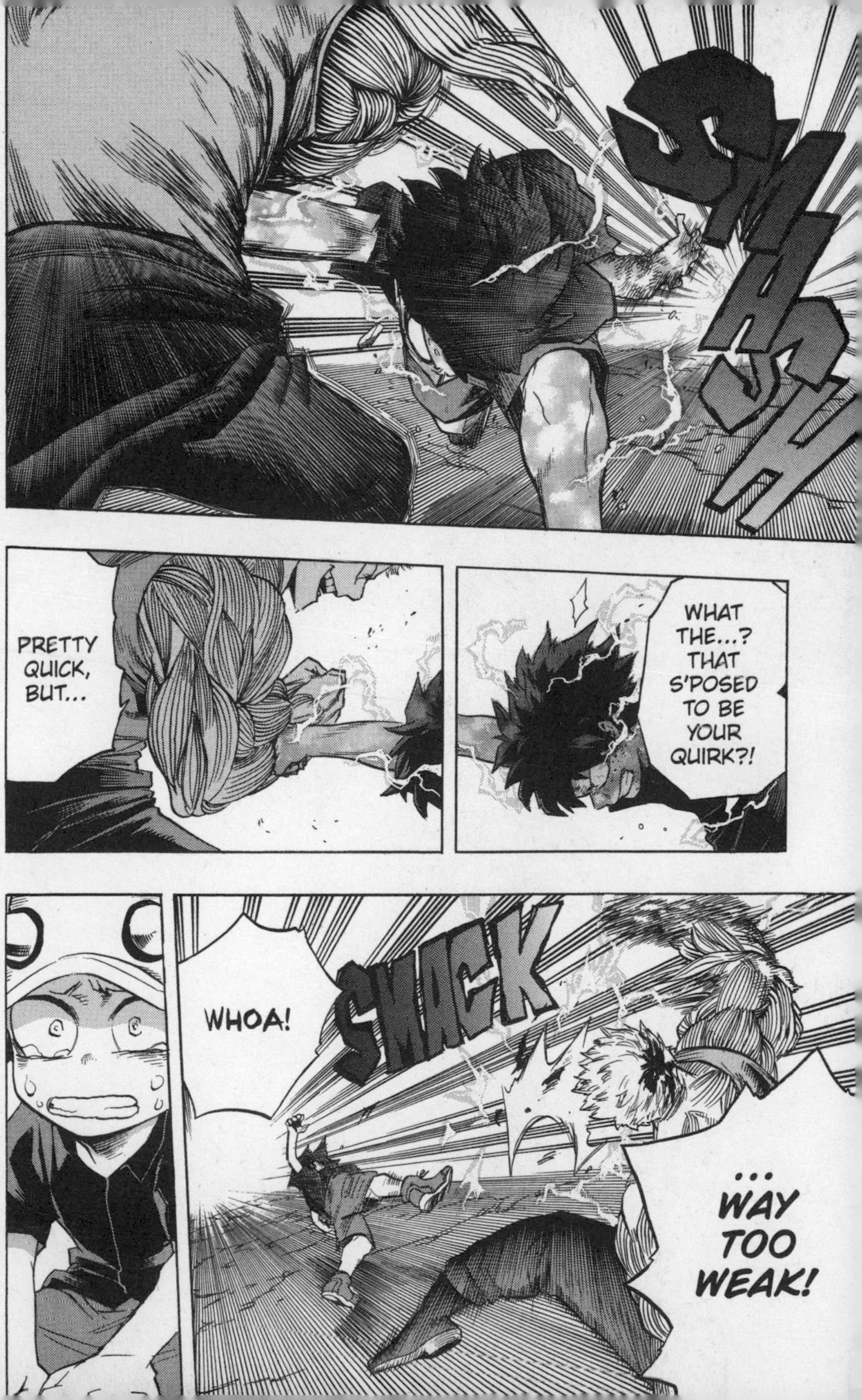
SMASH
WHAT THE...? THAT S'POSED TO BE YOUR QUIRK?!
PRETTY QUICK, BUT...
SMACK
WHOA!
...WAY TOO WEAK!

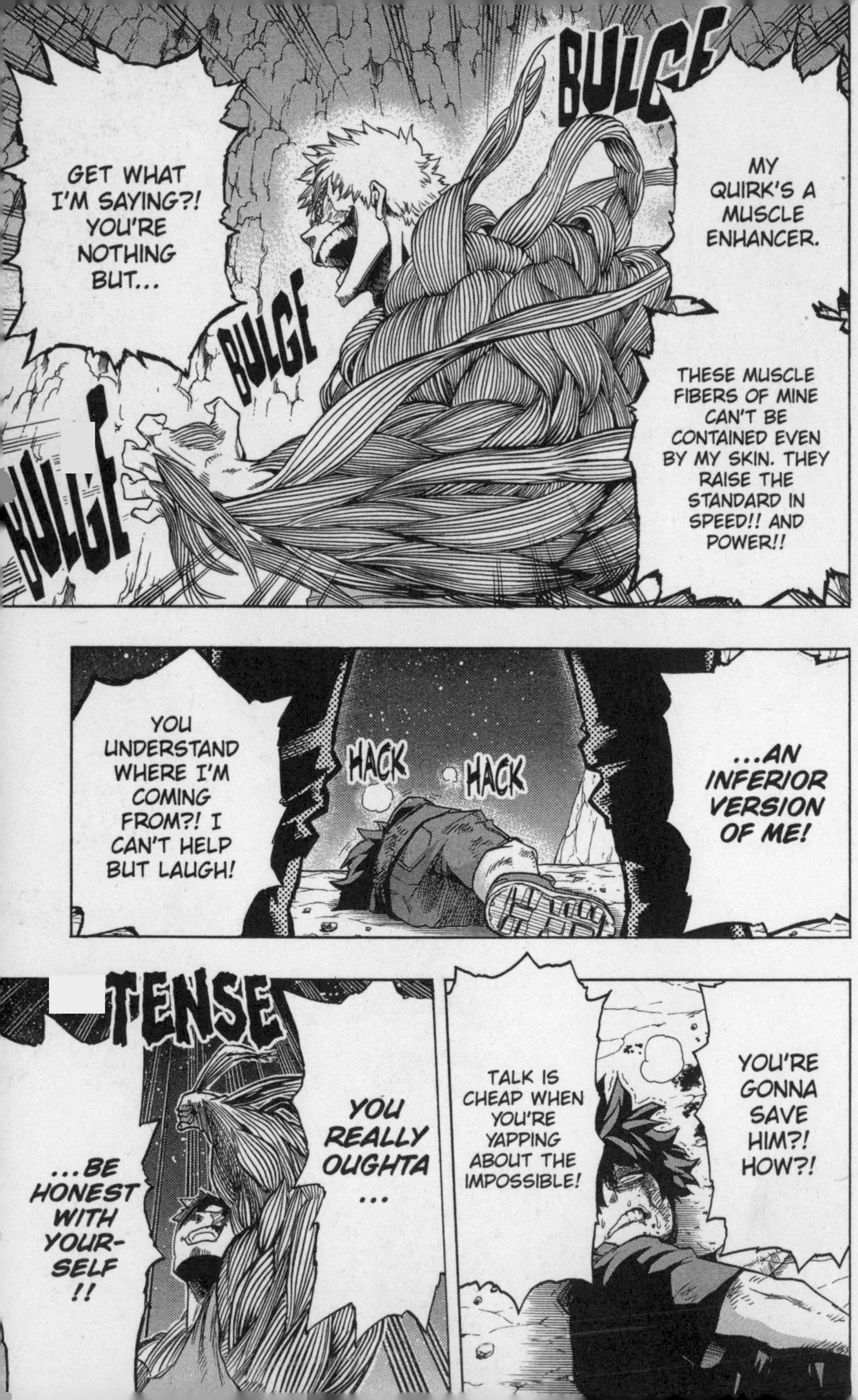
BULGE
MY QUIRK'S A MUSCLE ENHANCER.
THESE MUSCLE FIBERS OF MINE CAN'T BE CONTAINED EVEN BY MY SKIN. THEY RAISE THE STANDARD IN SPEED!! AND POWER!!
BULGE
BULGE
GET WHAT I'M SAYING?! YOU'RE NOTHING BUT...
...AN INFERIOR VERSION OF ME!
HACK
HACK
YOU UNDERSTAND WHERE I'M COMING FROM?! I CAN'T HELP BUT LAUGH!
YOU'RE GONNA SAVE HIM?! HOW?!
TALK IS CHEAP WHEN YOU'RE YAPPING ABOUT THE IMPOSSIBLE!
TENSE
YOU REALLY OUGHTA...
...BE HONEST WITH YOUR-SELF!!

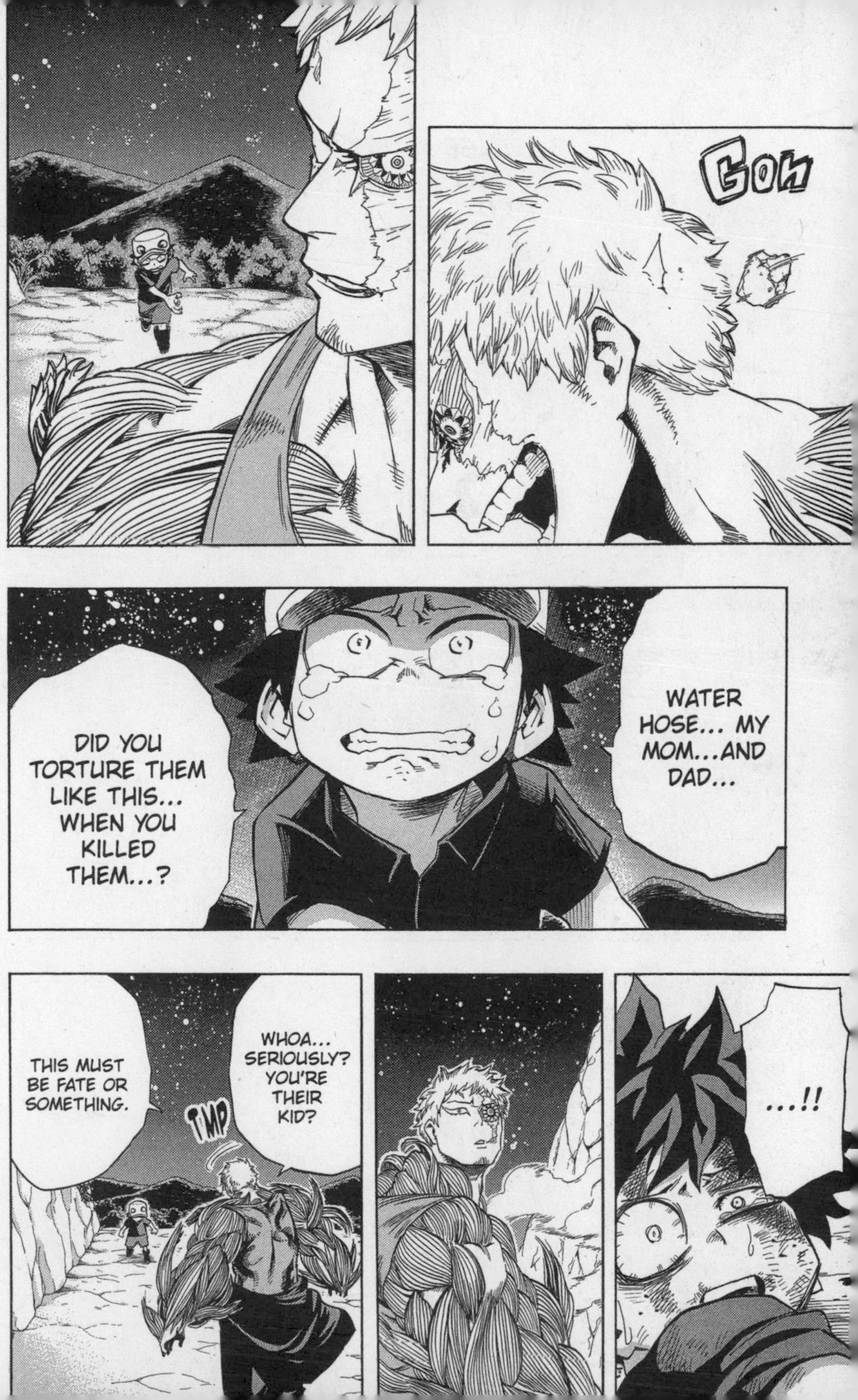
GOH
WATER HOSE... MY MOM...AND DAD...
DID YOU TORTURE THEM LIKE THIS... WHEN YOU KILLED THEM...?
...!!
WHOA... SERIOUSLY? YOU'RE THEIR KID?
TMP
THIS MUST BE FATE OR SOMETHING.

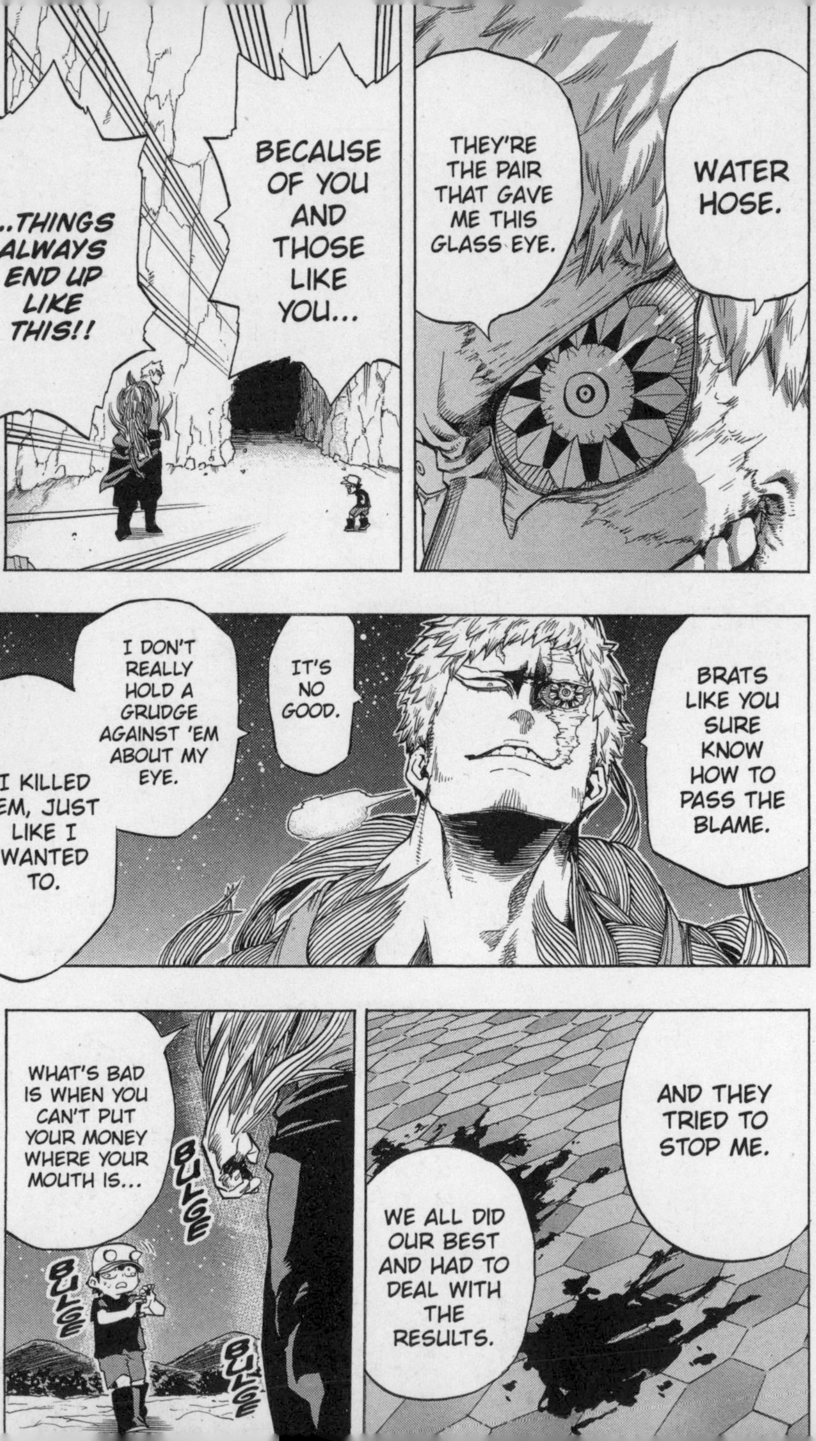
WATER HOSE.
THEY'RE THE PAIR THAT GAVE ME THIS GLASS EYE.
BECAUSE OF YOU AND THOSE LIKE YOU...
...THINGS ALWAYS END UP LIKE THIS!!
BRATS LIKE YOU SURE KNOW HOW TO PASS THE BLAME.
IT'S NO GOOD.
I DON'T REALLY HOLD A GRUDGE AGAINST 'EM ABOUT MY EYE.
I KILLED 'EM, JUST LIKE I WANTED TO.
AND THEY TRIED TO STOP ME.
WE ALL DID OUR BEST AND HAD TO DEAL WITH THE RESULTS.
WHAT'S BAD IS WHEN YOU CAN'T PUT YOUR MONEY WHERE YOUR MOUTH IS...
BULGE
BULGE
BULGE

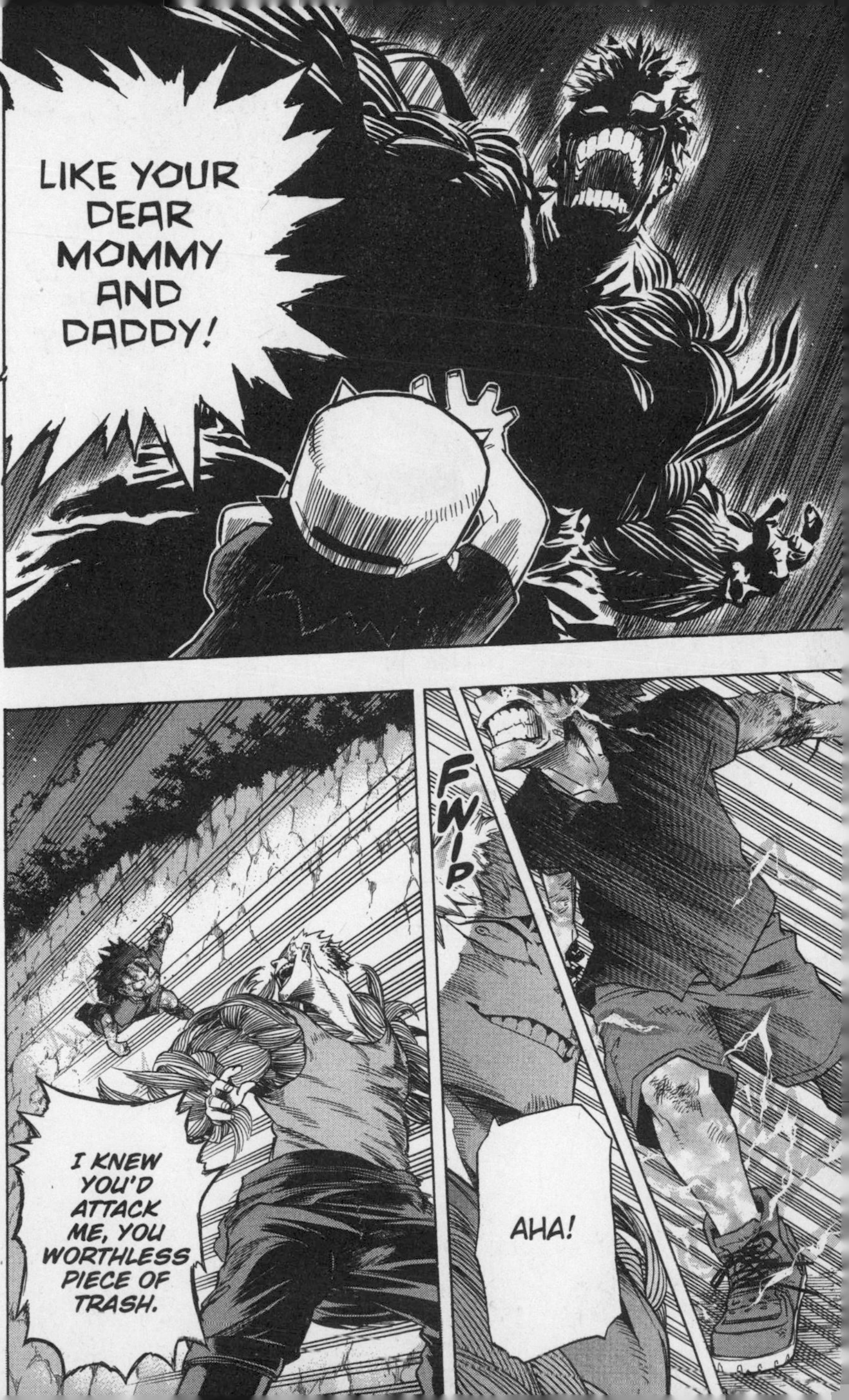
LIKE YOUR DEAR MOMMY AND DADDY!
FWIP
AHA!
I KNEW YOU'D ATTACK ME, YOU WORTHLESS PIECE OF TRASH.

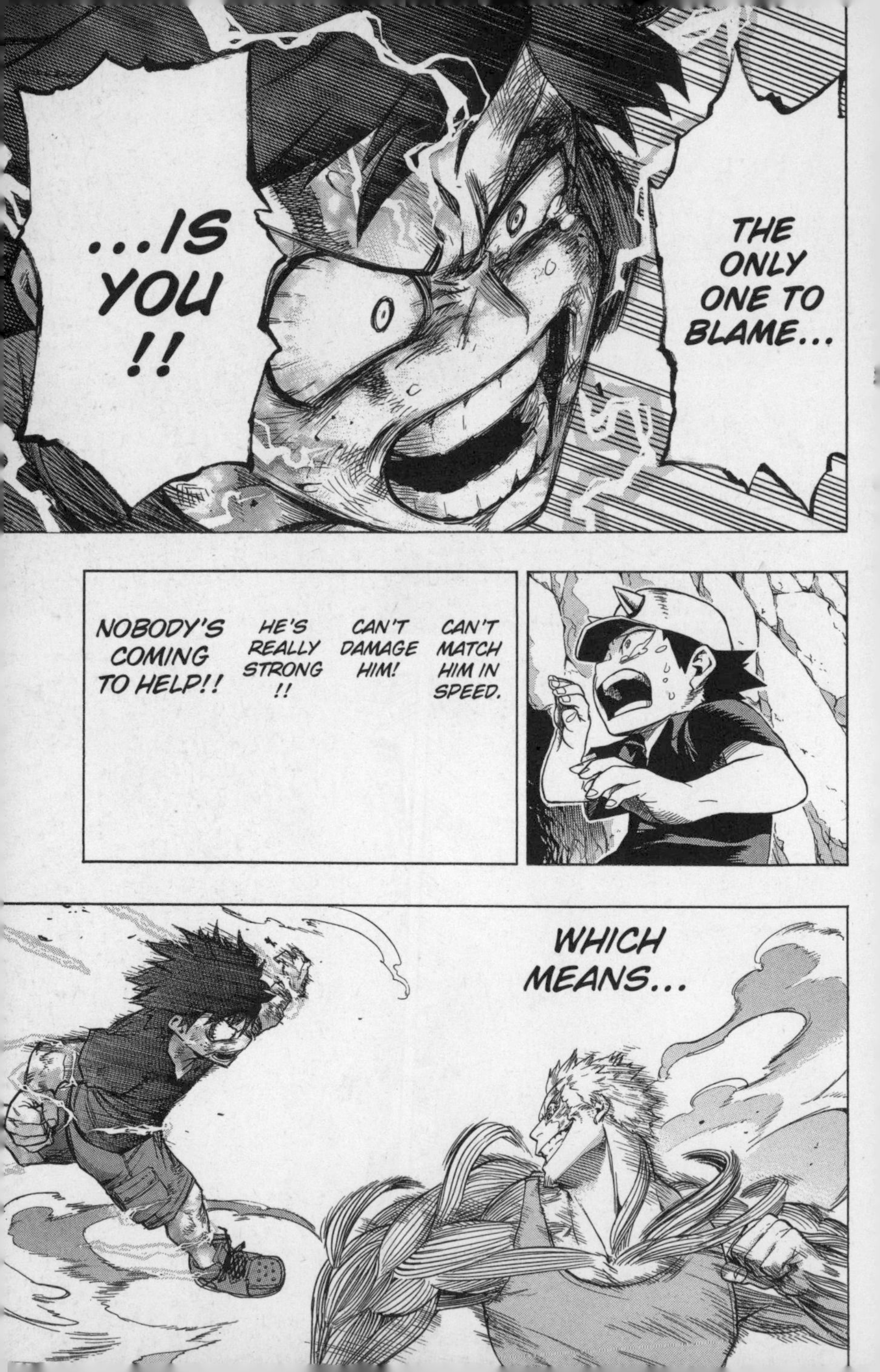
THE ONLY ONE TO BLAME...
...IS YOU!!
CAN'T MATCH HIM IN SPEED.
CAN'T DAMAGE HIM!
HE'S REALLY STRONG!!
NOBODY'S COMING TO HELP!!
WHICH MEANS...

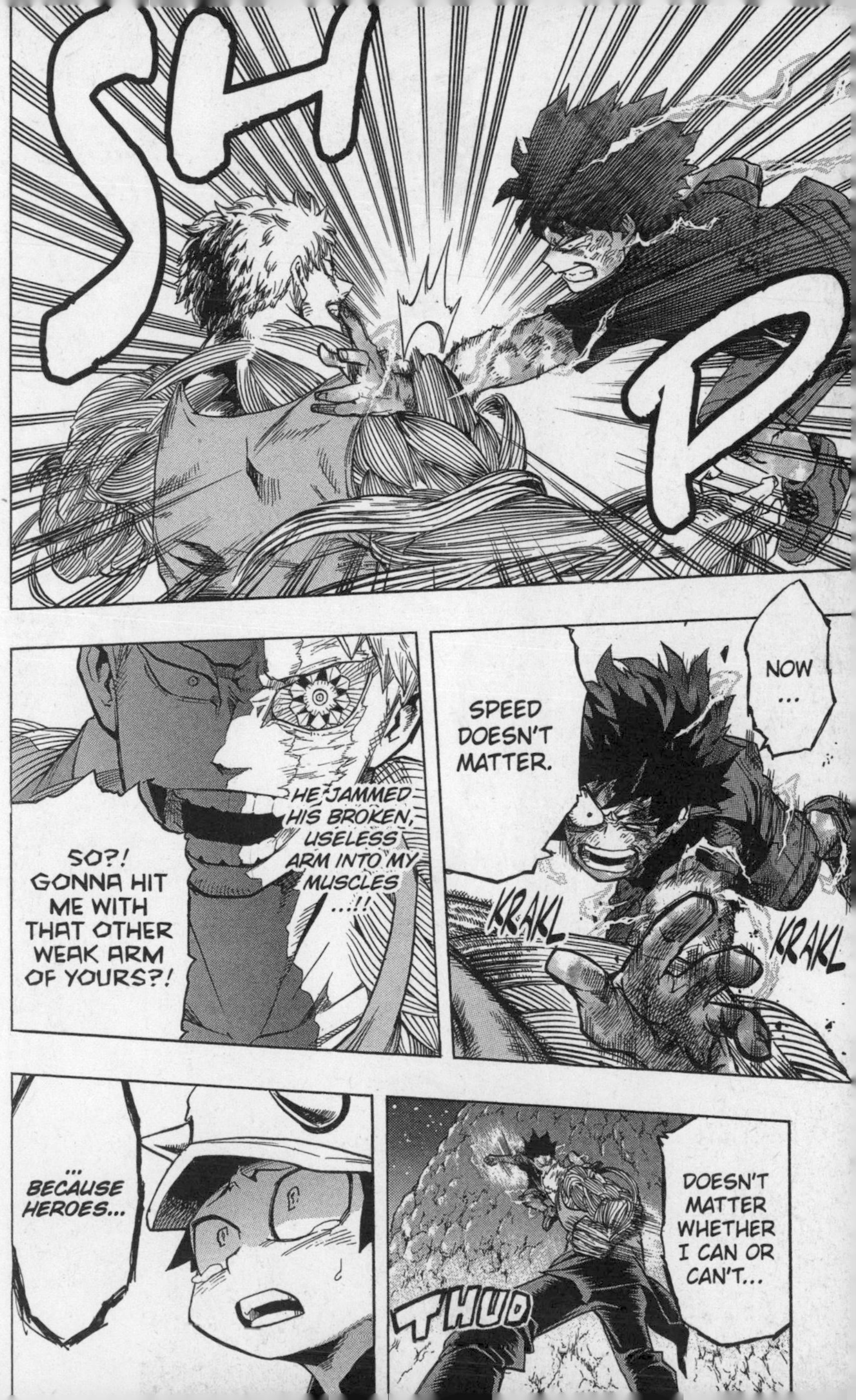
SHP
NOW...
SPEED DOESN'T MATTER.
KRAKL
KRAKL
HE JAMMED HIS BROKEN, USELESS ARM INTO MY MUSCLES...!!
SO?! GONNA HIT ME WITH THAT OTHER WEAK ARM OF YOURS?!
DOESN'T MATTER WHETHER I CAN OR CAN'T...
THUD
...BECAUSE HEROES...

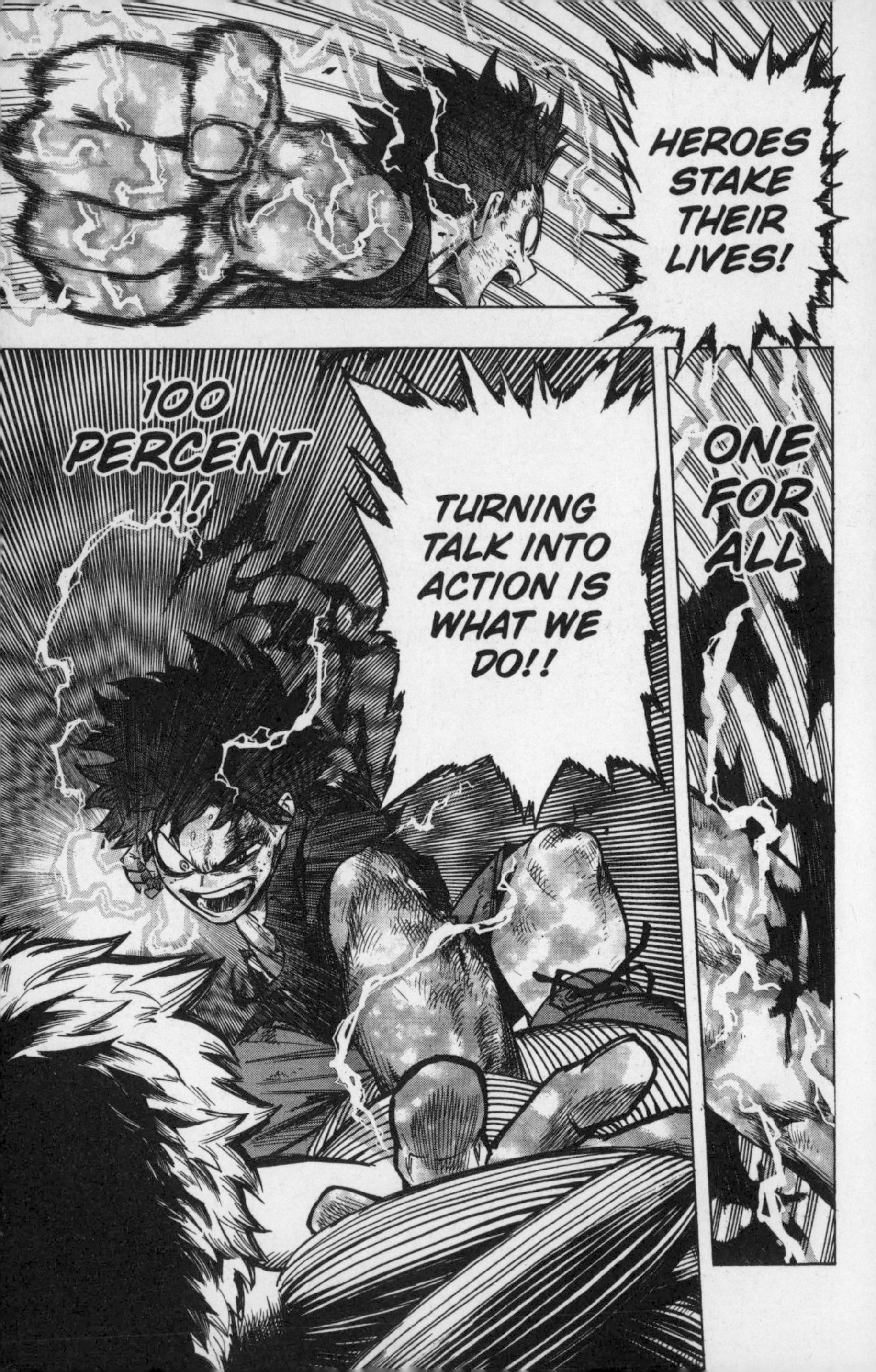
HEROES STAKE THEIR LIVES!
ONE FOR ALL
TURNING TALK INTO ACTION IS WHAT WE DO!!
100 PERCENT!!

HERO

WILD WILD PUSSYCATS
RAGDOLL (AGE 31)
(TOMOKO SHIRETOKO)

STREET CLOTHES

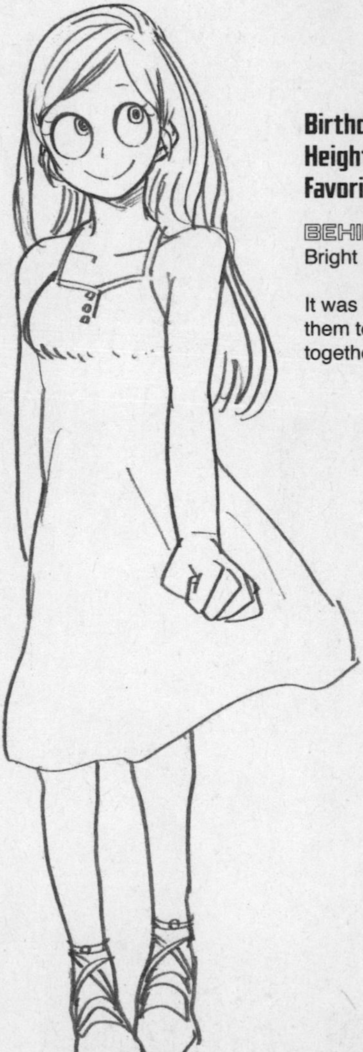

Birthday: 4/8
Height: 166 cm
Favorite Things: Tora, Mandalay, Pixie-Bob

BEHIND THE SCENES

Bright and cheery.

It was her idea for the four of them to form a pro hero team together.

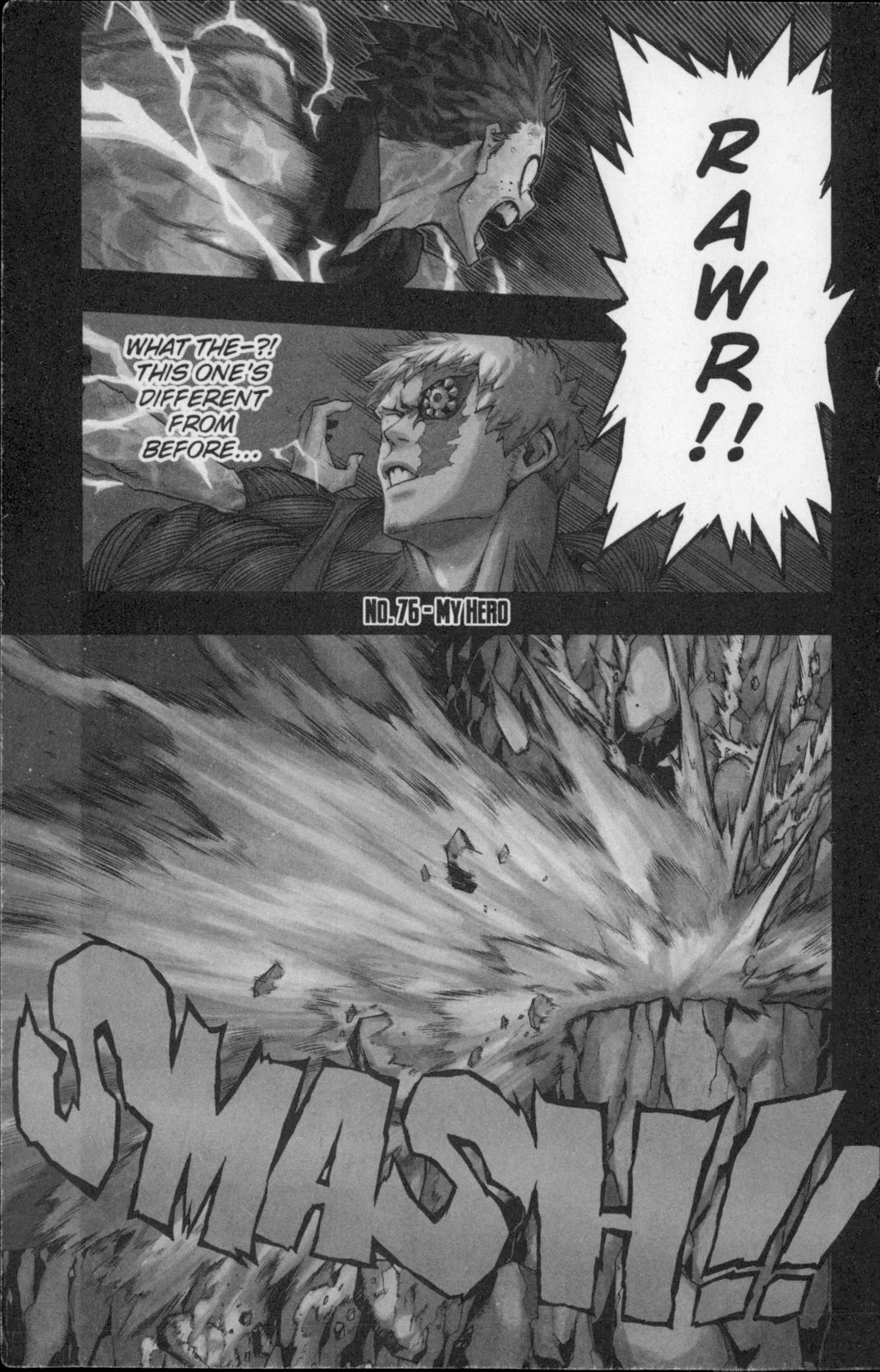
RAWR!!
WHAT THE-?! THIS ONE'S DIFFERENT FROM BEFORE...
No. 76 - My Hero
SMASH!!

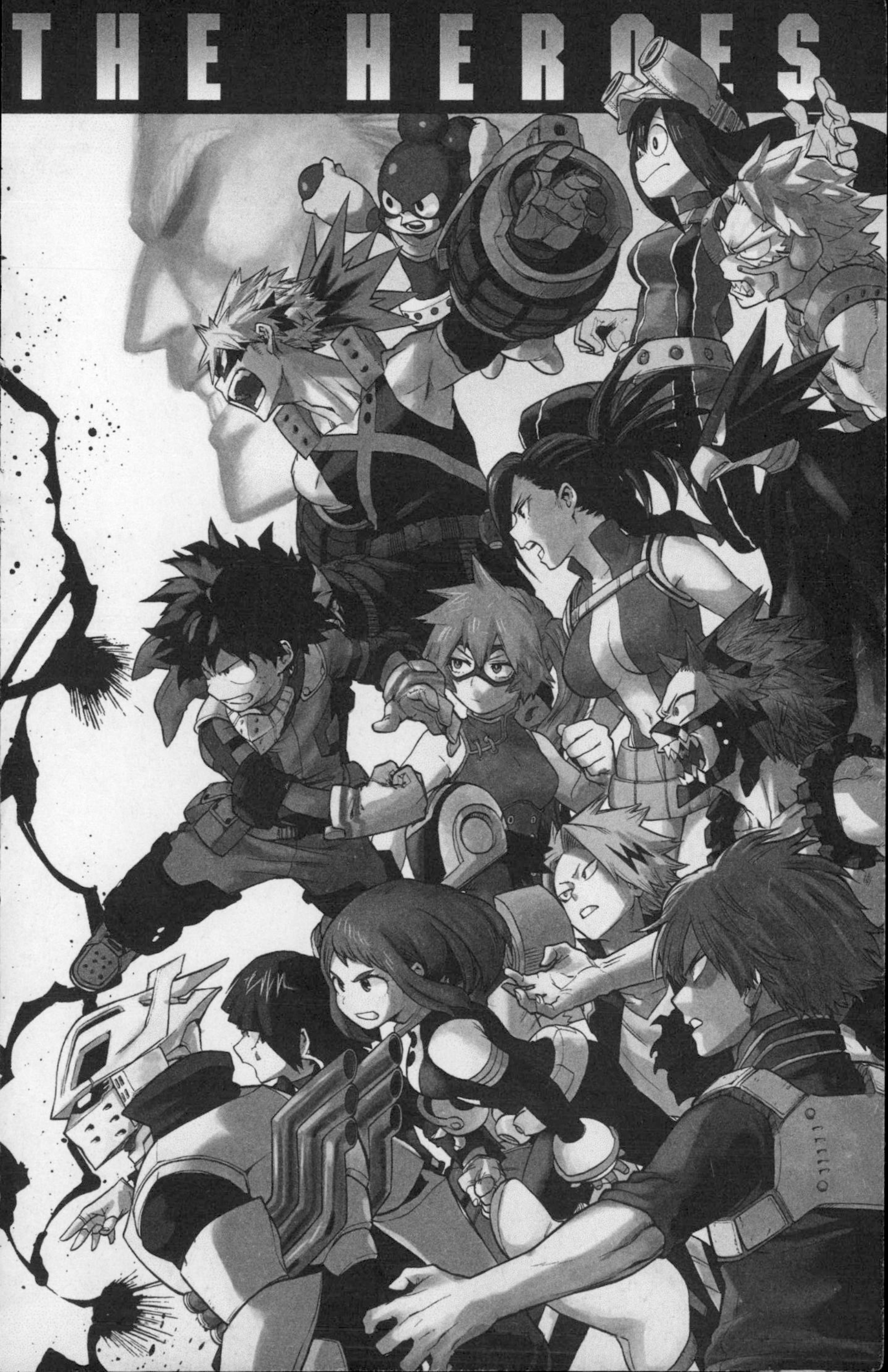
THE HEROES

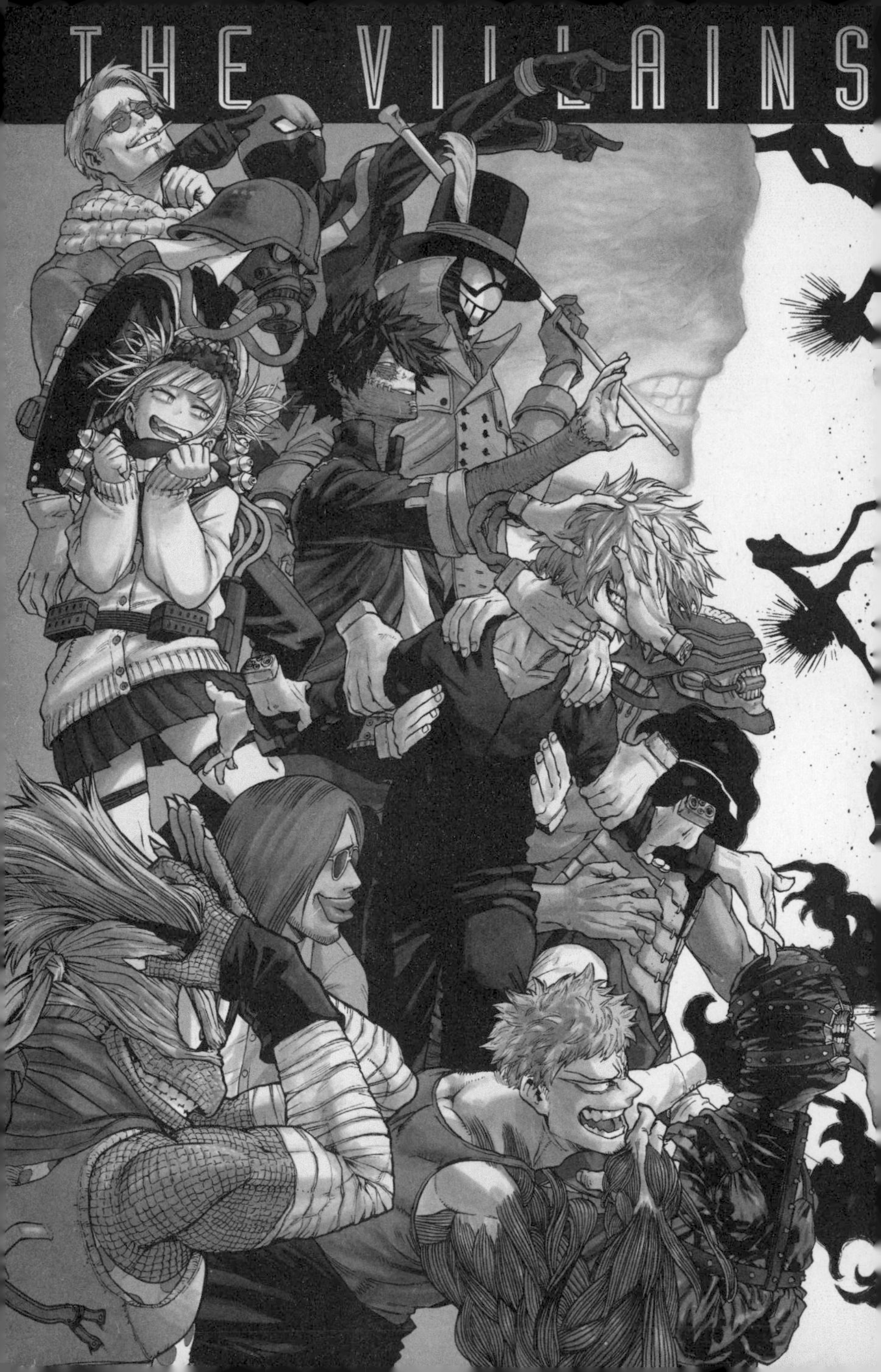
THE VILLAINS

MY HERO
ACADEMIA

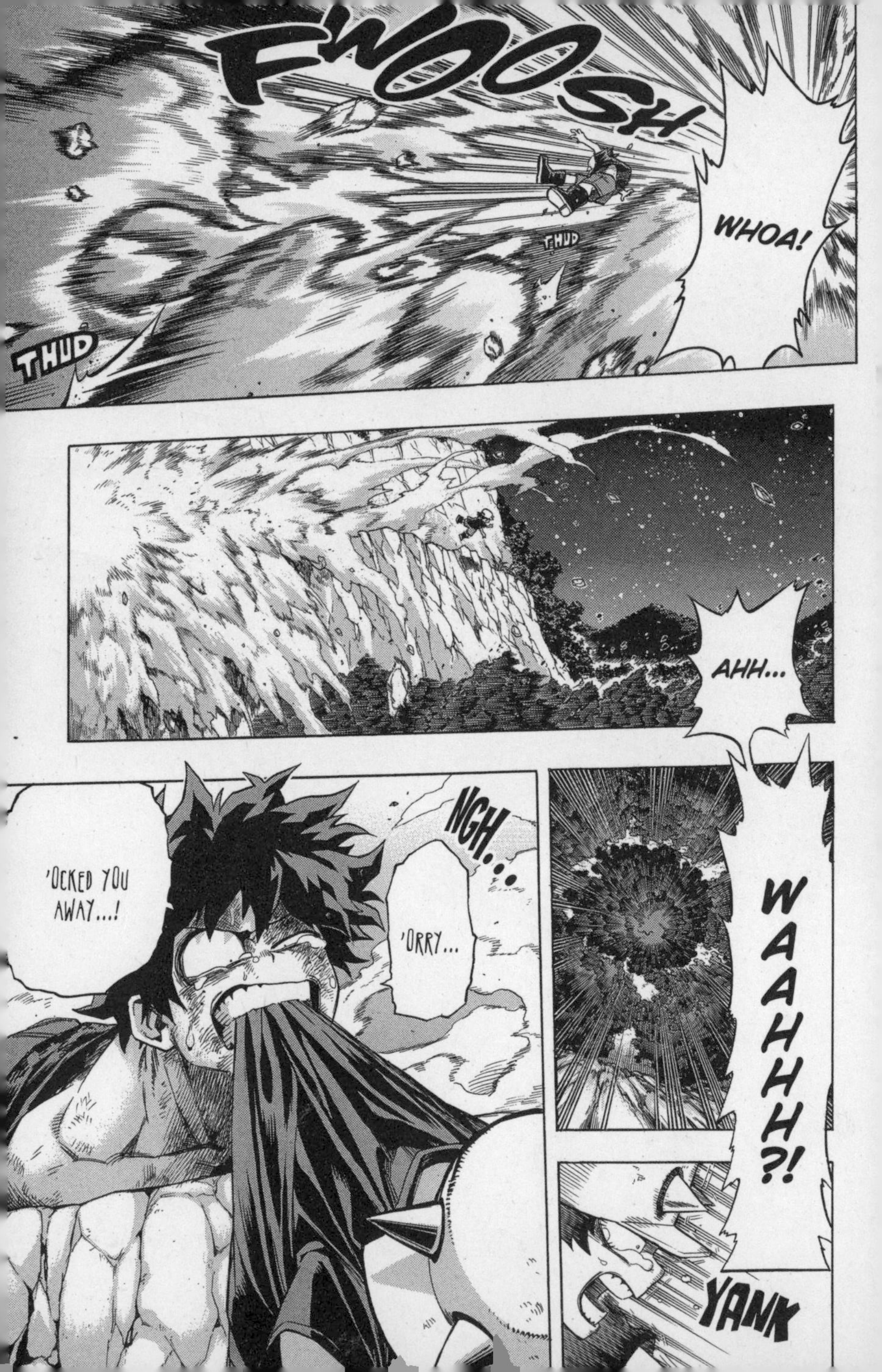
F'WOOSH
WHOA!
THUD
THUD
AHH...
WAAHHH?!
YANK
NGH...
'ORRY...
'OCKED YOU AWAY...!

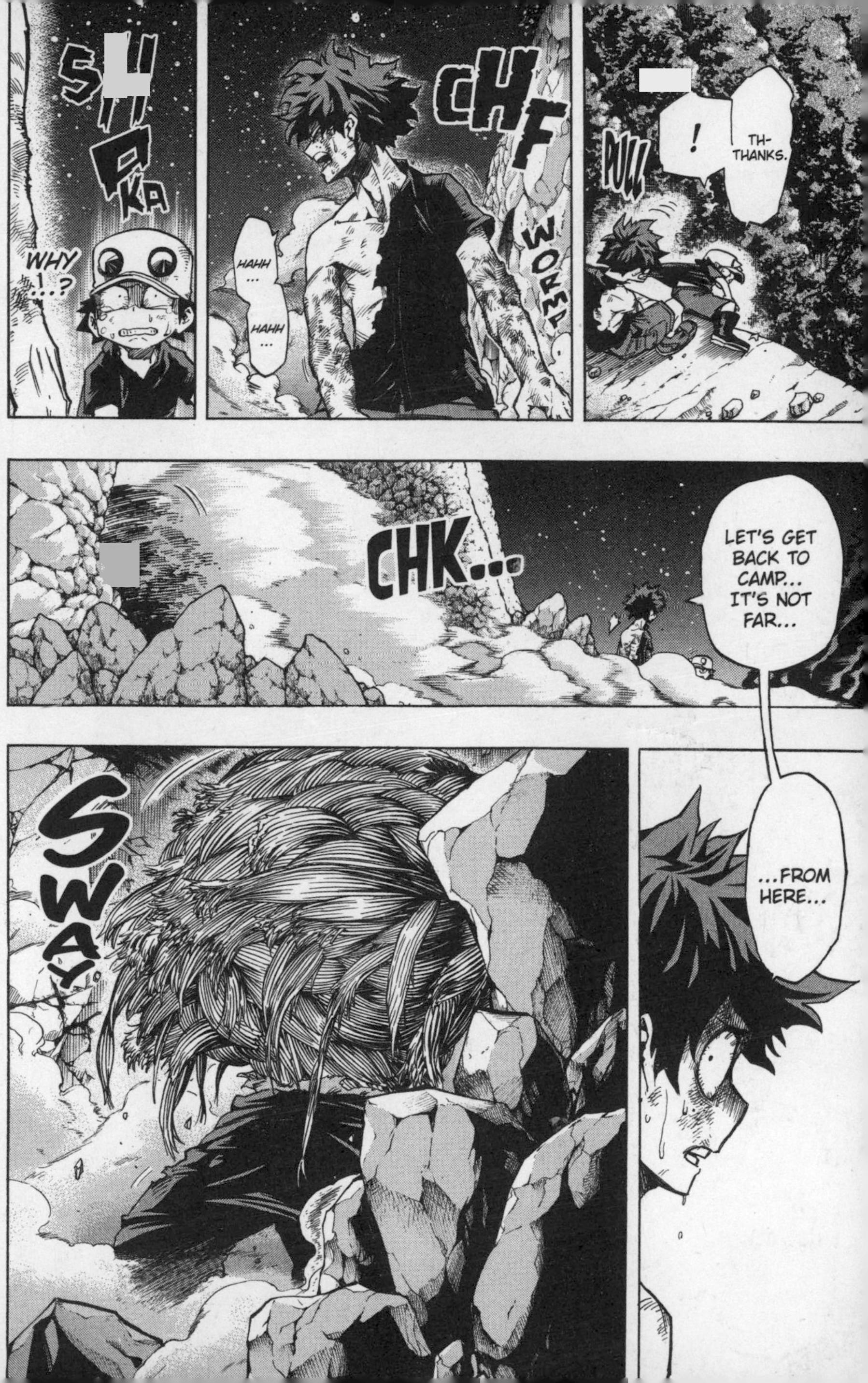
PULL
!
TH-THANKS.
CHF
WORMP
HAHH...
HAHH...
WHY...?
LET'S GET BACK TO CAMP... IT'S NOT FAR...
CHK...
...FROM HERE...
SWAY

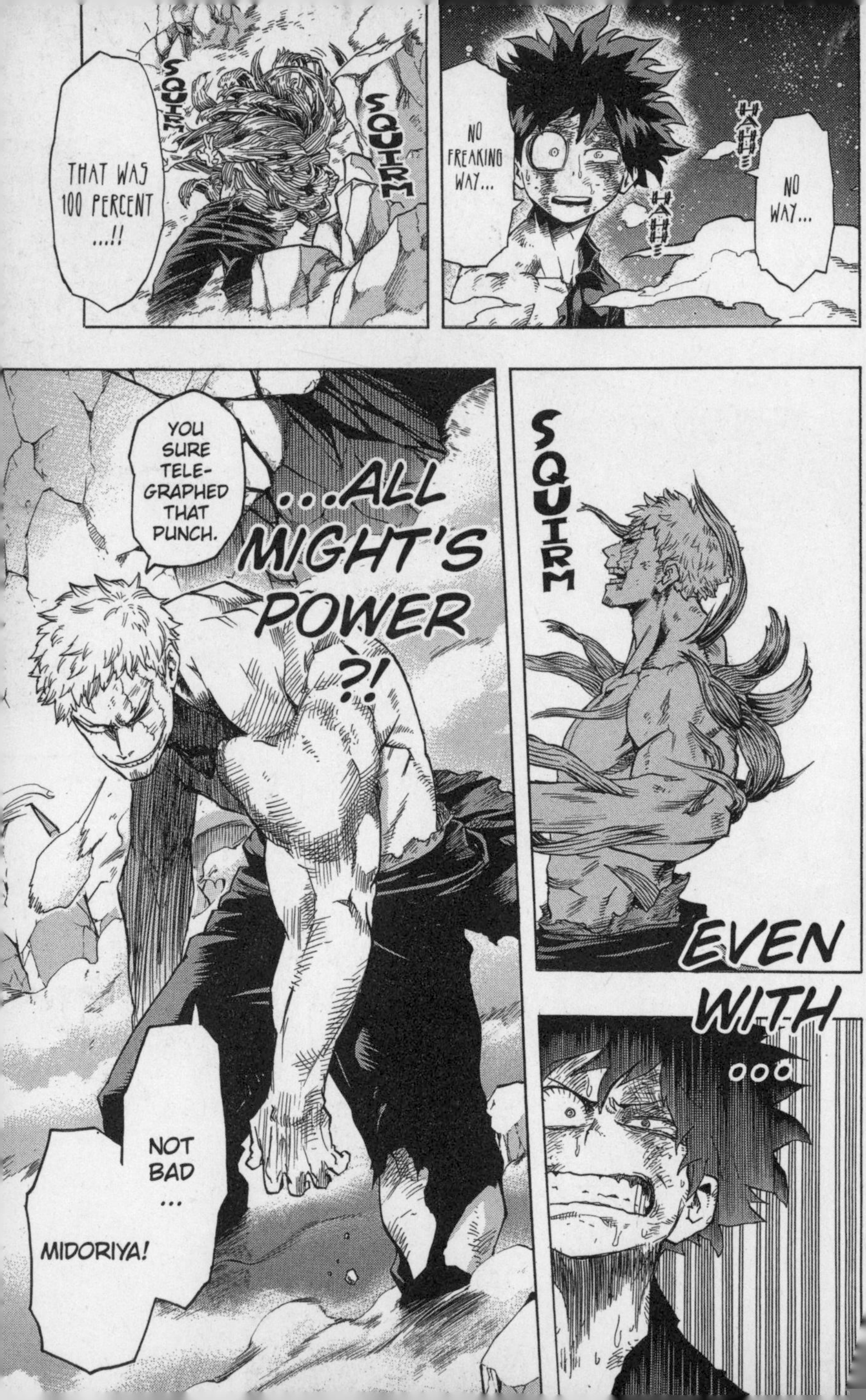
HAH
HAH
NO WAY...
NO FREAKING WAY...
SQUIRM
SQUIRM
THAT WAS 100 PERCENT ...!!
SQUIRM
EVEN WITH ...
...ALL MIGHT'S POWER ?!
YOU SURE TELEGRAPHED THAT PUNCH.
NOT BAD ... MIDORIYA!

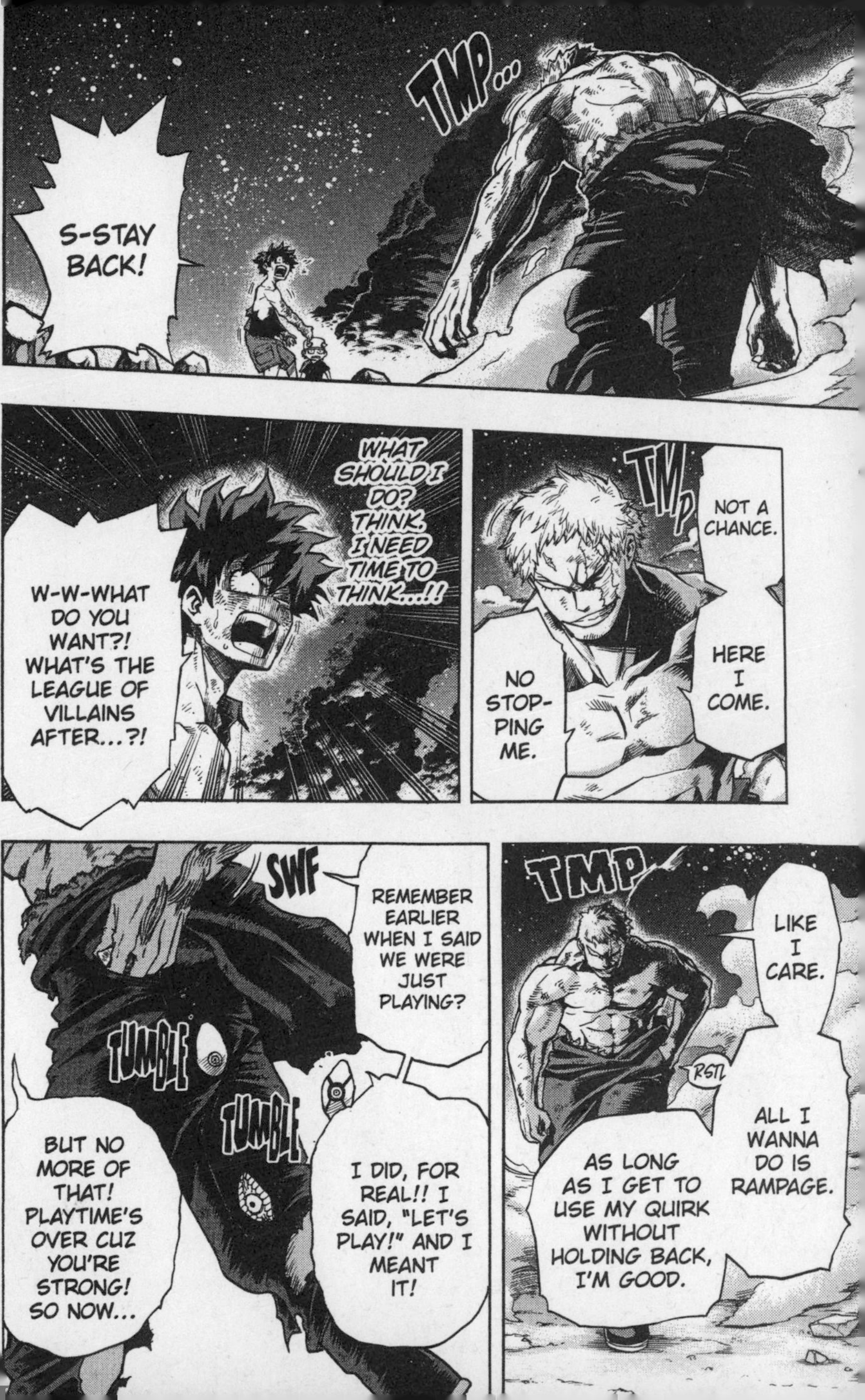
TMP...
S-STAY BACK!
TMP
NOT A CHANCE.
HERE I COME.
NO STOPPING ME.
WHAT SHOULD I DO? THINK. I NEED TIME TO THINK...!!
W-W-WHAT DO YOU WANT?! WHAT'S THE LEAGUE OF VILLAINS AFTER...?!
TMP
LIKE I CARE.
RSTL
ALL I WANNA DO IS RAMPAGE.
AS LONG AS I GET TO USE MY QUIRK WITHOUT HOLDING BACK, I'M GOOD.
SWF
REMEMBER EARLIER WHEN I SAID WE WERE JUST PLAYING?
TUMBLE
TUMBLE
I DID, FOR REAL!! I SAID, "LET'S PLAY!" AND I MEANT IT!
BUT NO MORE OF THAT! PLAYTIME'S OVER CUZ YOU'RE STRONG! SO NOW...

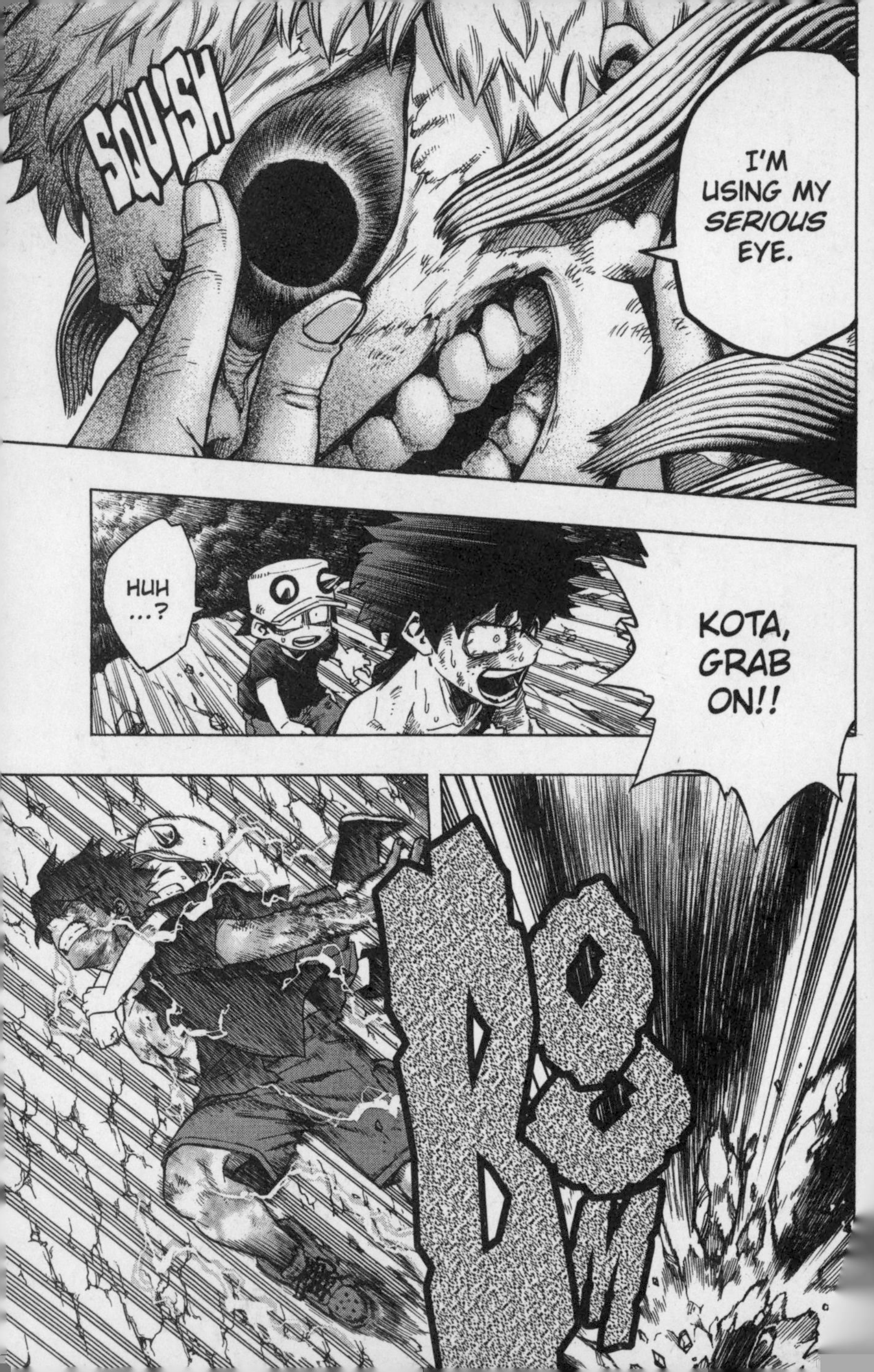
SQUISH
I'M USING MY SERIOUS EYE.
KOTA, GRAB ON!!
HUH ...?

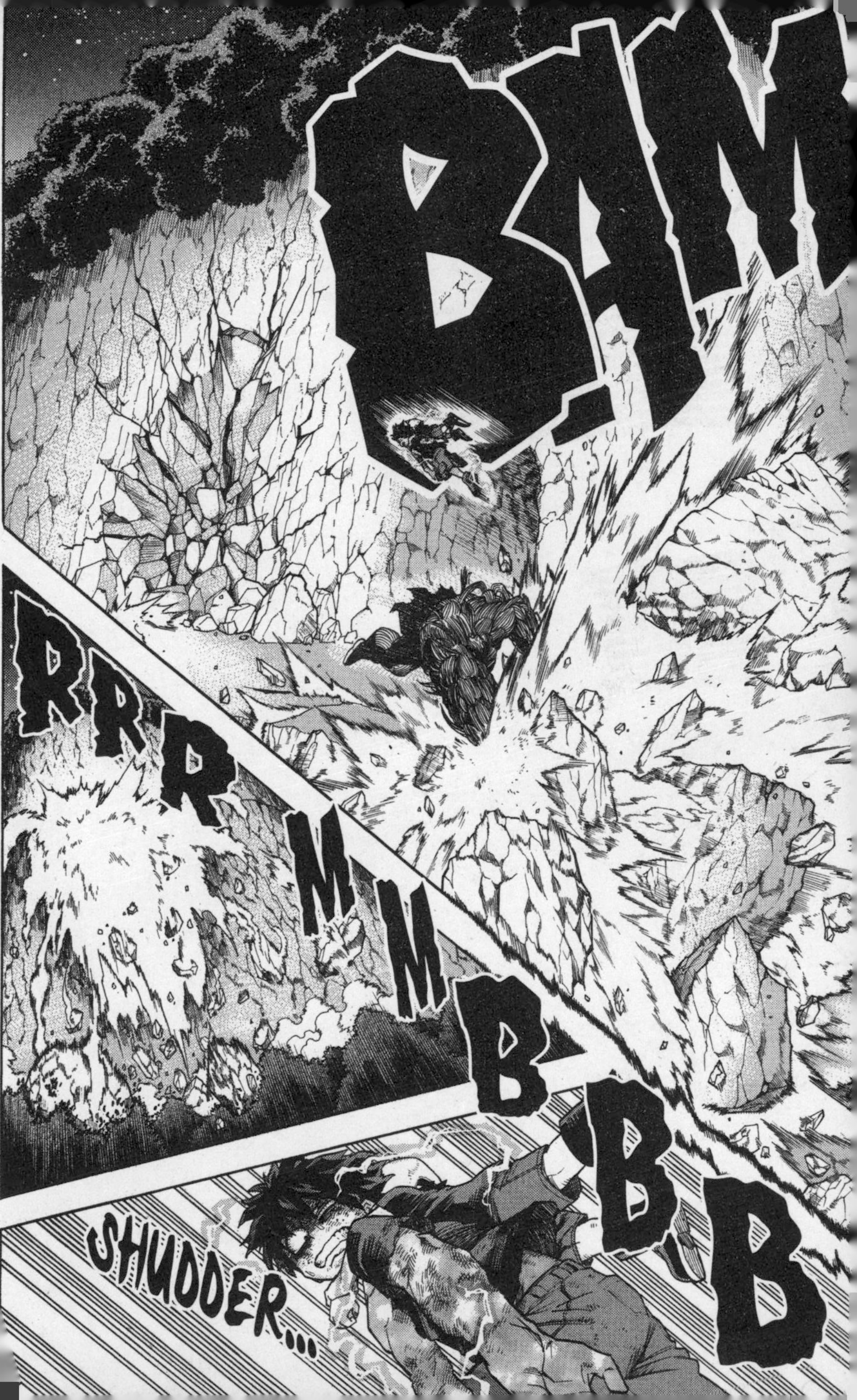
BAM
RRRMMMBBB
SHUDDER...

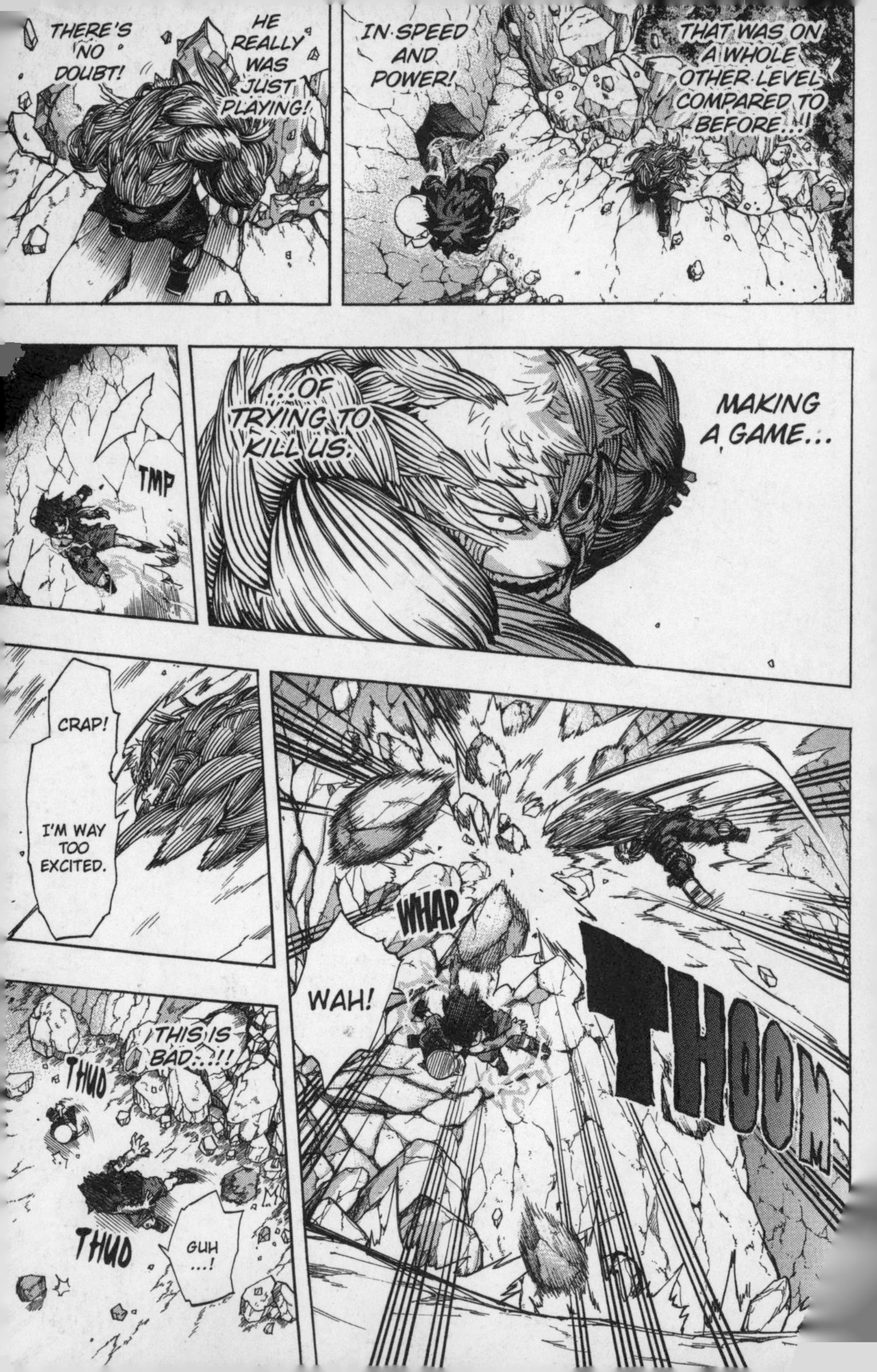
THAT WAS ON A WHOLE OTHER LEVEL COMPARED TO BEFORE...!!
IN SPEED AND POWER!
HE REALLY WAS JUST PLAYING!
THERE'S NO DOUBT!
MAKING A GAME...
...OF TRYING TO KILL US.
TMP
WHAP
THOOM
WAH!
CRAP!
I'M WAY TOO EXCITED.
THIS IS BAD...!!
THUD
THUD
GUH ...!

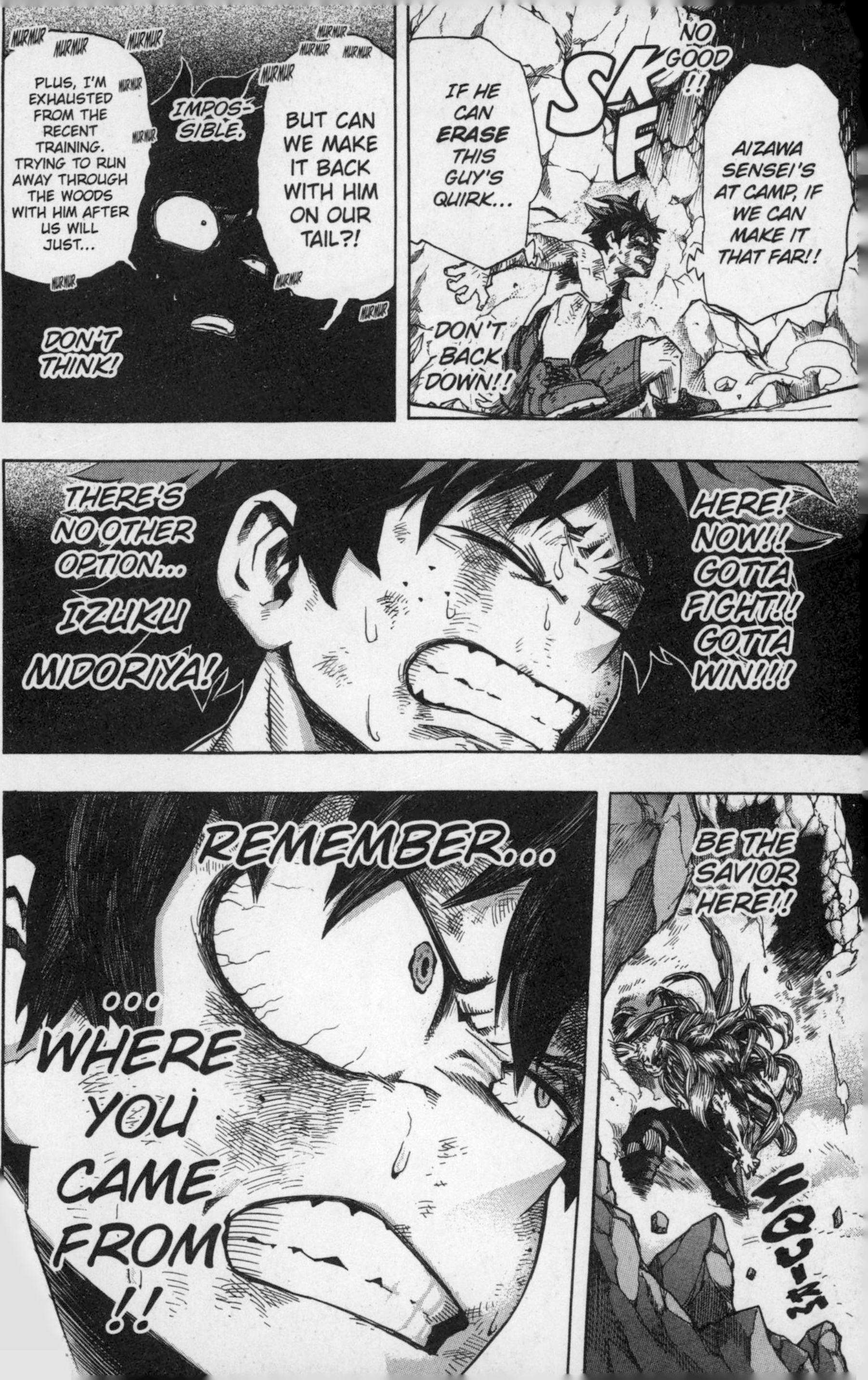
NO GOOD!!
SKF
AIZAWA SENSEI'S AT CAMP, IF WE CAN MAKE IT THAT FAR!!
IF HE CAN ERASE THIS GUY'S QUIRK...
DON'T BACK DOWN!!
MURMUR MURMUR
BUT CAN WE MAKE IT BACK WITH HIM ON OUR TAIL?!
IMPOS-SIBLE.
PLUS, I'M EXHAUSTED FROM THE RECENT TRAINING. TRYING TO RUN AWAY THROUGH THE WOODS WITH HIM AFTER US WILL JUST...
MURMUR MURMUR MURMUR
DON'T THINK!
HERE! NOW!! GOTTA FIGHT!! GOTTA WIN!!!
THERE'S NO OTHER OPTION... IZUKU MIDORIYA!
BE THE SAVIOR HERE!!
REMEMBER...
...WHERE YOU CAME FROM!!

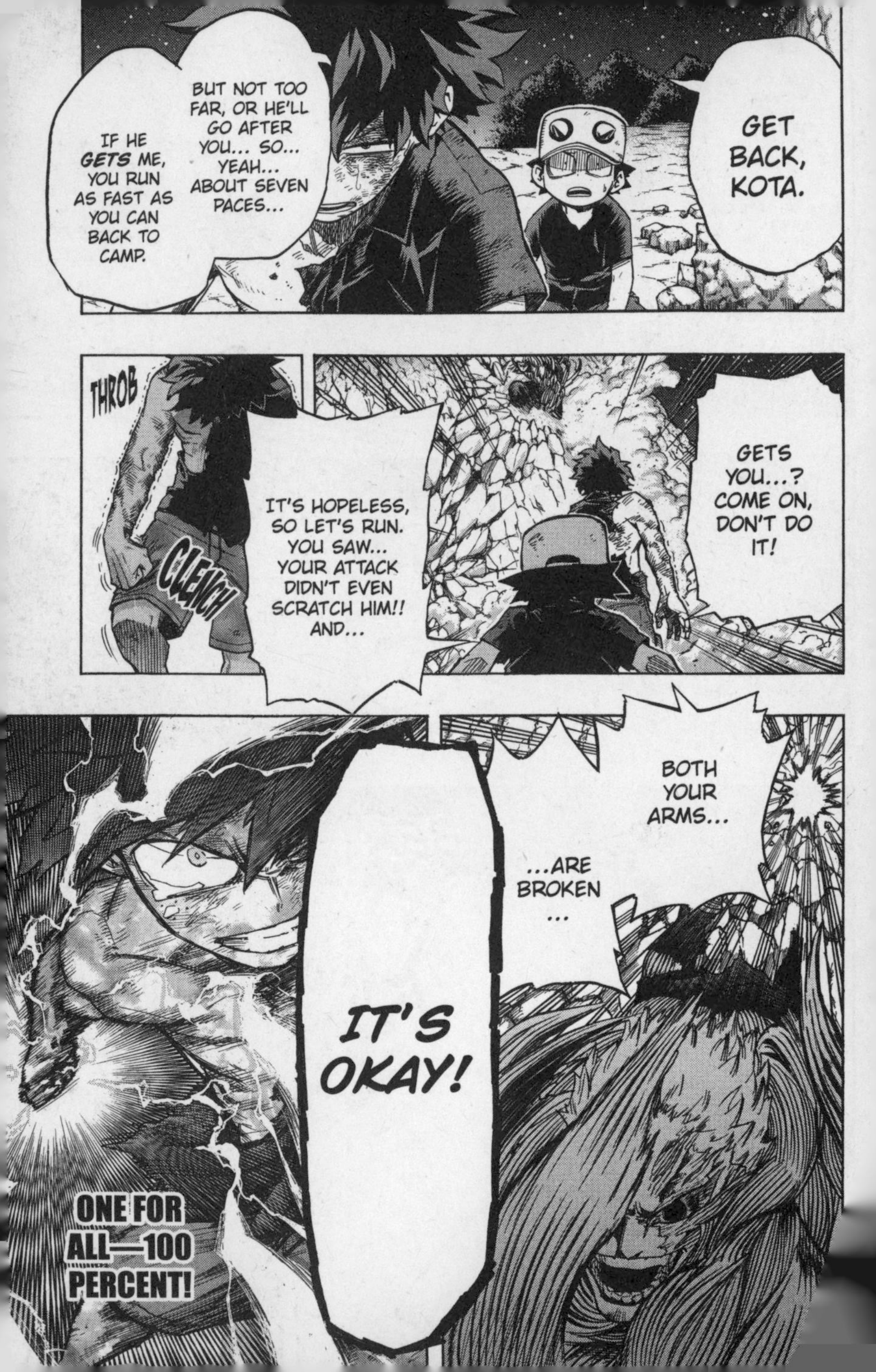
GET BACK, KOTA.
BUT NOT TOO FAR, OR HE'LL GO AFTER YOU... SO... YEAH... ABOUT SEVEN PACES...
IF HE *GETS* ME, YOU RUN AS FAST AS YOU CAN BACK TO CAMP.
GETS YOU...? COME ON, DON'T DO IT!
IT'S HOPELESS, SO LET'S RUN. YOU SAW... YOUR ATTACK DIDN'T EVEN SCRATCH HIM!! AND...
THROB
CLENCH
BOTH YOUR ARMS...
...ARE BROKEN...
IT'S OKAY!
ONE FOR ALL—100 PERCENT!

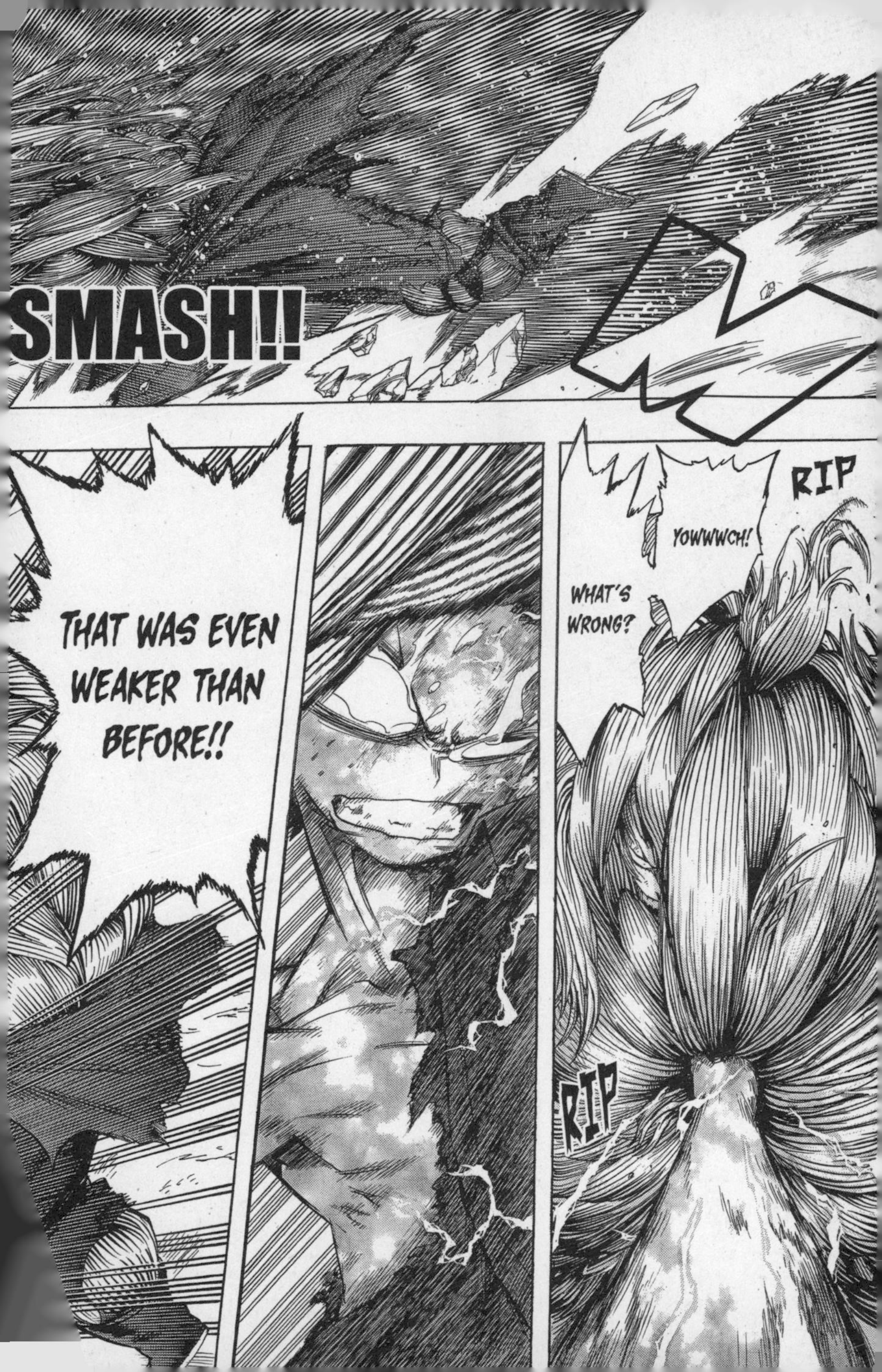
SMASH!!
RIP
YOWWWCH!
WHAT'S WRONG?
RIP
THAT WAS EVEN WEAKER THAN BEFORE!!

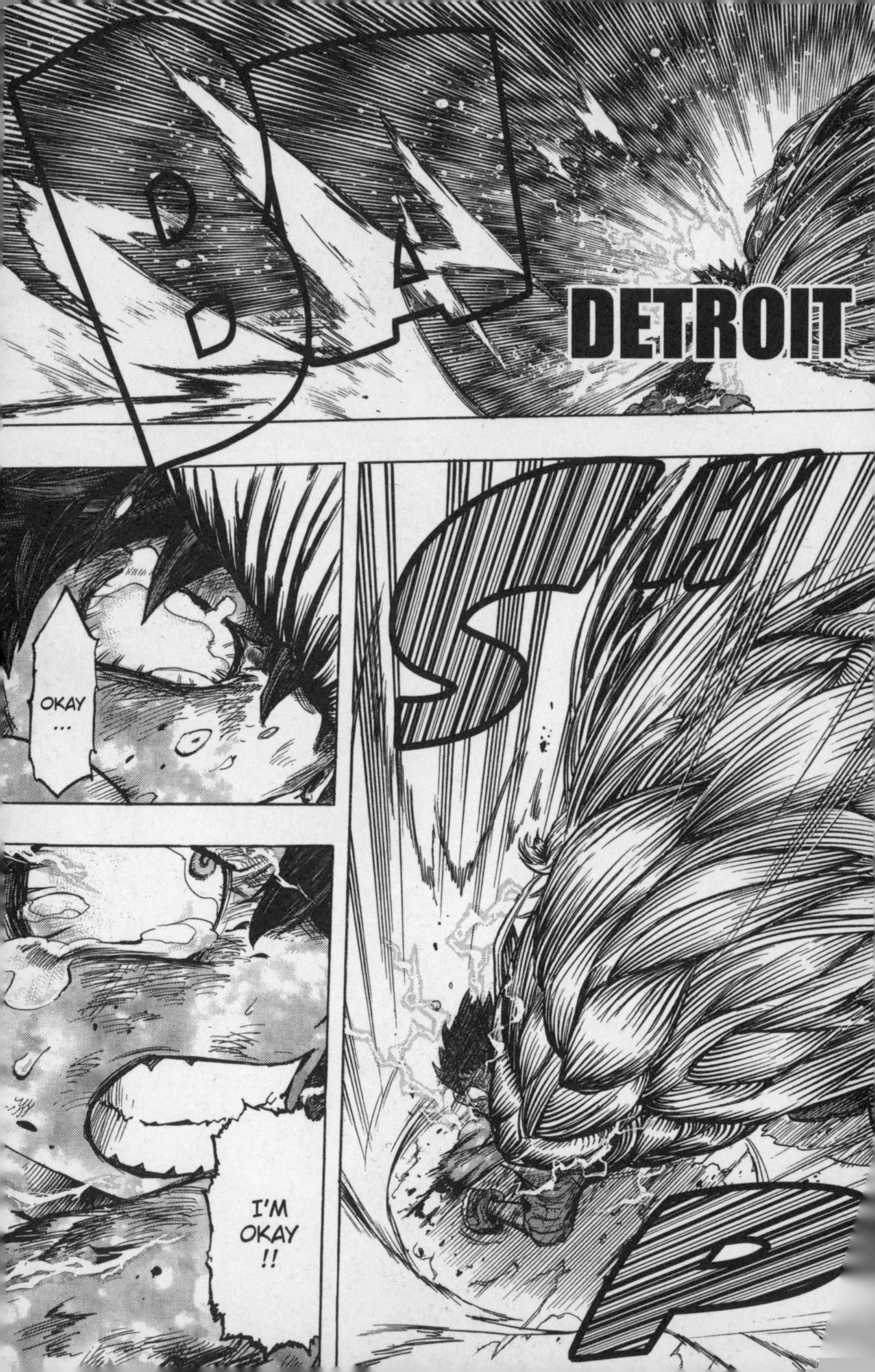
DETROIT
OKAY ...
I'M OKAY !!

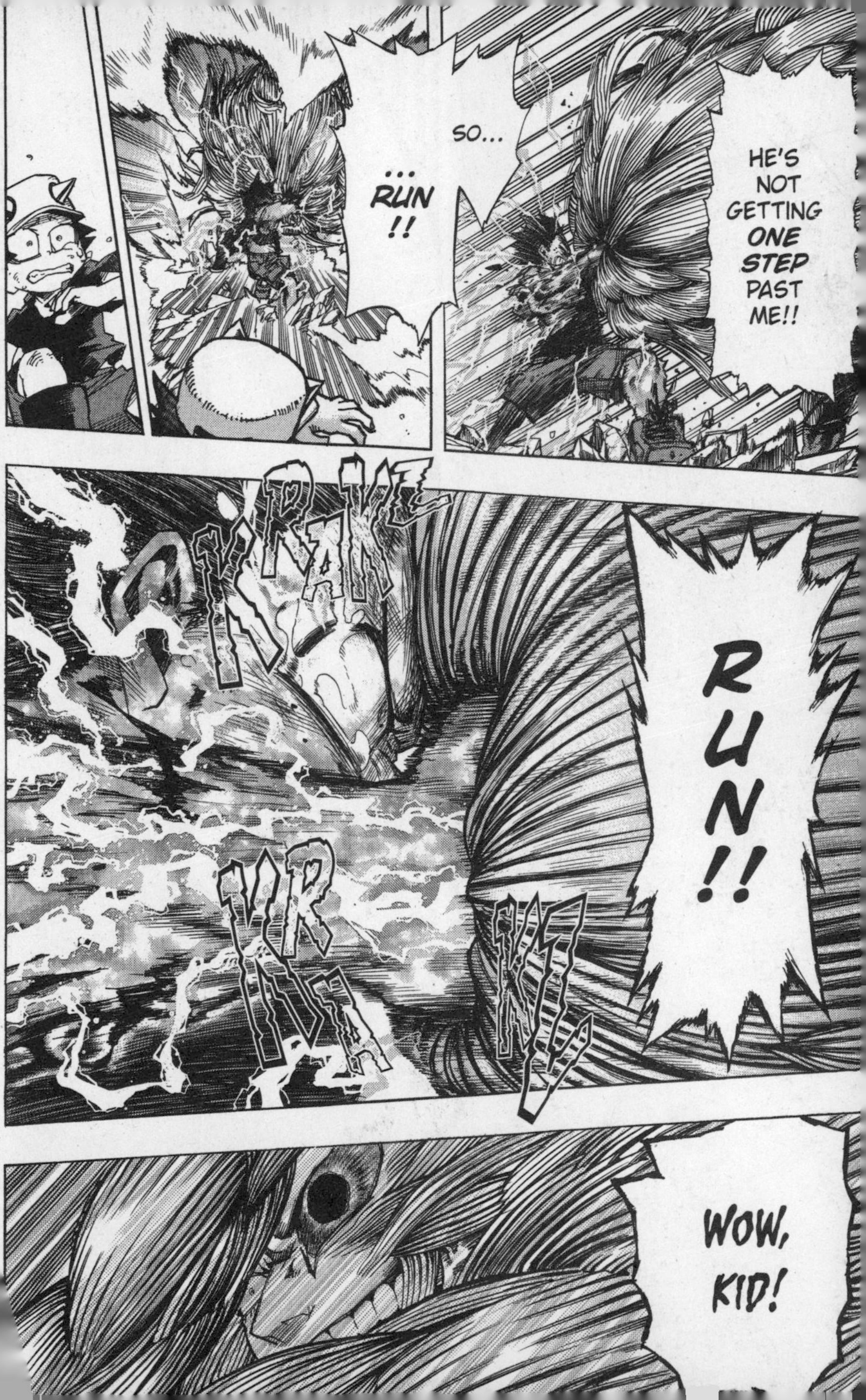
HE'S NOT GETTING ONE STEP PAST ME!!
SO...
...RUN!!
RUN!!
WOW, KID!

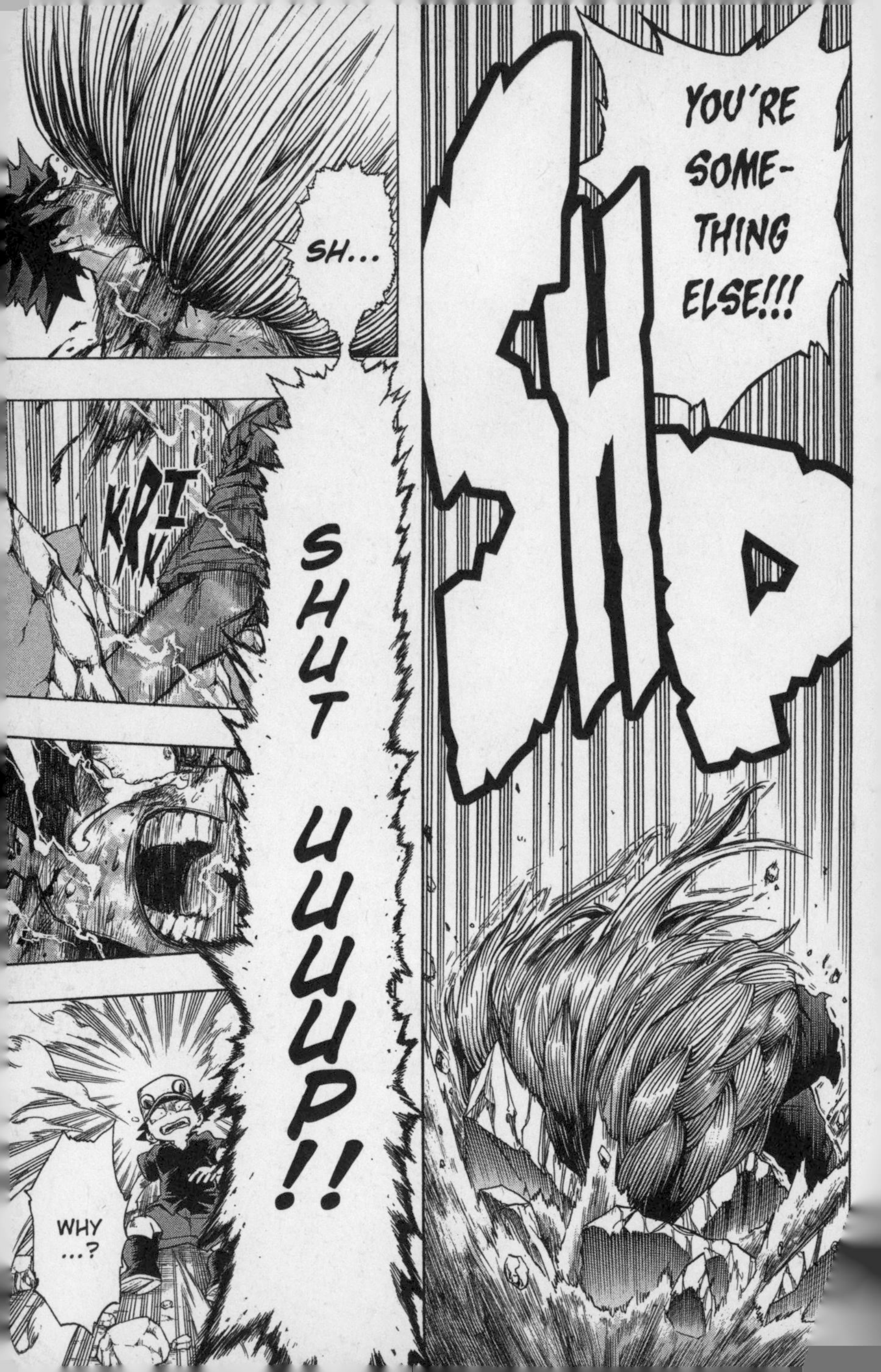
YOU'RE SOMETHING ELSE!!!
SH...
KRIK
SHUT UUUUP!!
WHY ...?

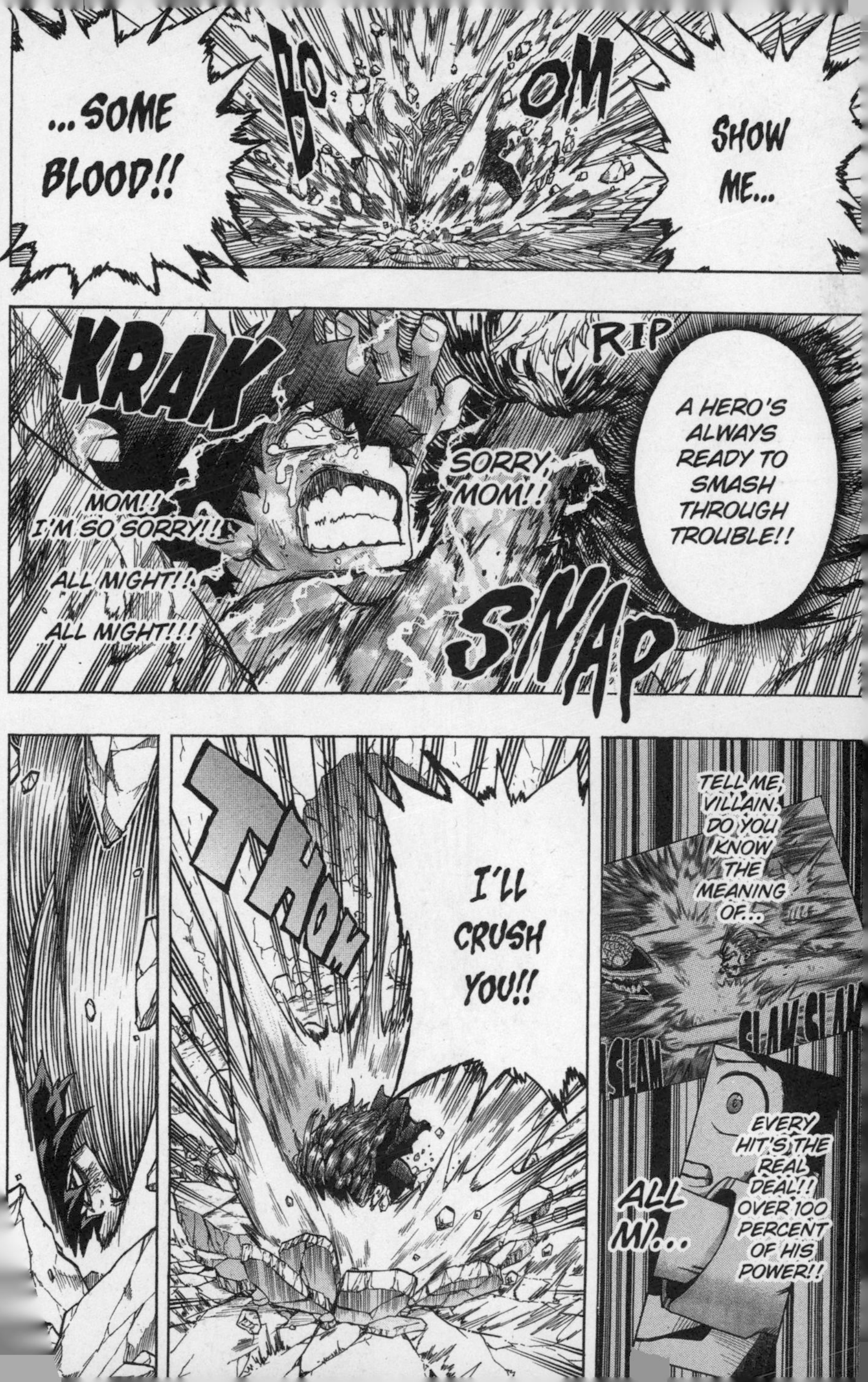
SHOW ME...
BOOM
...SOME BLOOD!!
A HERO'S ALWAYS READY TO SMASH THROUGH TROUBLE!!
RIP
SNAP
SORRY, MOM!!
KRAK
MOM!! I'M SO SORRY!!
ALL MIGHT!!
ALL MIGHT!!!
TELL ME, VILLAIN. DO YOU KNOW THE MEANING OF...
SLAM SLAM
SLAM
EVERY HIT'S THE REAL DEAL!! OVER 100 PERCENT OF HIS POWER!!
ALL MI...
THOOM
I'LL CRUSH YOU!!

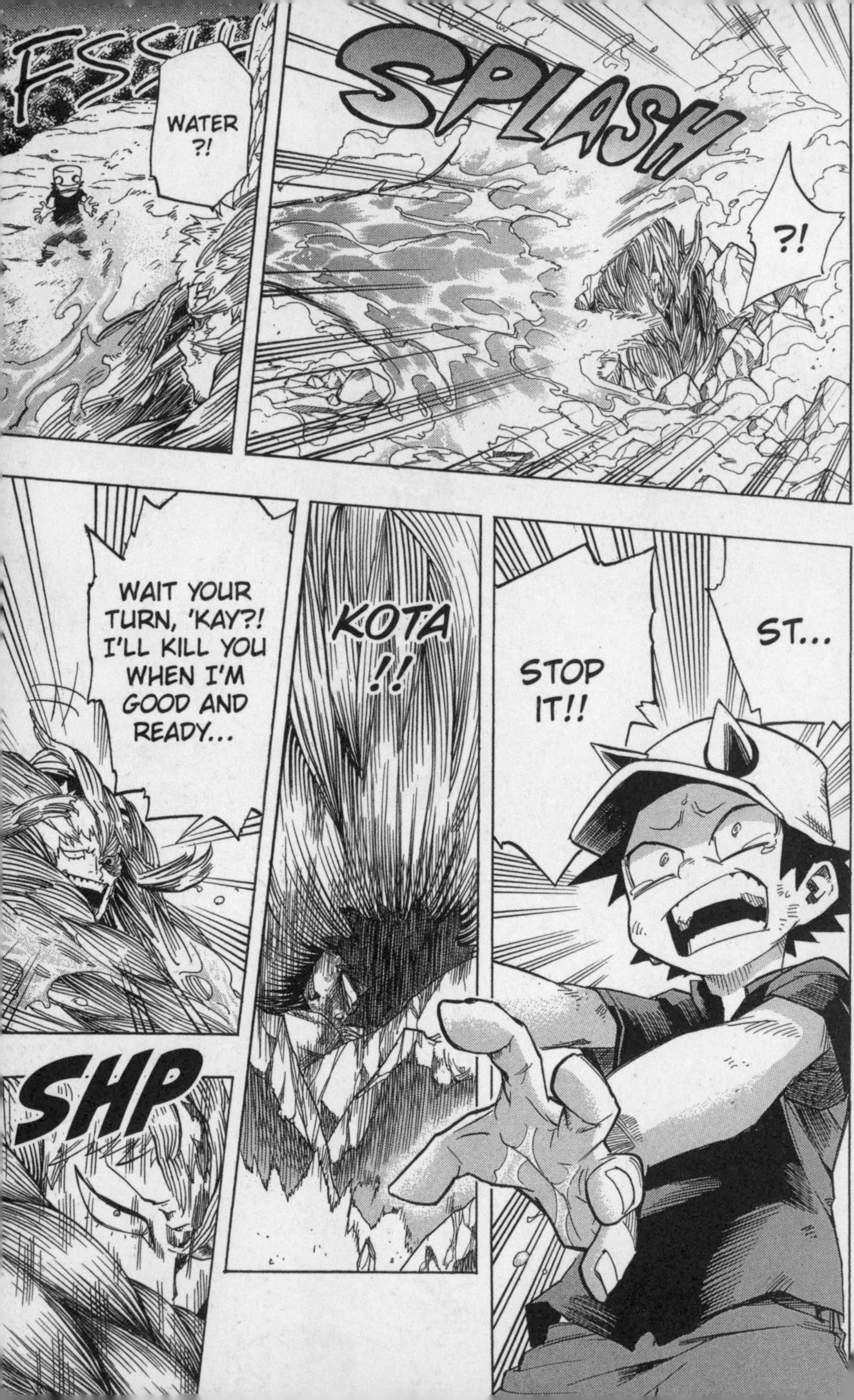
SPLASH
?!
FSSH
WATER ?!
ST...
STOP IT!!
KOTA !!
WAIT YOUR TURN, 'KAY?! I'LL KILL YOU WHEN I'M GOOD AND READY...
SHP

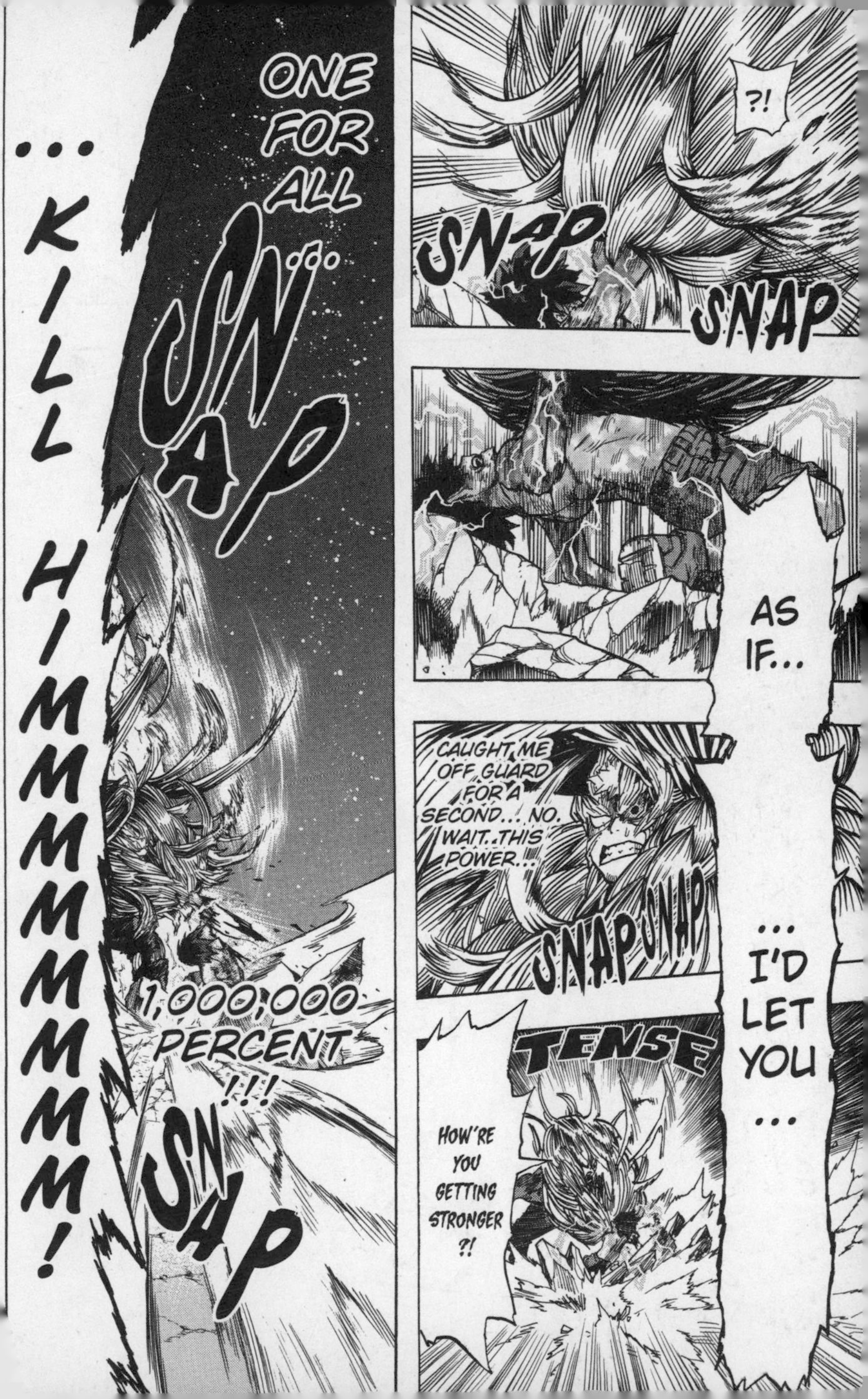
?!
SNAP
SNAP
AS IF...
CAUGHT ME OFF GUARD FOR A SECOND... NO. WAIT. THIS POWER...
SNAP SNAP
... I'D LET YOU ...
TENSE
HOW'RE YOU GETTING STRONGER ?!
ONE FOR ALL...
SNAP
...KILL HIMMMMMMMMM!
1,000,000 PERCENT !!!
SNAP

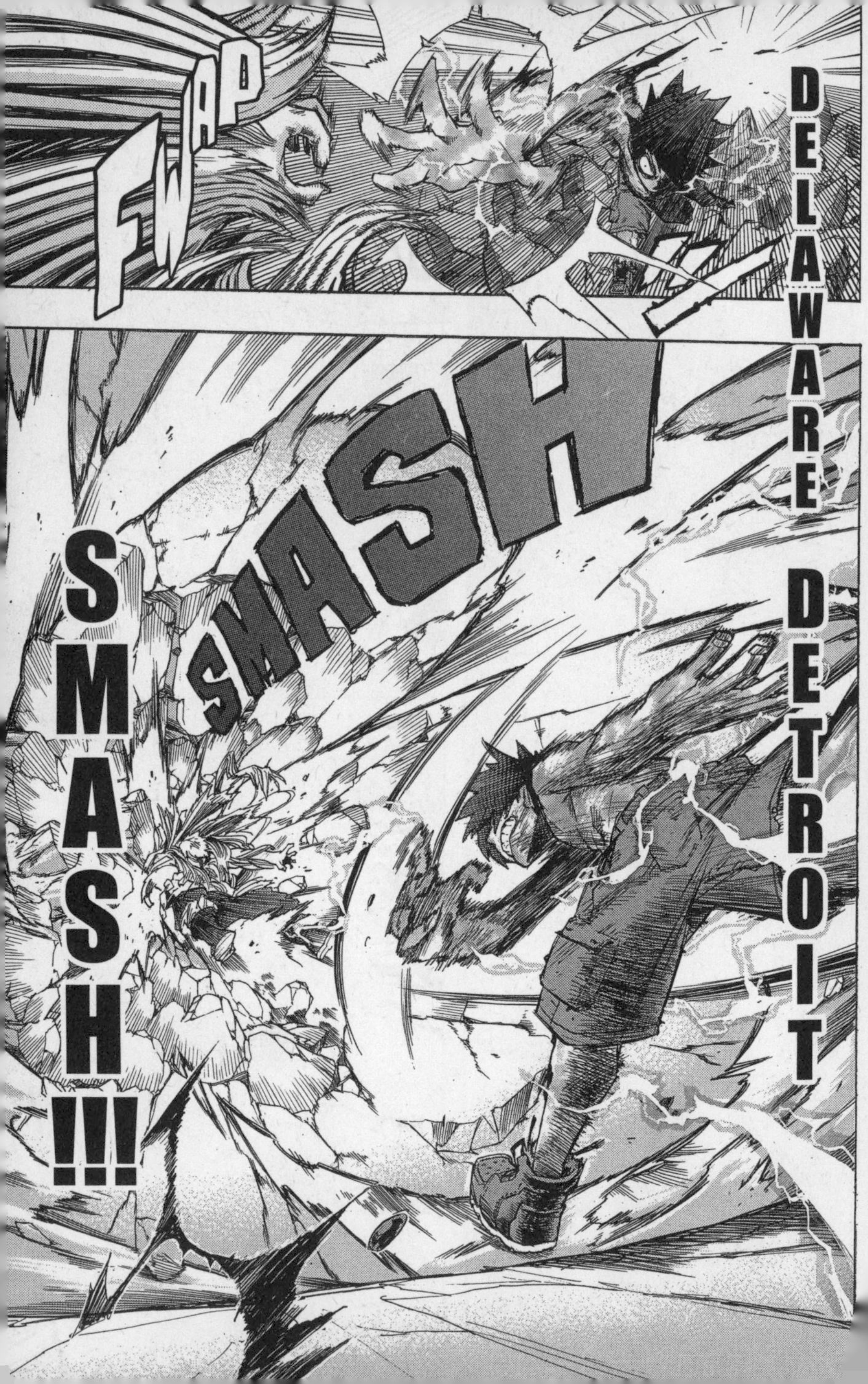
FWAP
DELAWARE DETROIT
SMASH
SMASH!!!

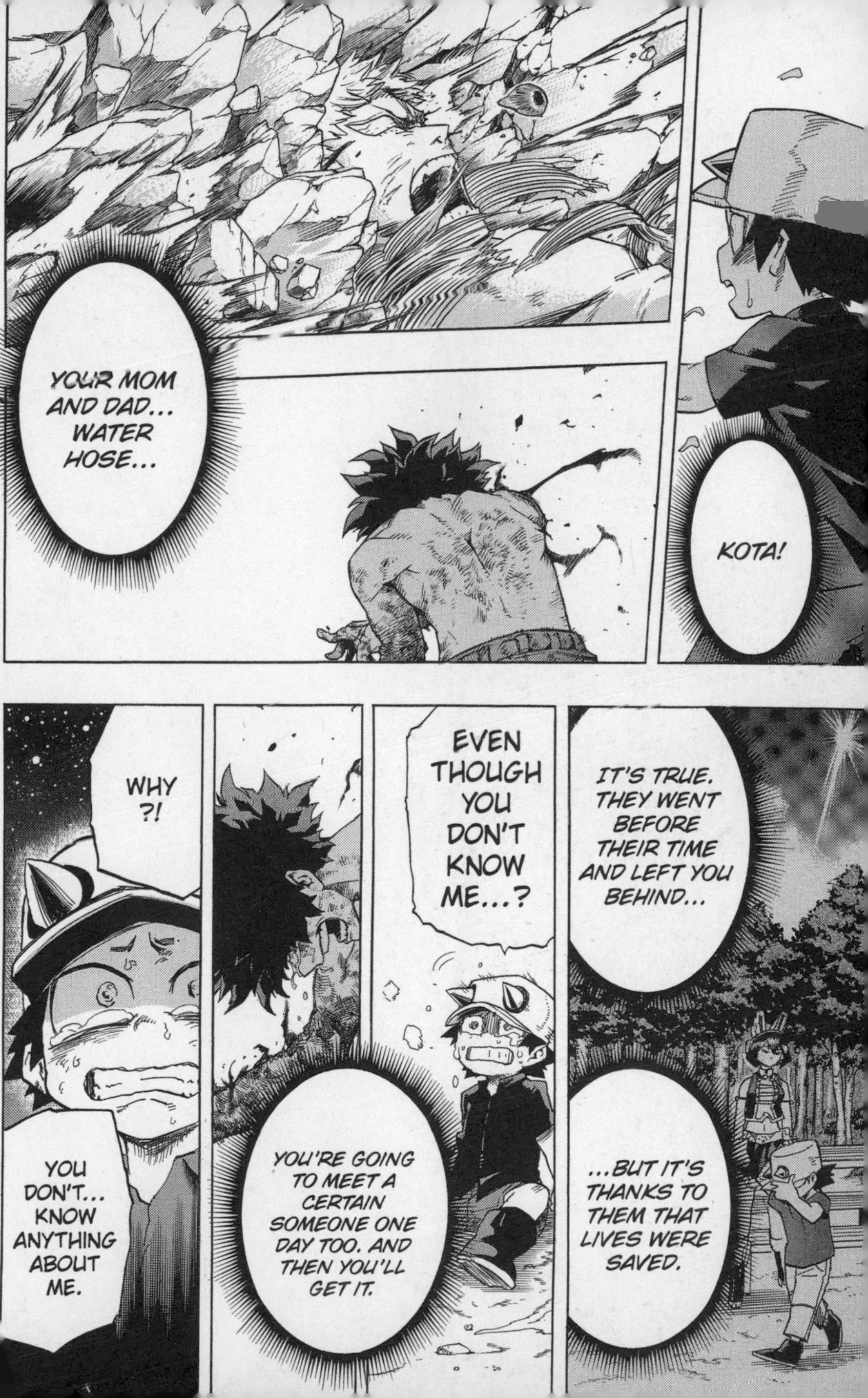
KOTA!
YOUR MOM AND DAD... WATER HOSE...
IT'S TRUE. THEY WENT BEFORE THEIR TIME AND LEFT YOU BEHIND...
...BUT IT'S THANKS TO THEM THAT LIVES WERE SAVED.
EVEN THOUGH YOU DON'T KNOW ME...?
YOU'RE GOING TO MEET A CERTAIN SOMEONE ONE DAY TOO. AND THEN YOU'LL GET IT.
WHY?!
YOU DON'T... KNOW ANYTHING ABOUT ME.

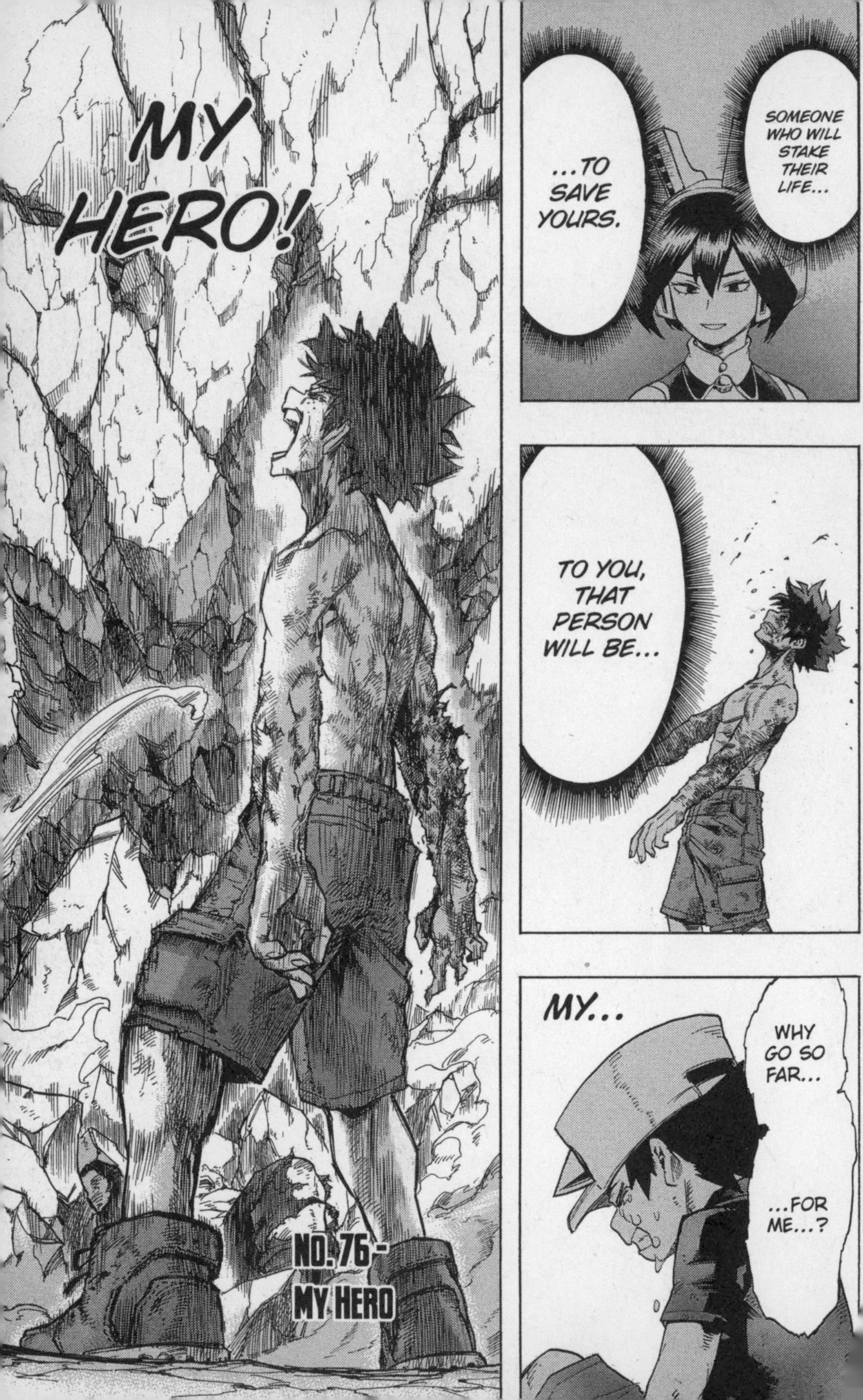
SOMEONE WHO WILL STAKE THEIR LIFE...
...TO SAVE YOURS.
TO YOU, THAT PERSON WILL BE...
WHY GO SO FAR...
...FOR ME...?
MY...
MY HERO!
NO. 76 - My Hero

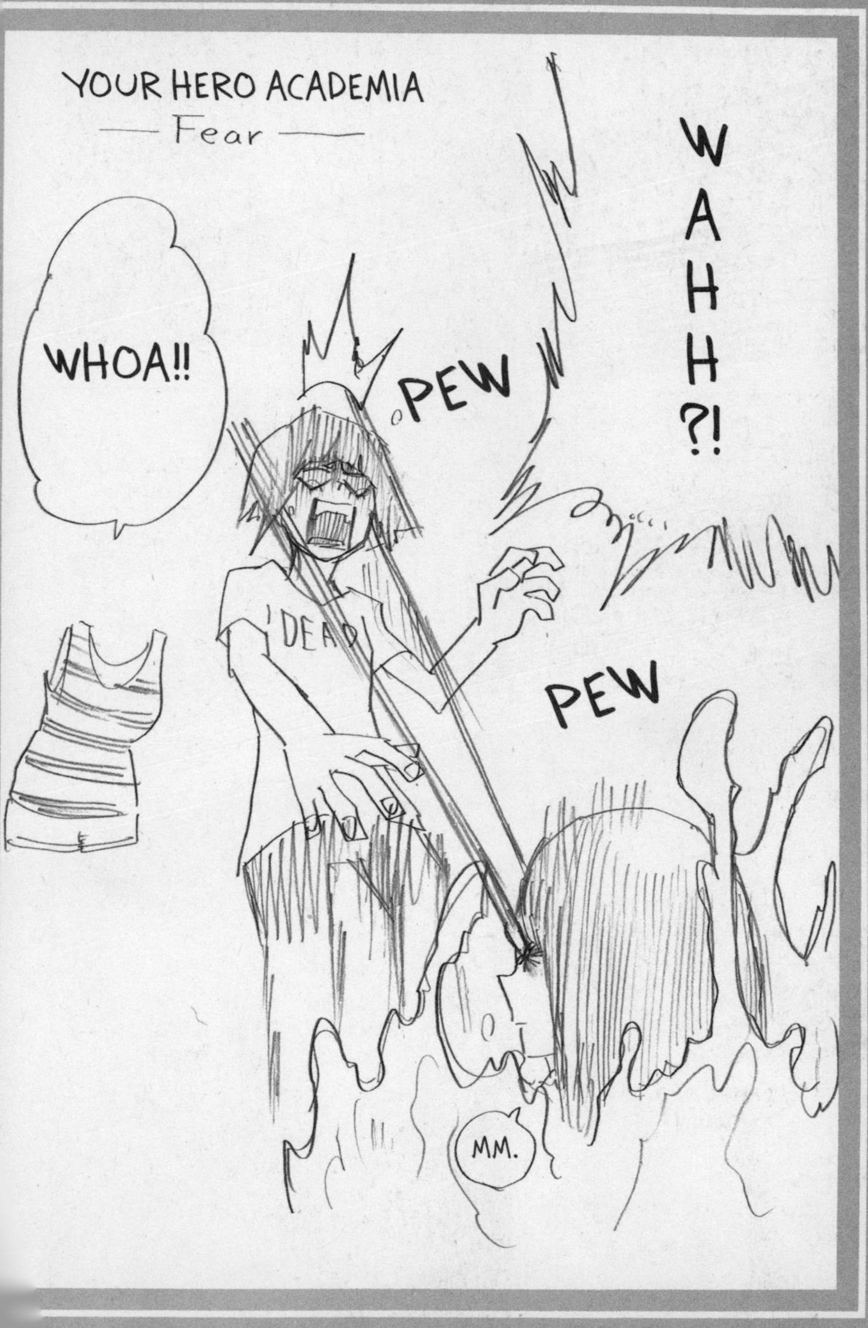
YOUR HERO ACADEMIA
—Fear—
WAHH?!
PEW
WHOA!!
DEAD
PEW
MM.

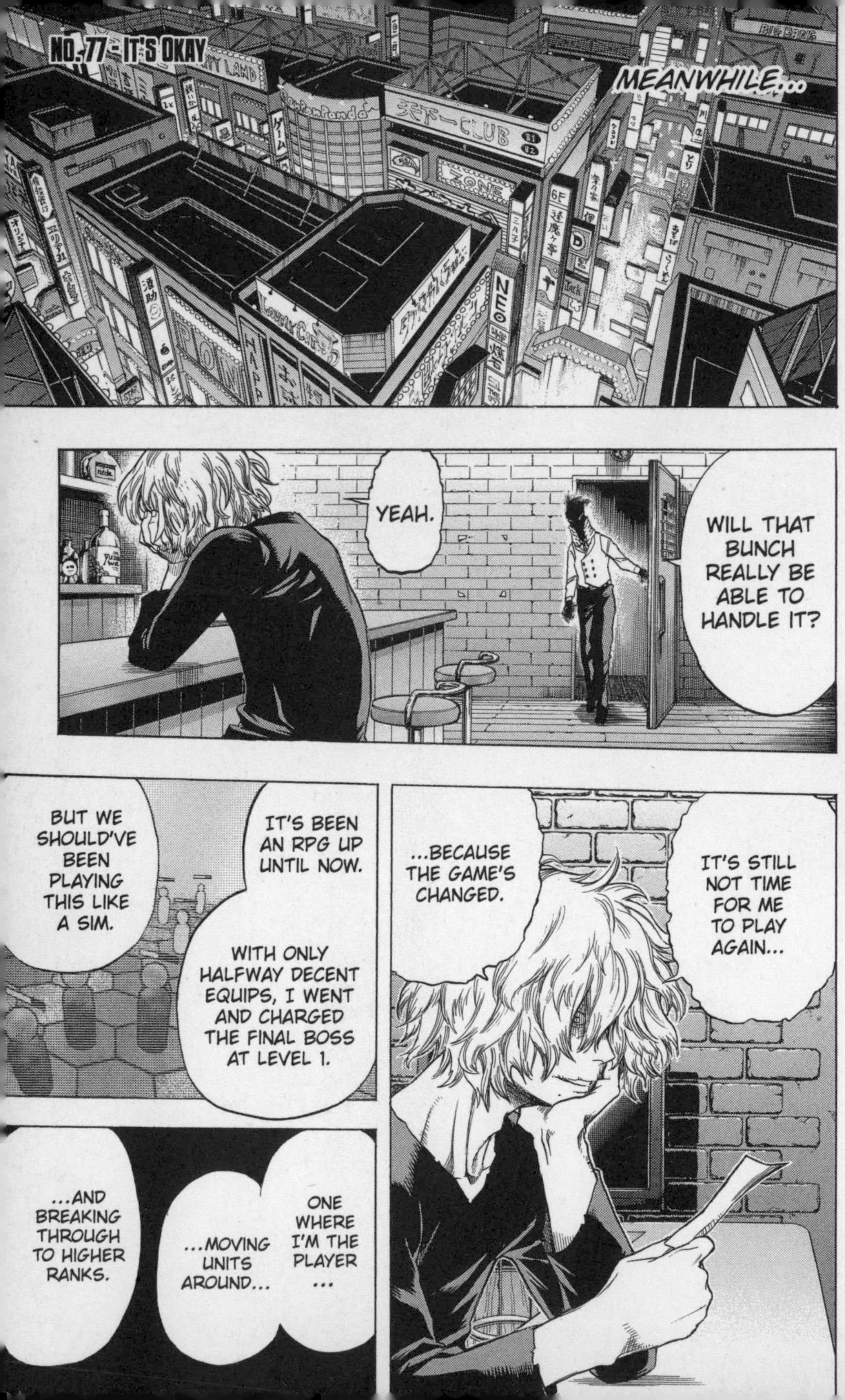
NO. 77 - IT'S OKAY
MEANWHILE...
WILL THAT BUNCH REALLY BE ABLE TO HANDLE IT?
YEAH.
IT'S STILL NOT TIME FOR ME TO PLAY AGAIN...
...BECAUSE THE GAME'S CHANGED.
IT'S BEEN AN RPG UP UNTIL NOW.
WITH ONLY HALFWAY DECENT EQUIPS, I WENT AND CHARGED THE FINAL BOSS AT LEVEL 1.
BUT WE SHOULD'VE BEEN PLAYING THIS LIKE A SIM.
ONE WHERE I'M THE PLAYER ...
...MOVING UNITS AROUND...
...AND BREAKING THROUGH TO HIGHER RANKS.

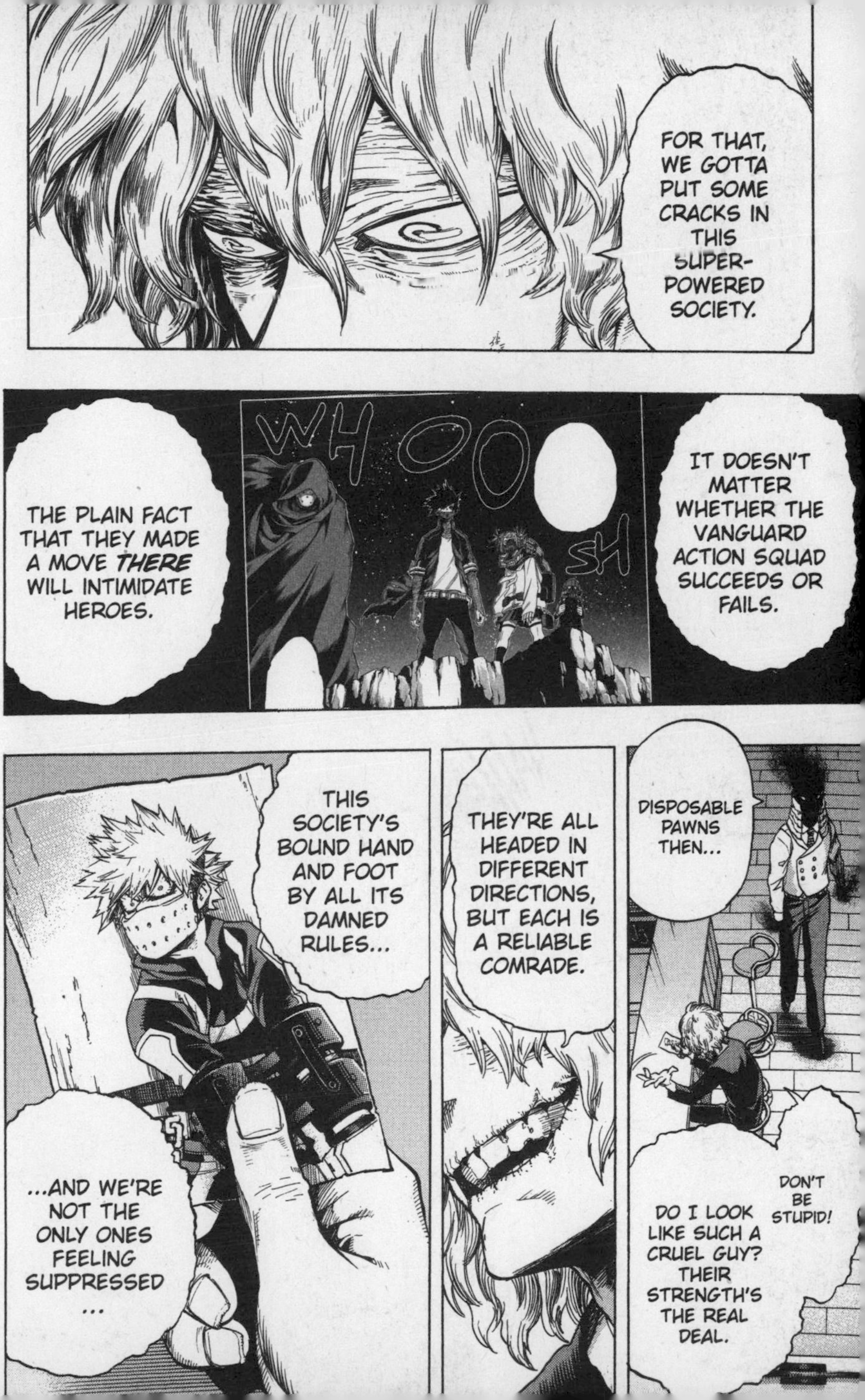
FOR THAT, WE GOTTA PUT SOME CRACKS IN THIS SUPER-POWERED SOCIETY.
IT DOESN'T MATTER WHETHER THE VANGUARD ACTION SQUAD SUCCEEDS OR FAILS.
WHOOOSH
THE PLAIN FACT THAT THEY MADE A MOVE *THERE* WILL INTIMIDATE HEROES.
DISPOSABLE PAWNS THEN...
DON'T BE STUPID!
DO I LOOK LIKE SUCH A CRUEL GUY? THEIR STRENGTH'S THE REAL DEAL.
THEY'RE ALL HEADED IN DIFFERENT DIRECTIONS, BUT EACH IS A RELIABLE COMRADE.
THIS SOCIETY'S BOUND HAND AND FOOT BY ALL ITS DAMNED RULES...
...AND WE'RE NOT THE ONLY ONES FEELING SUPPRESSED...

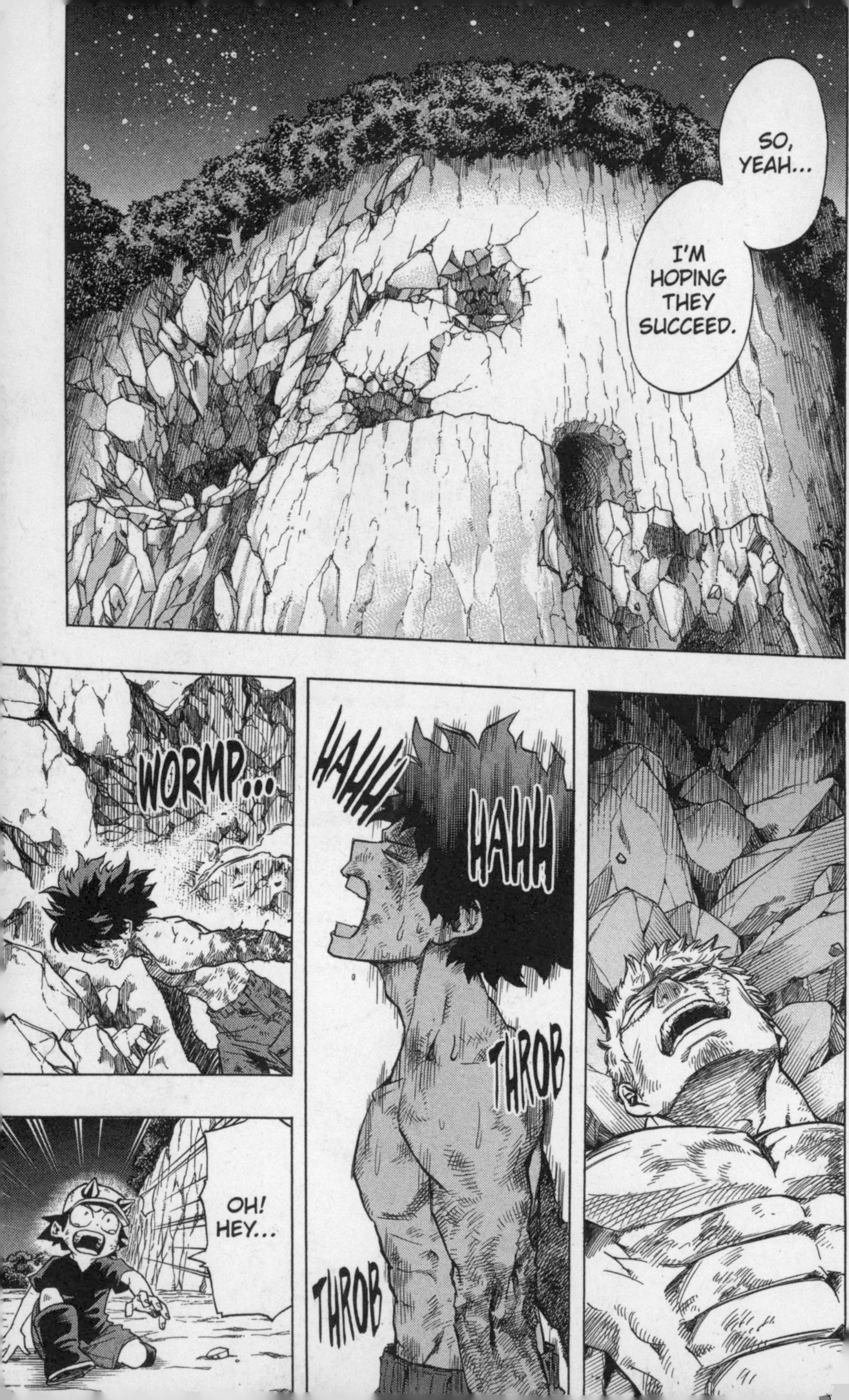
SO, YEAH...
I'M HOPING THEY SUCCEED.
HAHH
HAHH
THROB
THROB
WORMP...
OH! HEY...

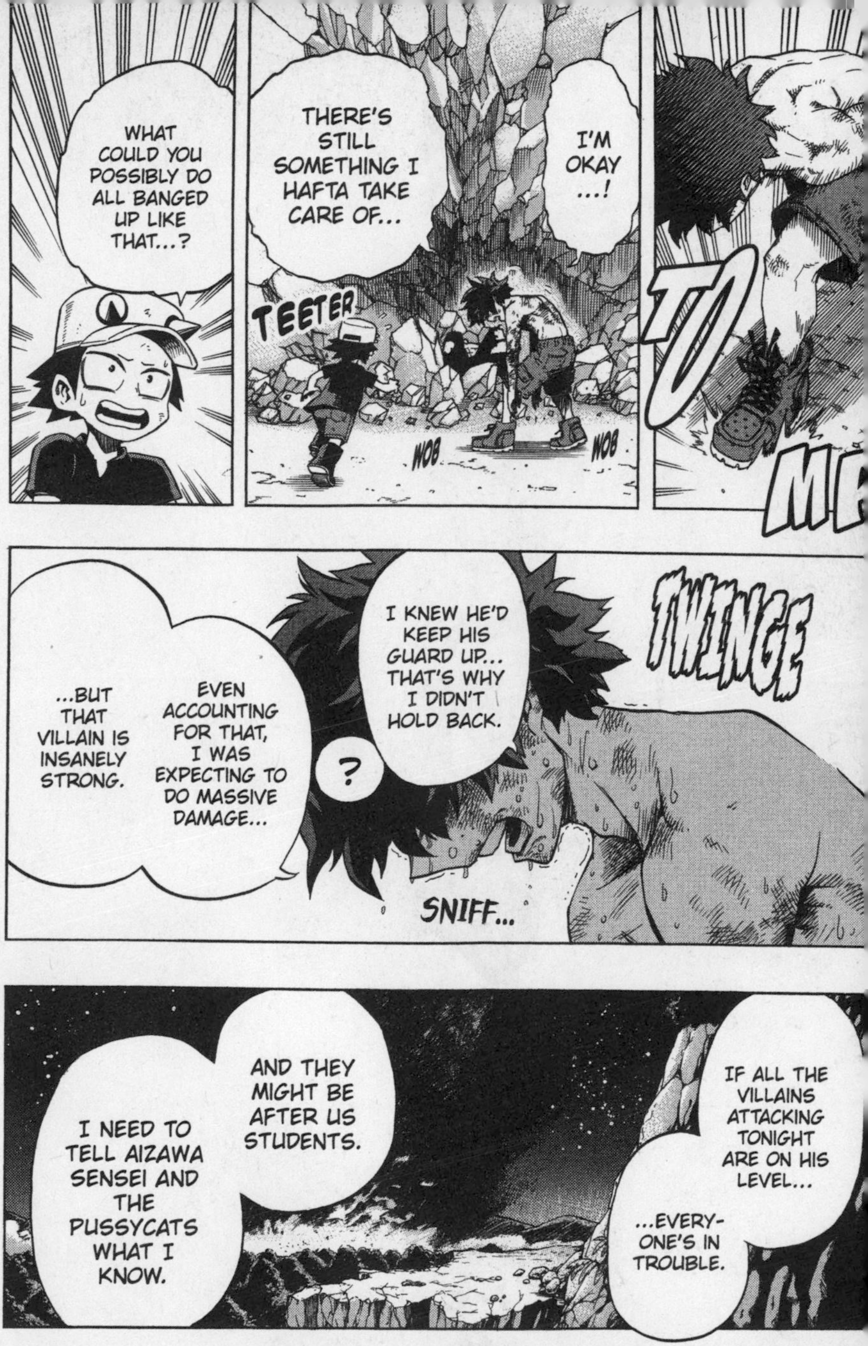
TO
M
I'M OKAY ...!
THERE'S STILL SOMETHING I HAFTA TAKE CARE OF...
TEETER
WOB
WOB
WHAT COULD YOU POSSIBLY DO ALL BANGED UP LIKE THAT...?
TWINGE
I KNEW HE'D KEEP HIS GUARD UP... THAT'S WHY I DIDN'T HOLD BACK.
?
EVEN ACCOUNTING FOR THAT, I WAS EXPECTING TO DO MASSIVE DAMAGE...
...BUT THAT VILLAIN IS INSANELY STRONG.
SNIFF...
IF ALL THE VILLAINS ATTACKING TONIGHT ARE ON HIS LEVEL...
...EVERYONE'S IN TROUBLE.
AND THEY MIGHT BE AFTER US STUDENTS.
I NEED TO TELL AIZAWA SENSEI AND THE PUSSYCATS WHAT I KNOW.

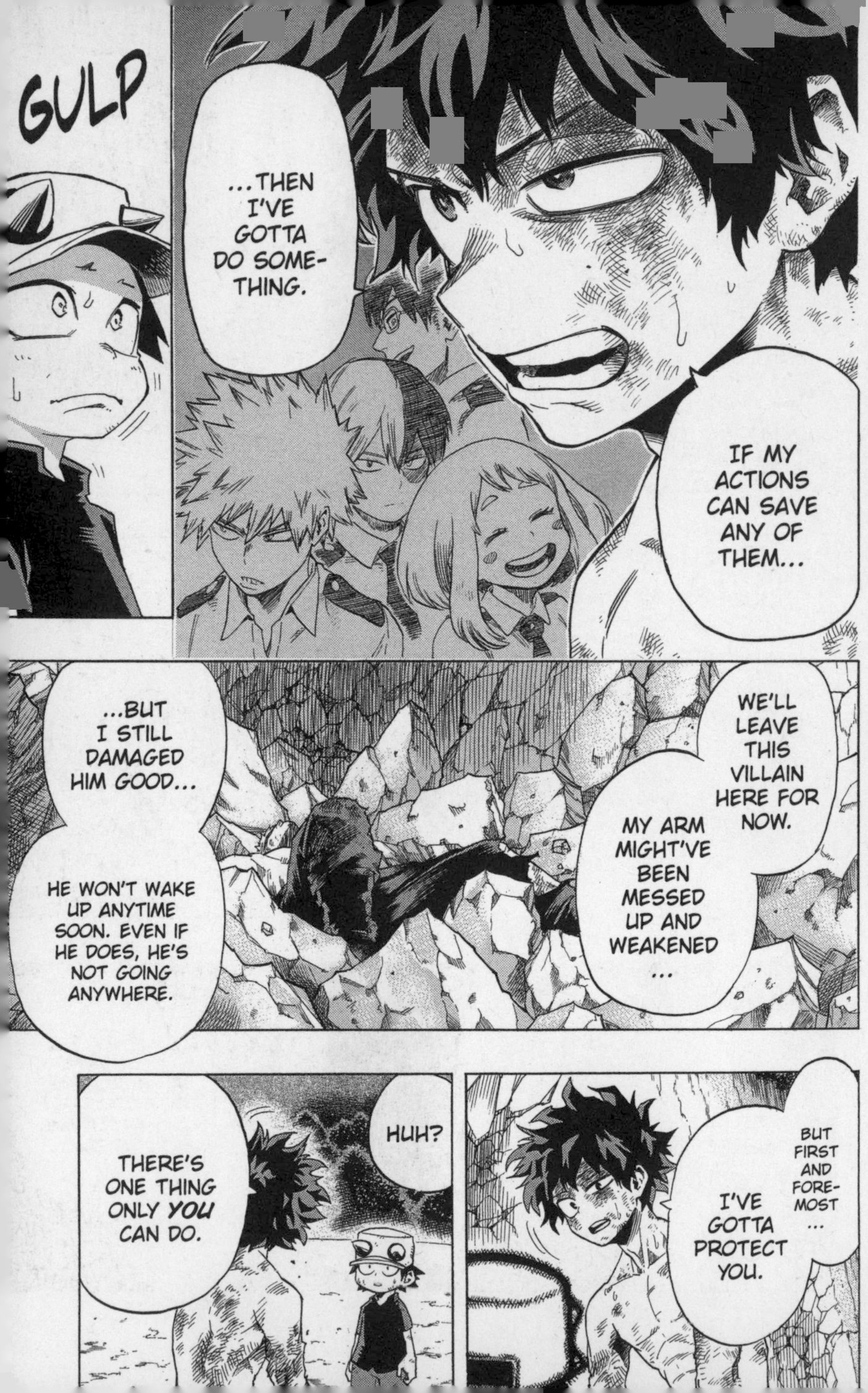
IF MY ACTIONS CAN SAVE ANY OF THEM...
...THEN I'VE GOTTA DO SOME-THING.
GULP
WE'LL LEAVE THIS VILLAIN HERE FOR NOW.
MY ARM MIGHT'VE BEEN MESSED UP AND WEAKENED...
...BUT I STILL DAMAGED HIM GOOD...
HE WON'T WAKE UP ANYTIME SOON. EVEN IF HE DOES, HE'S NOT GOING ANYWHERE.
BUT FIRST AND FORE-MOST...
I'VE GOTTA PROTECT YOU.
HUH?
THERE'S ONE THING ONLY *YOU* CAN DO.

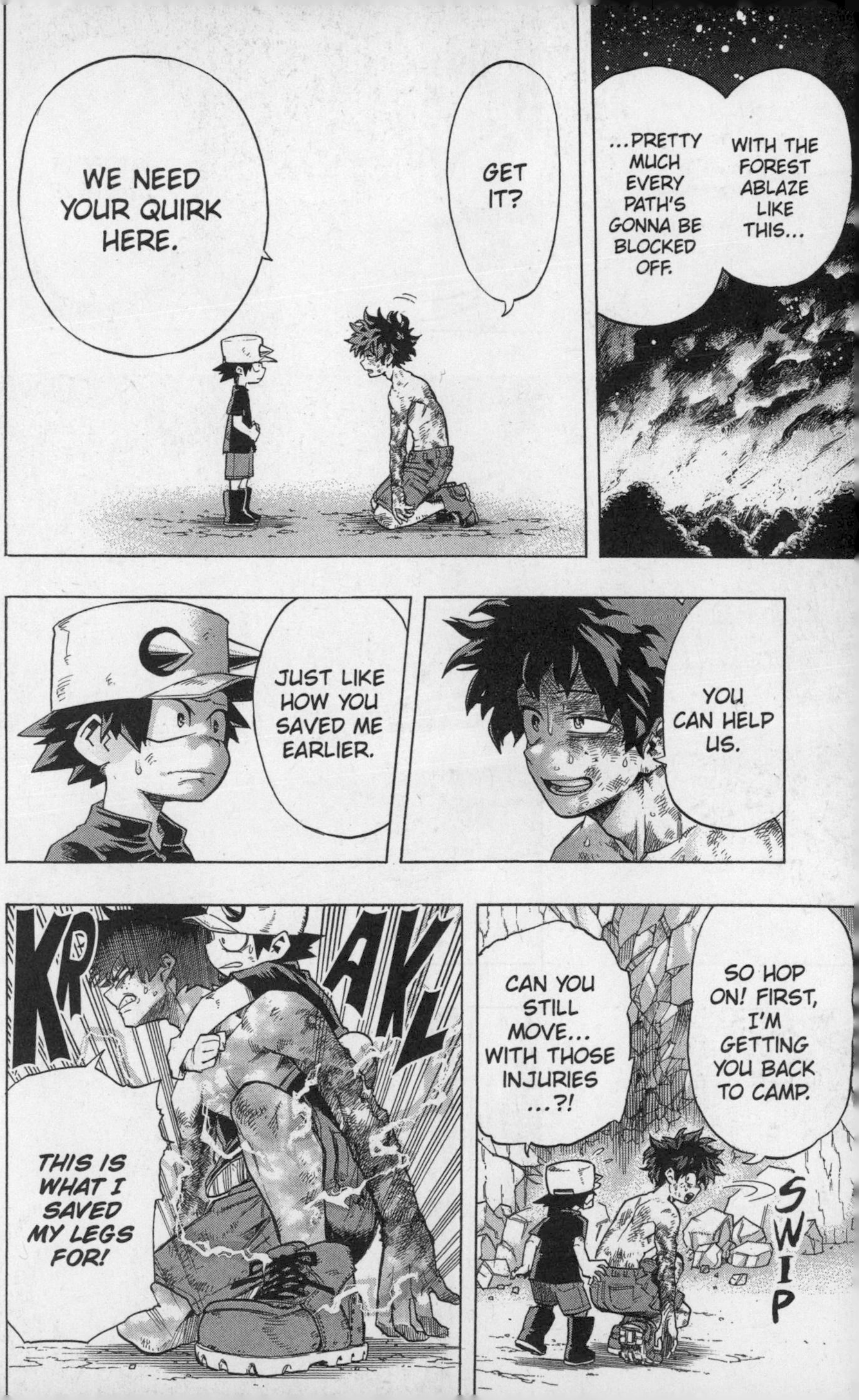
WITH THE FOREST ABLAZE LIKE THIS...
...PRETTY MUCH EVERY PATH'S GONNA BE BLOCKED OFF.
GET IT?
WE NEED YOUR QUIRK HERE.
YOU CAN HELP US.
JUST LIKE HOW YOU SAVED ME EARLIER.
SO HOP ON! FIRST, I'M GETTING YOU BACK TO CAMP.
CAN YOU STILL MOVE... WITH THOSE INJURIES ...?!
SWIP
KRAK
THIS IS WHAT I SAVED MY LEGS FOR!

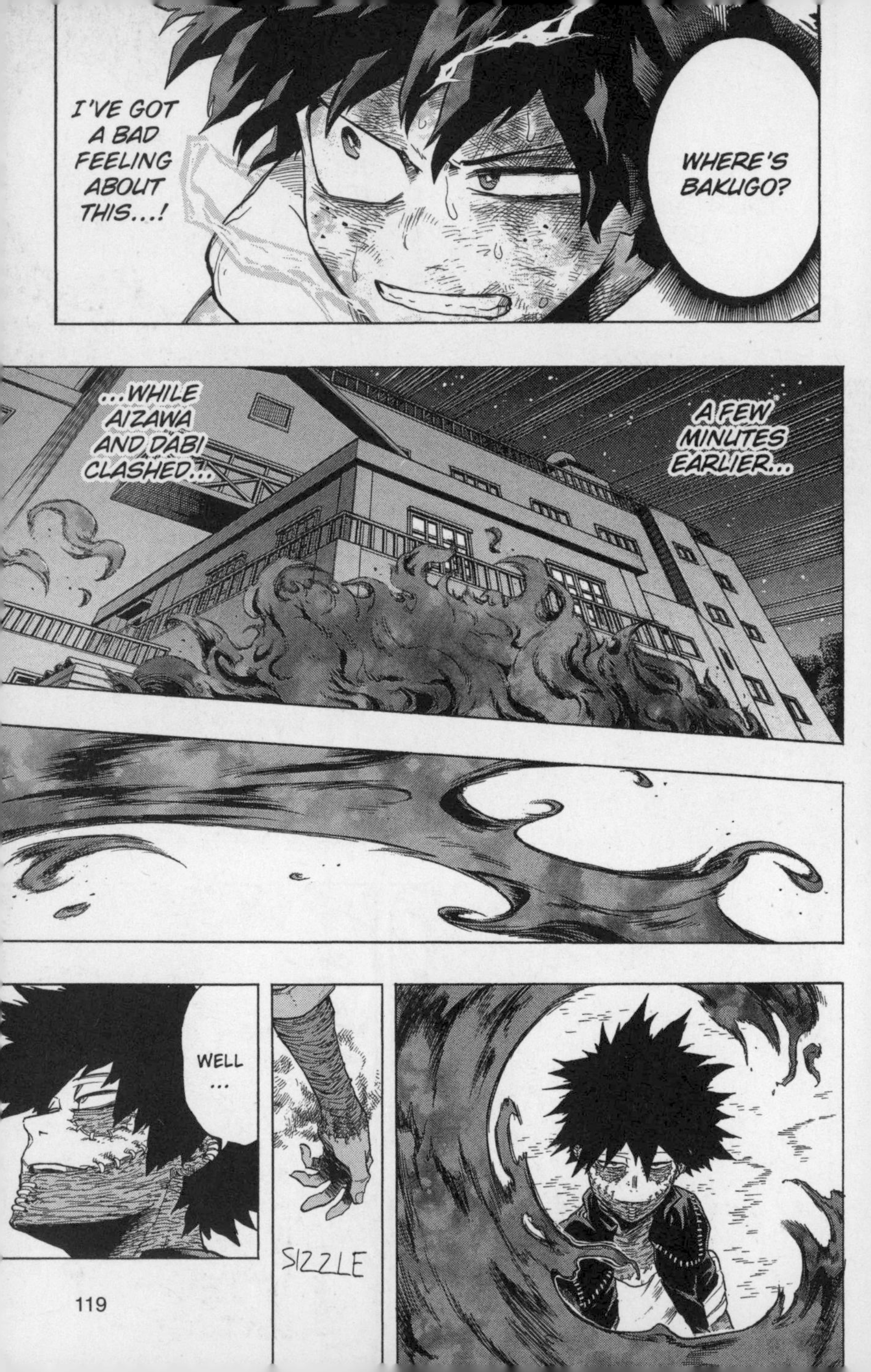

WHERE'S BAKUGO?
I'VE GOT A BAD FEELING ABOUT THIS...!
A FEW MINUTES EARLIER...
...WHILE AIZAWA AND DABI CLASHED...
SIZZLE
WELL...

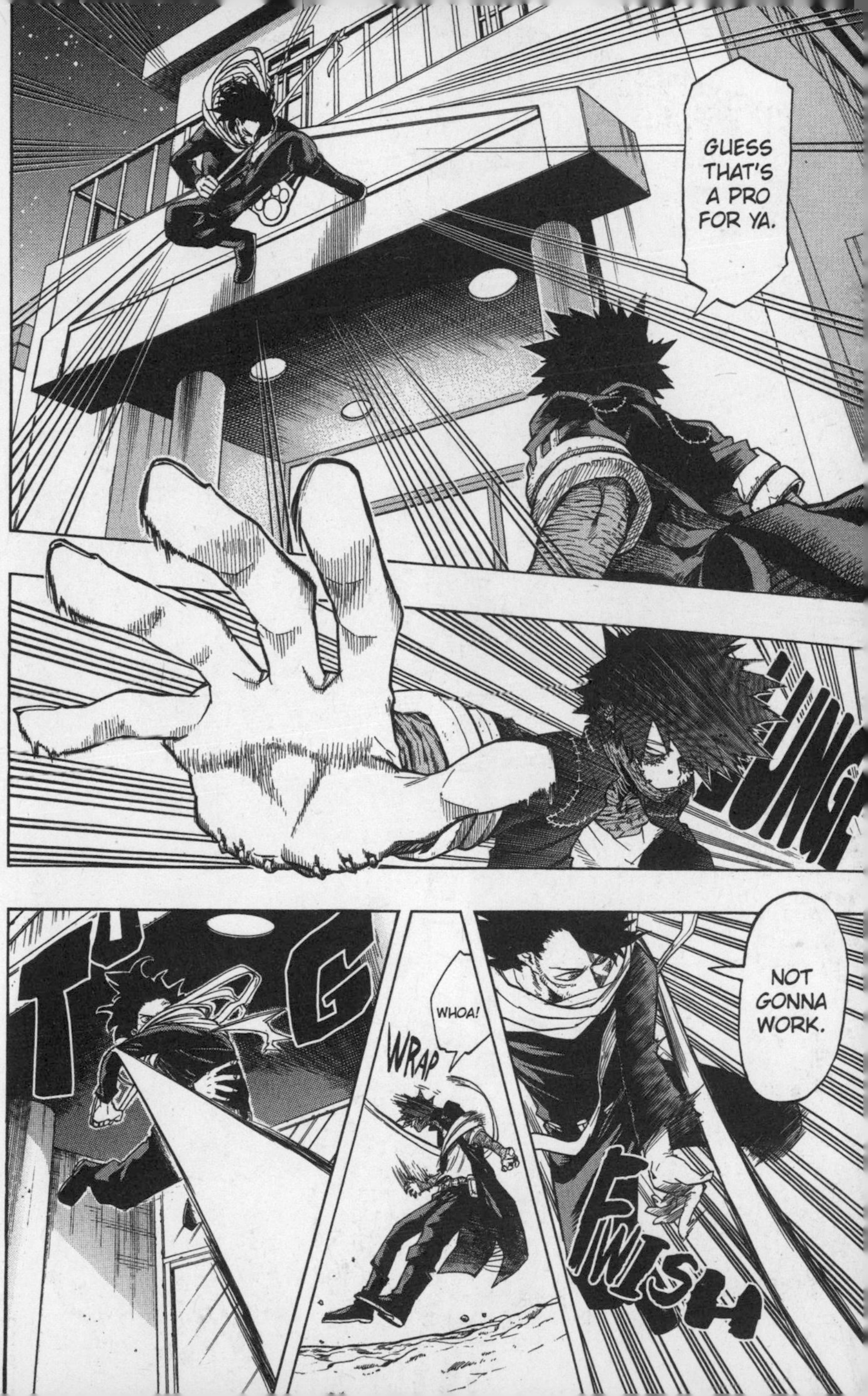
GUESS THAT'S A PRO FOR YA.
LUNGE
NOT GONNA WORK.
FWISH
WHOA!
WRAP

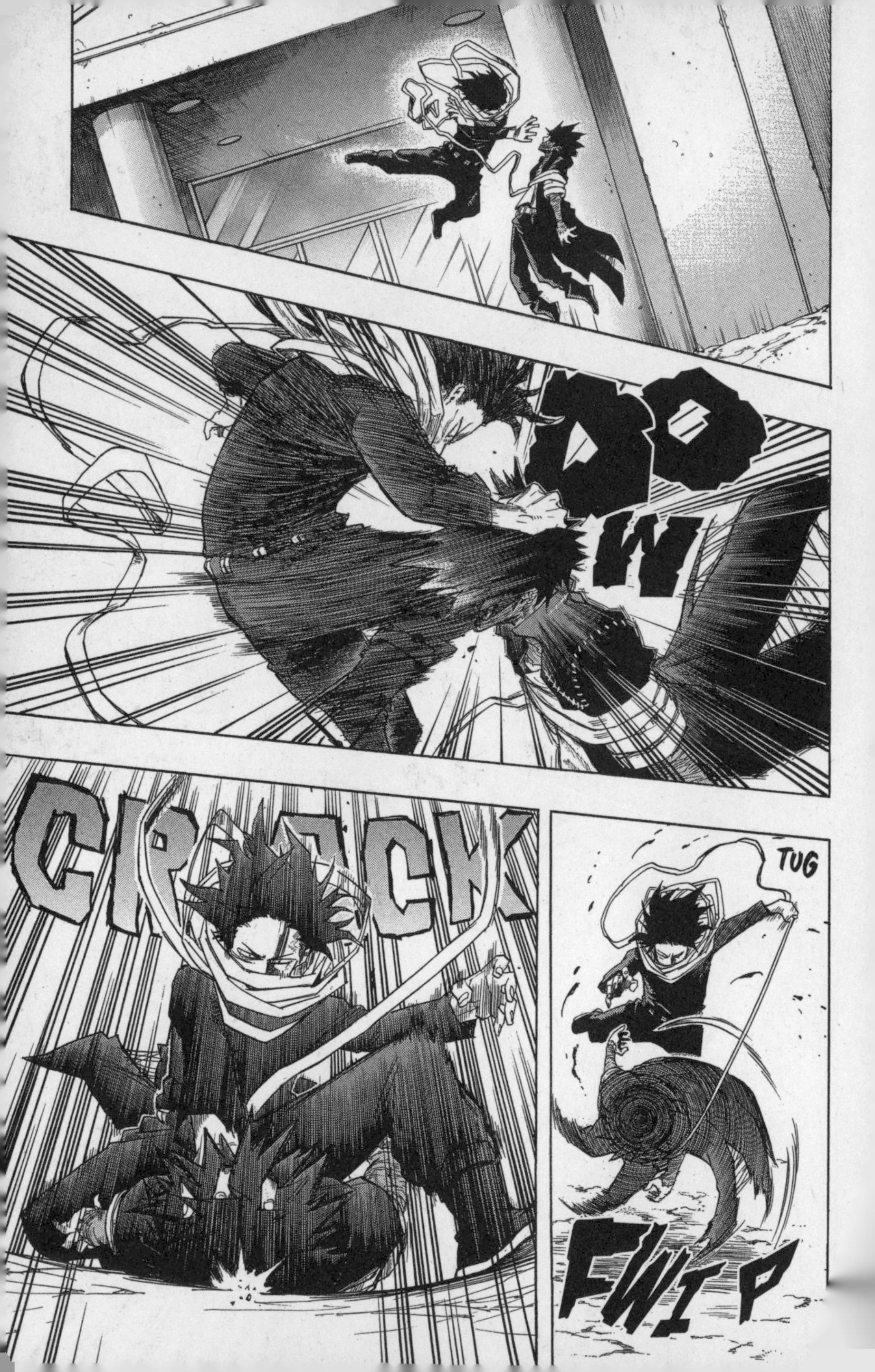
TUG
FWIP
CRACK

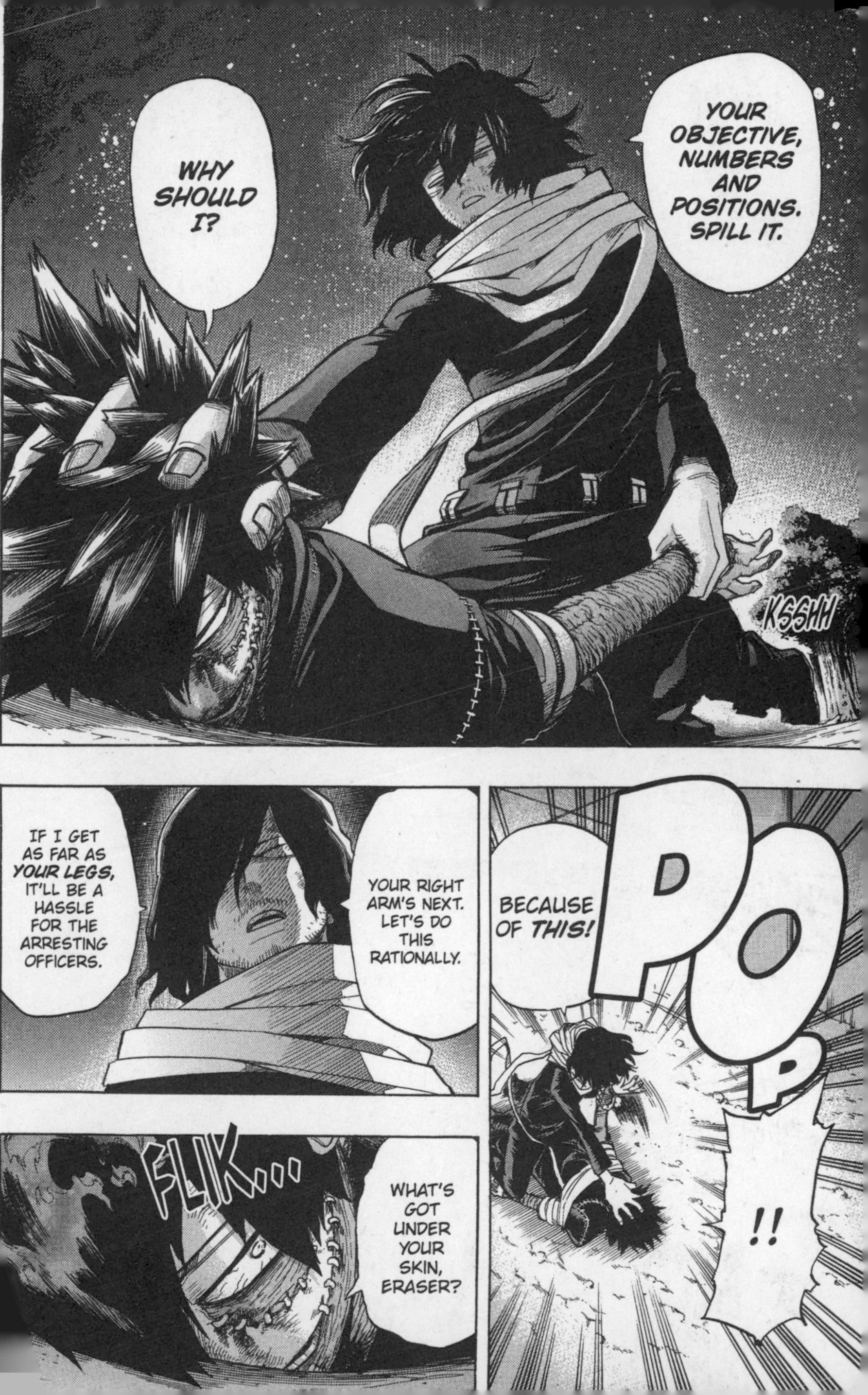

YOUR OBJECTIVE, NUMBERS AND POSITIONS. SPILL IT.
WHY SHOULD I?
KSSHH
POP
BECAUSE OF *THIS!*
!!
YOUR RIGHT ARM'S NEXT. LET'S DO THIS RATIONALLY.
IF I GET AS FAR AS ***YOUR LEGS,*** IT'LL BE A HASSLE FOR THE ARRESTING OFFICERS.
FLIK...
WHAT'S GOT UNDER YOUR SKIN, ERASER?

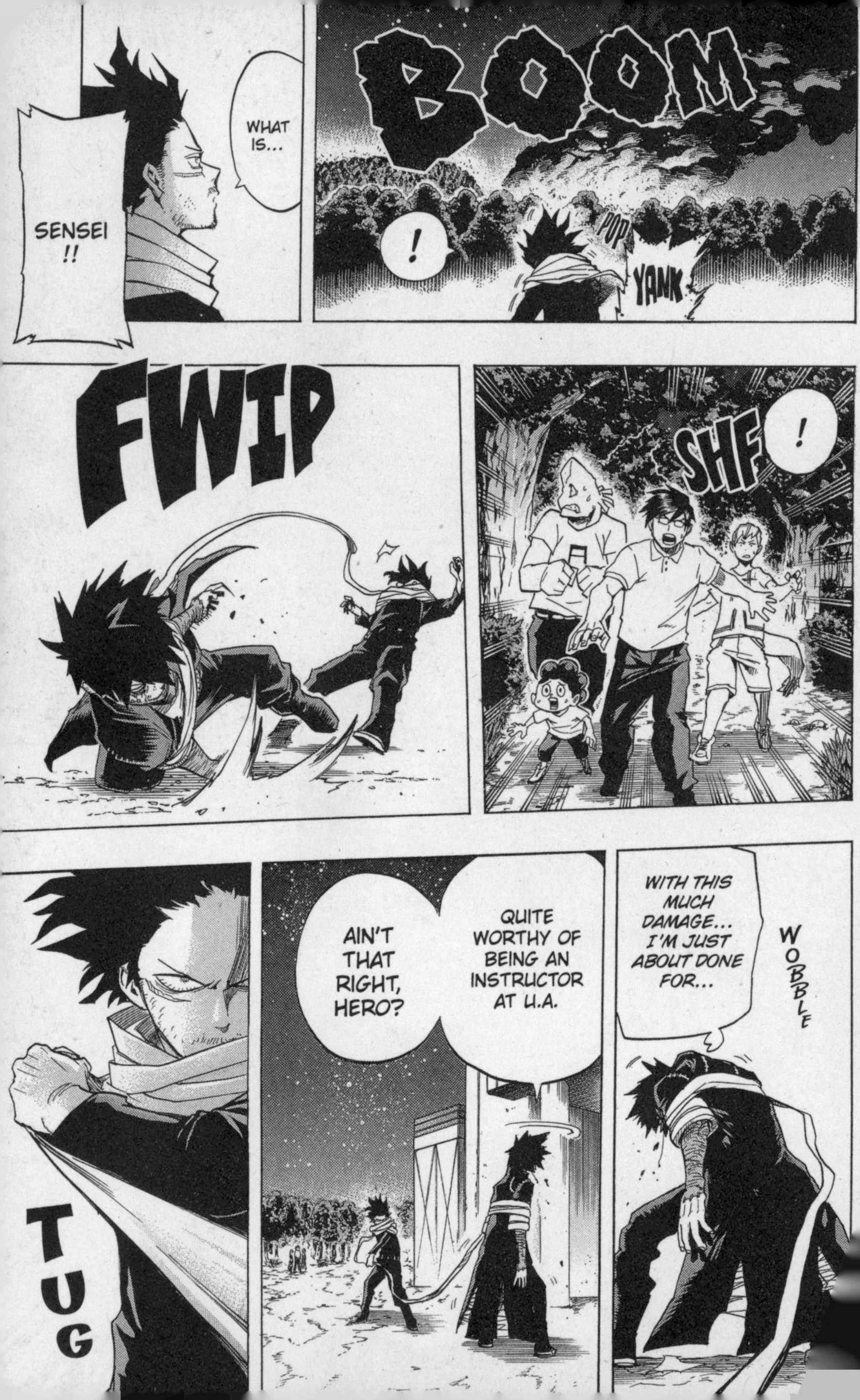
BOOM
!
POP
YANK
WHAT IS...
SENSEI !!
SHF
!
FWIP
WITH THIS MUCH DAMAGE... I'M JUST ABOUT DONE FOR...
WOBBLE
QUITE WORTHY OF BEING AN INSTRUCTOR AT U.A.
AIN'T THAT RIGHT, HERO?
TUG

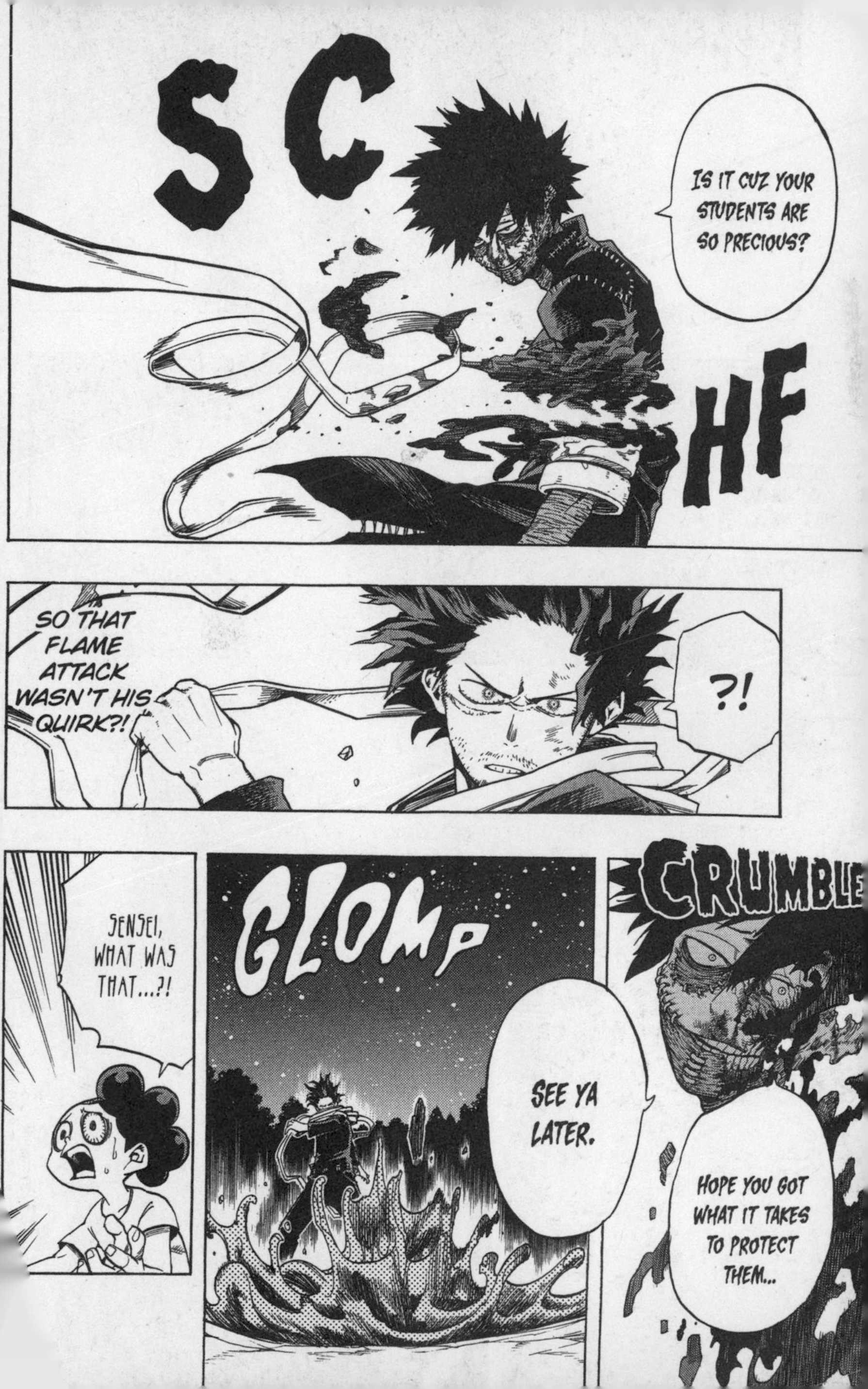
IS IT CUZ YOUR STUDENTS ARE SO PRECIOUS?
SCHF
?!
SO THAT FLAME ATTACK WASN'T HIS QUIRK?!
CRUMBLE
SEE YA LATER.
HOPE YOU GOT WHAT IT TAKES TO PROTECT THEM...
GLOMP
SENSEI, WHAT WAS THAT...?!

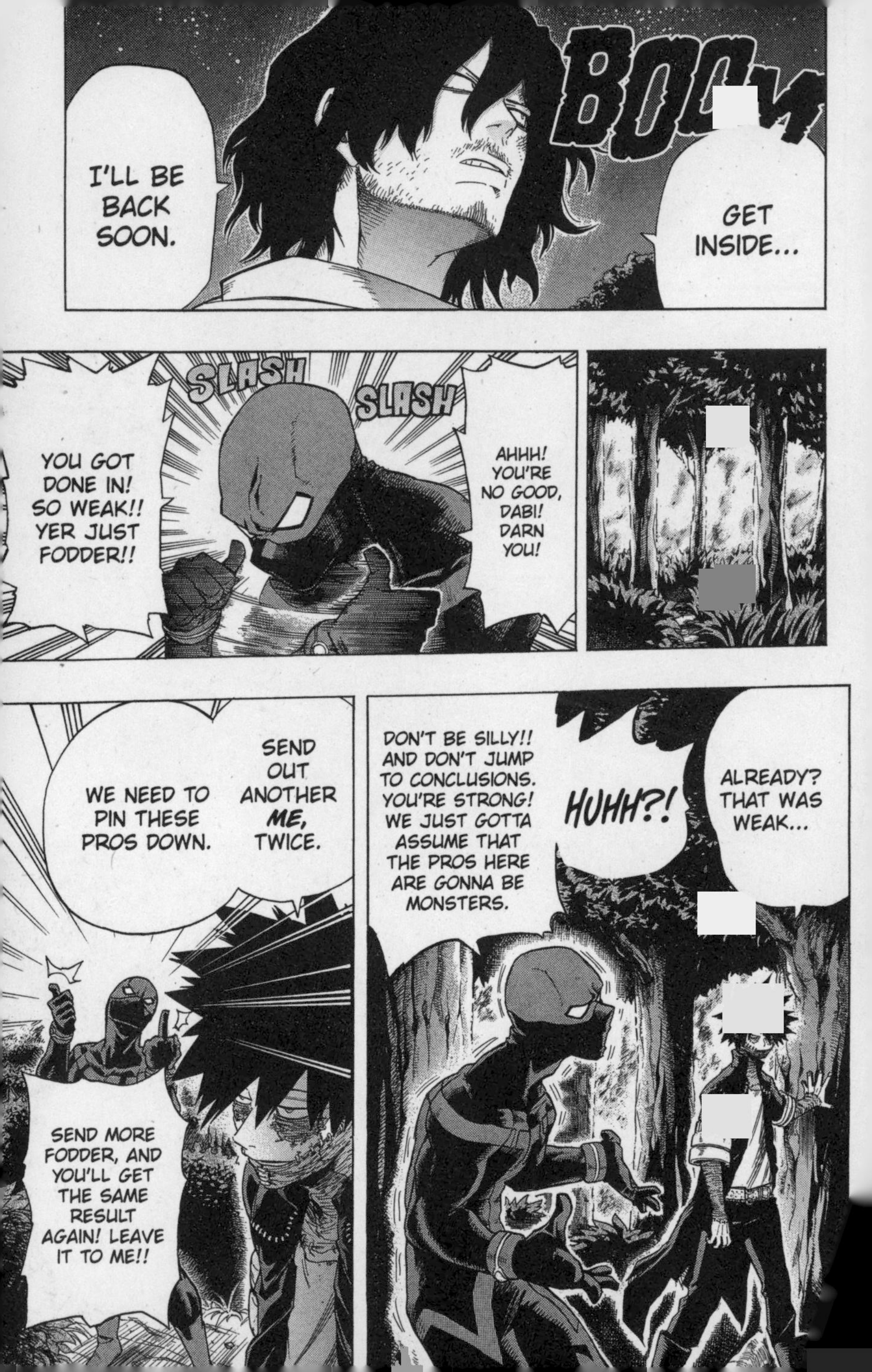
BOOM
GET INSIDE...
I'LL BE BACK SOON.
SLASH
SLASH
AHHH! YOU'RE NO GOOD, DABI! DARN YOU!
YOU GOT DONE IN! SO WEAK!! YER JUST FODDER!!
ALREADY? THAT WAS WEAK...
HUHH?!
DON'T BE SILLY!! AND DON'T JUMP TO CONCLUSIONS. YOU'RE STRONG! WE JUST GOTTA ASSUME THAT THE PROS HERE ARE GONNA BE MONSTERS.
SEND OUT ANOTHER *ME,* TWICE.
WE NEED TO PIN THESE PROS DOWN.
SEND MORE FODDER, AND YOU'LL GET THE SAME RESULT AGAIN! LEAVE IT TO ME!!

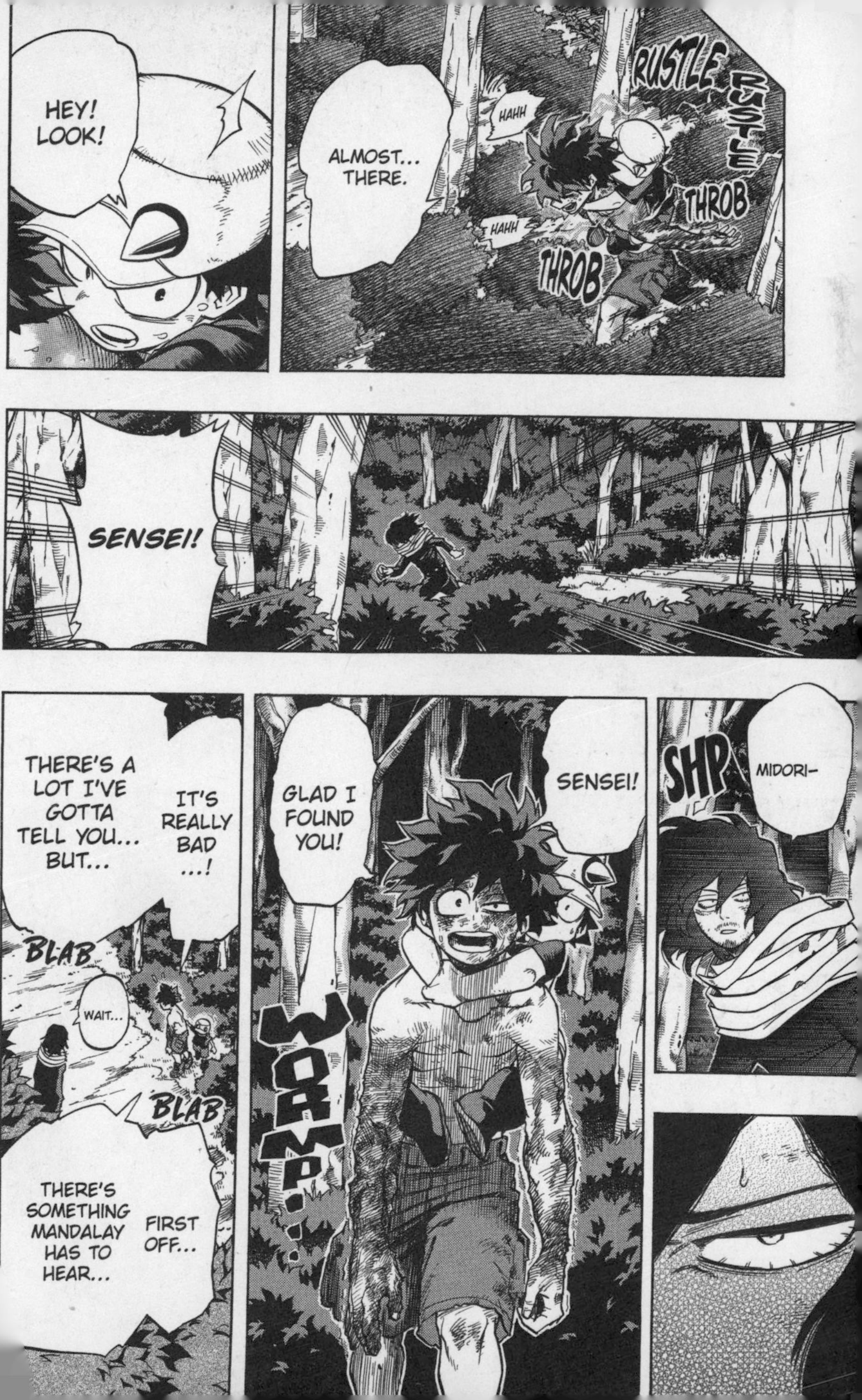
RUSTLE
RUSTLE
HAHH
ALMOST... THERE.
THROB
HAHH
THROB
HEY! LOOK!
SENSEI!
SHP
MIDORI-
SENSEI!
GLAD I FOUND YOU!
WOMP...
IT'S REALLY BAD ...!
THERE'S A LOT I'VE GOTTA TELL YOU... BUT...
BLAB
WAIT...
BLAB
FIRST OFF...
THERE'S SOMETHING MANDALAY HAS TO HEAR...

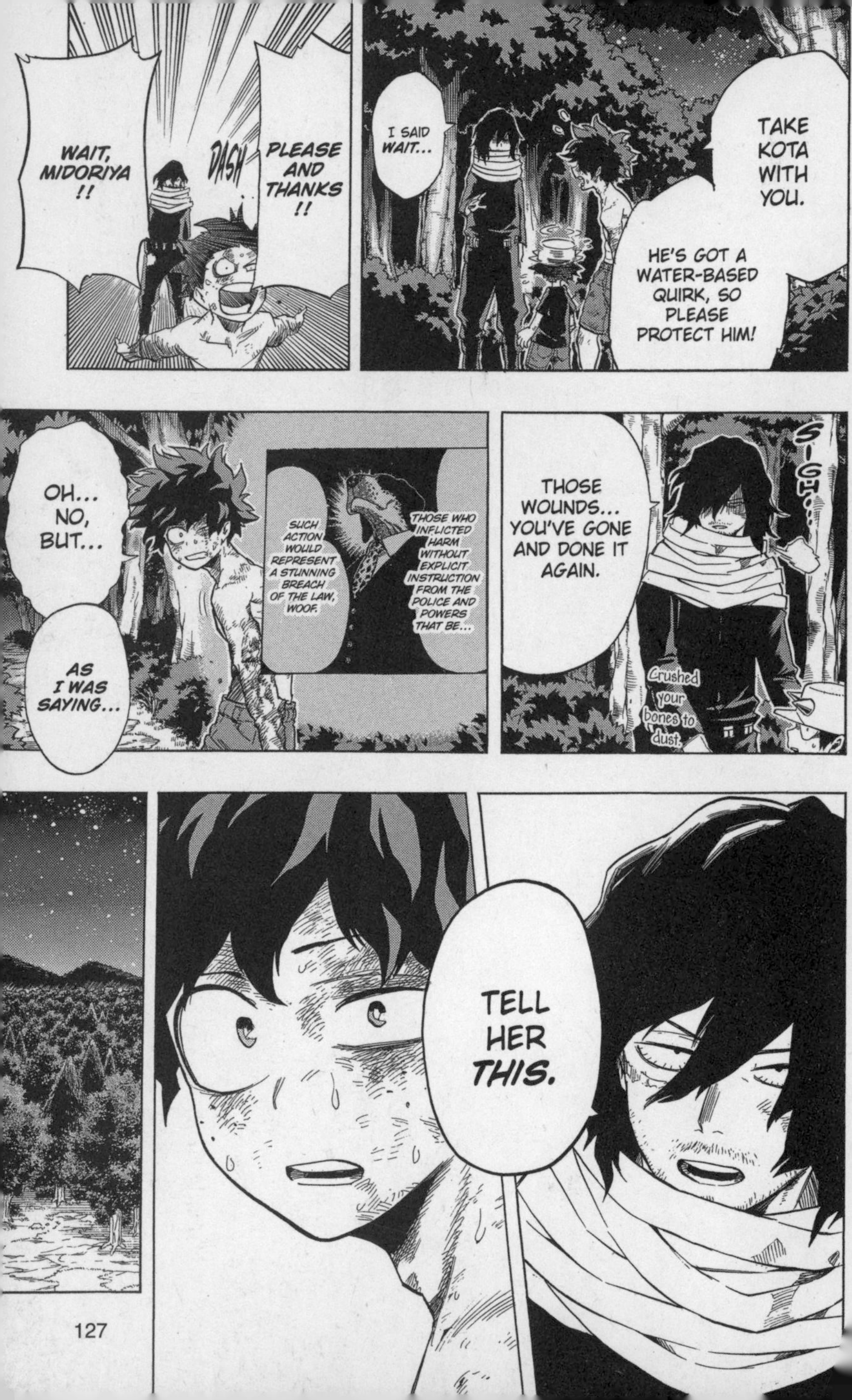
TAKE KOTA WITH YOU.
HE'S GOT A WATER-BASED QUIRK, SO PLEASE PROTECT HIM!
I SAID WAIT...
PLEASE AND THANKS !!
DASH
WAIT, MIDORIYA !!
SIGH...
THOSE WOUNDS... YOU'VE GONE AND DONE IT AGAIN.
Crushed your bones to dust.
THOSE WHO INFLICTED HARM WITHOUT EXPLICIT INSTRUCTION FROM THE POLICE AND POWERS THAT BE...
SUCH ACTION WOULD REPRESENT A STUNNING BREACH OF THE LAW, WOOF.
OH... NO, BUT...
AS I WAS SAYING...
TELL HER THIS.

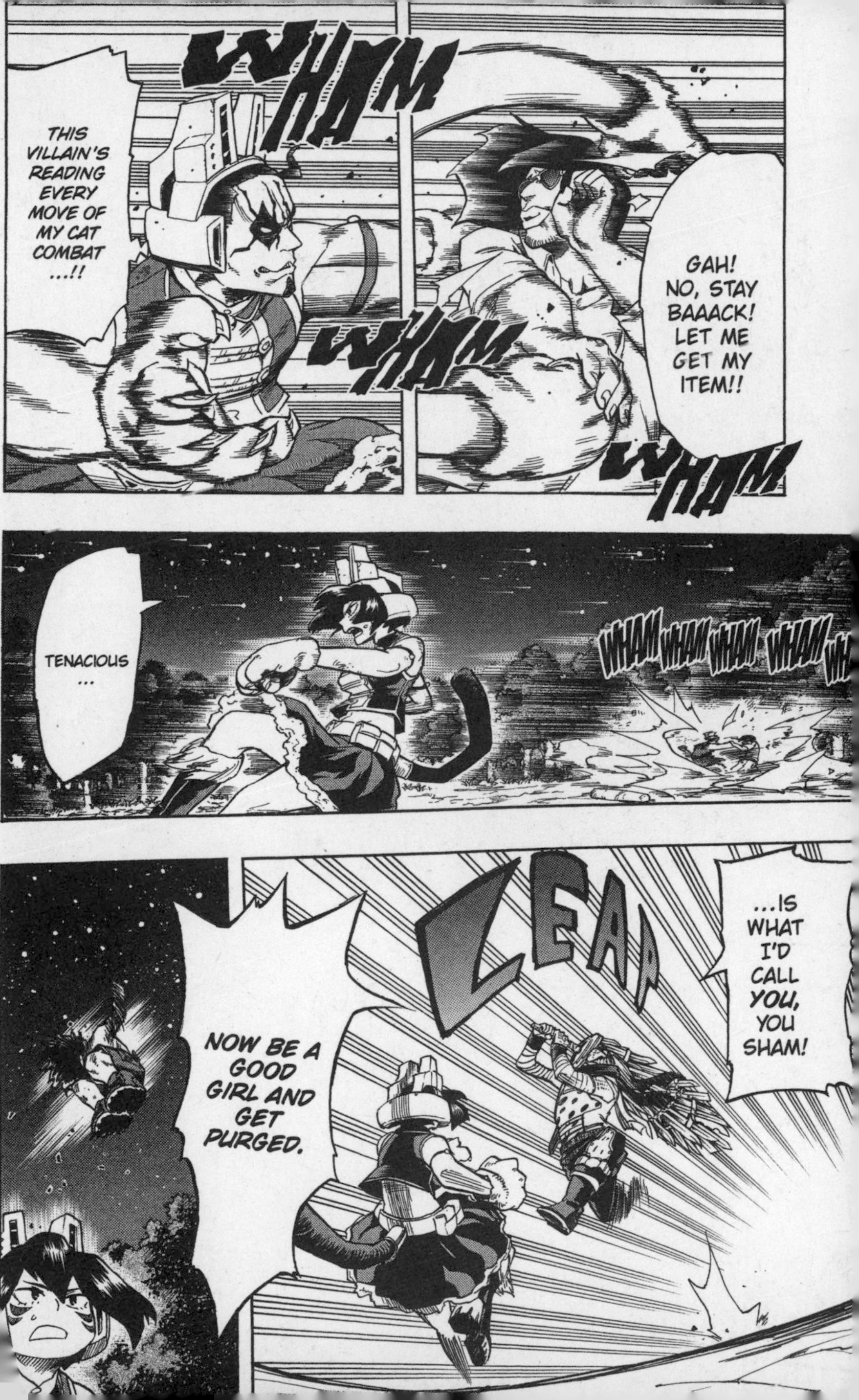
WHAM
GAH! NO, STAY BAAACK! LET ME GET MY ITEM!!
WHAM
THIS VILLAIN'S READING EVERY MOVE OF MY CAT COMBAT ...!!
WHAM
TENACIOUS ...
WHAM WHAM WHAM WHAM
LEAP
...IS WHAT I'D CALL YOU, YOU SHAM!
NOW BE A GOOD GIRL AND GET PURGED.

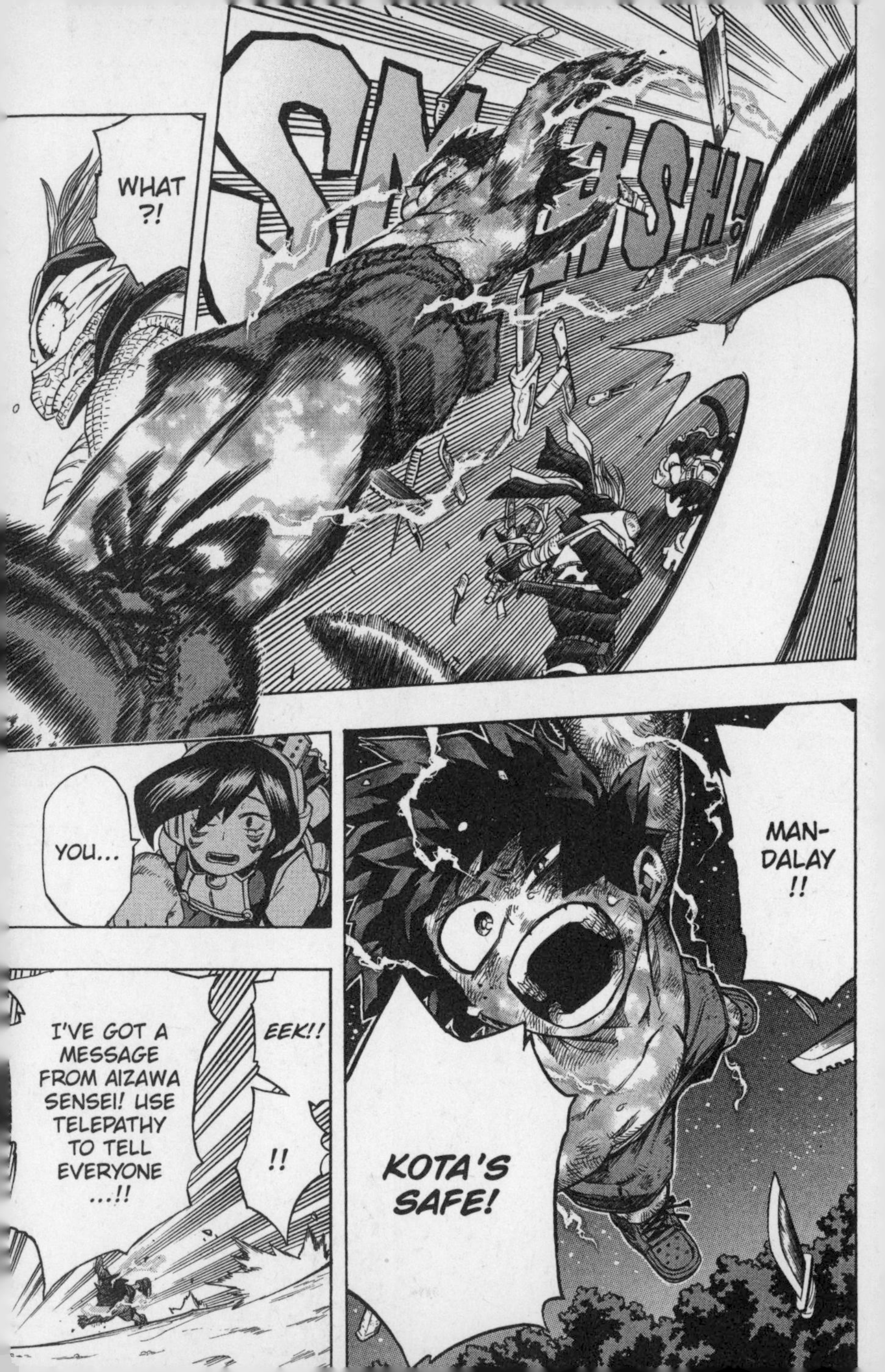
SMASH!!
WHAT ?!
MAN-DALAY !!
KOTA'S SAFE!
YOU...
EEK!!
I'VE GOT A MESSAGE FROM AIZAWA SENSEI! USE TELEPATHY TO TELL EVERYONE ...!!
!!

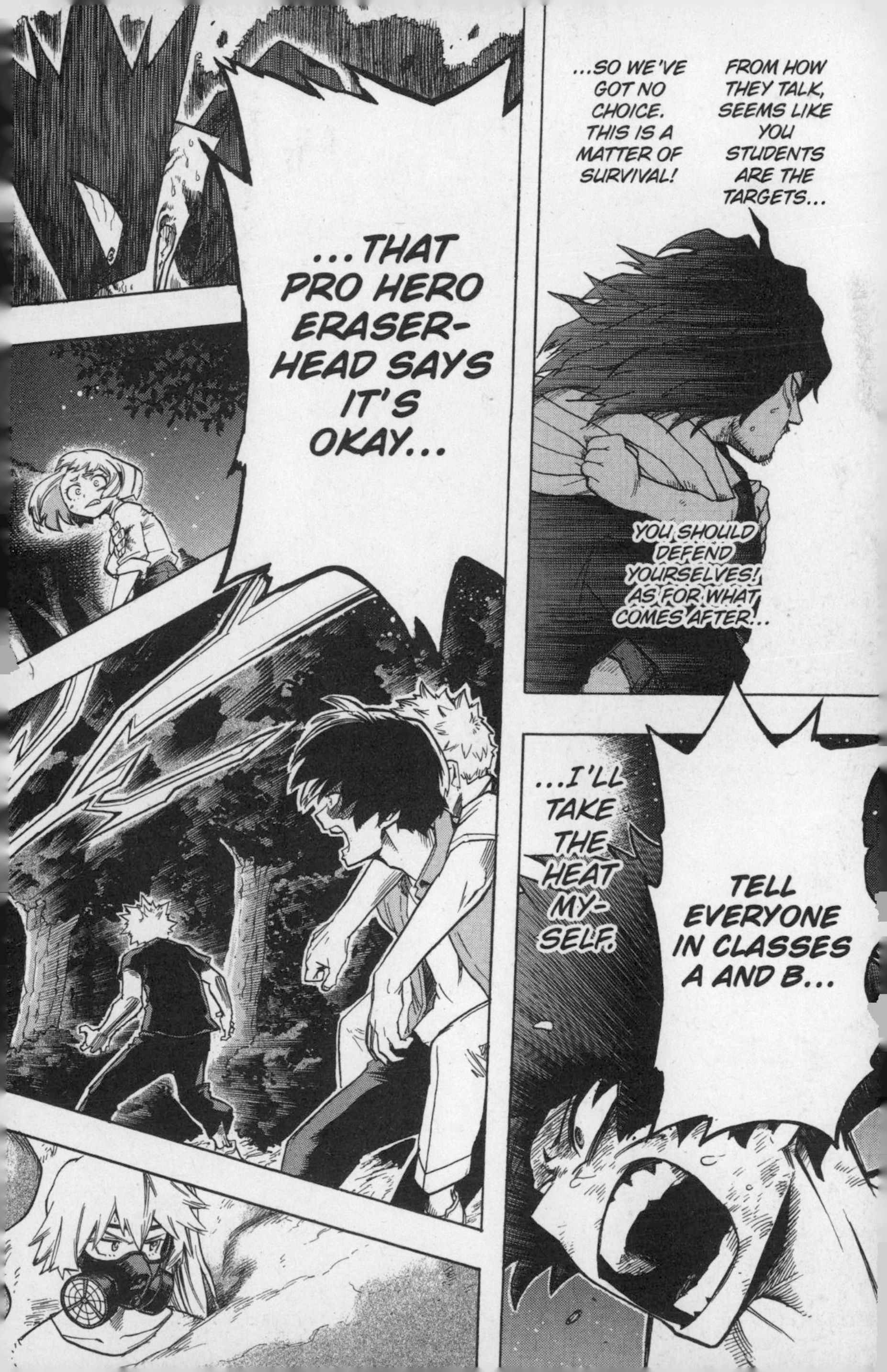
FROM HOW THEY TALK, SEEMS LIKE YOU STUDENTS ARE THE TARGETS...
...SO WE'VE GOT NO CHOICE. THIS IS A MATTER OF SURVIVAL!
YOU SHOULD DEFEND YOURSELVES! AS FOR WHAT COMES AFTER...
TELL EVERYONE IN CLASSES A AND B...
...I'LL TAKE THE HEAT MY-SELF.
...THAT PRO HERO ERASER-HEAD SAYS IT'S OKAY...

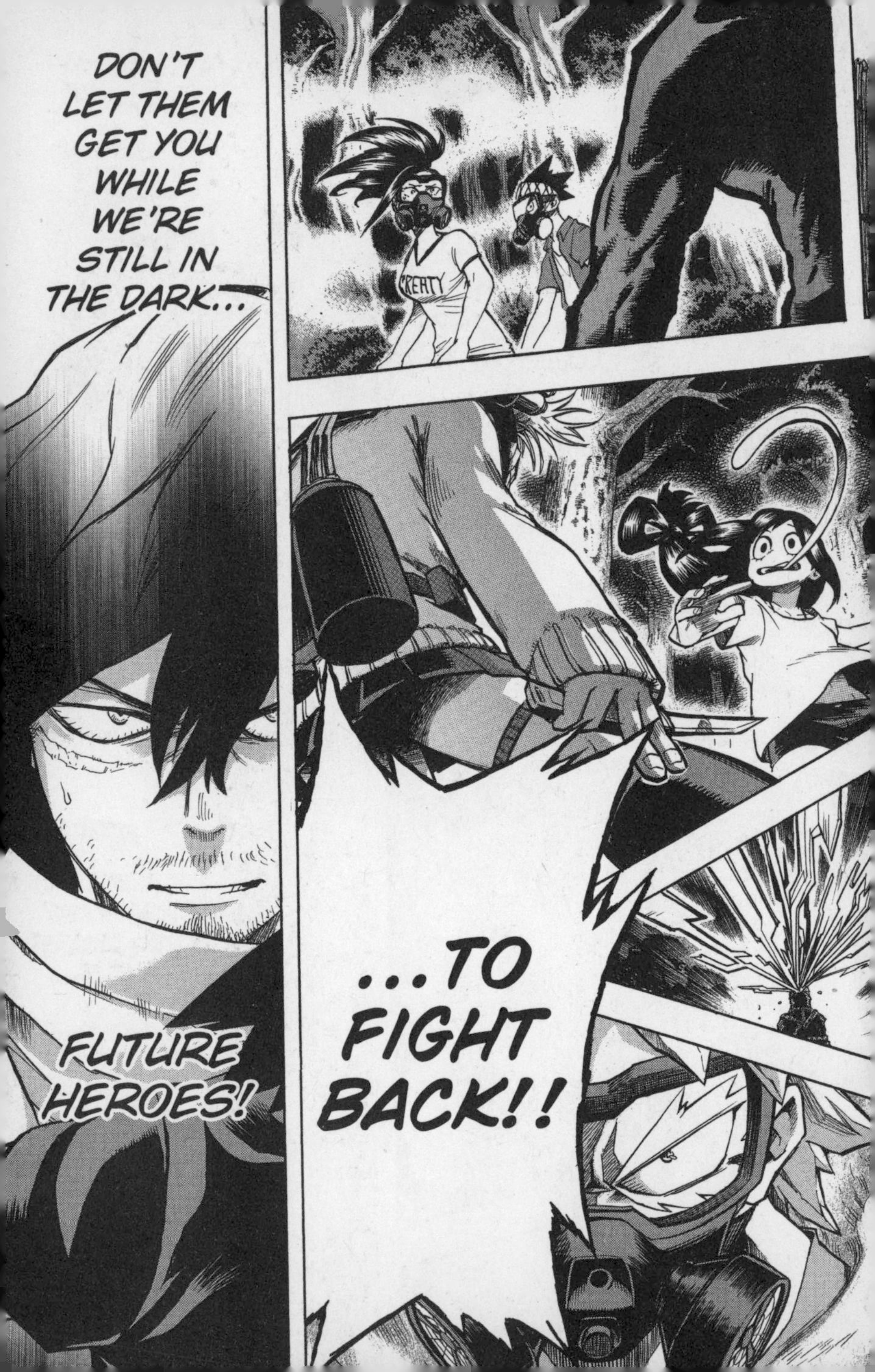
...TO FIGHT BACK!!
DON'T LET THEM GET YOU WHILE WE'RE STILL IN THE DARK...
FUTURE HEROES!
CREATY

ABOUT "IT'S OKAY"

Harming another with one's Quirk is fundamentally against the rules, which is why the use of Quirks in public places is forbidden by law (self-defense is an exception—if someone is attacked first, they're allowed to defend themselves). It's different than ordinary self-defense though, which might involve punching someone or pinning them down. This is because Quirks vary so much in nature and because some Quirks are capable of killing in an instant. Attempting to account for every given Quirk in the law books is essentially impossible due to the varying degrees of harm that different Quirks can cause. This is what led to the current heavy-handed law, which states, "No one may use his/her Quirk to harm another!"

However, the law that forbids Quirk use in public spaces is viewed much like the old rule that states, "Bicycles are not to be ridden on sidewalks." That is to say, if Izuku's mother dropped her cell phone on the ground outside, she might use her telekinetic Quirk to draw it back to her. Strictly speaking, this would constitute a violation of the rules, but few people would actually give her any guff about it.

Naturally, a stricter approach would be taken with Quirks that could actually harm bystanders (Bakugo would probably get in trouble for using his explosions to boost himself down the street).

As for the battle fought at USJ, anti-personnel Quirk use is permitted on school grounds, which are meant to be spaces for education and training. As such, there was no issue in that case. Still, it would've been a different story if any of the students had killed or nearly killed anyone.

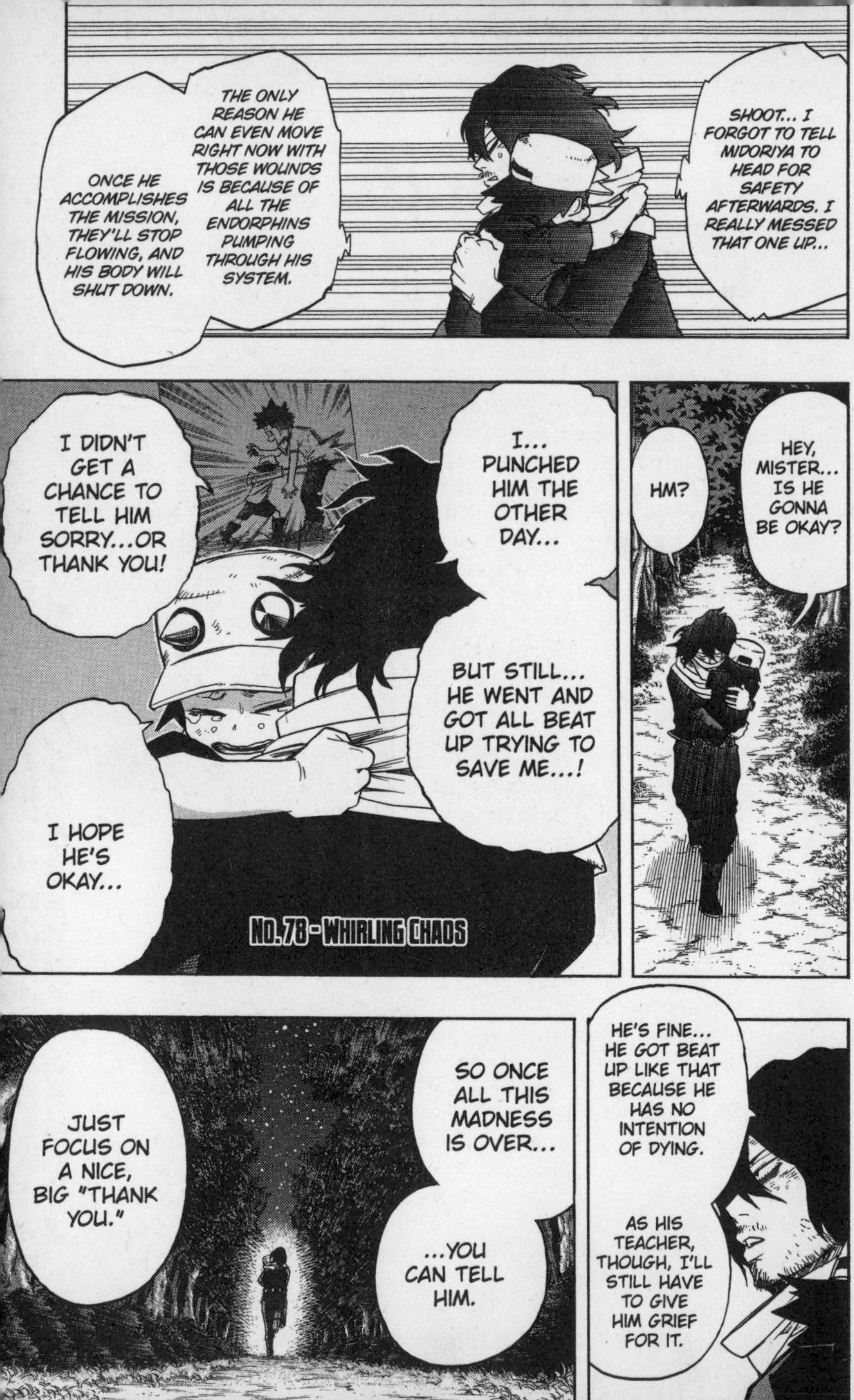
SHOOT... I FORGOT TO TELL MIDORIYA TO HEAD FOR SAFETY AFTERWARDS. I REALLY MESSED THAT ONE UP...
THE ONLY REASON HE CAN EVEN MOVE RIGHT NOW WITH THOSE WOUNDS IS BECAUSE OF ALL THE ENDORPHINS PUMPING THROUGH HIS SYSTEM.
ONCE HE ACCOMPLISHES THE MISSION, THEY'LL STOP FLOWING, AND HIS BODY WILL SHUT DOWN.
HEY, MISTER... IS HE GONNA BE OKAY?
HM?
I... PUNCHED HIM THE OTHER DAY...
I DIDN'T GET A CHANCE TO TELL HIM SORRY...OR THANK YOU!
BUT STILL... HE WENT AND GOT ALL BEAT UP TRYING TO SAVE ME...!
I HOPE HE'S OKAY...
NO. 78 - WHIRLING CHAOS
HE'S FINE... HE GOT BEAT UP LIKE THAT BECAUSE HE HAS NO INTENTION OF DYING.
AS HIS TEACHER, THOUGH, I'LL STILL HAVE TO GIVE HIM GRIEF FOR IT.
SO ONCE ALL THIS MADNESS IS OVER...
JUST FOCUS ON A NICE, BIG "THANK YOU."
...YOU CAN TELL HIM.

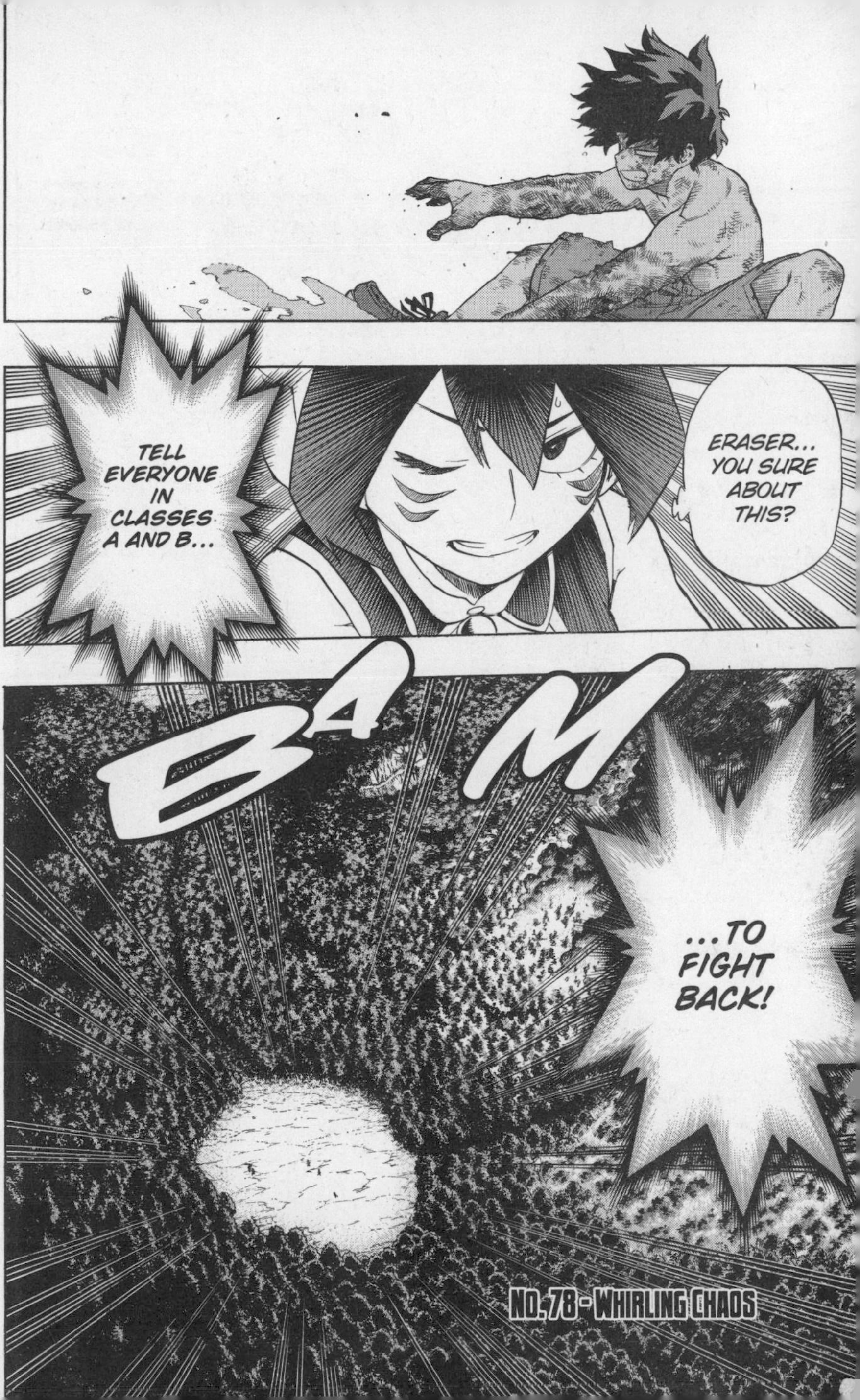
ERASER... YOU SURE ABOUT THIS?
TELL EVERYONE IN CLASSES A AND B...
BAM
...TO FIGHT BACK!

No. 78 - Whirling Chaos

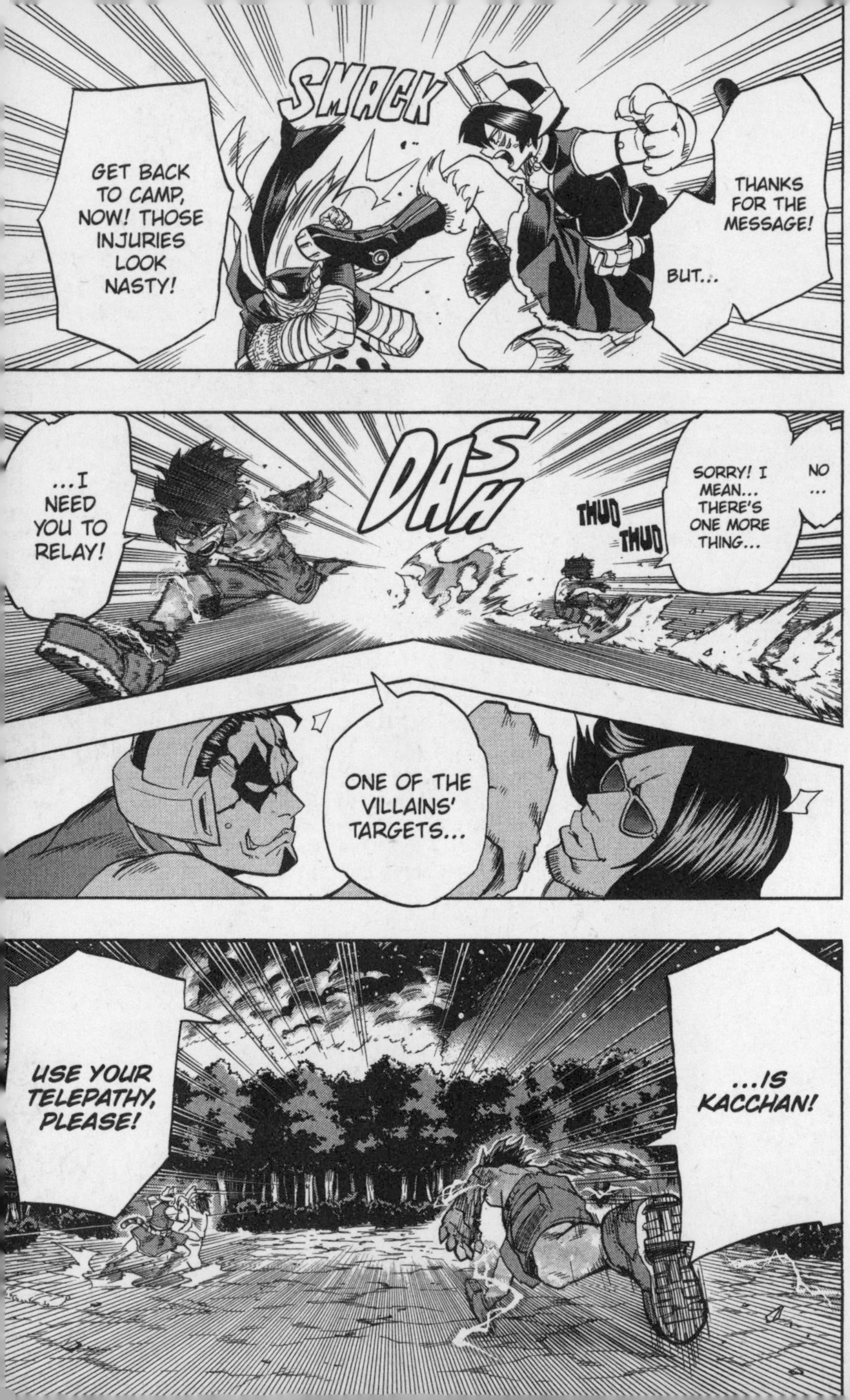
THANKS FOR THE MESSAGE!
BUT...
SMACK
GET BACK TO CAMP, NOW! THOSE INJURIES LOOK NASTY!
NO...
SORRY! I MEAN... THERE'S ONE MORE THING...
THUD
THUD
DASH
...I NEED YOU TO RELAY!
ONE OF THE VILLAINS' TARGETS...
...IS KACCHAN!
USE YOUR TELEPATHY, PLEASE!

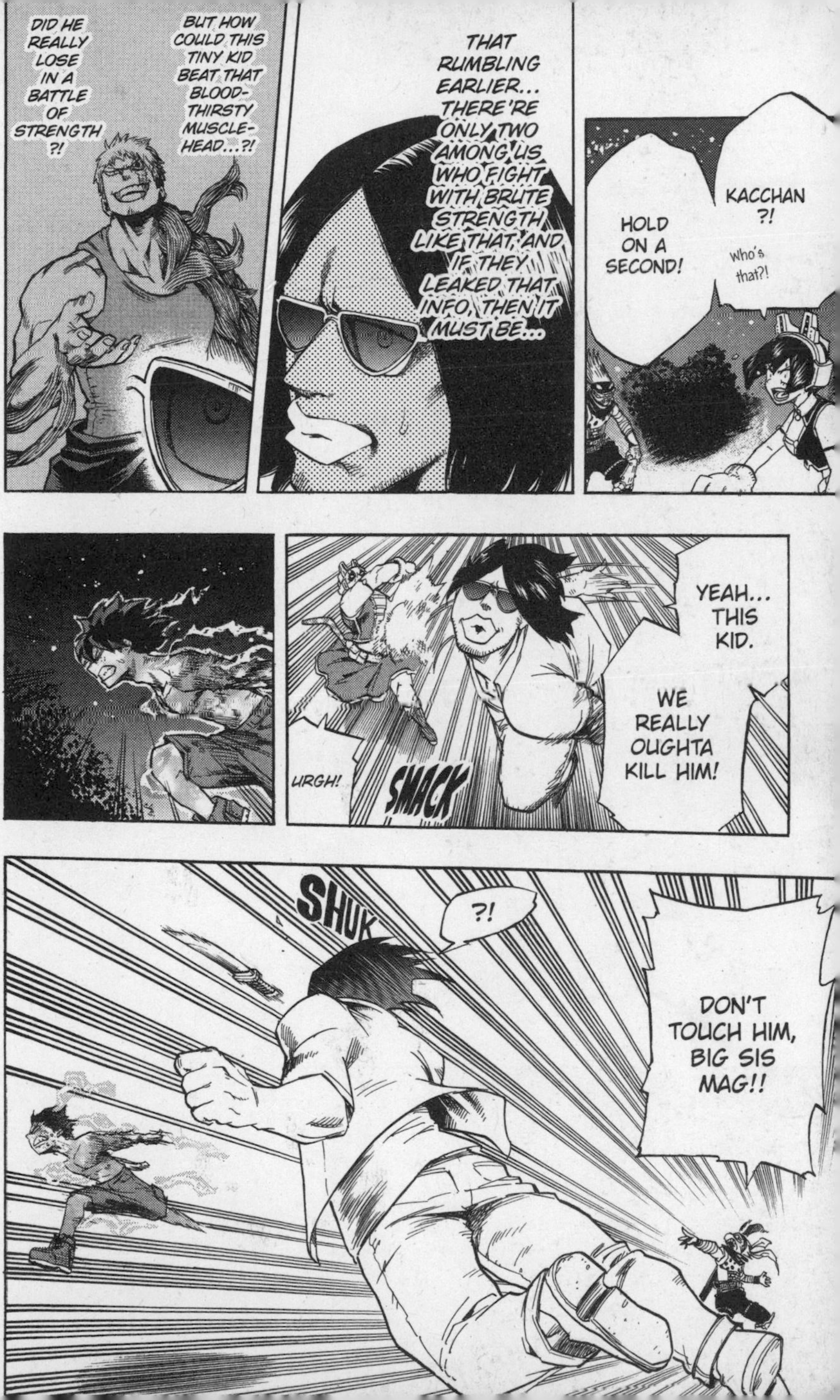
KACCHAN ?!
Who's that?!
HOLD ON A SECOND!
THAT RUMBLING EARLIER... THERE'RE ONLY TWO AMONG US WHO FIGHT WITH BRUTE STRENGTH LIKE THAT, AND IF THEY LEAKED THAT INFO, THEN IT MUST BE...
BUT HOW COULD THIS TINY KID BEAT THAT BLOOD-THIRSTY MUSCLE-HEAD...?!
DID HE REALLY LOSE IN A BATTLE OF STRENGTH ?!
YEAH... THIS KID.
WE REALLY OUGHTA KILL HIM!
SMACK
URGH!
DON'T TOUCH HIM, BIG SIS MAG!!
?!
SHUK

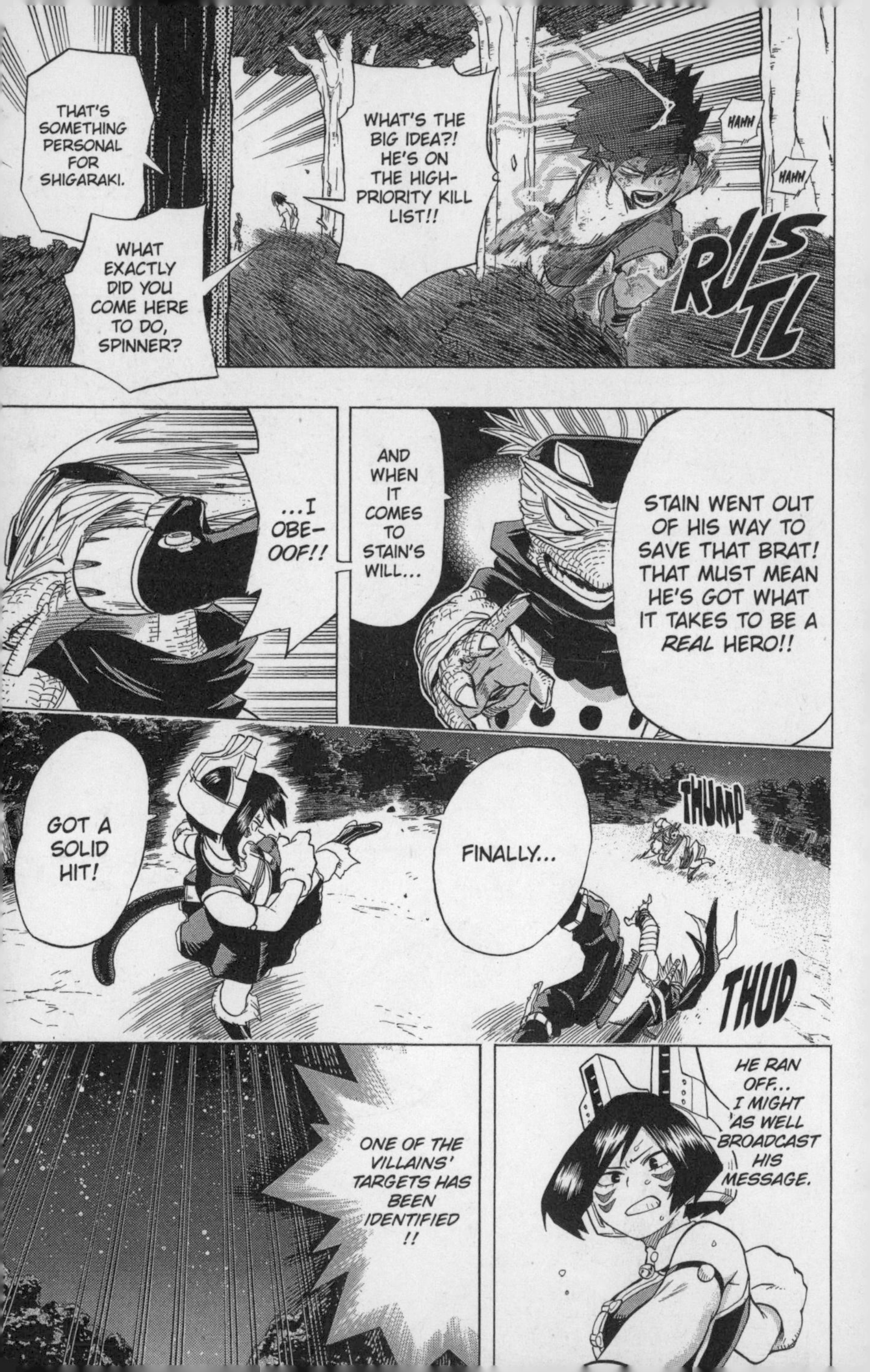
HAHH
HAHH
WHAT'S THE BIG IDEA?! HE'S ON THE HIGH-PRIORITY KILL LIST!!
THAT'S SOMETHING PERSONAL FOR SHIGARAKI.
WHAT EXACTLY DID YOU COME HERE TO DO, SPINNER?
RUSTL
STAIN WENT OUT OF HIS WAY TO SAVE THAT BRAT! THAT MUST MEAN HE'S GOT WHAT IT TAKES TO BE A *REAL* HERO!!
AND WHEN IT COMES TO STAIN'S WILL...
...I OBE-*OOF!!*
THUMP
FINALLY...
THUD
GOT A SOLID HIT!
HE RAN OFF... I MIGHT AS WELL BROADCAST HIS MESSAGE.
ONE OF THE VILLAINS' TARGETS HAS BEEN IDENTIFIED!!

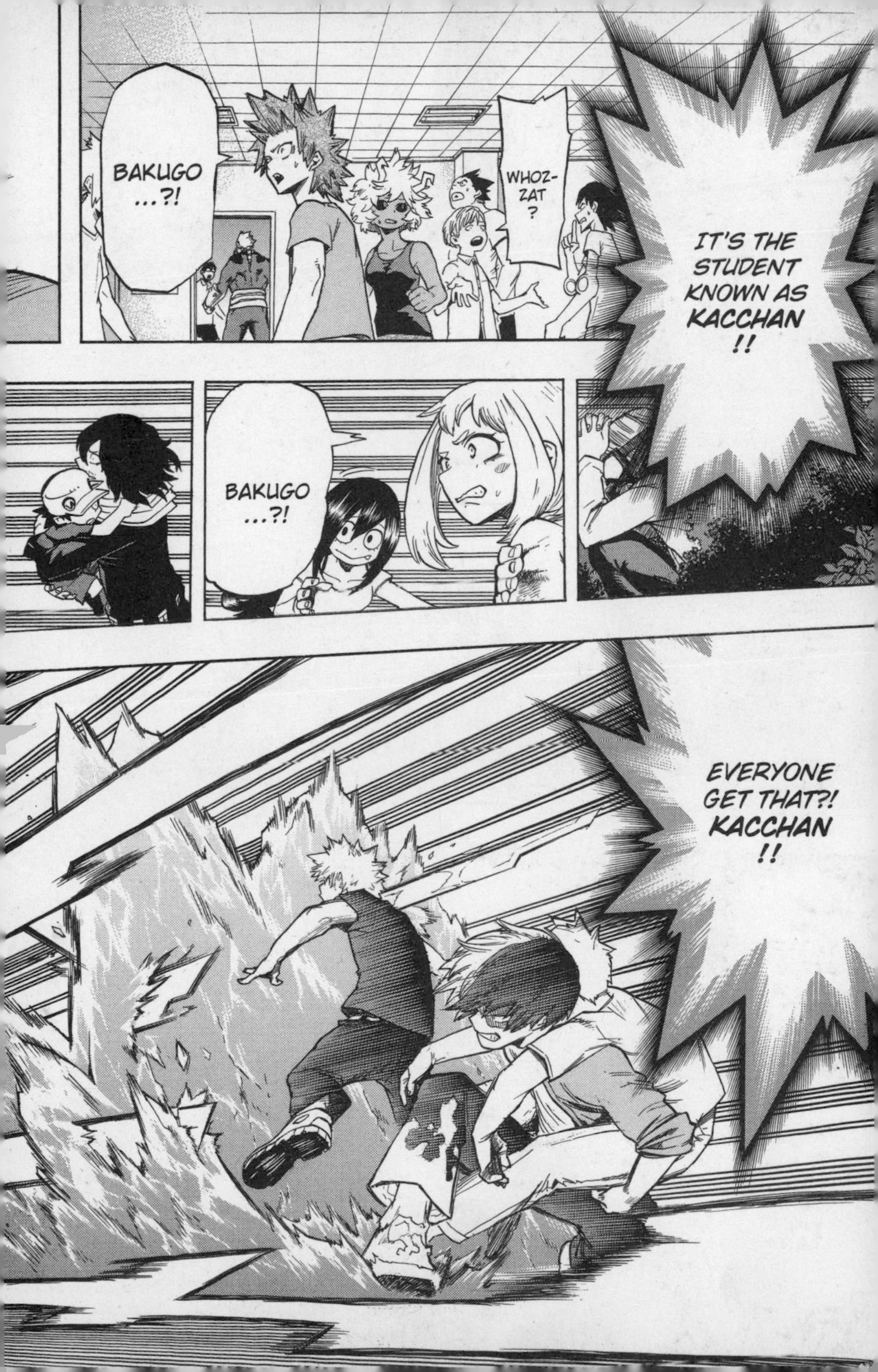
IT'S THE STUDENT KNOWN AS KACCHAN!!
WHOZ-ZAT?
BAKUGO...?!
BAKUGO...?!
EVERYONE GET THAT?! KACCHAN!!

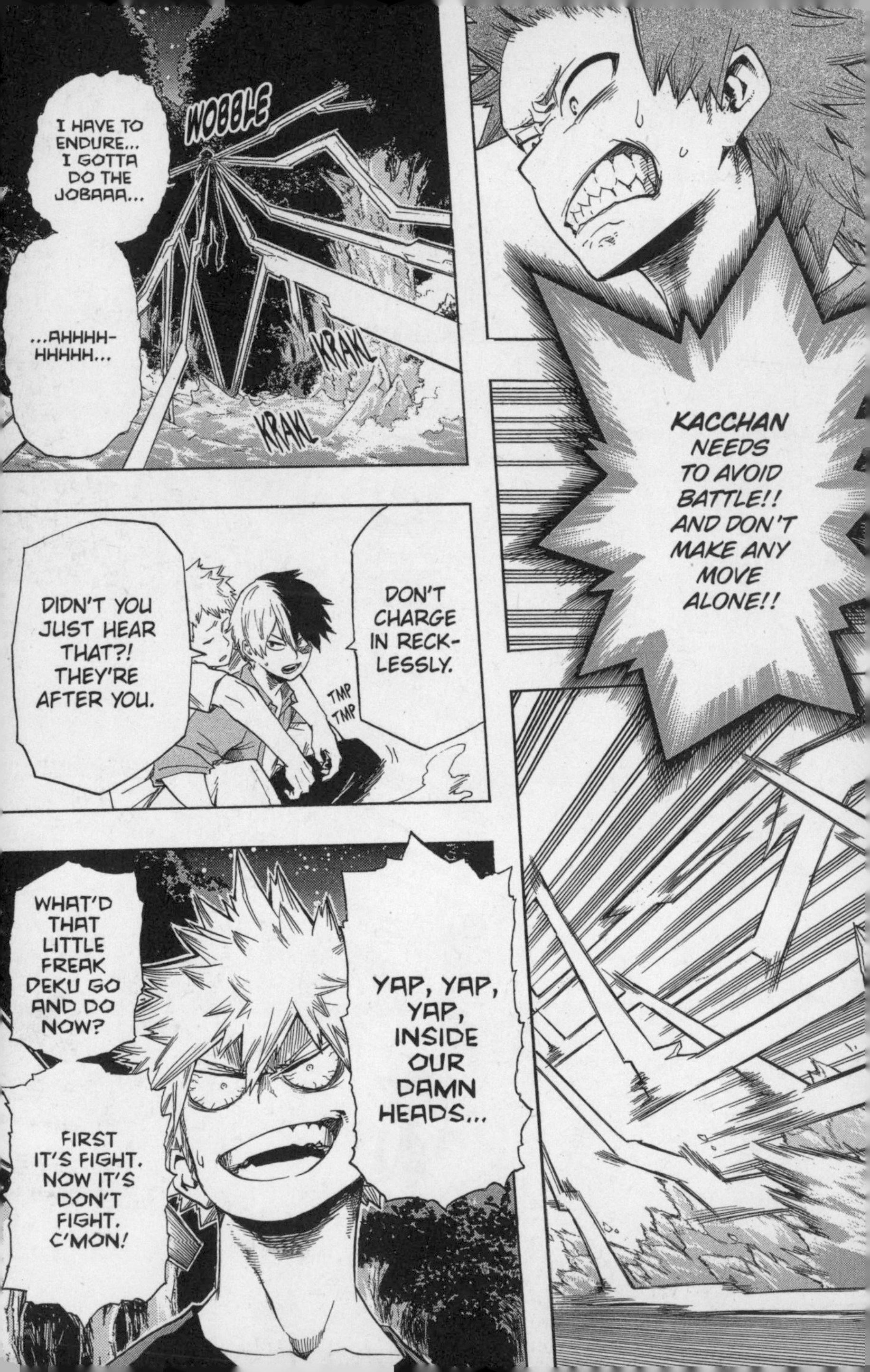
KACCHAN NEEDS TO AVOID BATTLE!! AND DON'T MAKE ANY MOVE ALONE!!
WOBBLE
I HAVE TO ENDURE... I GOTTA DO THE JOBAAA...
KRAKL
KRAKL
...AHHHH-HHHHH...
DON'T CHARGE IN RECK-LESSLY.
TMP TMP
DIDN'T YOU JUST HEAR THAT?! THEY'RE AFTER YOU.
WHAT'D THAT LITTLE FREAK DEKU GO AND DO NOW?
YAP, YAP, YAP, INSIDE OUR DAMN HEADS...
FIRST IT'S FIGHT. NOW IT'S DON'T FIGHT. C'MON!

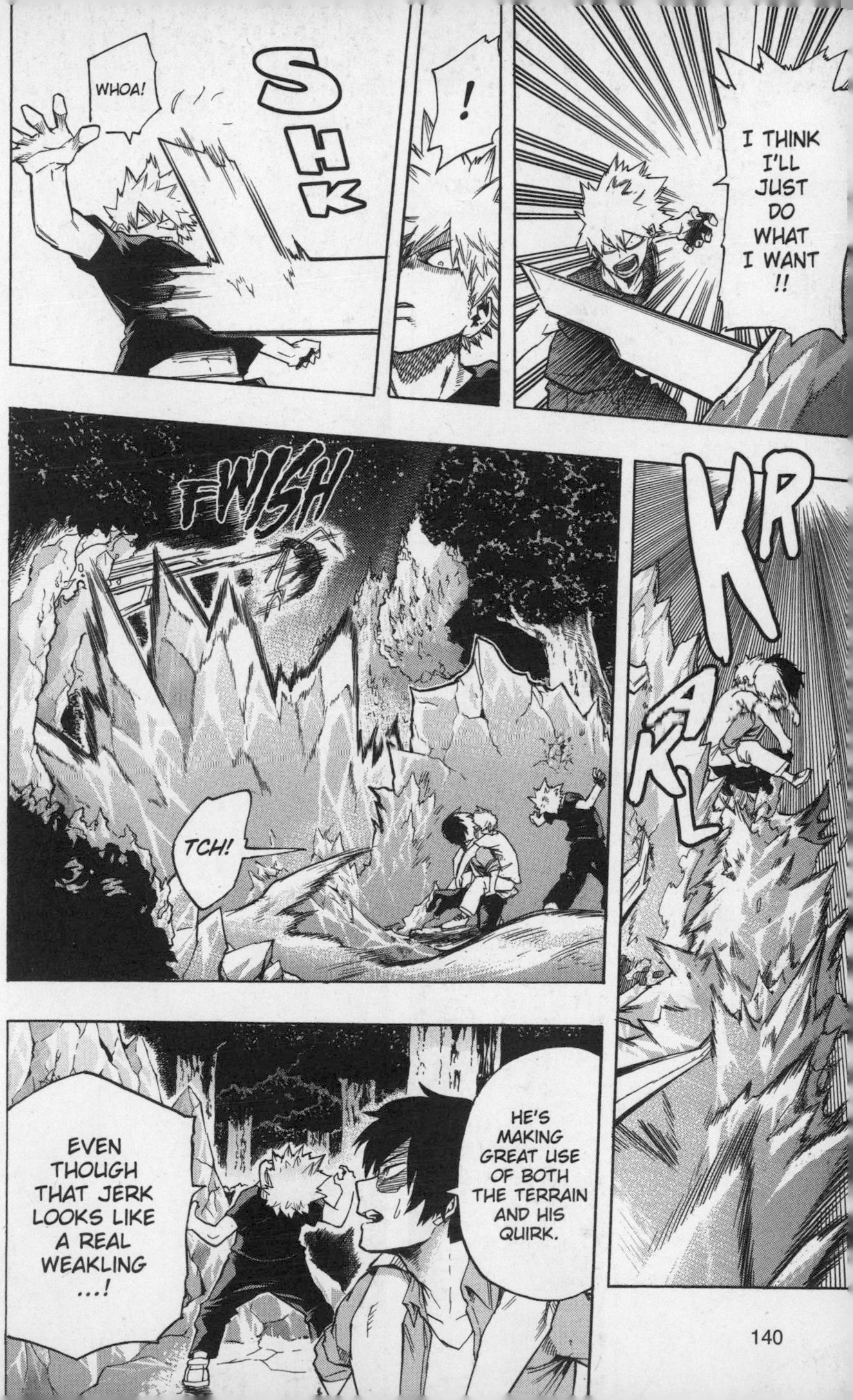
I THINK I'LL JUST DO WHAT I WANT!!
!
SHK
WHOA!
KRAKL
FWISH
TCH!
HE'S MAKING GREAT USE OF BOTH THE TERRAIN AND HIS QUIRK.
EVEN THOUGH THAT JERK LOOKS LIKE A REAL WEAKLING...!

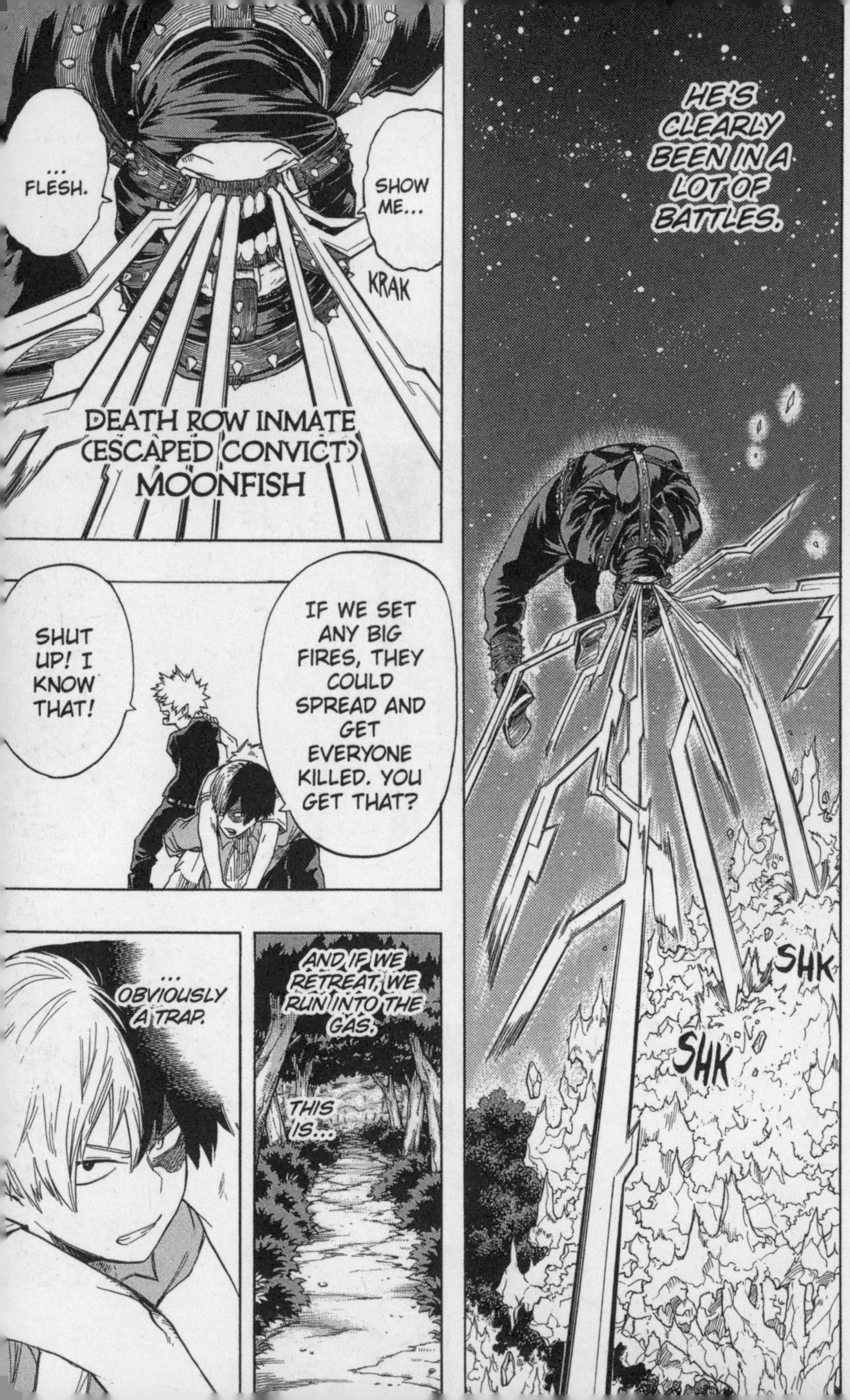
HE'S CLEARLY BEEN IN A LOT OF BATTLES.
SHK
SHK
SHOW ME...
... FLESH.
KRAK
DEATH ROW INMATE (ESCAPED CONVICT) MOONFISH
IF WE SET ANY BIG FIRES, THEY COULD SPREAD AND GET EVERYONE KILLED. YOU GET THAT?
SHUT UP! I KNOW THAT!
AND IF WE RETREAT, WE RUN INTO THE GAS.
THIS IS...
... OBVIOUSLY A TRAP.

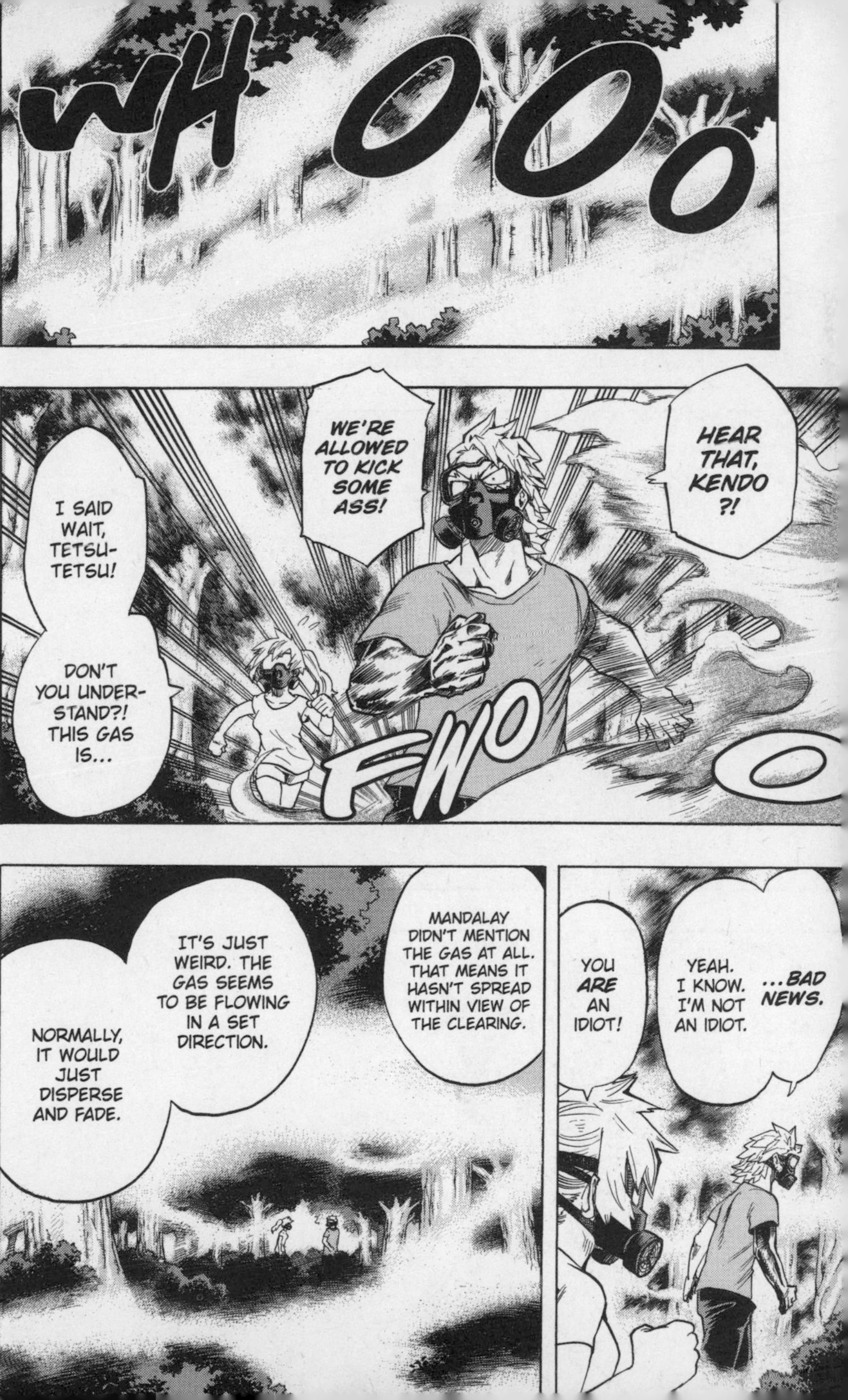
WHOOOO
HEAR THAT, KENDO?!
WE'RE ALLOWED TO KICK SOME ASS!
I SAID WAIT, TETSU-TETSU!
DON'T YOU UNDER-STAND?! THIS GAS IS...
FWOO
...BAD NEWS.
YEAH. I KNOW. I'M NOT AN IDIOT.
YOU ARE AN IDIOT!
MANDALAY DIDN'T MENTION THE GAS AT ALL. THAT MEANS IT HASN'T SPREAD WITHIN VIEW OF THE CLEARING.
IT'S JUST WEIRD. THE GAS SEEMS TO BE FLOWING IN A SET DIRECTION.
NORMALLY, IT WOULD JUST DISPERSE AND FADE.

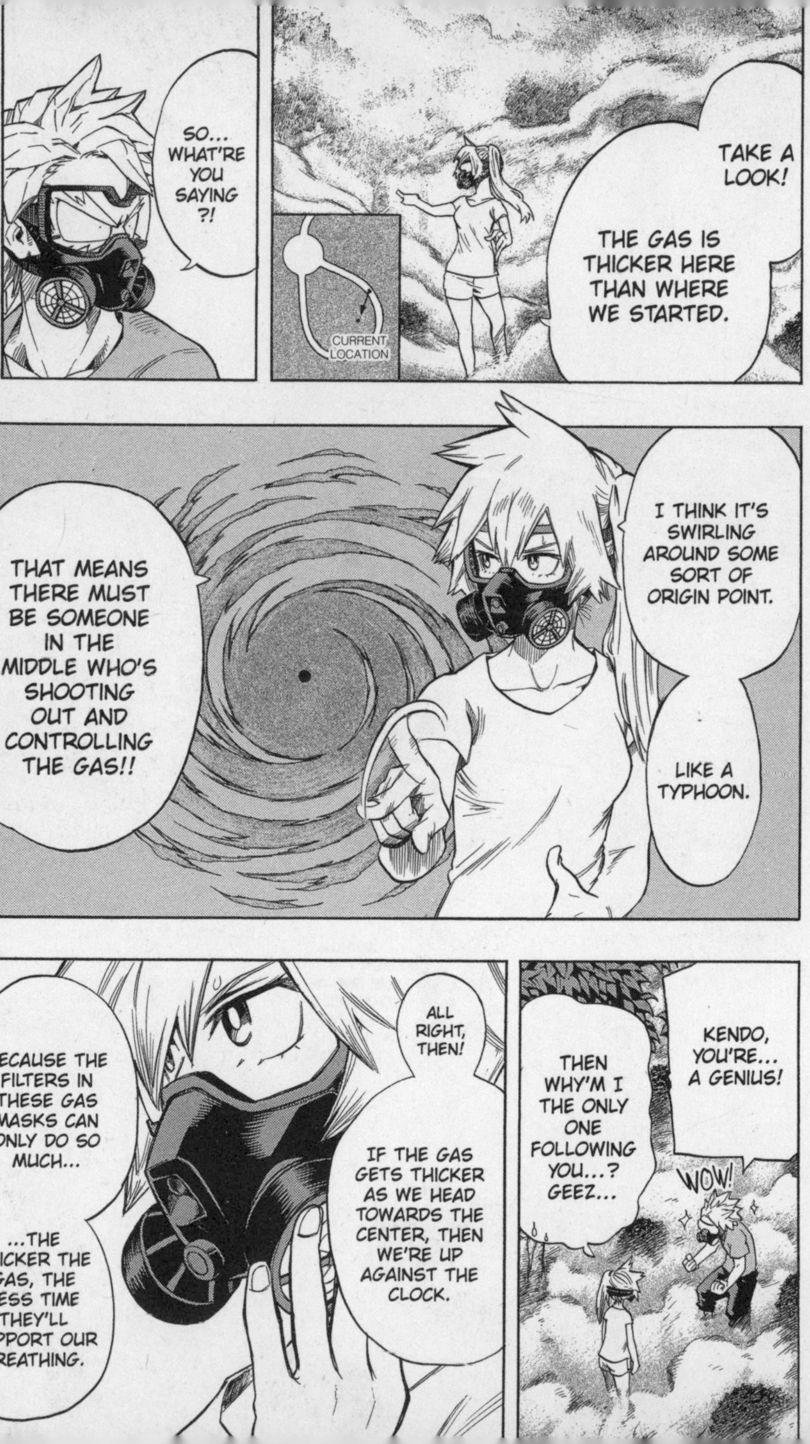
TAKE A LOOK!
THE GAS IS THICKER HERE THAN WHERE WE STARTED.
CURRENT LOCATION
SO... WHAT'RE YOU SAYING ?!
I THINK IT'S SWIRLING AROUND SOME SORT OF ORIGIN POINT.
LIKE A TYPHOON.
THAT MEANS THERE MUST BE SOMEONE IN THE MIDDLE WHO'S SHOOTING OUT AND CONTROLLING THE GAS!!
KENDO, YOU'RE... A GENIUS!
WOW!
THEN WHY'M I THE ONLY ONE FOLLOWING YOU...? GEEZ...
ALL RIGHT, THEN!
IF THE GAS GETS THICKER AS WE HEAD TOWARDS THE CENTER, THEN WE'RE UP AGAINST THE CLOCK.
BECAUSE THE FILTERS IN THESE GAS MASKS CAN ONLY DO SO MUCH...
...THE THICKER THE GAS, THE LESS TIME THEY'LL SUPPORT OUR BREATHING.

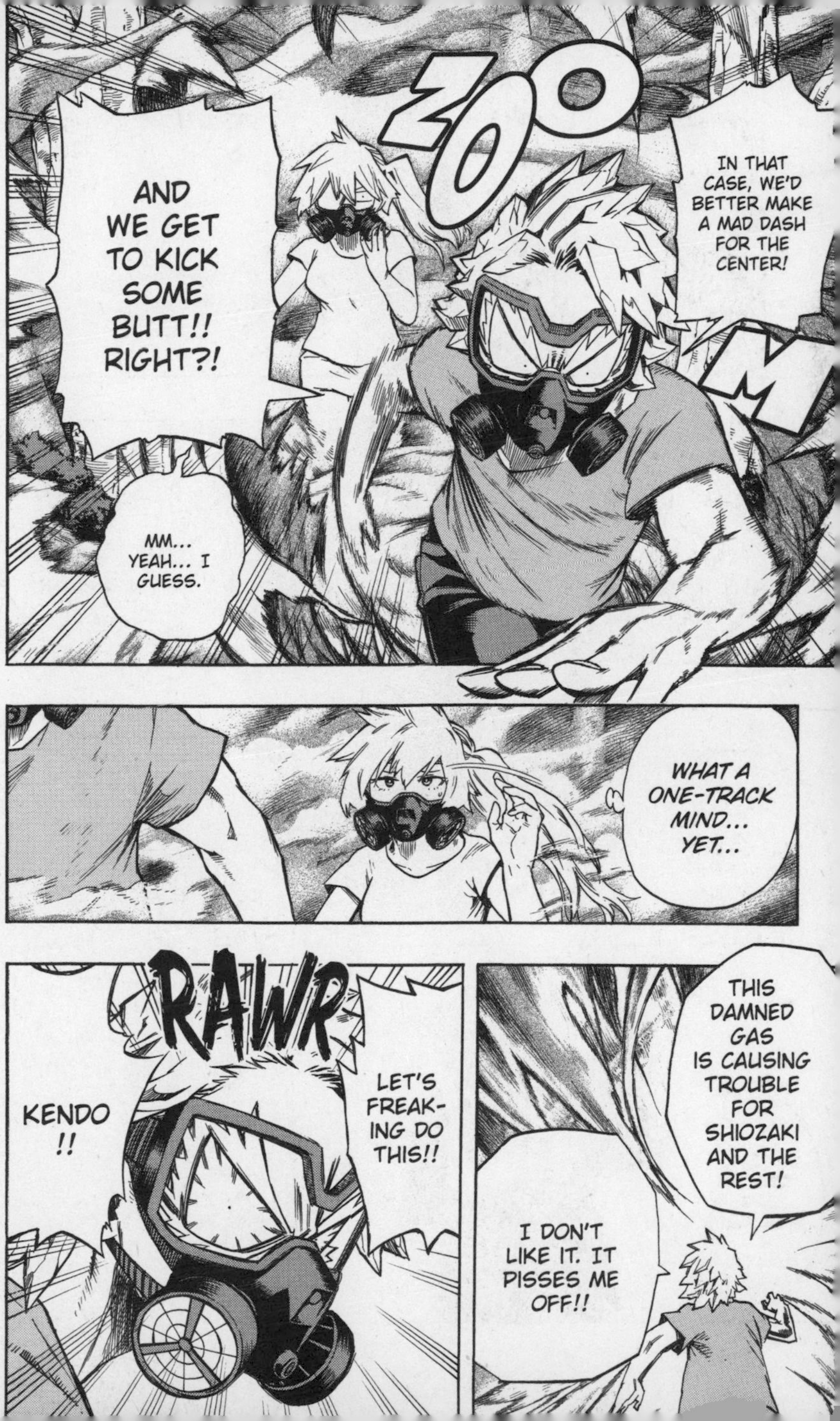
ZOOM
IN THAT CASE, WE'D BETTER MAKE A MAD DASH FOR THE CENTER!
AND WE GET TO KICK SOME BUTT!! RIGHT?!
MM... YEAH... I GUESS.
WHAT A ONE-TRACK MIND... YET...
THIS DAMNED GAS IS CAUSING TROUBLE FOR SHIOZAKI AND THE REST!
I DON'T LIKE IT. IT PISSES ME OFF!!
RAWR
LET'S FREAKING DO THIS!!
KENDO!!

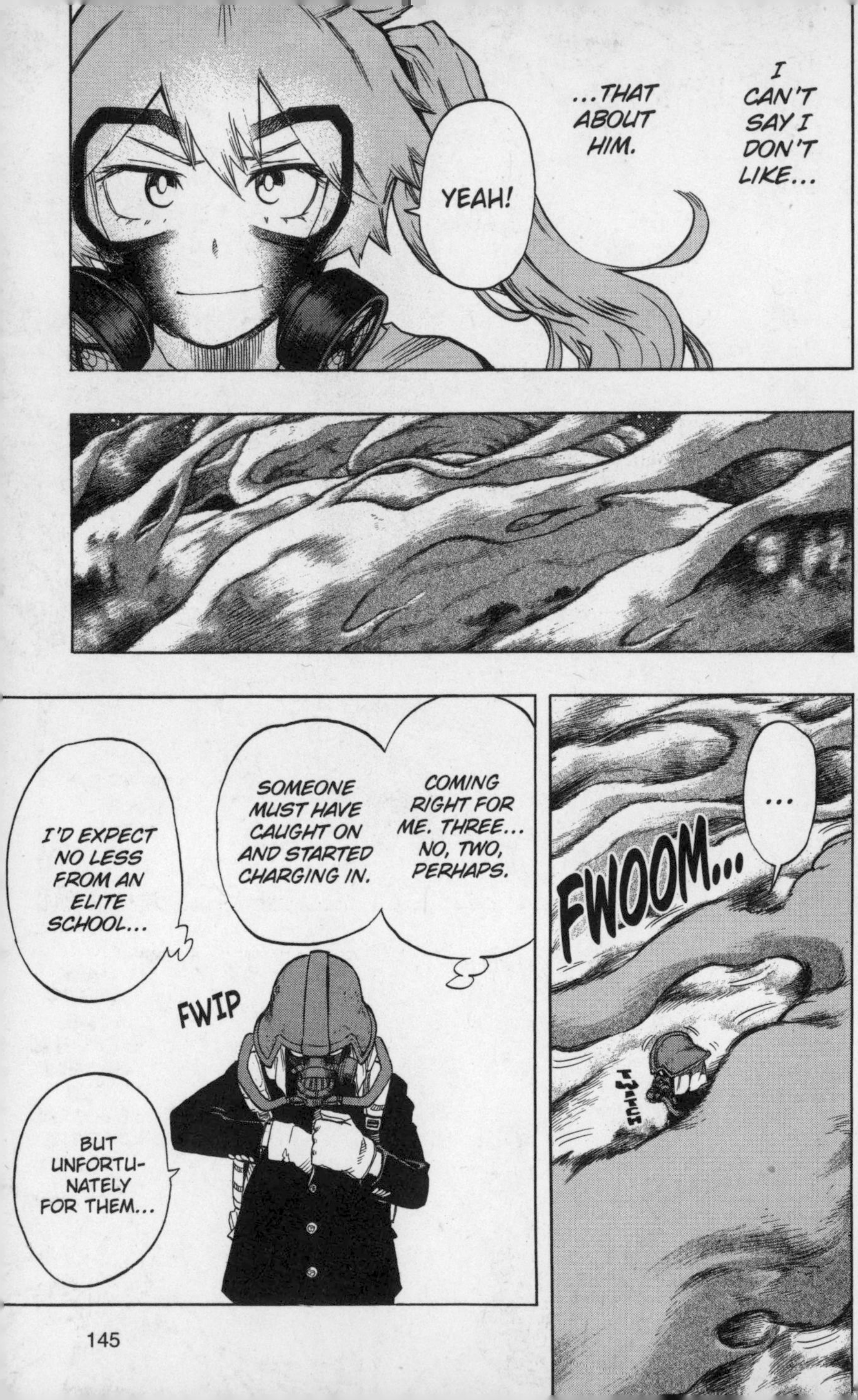

I CAN'T SAY I DON'T LIKE...
...THAT ABOUT HIM.
YEAH!
...
FWOOM...
SOMEONE MUST HAVE CAUGHT ON AND STARTED CHARGING IN. COMING RIGHT FOR ME. THREE... NO, TWO, PERHAPS.
I'D EXPECT NO LESS FROM AN ELITE SCHOOL...
FWIP
BUT UNFORTUNATELY FOR THEM...

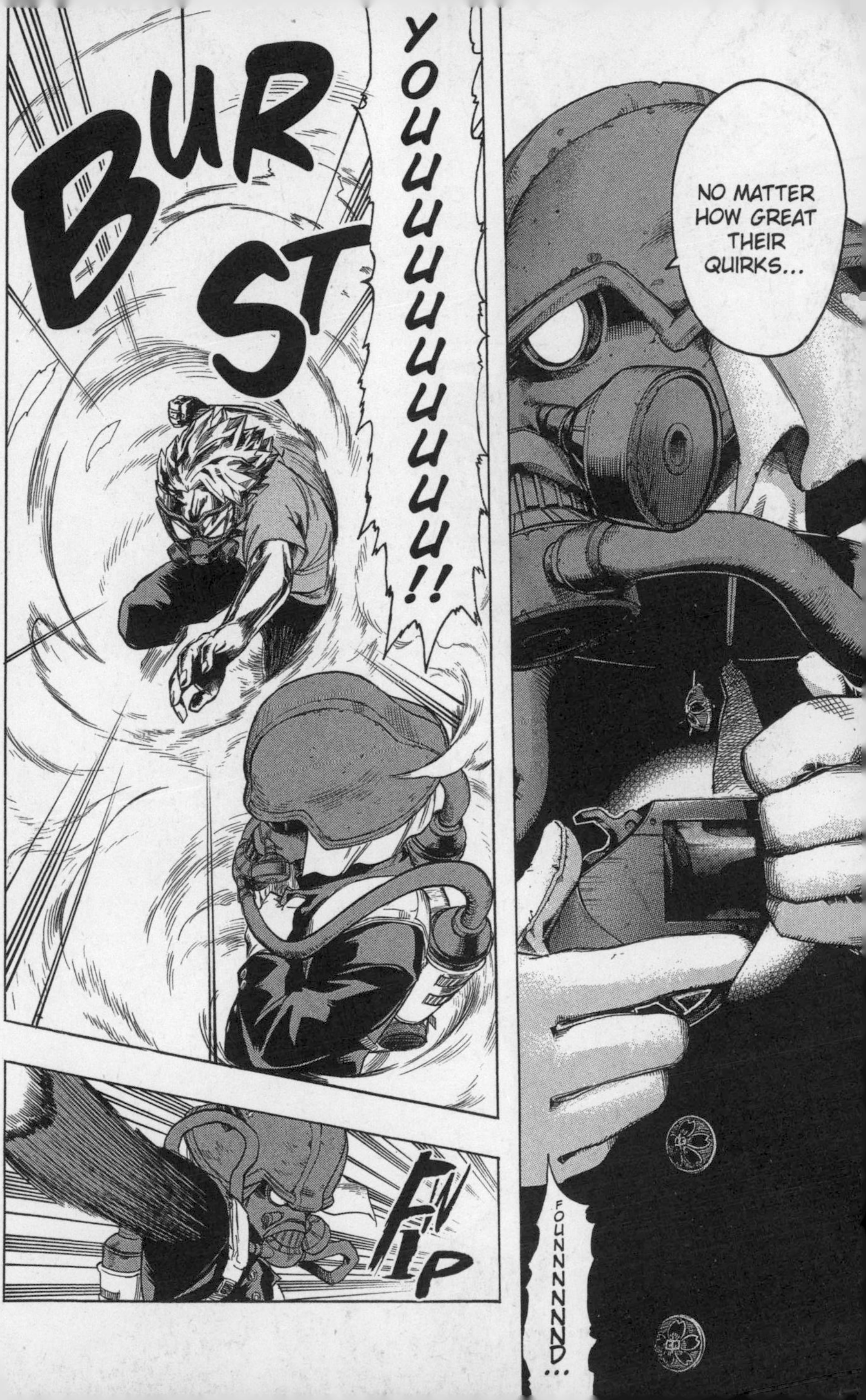
NO MATTER HOW GREAT THEIR QUIRKS...
FOUNNNNNND...
BURST
YOUUUUUUUUUUUUU!!
FWIP

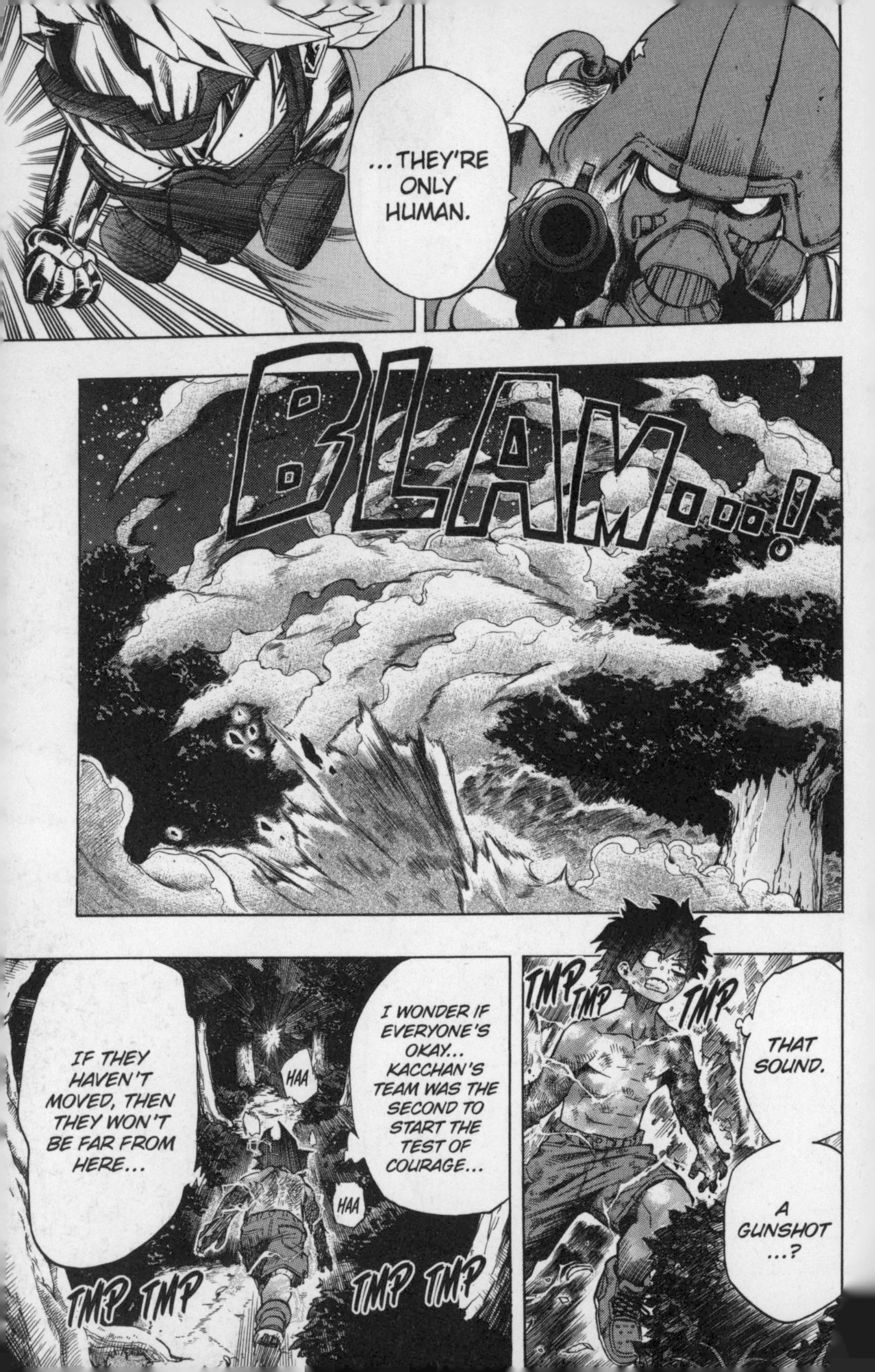
...THEY'RE ONLY HUMAN.
BLAM...!
TMP TMP TMP
THAT SOUND.
A GUNSHOT ...?
I WONDER IF EVERYONE'S OKAY... KACCHAN'S TEAM WAS THE SECOND TO START THE TEST OF COURAGE...
HAA
IF THEY HAVEN'T MOVED, THEN THEY WON'T BE FAR FROM HERE...
HAA
TMP TMP
TMP TMP

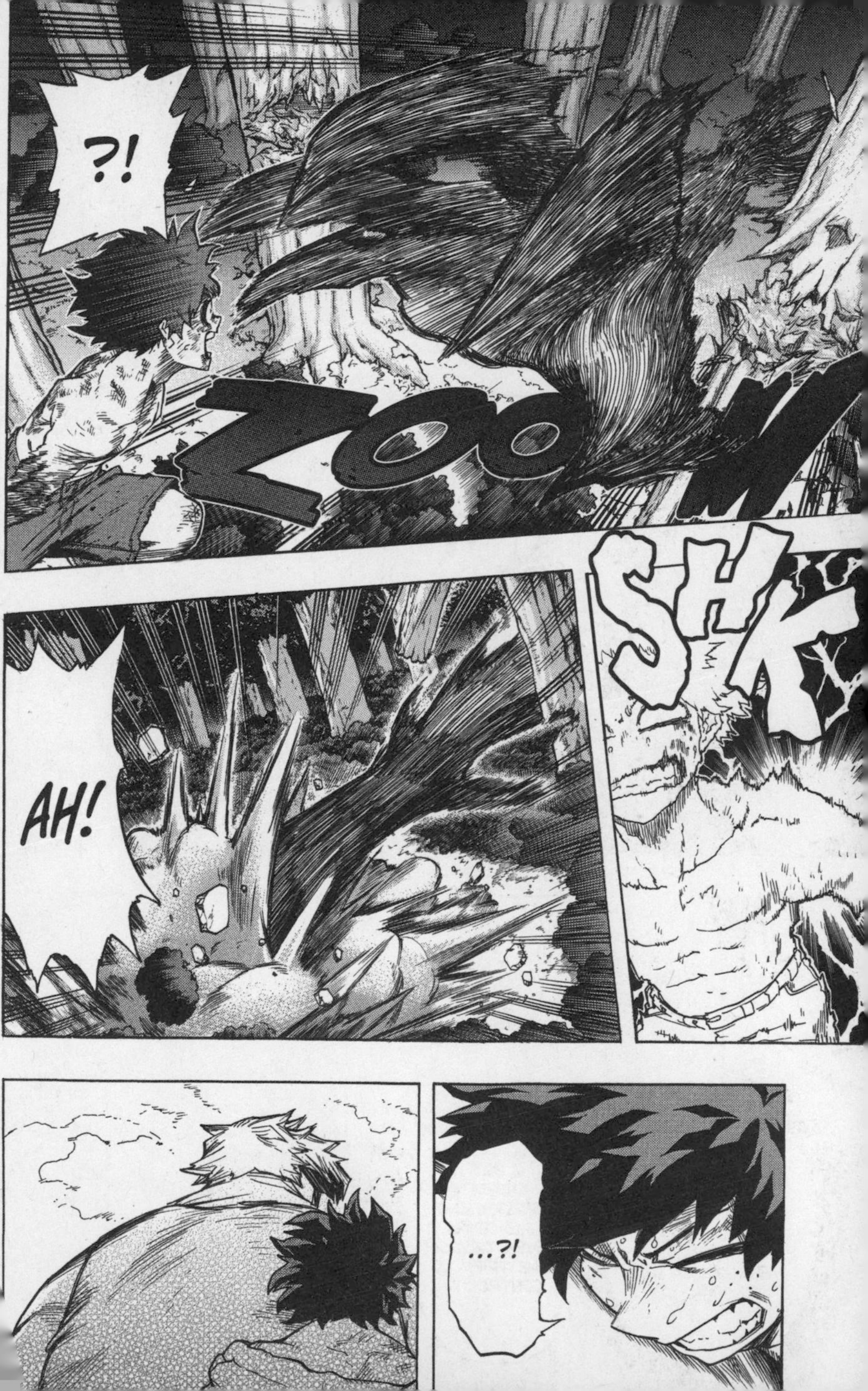
?!
ZOOM
SHK
AH!
...?!

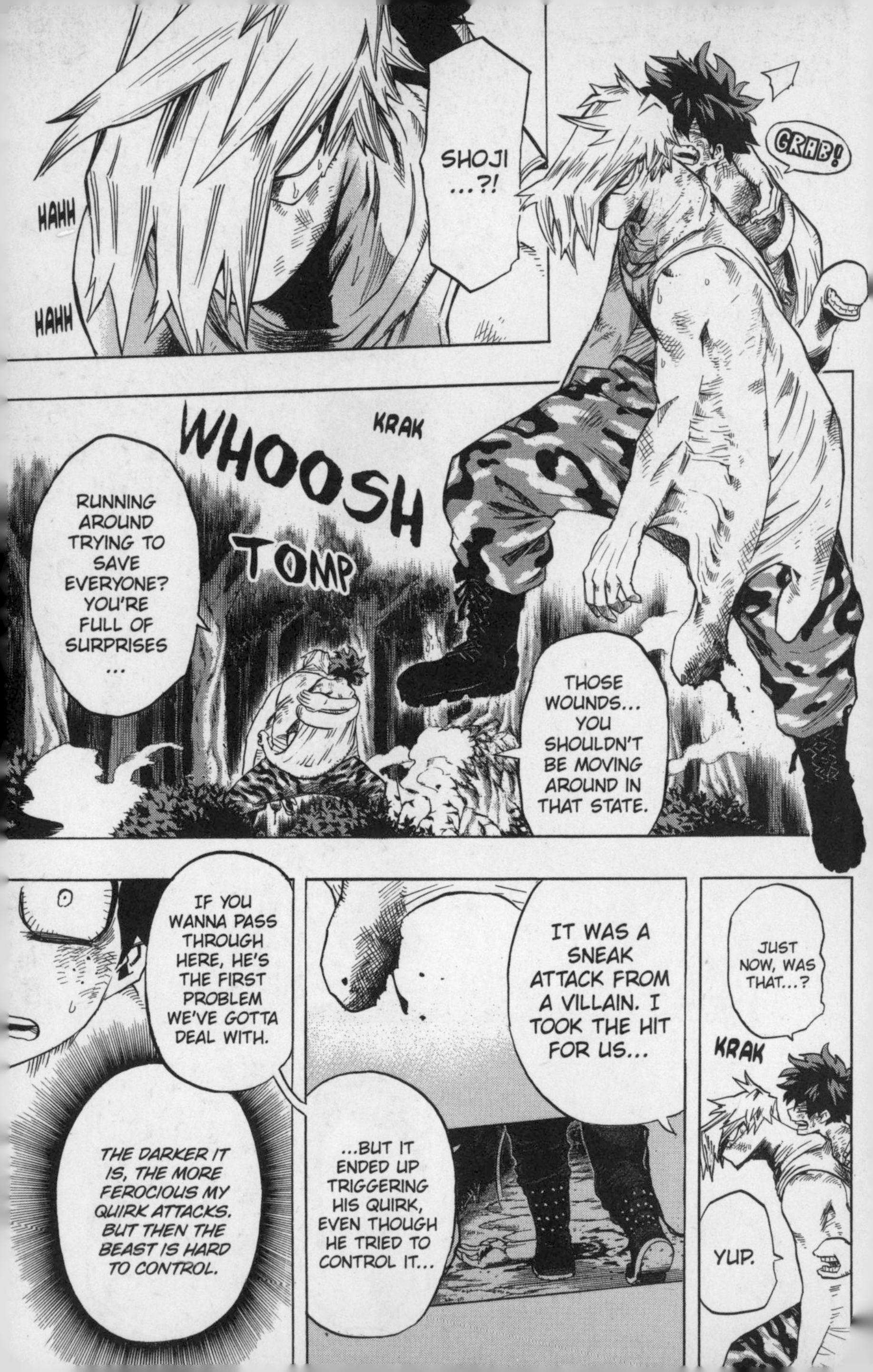
GRAB!
SHOJI ...?!
HAHH
HAHH
KRAK
WHOOSH
TOMP
RUNNING AROUND TRYING TO SAVE EVERYONE? YOU'RE FULL OF SURPRISES ...
THOSE WOUNDS... YOU SHOULDN'T BE MOVING AROUND IN THAT STATE.
JUST NOW, WAS THAT...?
KRAK
YUP.
IT WAS A SNEAK ATTACK FROM A VILLAIN. I TOOK THE HIT FOR US...
...BUT IT ENDED UP TRIGGERING HIS QUIRK, EVEN THOUGH HE TRIED TO CONTROL IT...
IF YOU WANNA PASS THROUGH HERE, HE'S THE FIRST PROBLEM WE'VE GOTTA DEAL WITH.
THE DARKER IT IS, THE MORE FEROCIOUS MY QUIRK ATTACKS. BUT THEN THE BEAST IS HARD TO CONTROL.

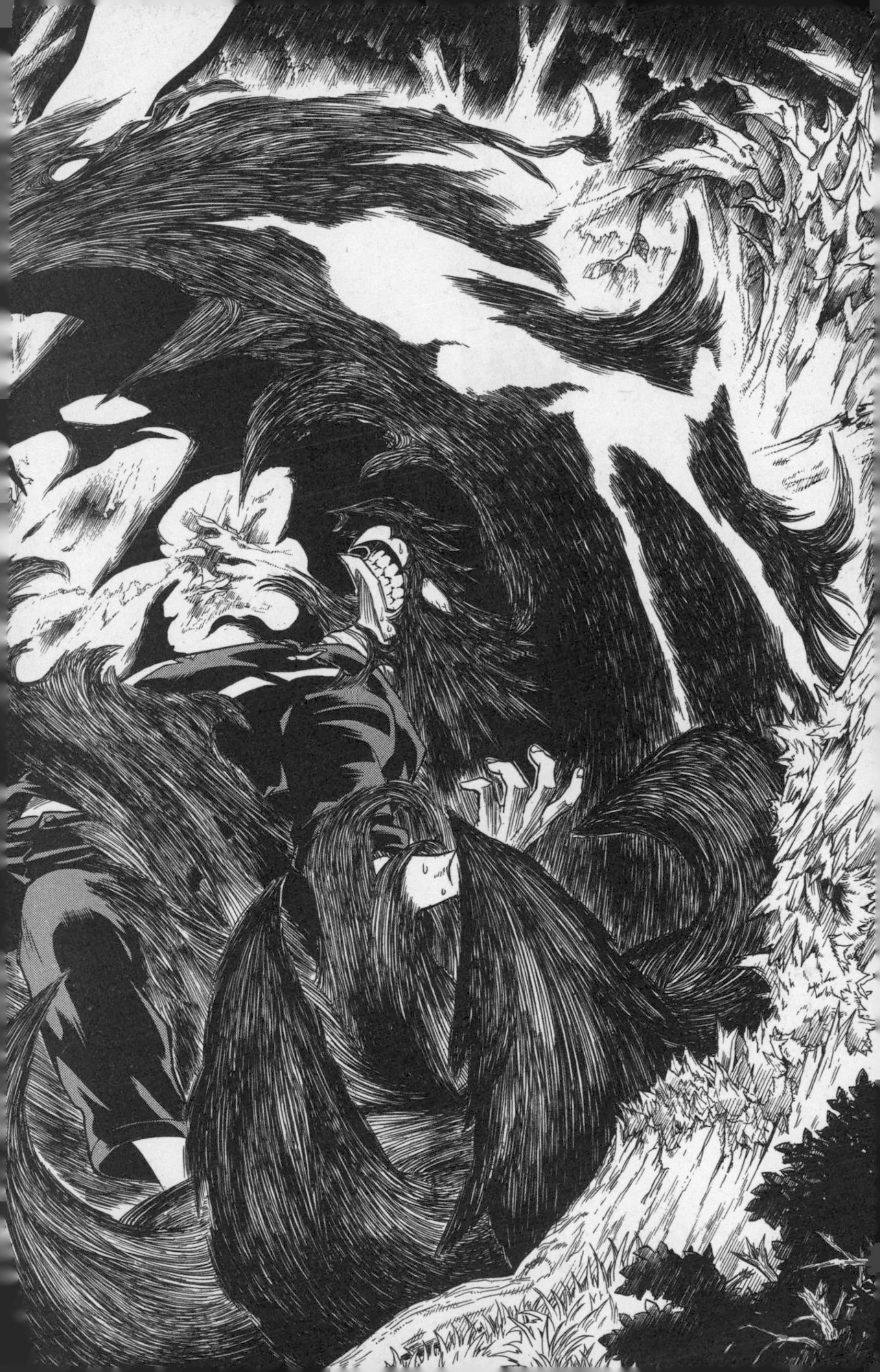

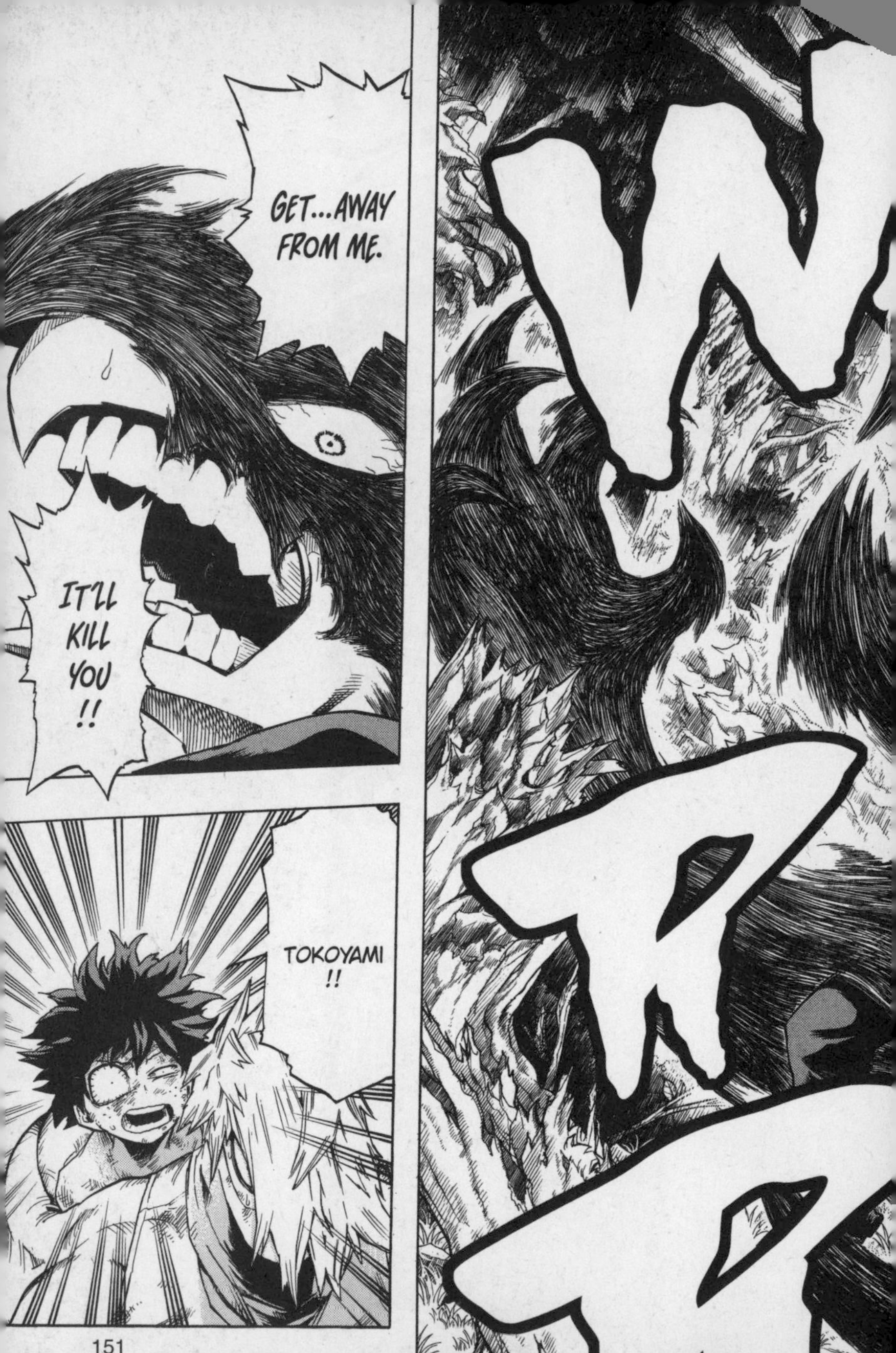
GET...AWAY FROM ME.
IT'LL KILL YOU!!
TOKOYAMI!!

THE SUPPLEMENT

CONCERNING IZUKU'S DETROIT SMASH 1,000,000 PERCENT

Fans and colleagues alike have asked me, "What's that mean? I totally don't get it." I'm really sorry if it was hard to understand. Of course it wasn't actually 1,000,000 percent—that was just a way of expressing Izuku's intense emotions and energy. Like when someone summons incredible strength in a crisis.

I'll be working hard to make everything going forward easier to understand, more cheery, openhearted and fun—in the hopes that I can eventually do away with this supplement column. Ahhhhhhh!!

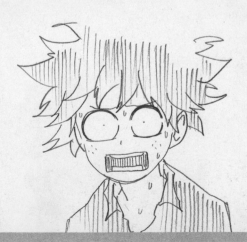

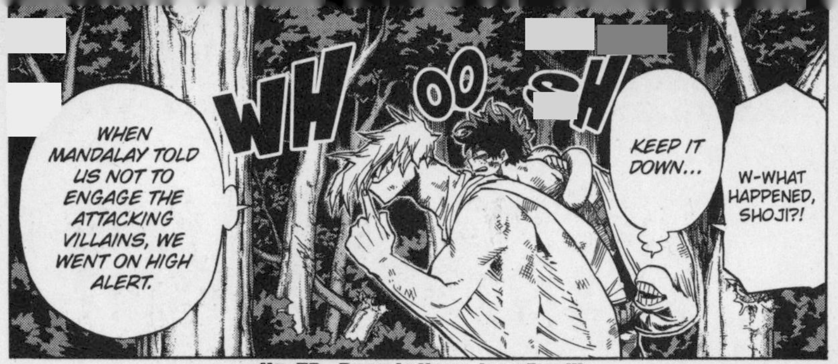
W-WHAT HAPPENED, SHOJI?!
KEEP IT DOWN...
WHOOSH
WHEN MANDALAY TOLD US NOT TO ENGAGE THE ATTACKING VILLAINS, WE WENT ON HIGH ALERT.

No. 79 - Drive It Home, Iron Fist!!!

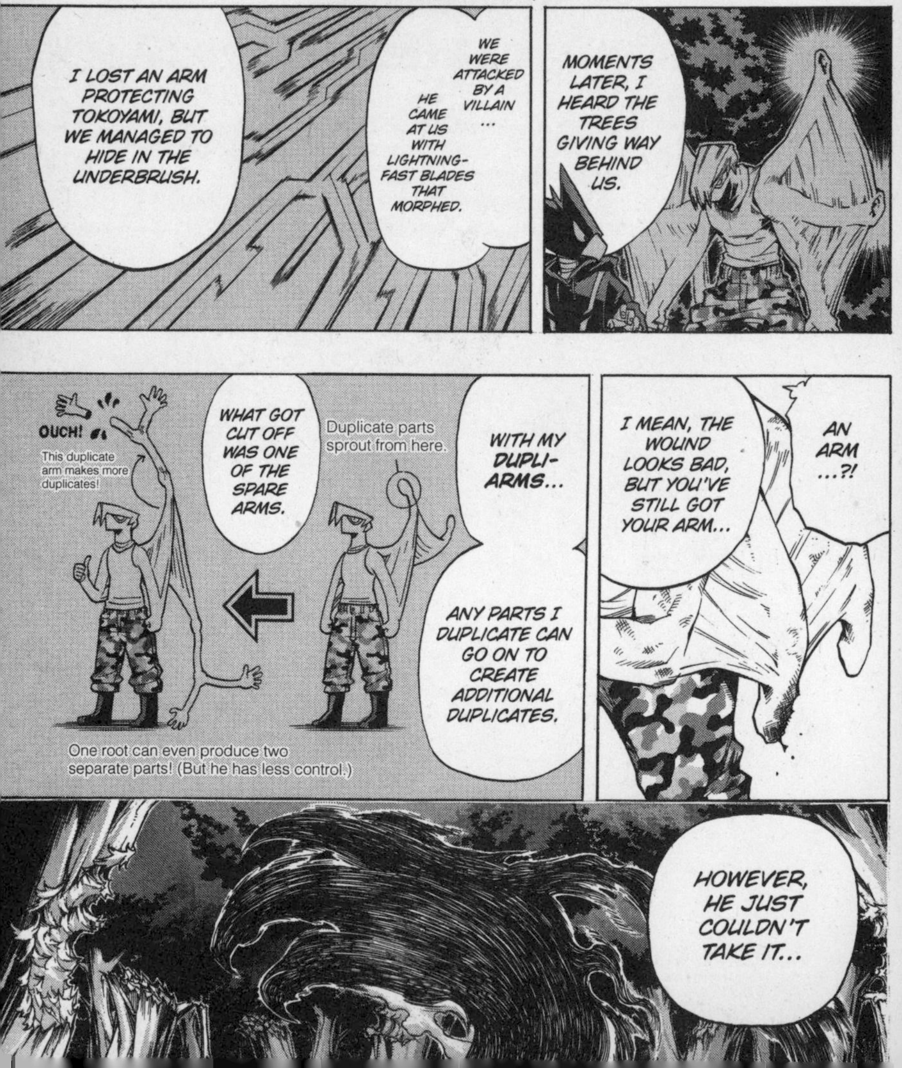
MOMENTS LATER, I HEARD THE TREES GIVING WAY BEHIND US.
WE WERE ATTACKED BY A VILLAIN...
HE CAME AT US WITH LIGHTNING-FAST BLADES THAT MORPHED.
I LOST AN ARM PROTECTING TOKOYAMI, BUT WE MANAGED TO HIDE IN THE UNDERBRUSH.
AN ARM...?!
I MEAN, THE WOUND LOOKS BAD, BUT YOU'VE STILL GOT YOUR ARM...
WITH MY DUPLI-ARMS...
ANY PARTS I DUPLICATE CAN GO ON TO CREATE ADDITIONAL DUPLICATES.
WHAT GOT CUT OFF WAS ONE OF THE SPARE ARMS.
Duplicate parts sprout from here.
OUCH!
This duplicate arm makes more duplicates!
One root can even produce two separate parts! (But he has less control.)
HOWEVER, HE JUST COULDN'T TAKE IT...

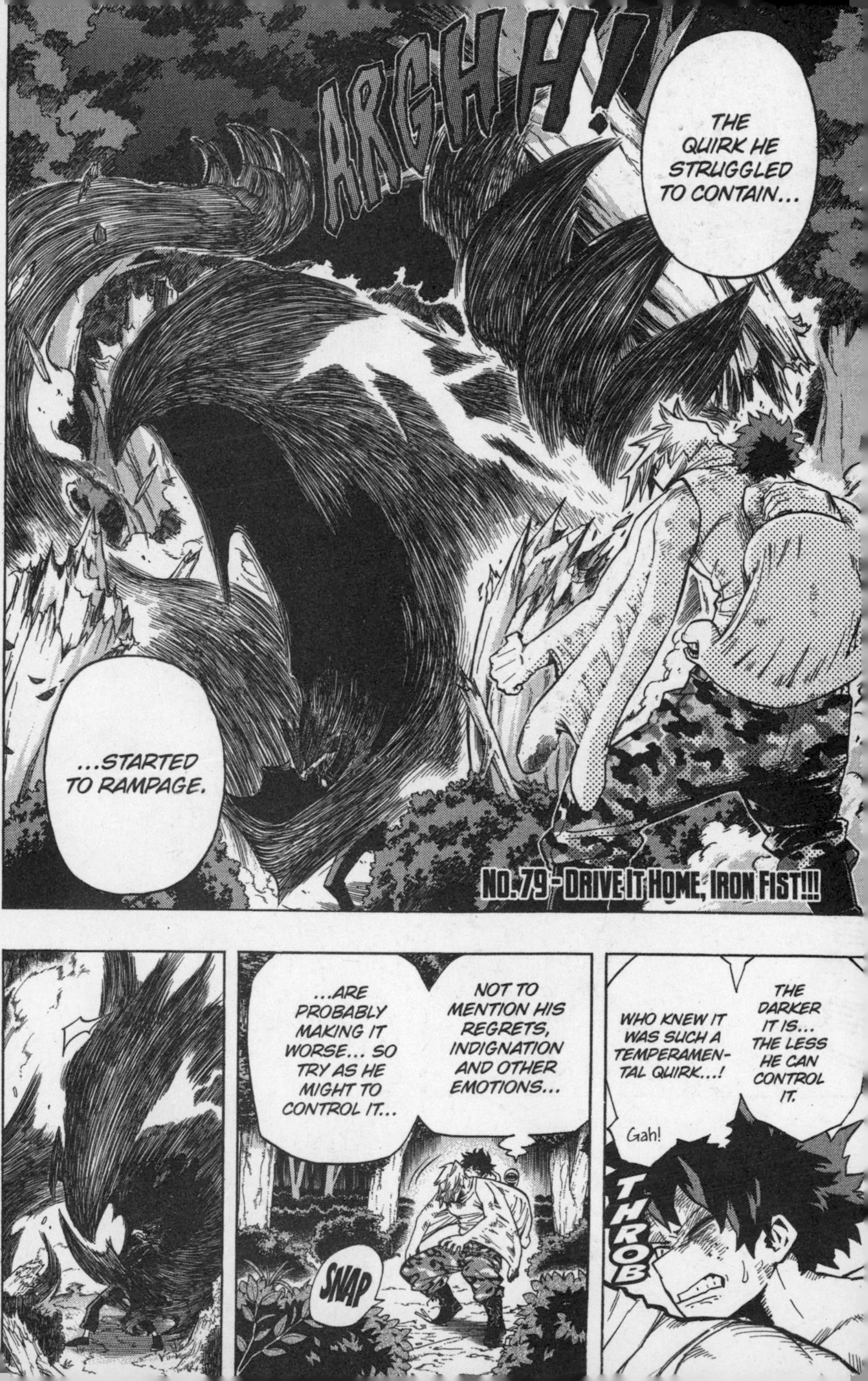
ARGHH!!
THE QUIRK HE STRUGGLED TO CONTAIN...
...STARTED TO RAMPAGE.
No. 79 - Drive It Home, Iron Fist!!!
THE DARKER IT IS... THE LESS HE CAN CONTROL IT.
WHO KNEW IT WAS SUCH A TEMPERAMENTAL QUIRK...!
Gah!
THROB
NOT TO MENTION HIS REGRETS, INDIGNATION AND OTHER EMOTIONS...
...ARE PROBABLY MAKING IT WORSE... SO TRY AS HE MIGHT TO CONTROL IT...
SNAP

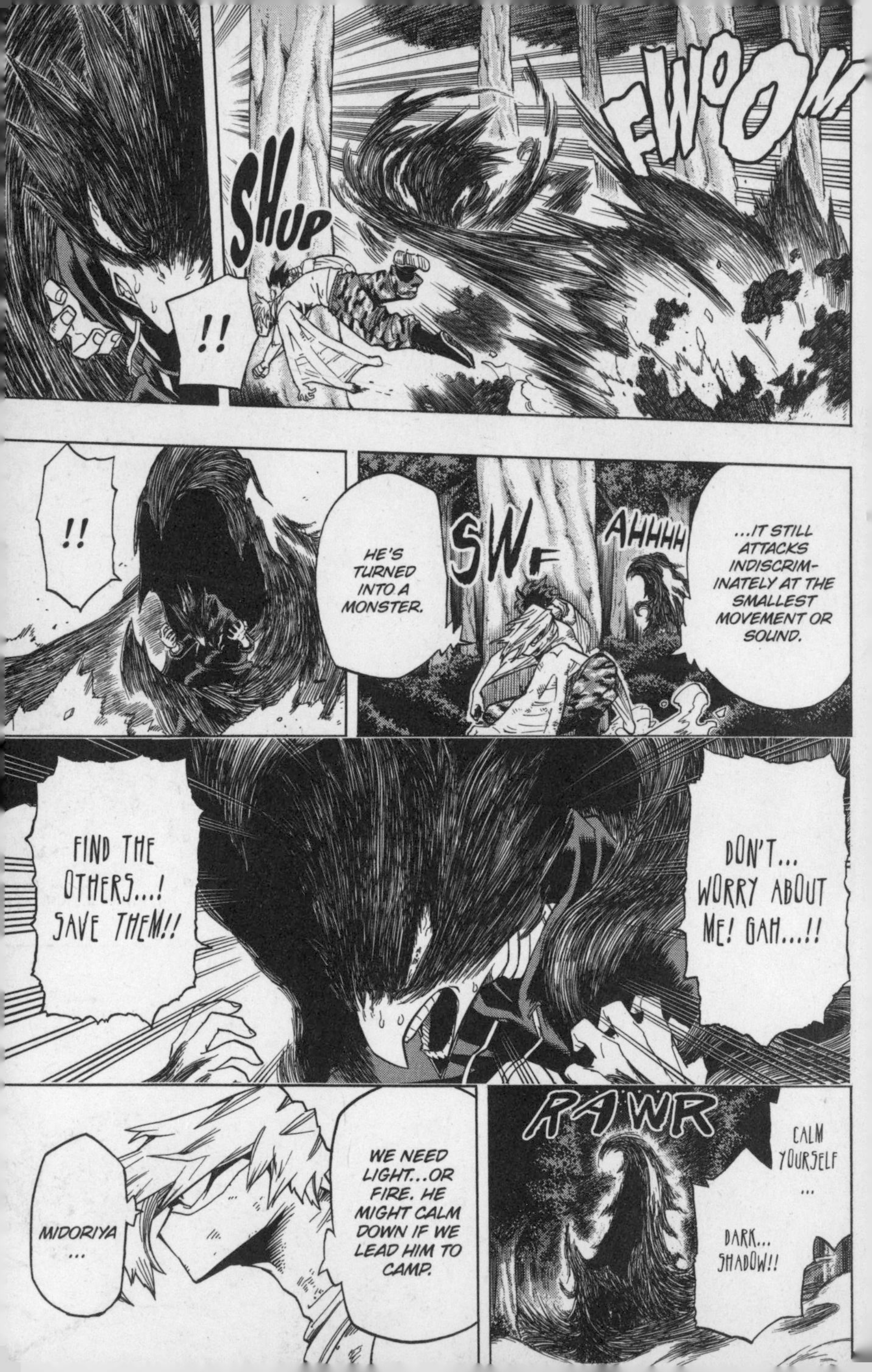
FWOOM
SHUP
!!
...IT STILL ATTACKS INDISCRIM-INATELY AT THE SMALLEST MOVEMENT OR SOUND.
AHHHH
SWF
HE'S TURNED INTO A MONSTER.
!!
DON'T... WORRY ABOUT ME! GAH...!!
FIND THE OTHERS...! SAVE THEM!!
RAWR
CALM YOURSELF ...
DARK... SHADOW!!
WE NEED LIGHT...OR FIRE. HE MIGHT CALM DOWN IF WE LEAD HIM TO CAMP.
MIDORIYA ...

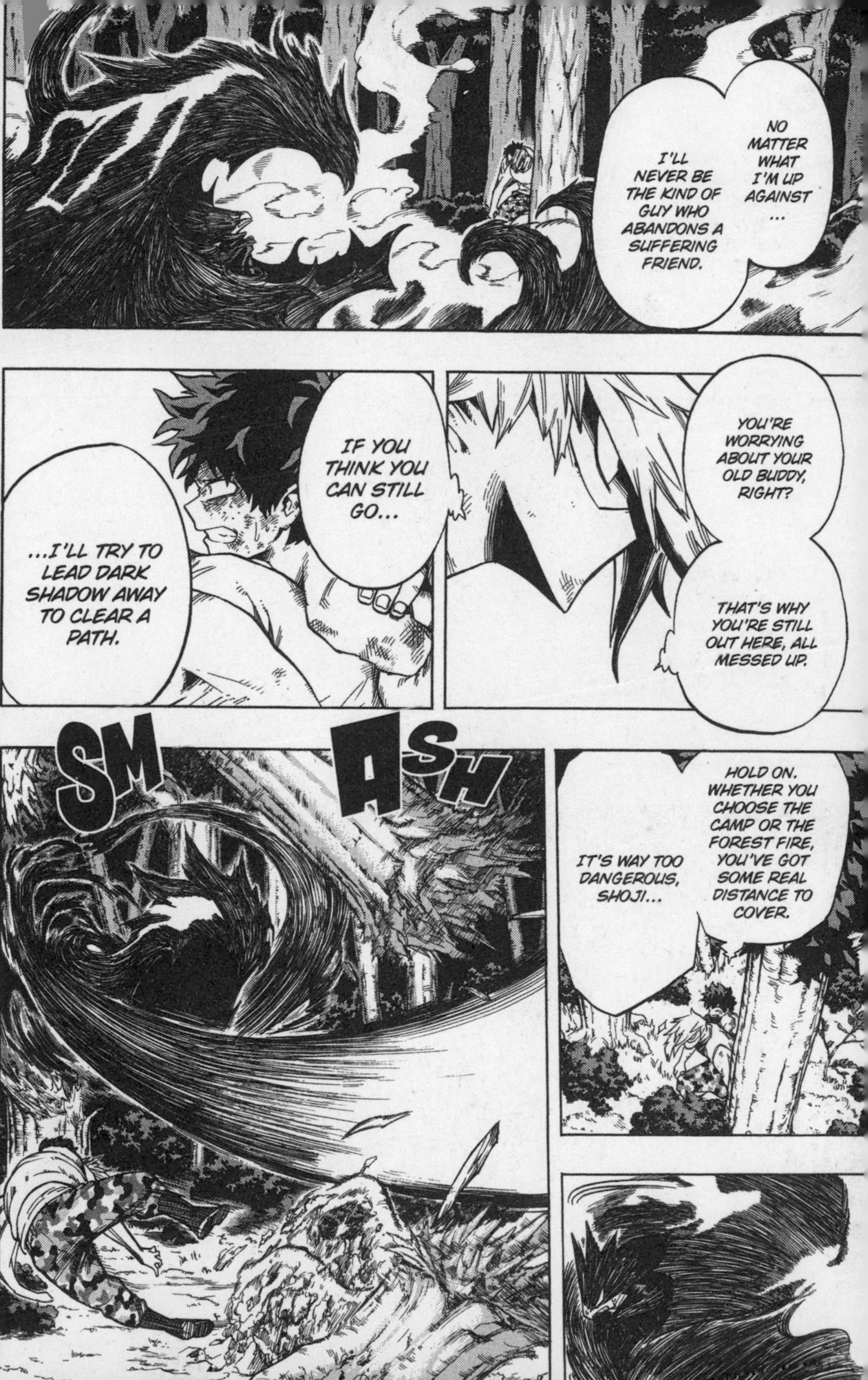
NO MATTER WHAT I'M UP AGAINST...
I'LL NEVER BE THE KIND OF GUY WHO ABANDONS A SUFFERING FRIEND.
YOU'RE WORRYING ABOUT YOUR OLD BUDDY, RIGHT?
THAT'S WHY YOU'RE STILL OUT HERE, ALL MESSED UP.
IF YOU THINK YOU CAN STILL GO...
...I'LL TRY TO LEAD DARK SHADOW AWAY TO CLEAR A PATH.
HOLD ON. WHETHER YOU CHOOSE THE CAMP OR THE FOREST FIRE, YOU'VE GOT SOME REAL DISTANCE TO COVER.
IT'S WAY TOO DANGEROUS, SHOJI...
SMASH

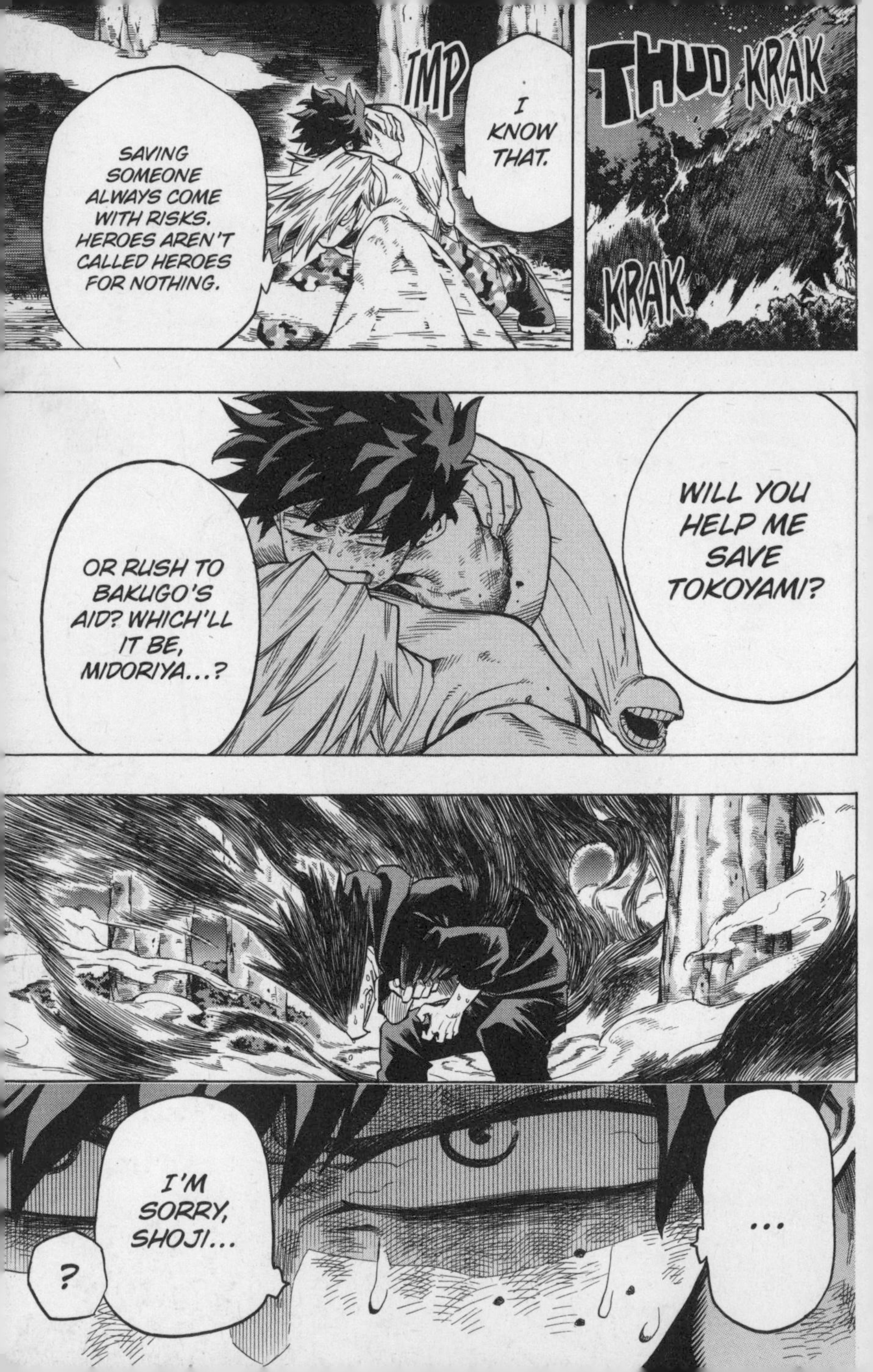
THUD KRAK
KRAK
IMP
I KNOW THAT.
SAVING SOMEONE ALWAYS COME WITH RISKS. HEROES AREN'T CALLED HEROES FOR NOTHING.
WILL YOU HELP ME SAVE TOKOYAMI?
OR RUSH TO BAKUGO'S AID? WHICH'LL IT BE, MIDORIYA...?
...
I'M SORRY, SHOJI...
?

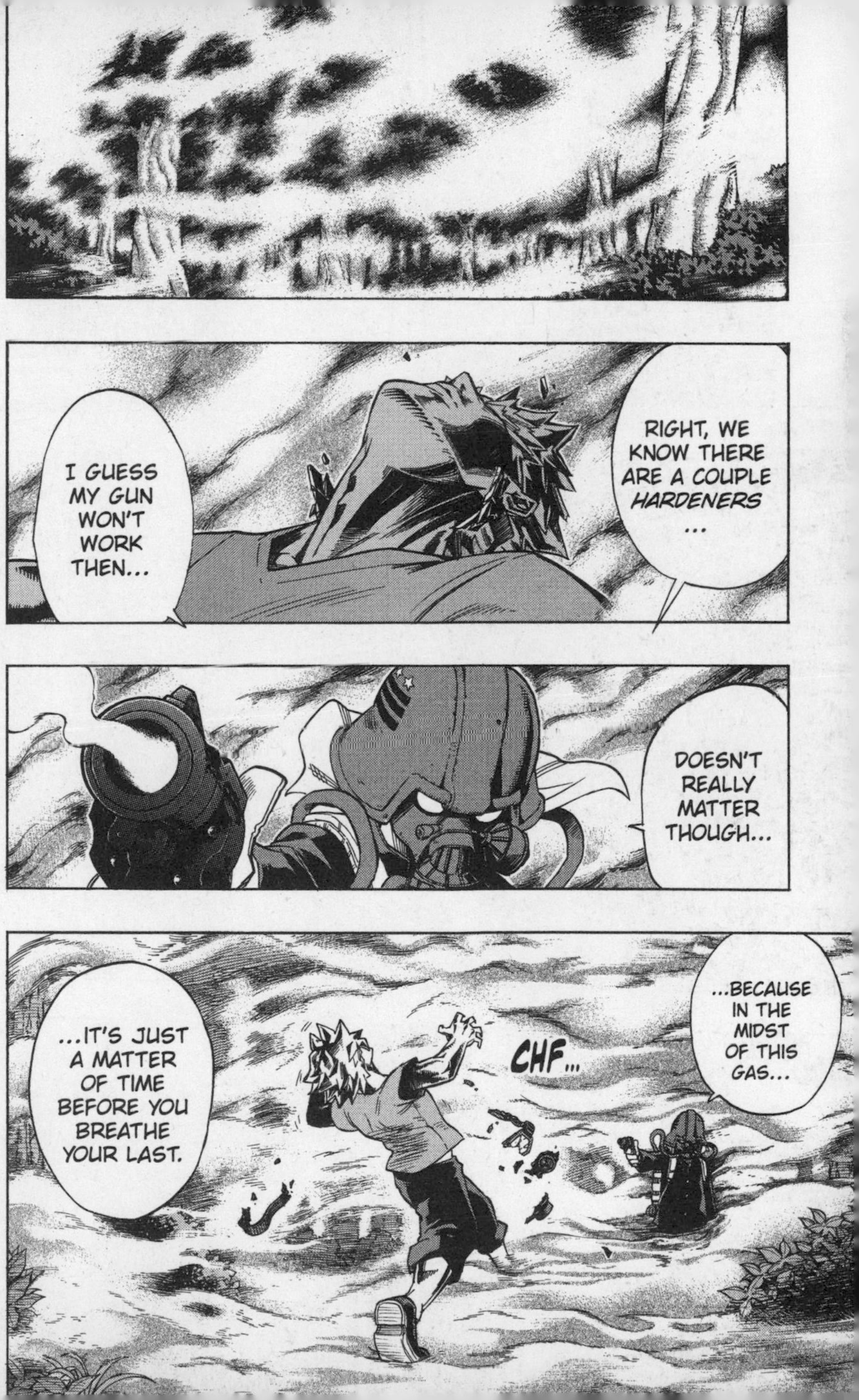
RIGHT, WE KNOW THERE ARE A COUPLE *HARDENERS* ...
I GUESS MY GUN WON'T WORK THEN...
DOESN'T REALLY MATTER THOUGH...
...BECAUSE IN THE MIDST OF THIS GAS...
CHF...
...IT'S JUST A MATTER OF TIME BEFORE YOU BREATHE YOUR LAST.

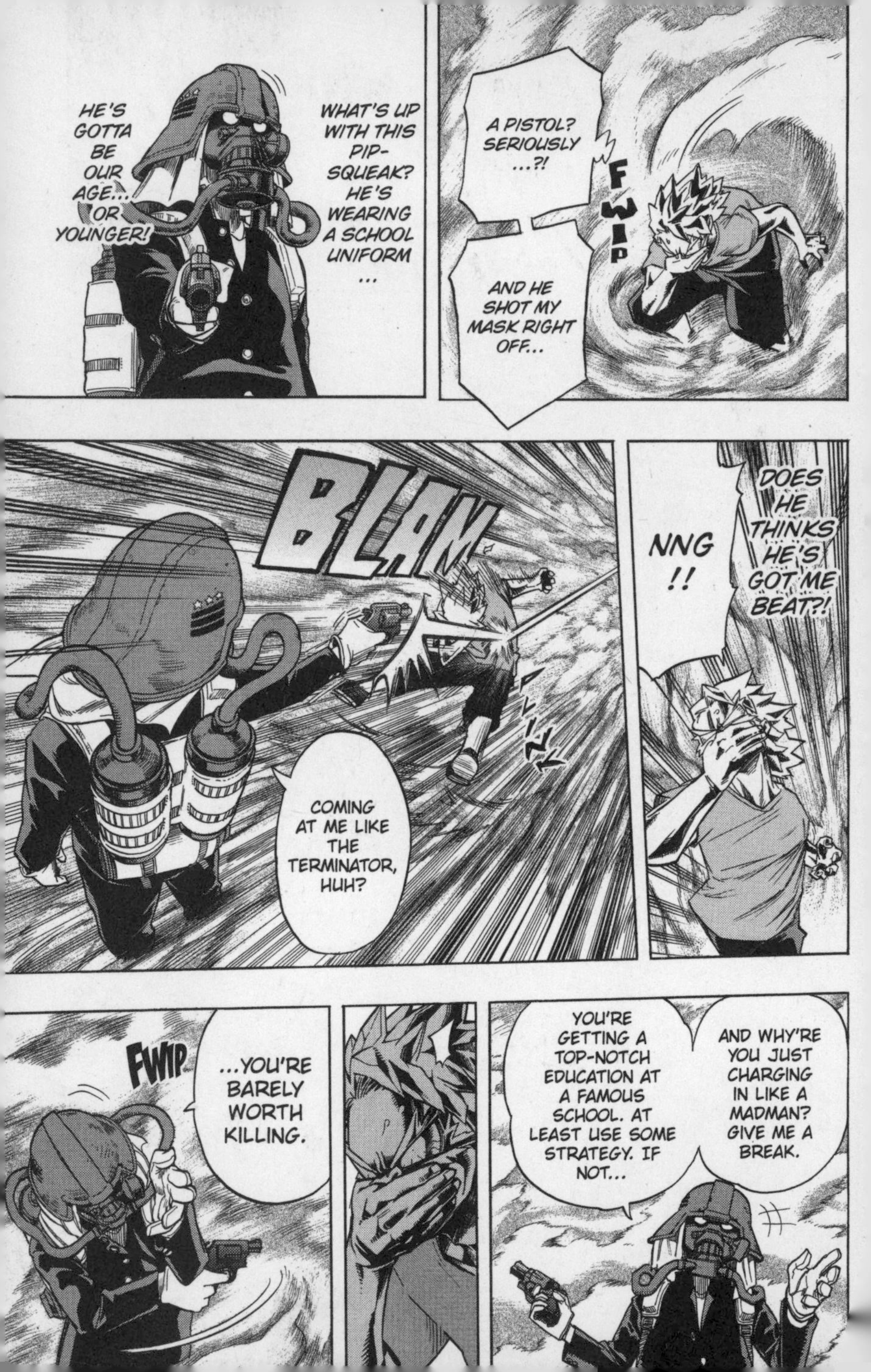
A PISTOL? SERIOUSLY ...?!
FWIP
AND HE SHOT MY MASK RIGHT OFF...
WHAT'S UP WITH THIS PIP-SQUEAK? HE'S WEARING A SCHOOL UNIFORM ...
HE'S GOTTA BE OUR AGE... OR YOUNGER!
DOES HE THINKS HE'S GOT ME BEAT?!
NNG !!
BLAM
COMING AT ME LIKE THE TERMINATOR, HUH?
AND WHY'RE YOU JUST CHARGING IN LIKE A MADMAN? GIVE ME A BREAK.
YOU'RE GETTING A TOP-NOTCH EDUCATION AT A FAMOUS SCHOOL. AT LEAST USE SOME STRATEGY. IF NOT...
FWIP
...YOU'RE BARELY WORTH KILLING.

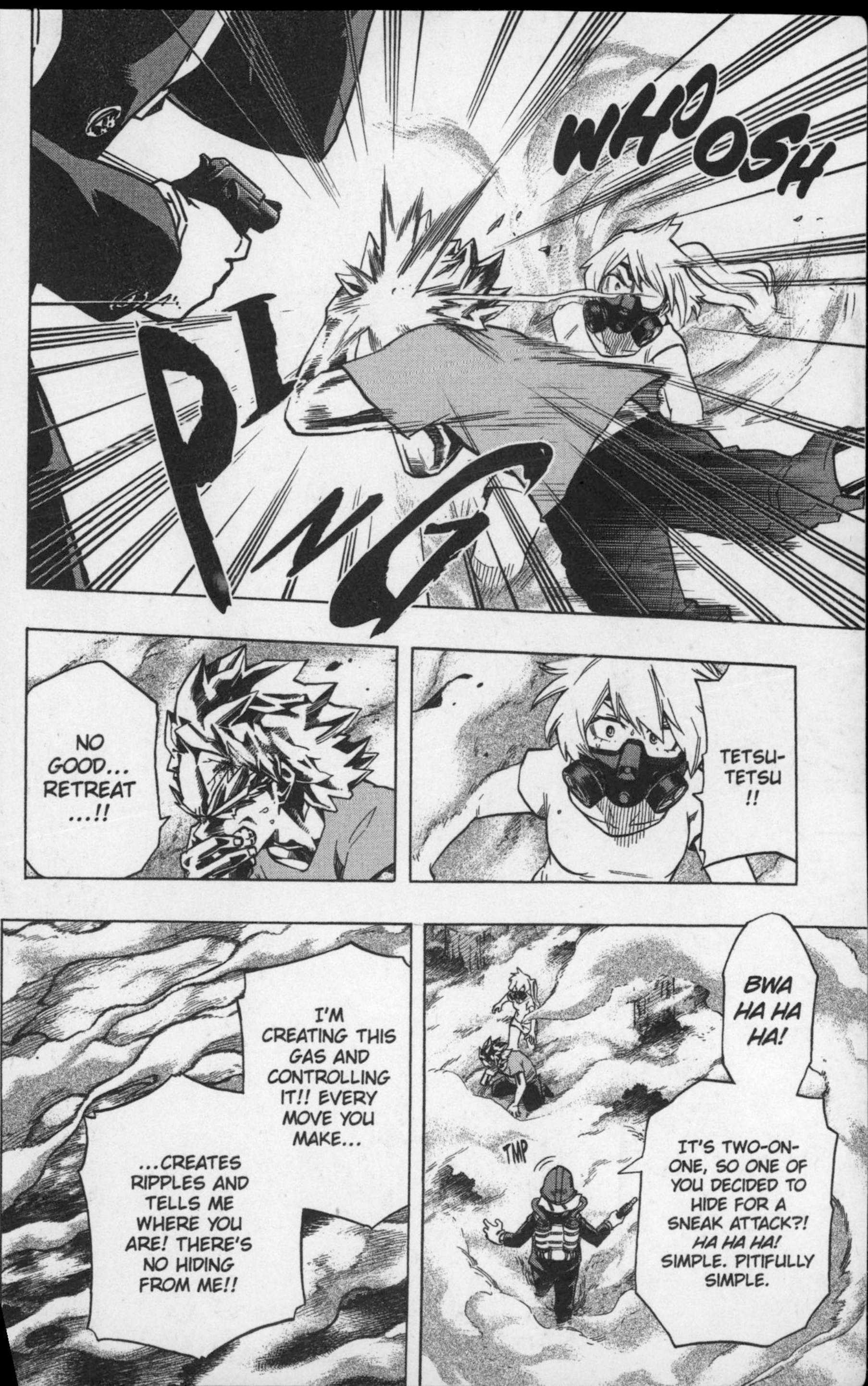
WHOOSH
PING
TETSU-TETSU!!
NO GOOD... RETREAT...!!
BWA HA HA HA!
TMP
IT'S TWO-ON-ONE, SO ONE OF YOU DECIDED TO HIDE FOR A SNEAK ATTACK?! HA HA HA! SIMPLE. PITIFULLY SIMPLE.
I'M CREATING THIS GAS AND CONTROLLING IT!! EVERY MOVE YOU MAKE...
...CREATES RIPPLES AND TELLS ME WHERE YOU ARE! THERE'S NO HIDING FROM ME!!

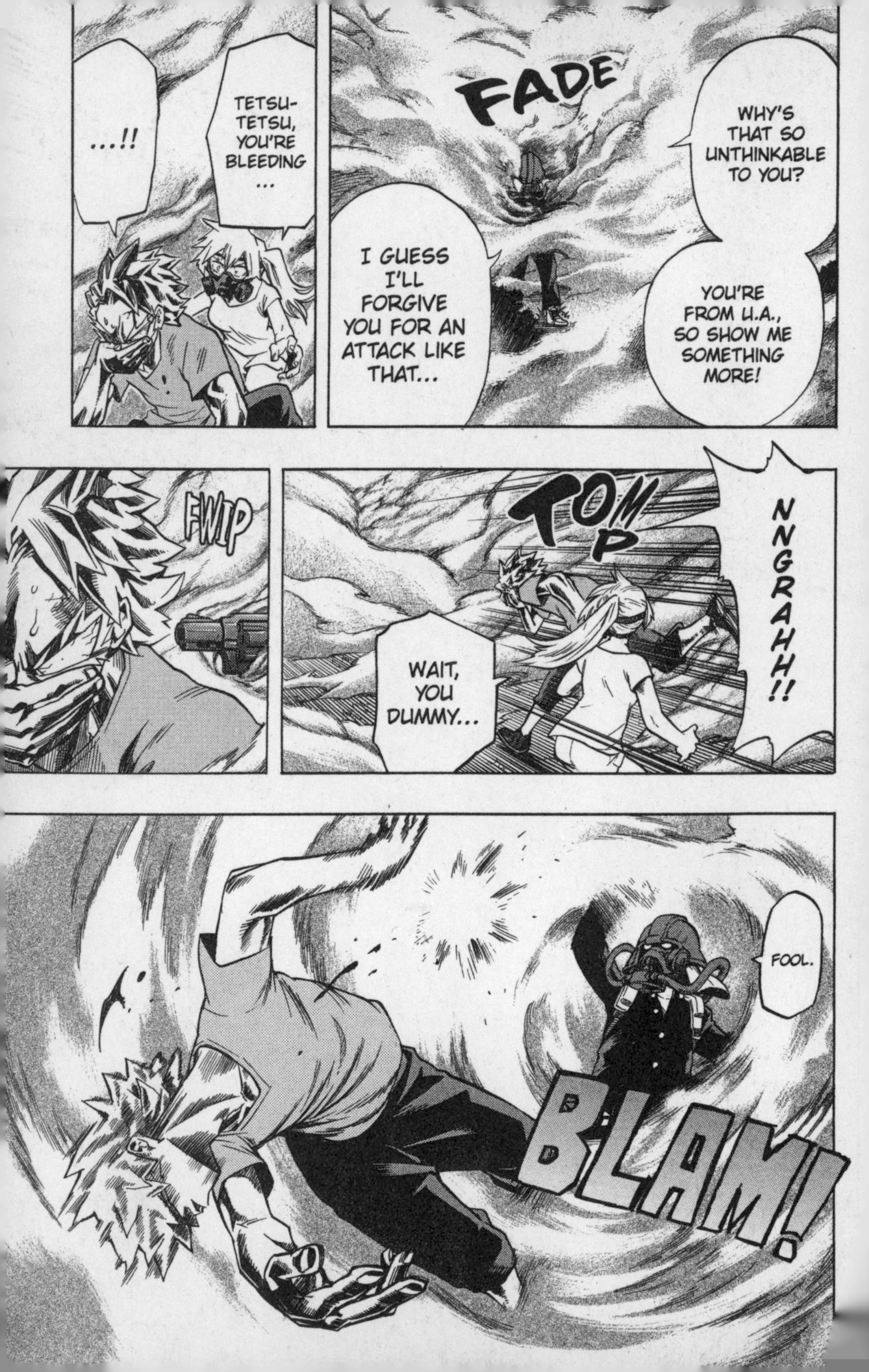
WHY'S THAT SO UNTHINKABLE TO YOU?
FADE
I GUESS I'LL FORGIVE YOU FOR AN ATTACK LIKE THAT...
YOU'RE FROM U.A., SO SHOW ME SOMETHING MORE!
TETSU-TETSU, YOU'RE BLEEDING...
...!!
NNGRAHH!!
TOMP
WAIT, YOU DUMMY...
FWIP
FOOL.
BLAM!

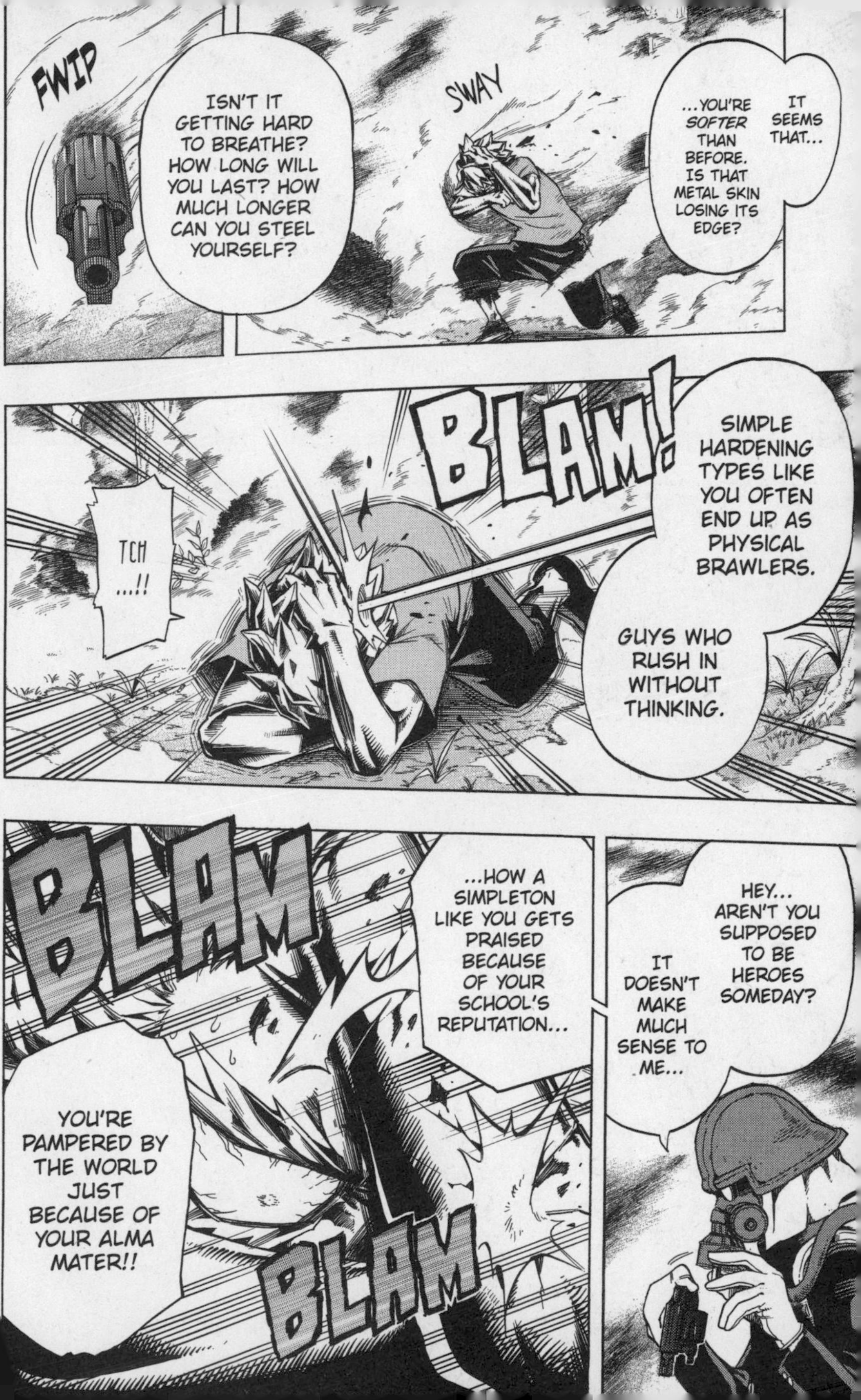
SWAY
IT SEEMS THAT...
...YOU'RE SOFTER THAN BEFORE. IS THAT METAL SKIN LOSING ITS EDGE?
FWIP
ISN'T IT GETTING HARD TO BREATHE? HOW LONG WILL YOU LAST? HOW MUCH LONGER CAN YOU STEEL YOURSELF?
BLAM!
SIMPLE HARDENING TYPES LIKE YOU OFTEN END UP AS PHYSICAL BRAWLERS.
GUYS WHO RUSH IN WITHOUT THINKING.
TCH ...!!
HEY... AREN'T YOU SUPPOSED TO BE HEROES SOMEDAY?
IT DOESN'T MAKE MUCH SENSE TO ME...
BLAM
...HOW A SIMPLETON LIKE YOU GETS PRAISED BECAUSE OF YOUR SCHOOL'S REPUTATION...
YOU'RE PAMPERED BY THE WORLD JUST BECAUSE OF YOUR ALMA MATER!!
BLAM

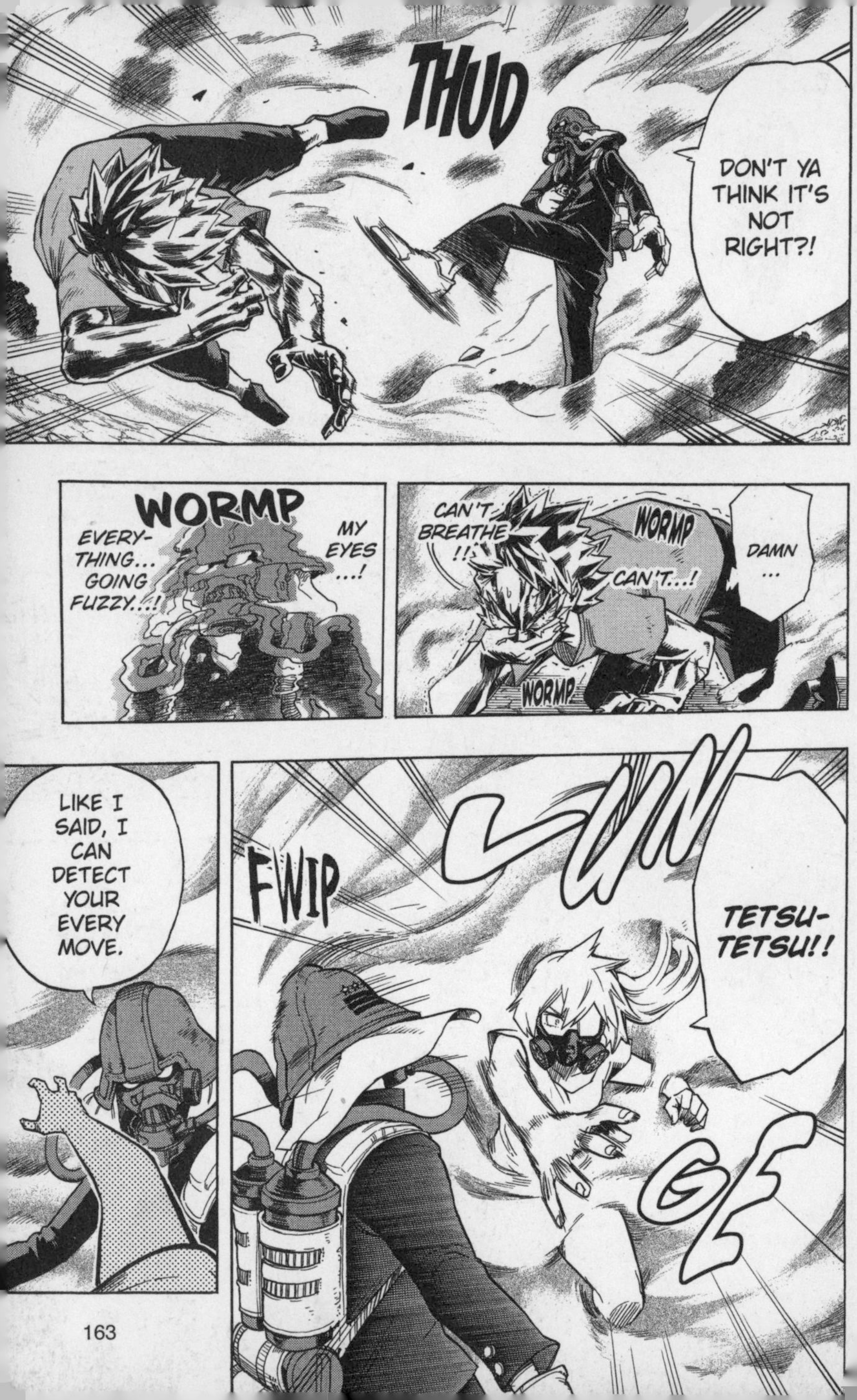
THUD
DON'T YA THINK IT'S NOT RIGHT?!
DAMN ...
CAN'T BREATHE !!
WORMP
CAN'T...!
WORMP
WORMP
MY EYES ...!
EVERY-THING... GOING FUZZY...!
TETSU-TETSU!!
FWIP
LIKE I SAID, I CAN DETECT YOUR EVERY MOVE.

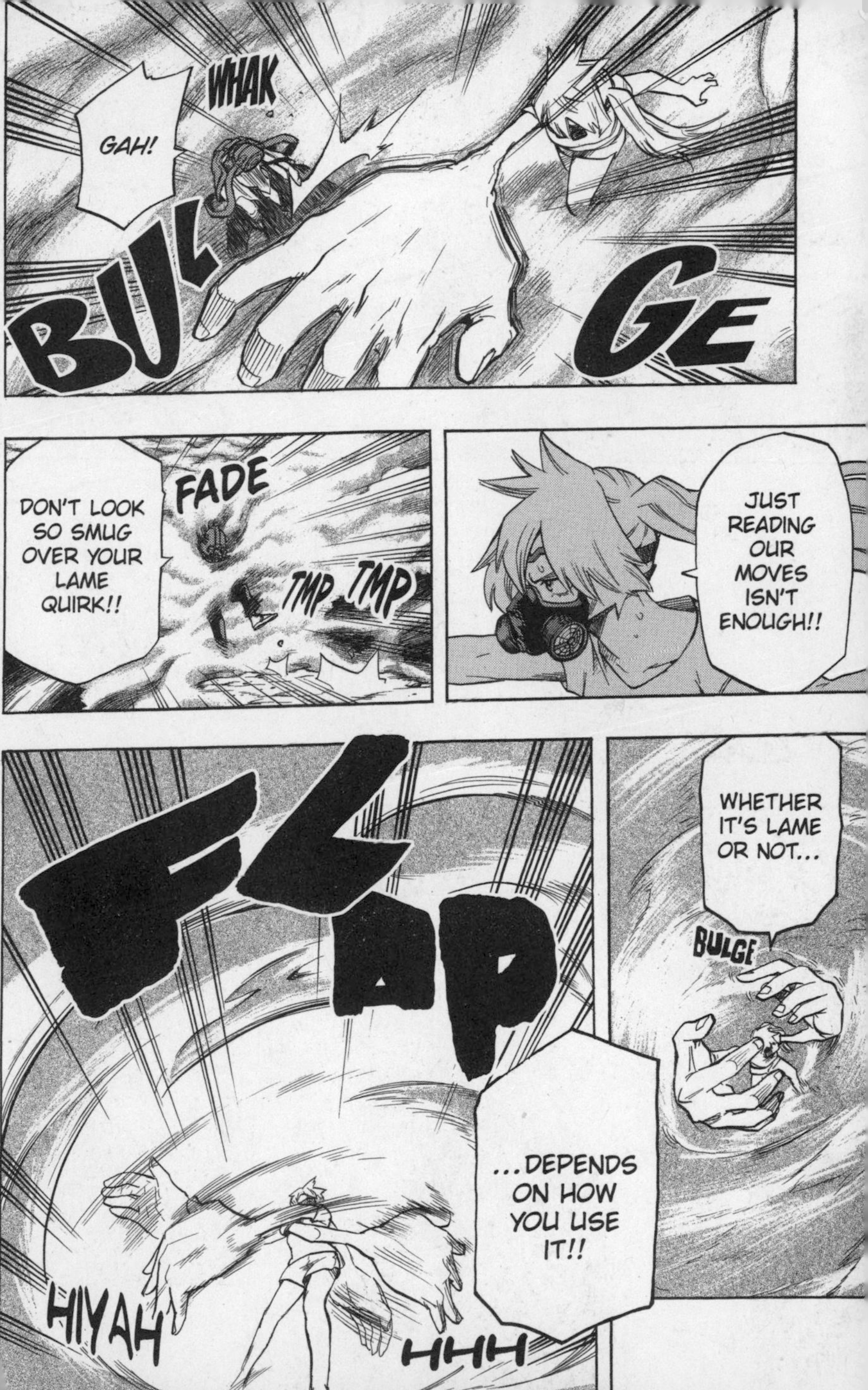
WHAK
GAH!
BU
GE
JUST READING OUR MOVES ISN'T ENOUGH!!
DON'T LOOK SO SMUG OVER YOUR LAME QUIRK!!
FADE
TMP TMP
WHETHER IT'S LAME OR NOT...
BULGE
FLAP
...DEPENDS ON HOW YOU USE IT!!
HIYAH
HHH

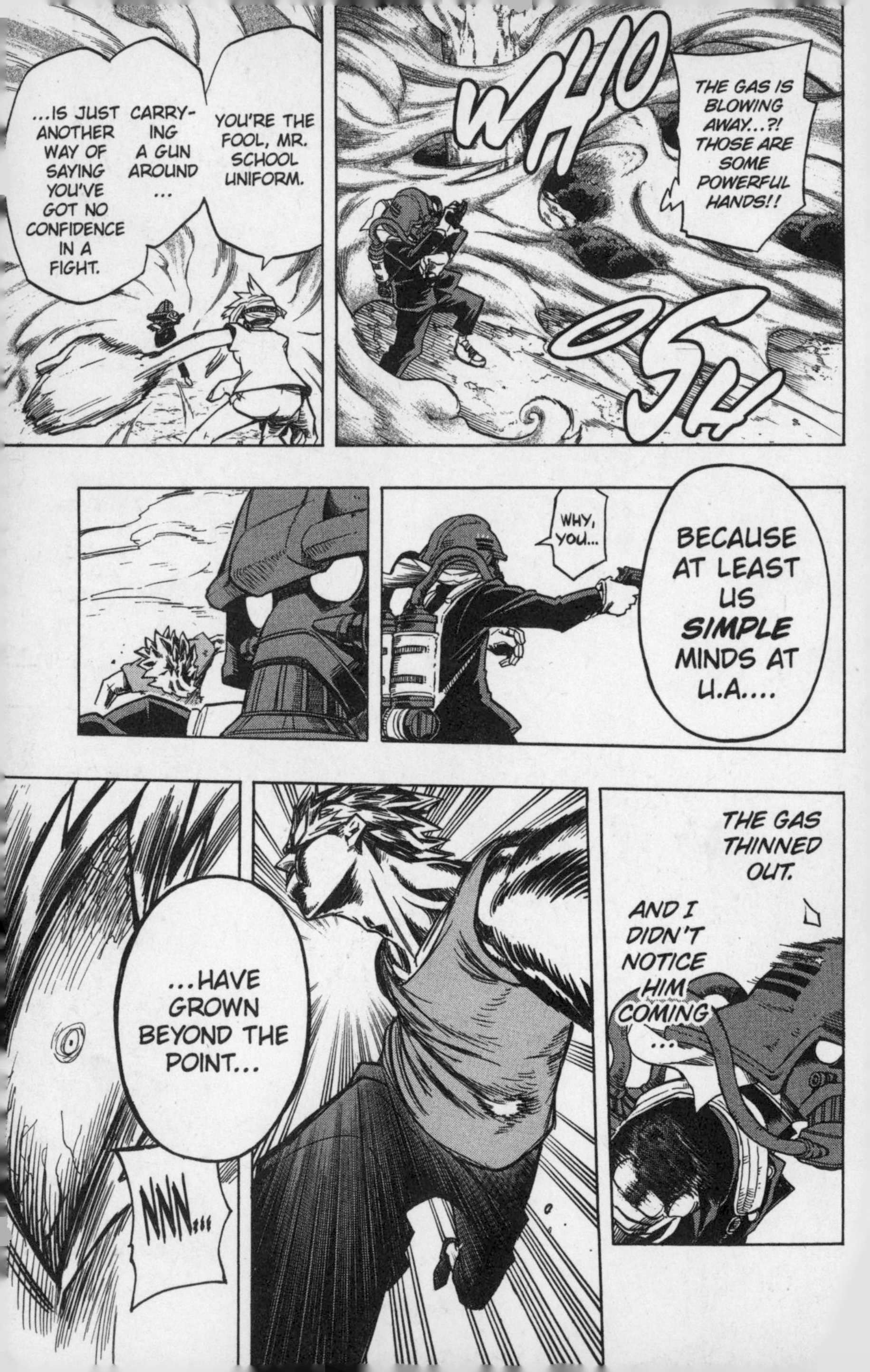
WHO
OSH
THE GAS IS BLOWING AWAY...?! THOSE ARE SOME POWERFUL HANDS!!
YOU'RE THE FOOL, MR. SCHOOL UNIFORM.
CARRY-ING A GUN AROUND...
...IS JUST ANOTHER WAY OF SAYING YOU'VE GOT NO CONFIDENCE IN A FIGHT.
WHY, YOU...
BECAUSE AT LEAST US SIMPLE MINDS AT U.A....
THE GAS THINNED OUT.
AND I DIDN'T NOTICE HIM COMING...
...HAVE GROWN BEYOND THE POINT...
NNN...

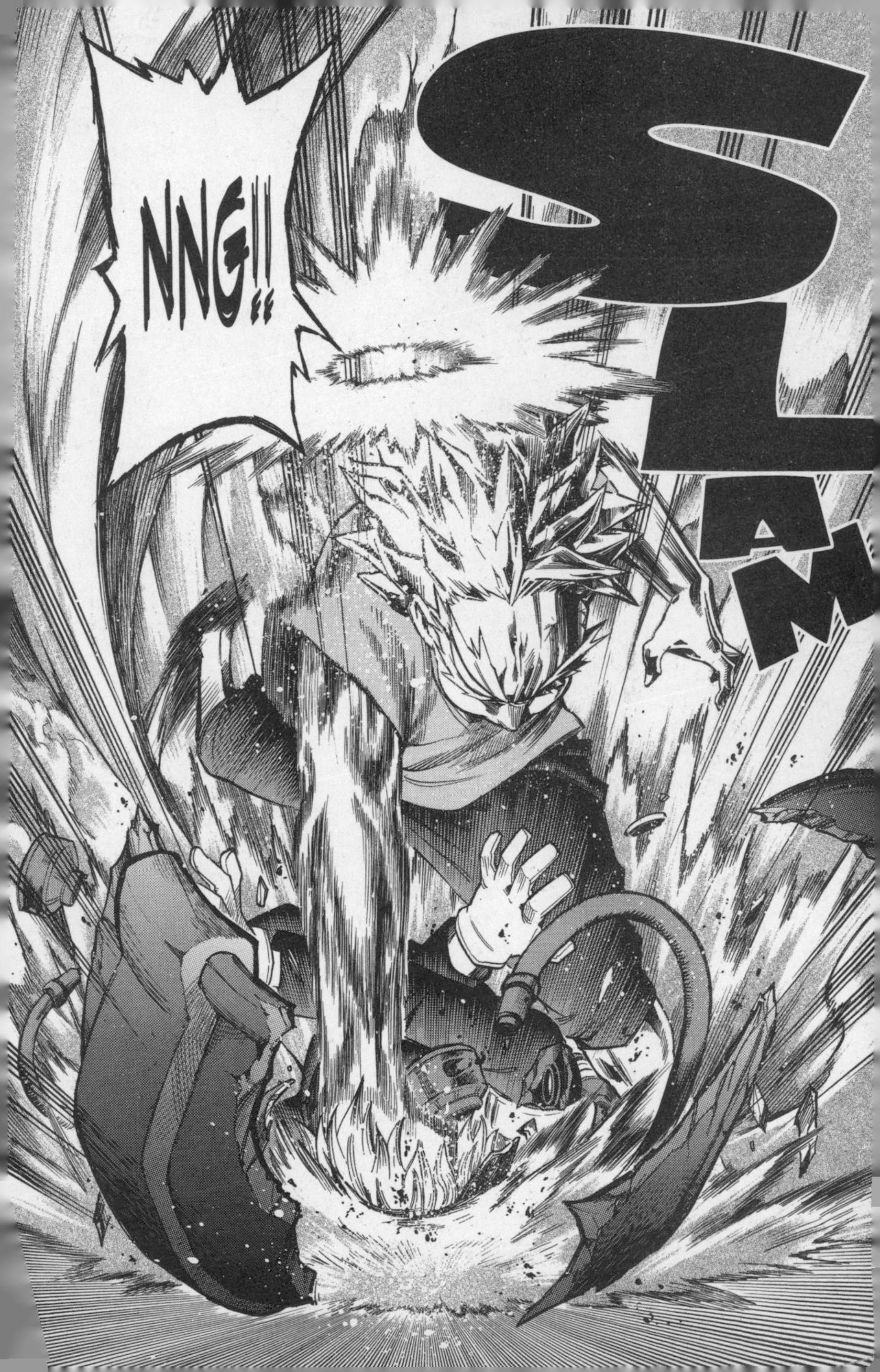
SLAM
NNG!!

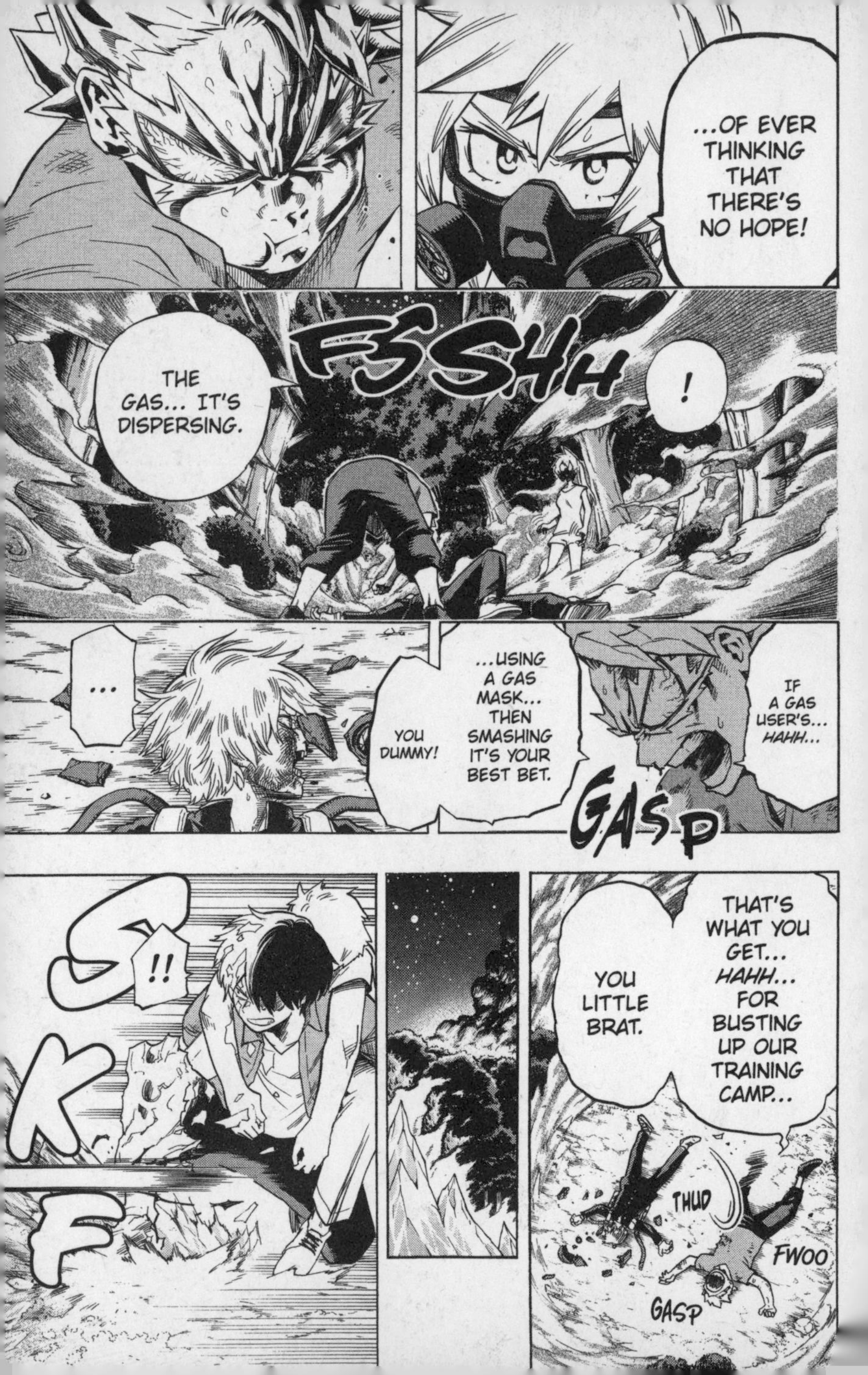
...OF EVER THINKING THAT THERE'S NO HOPE!
FSSHH
!
THE GAS... IT'S DISPERSING.
IF A GAS USER'S... HAHH...
GASP
...USING A GAS MASK... THEN SMASHING IT'S YOUR BEST BET.
YOU DUMMY!
...
THAT'S WHAT YOU GET... HAHH... FOR BUSTING UP OUR TRAINING CAMP...
YOU LITTLE BRAT.
THUD
FWOO
GASP
!!
SKF

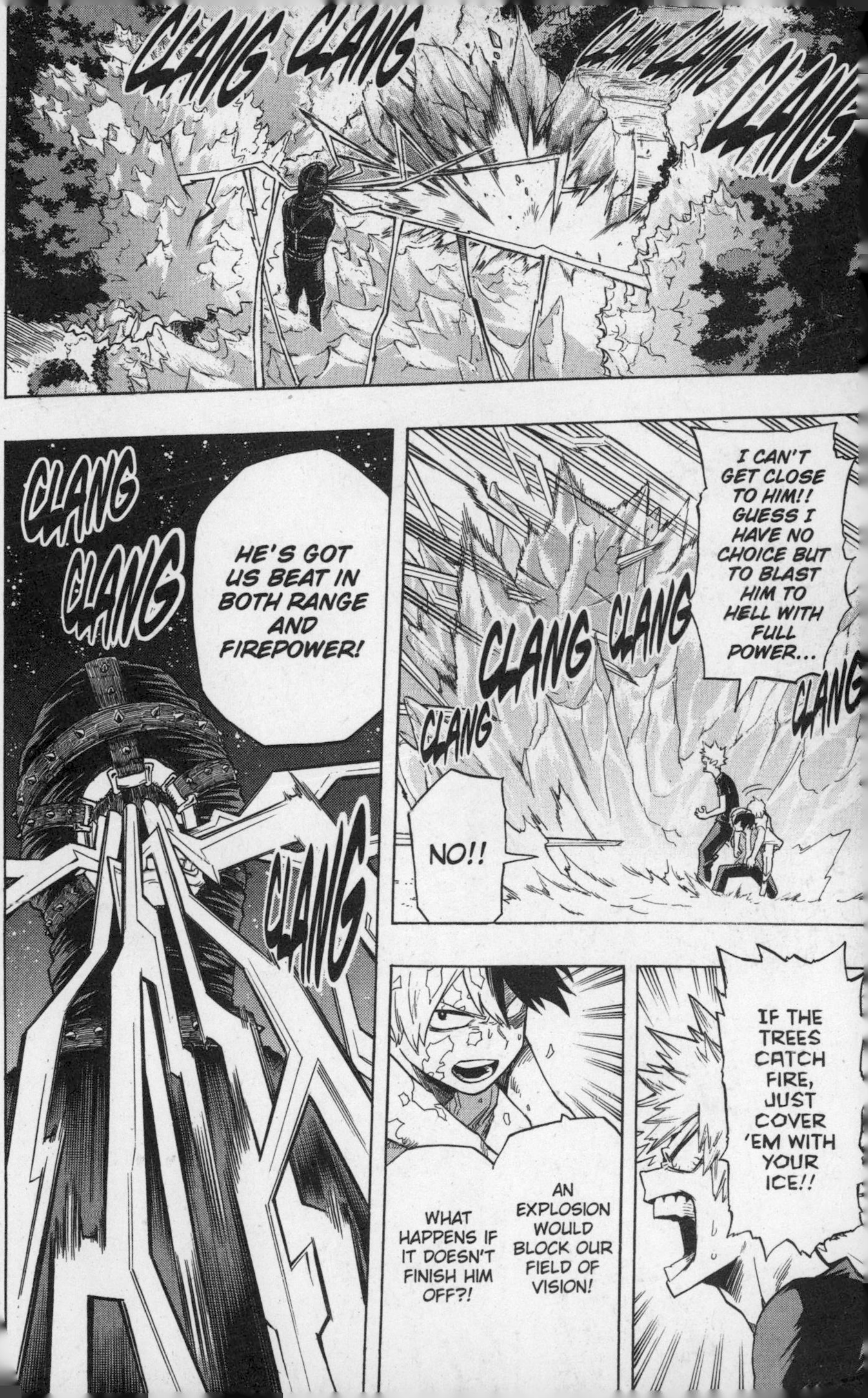
CLANG CLANG CLANG
CLANG CLANG
I CAN'T GET CLOSE TO HIM!! GUESS I HAVE NO CHOICE BUT TO BLAST HIM TO HELL WITH FULL POWER...
CLANG
CLANG CLANG
CLANG
NO!!
IF THE TREES CATCH FIRE, JUST COVER 'EM WITH YOUR ICE!!
AN EXPLOSION WOULD BLOCK OUR FIELD OF VISION!
WHAT HAPPENS IF IT DOESN'T FINISH HIM OFF?!
HE'S GOT US BEAT IN BOTH RANGE AND FIREPOWER!
CLANG CLANG
CLANG

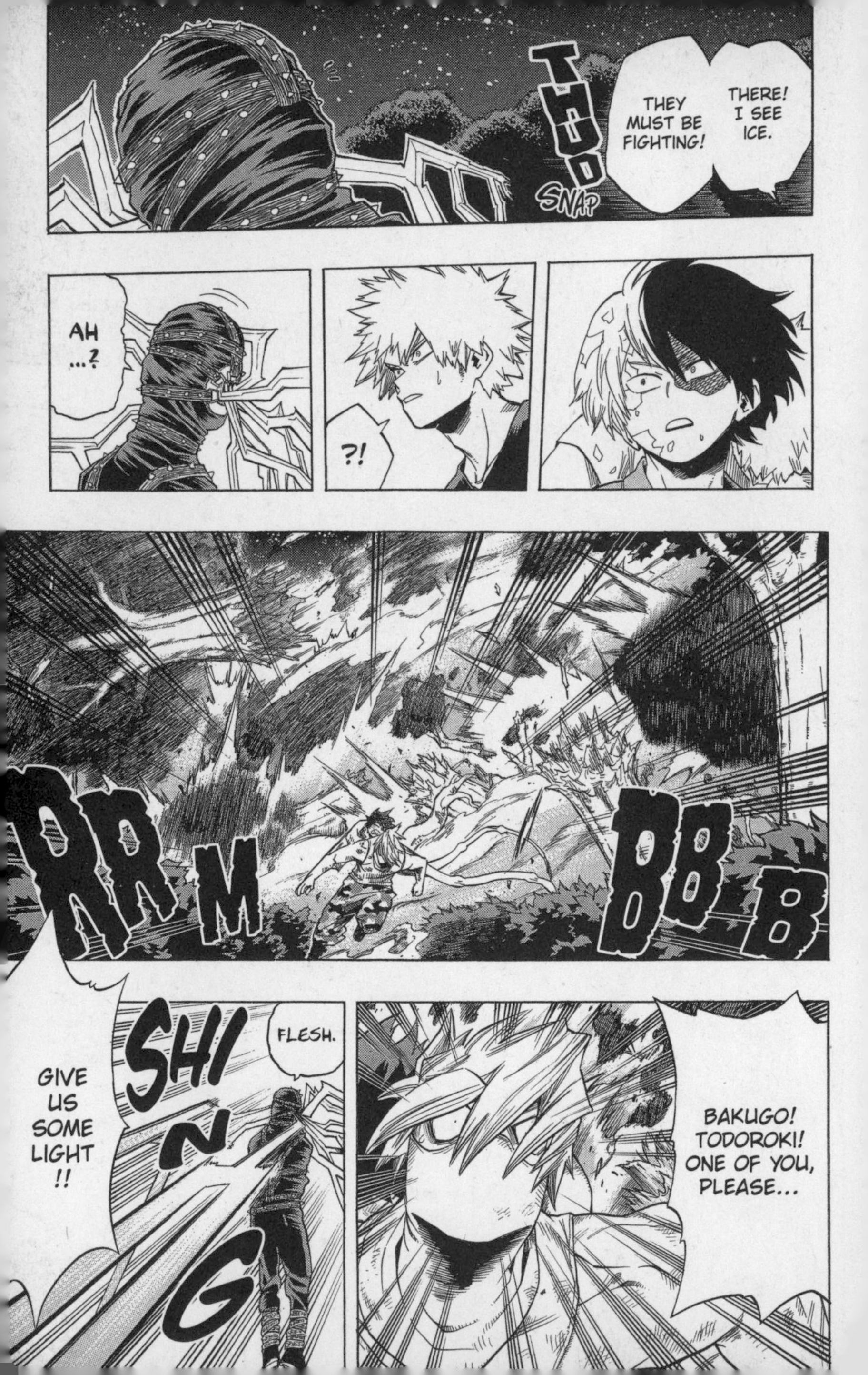
THERE! I SEE ICE.
THEY MUST BE FIGHTING!
THUD
SNAP
?!
AH ...?
BBB
RRRM
BAKUGO! TODOROKI! ONE OF YOU, PLEASE...
FLESH.
SHING
GIVE US SOME LIGHT!!

SLAM
GAH!

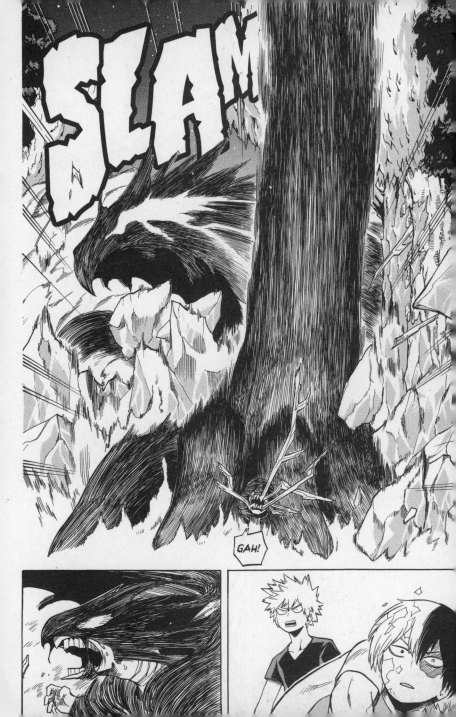

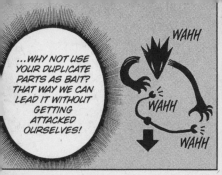

...WHY NOT USE YOUR DUPLICATE PARTS AS BAIT? THAT WAY WE CAN LEAD IT WITHOUT GETTING ATTACKED OURSELVES!

WAHH

WAHH

WAHH

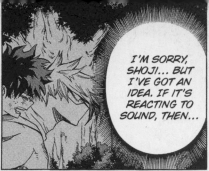

I'M SORRY, SHOJI... BUT I'VE GOT AN IDEA. IF IT'S REACTING TO SOUND, THEN...

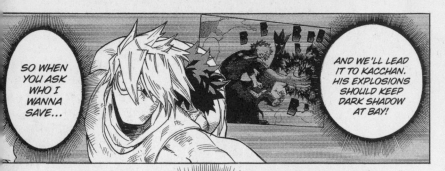

SO WHEN YOU ASK WHO I WANNA SAVE...

AND WE'LL LEAD IT TO KACCHAN. HIS EXPLOSIONS SHOULD KEEP DARK SHADOW AT BAY!

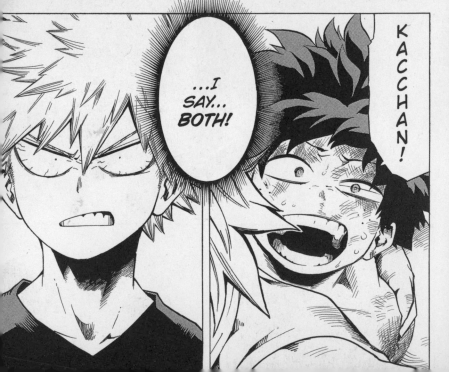

...I SAY... BOTH!

KACCHAN!

HORIKOSHI'S ASSISTANTS !!
FUJIYA-KUN
COOL.
SUPERVISING EDITOR: MONJI-SAN
BIG.
WILD, WILD...
NOGUCHI-KUN
COOL.
IKEDA-KUN
COOL.
FUSHIMI-KUN
COOL.
YOKOYAMA-SAN
STRONG.
YUZAWA-SAN
BIG.

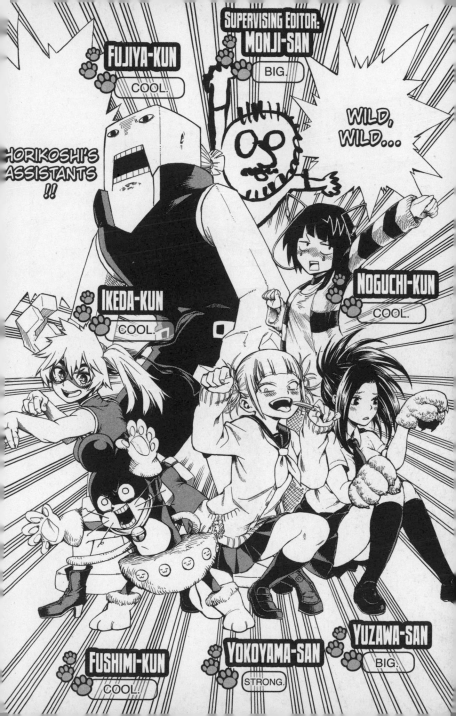

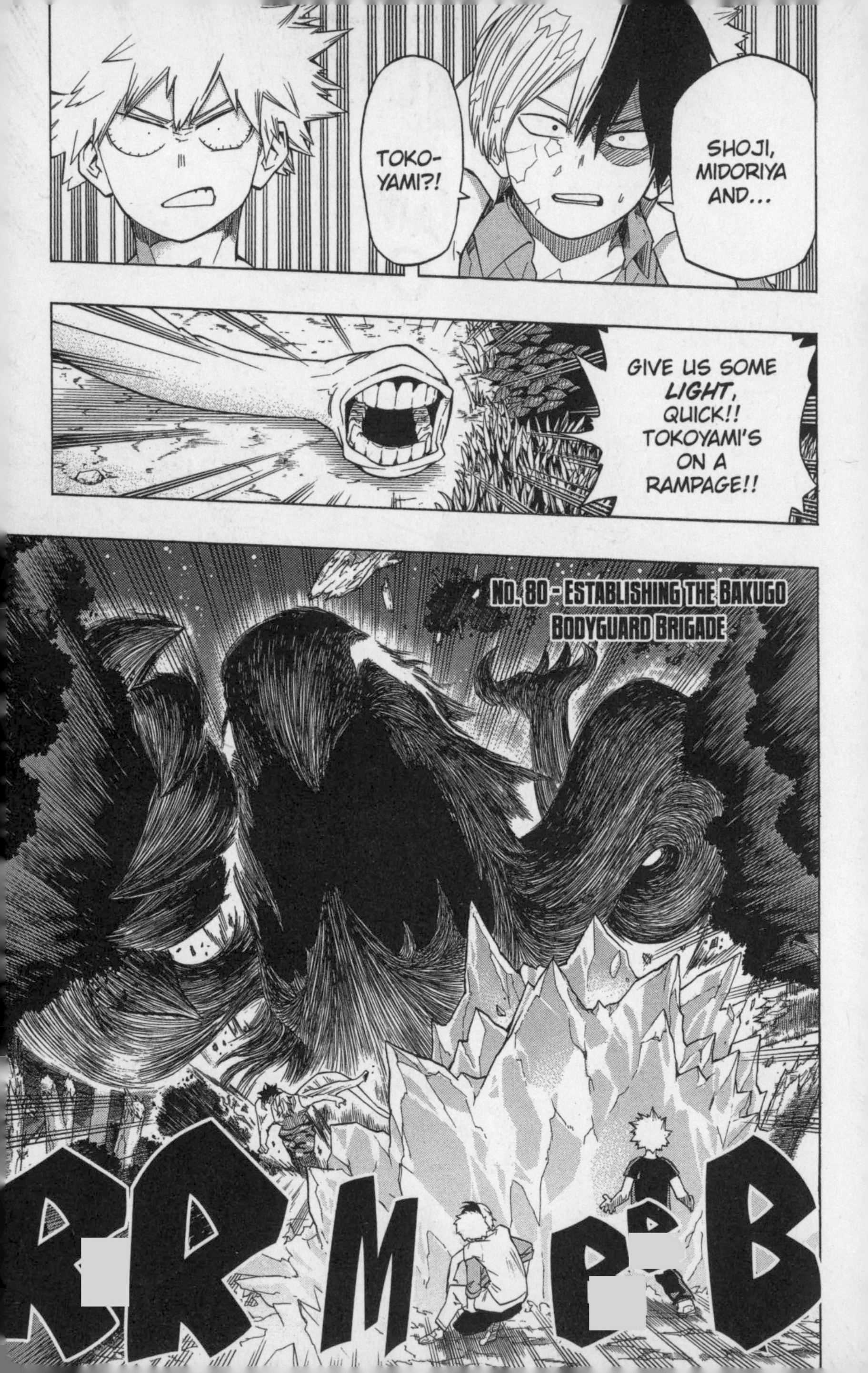
SHOJI, MIDORIYA AND...
TOKO-YAMI?!
GIVE US SOME LIGHT, QUICK!! TOKOYAMI'S ON A RAMPAGE!!
No. 80 - Establishing the Bakugo Bodyguard Brigade

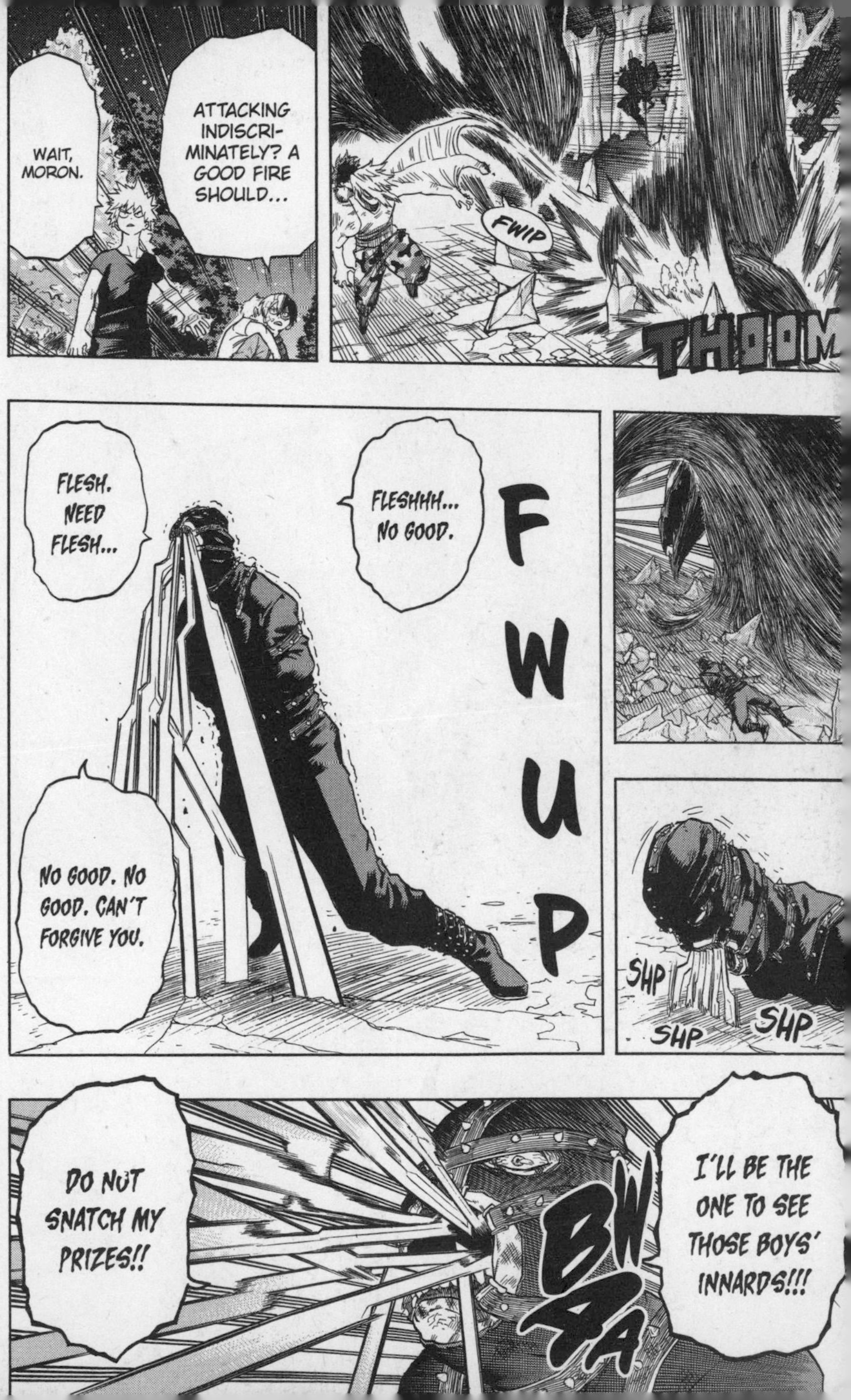
FWIP
THOOM
ATTACKING INDISCRIMINATELY? A GOOD FIRE SHOULD...
WAIT, MORON.
SHP
SHP
SHP
FWUP
FLESHHH... NO GOOD.
FLESH. NEED FLESH...
NO GOOD. NO GOOD. CAN'T FORGIVE YOU.
I'LL BE THE ONE TO SEE THOSE BOYS' INNARDS!!!
BWAA
DO NOT SNATCH MY PRIZES!!

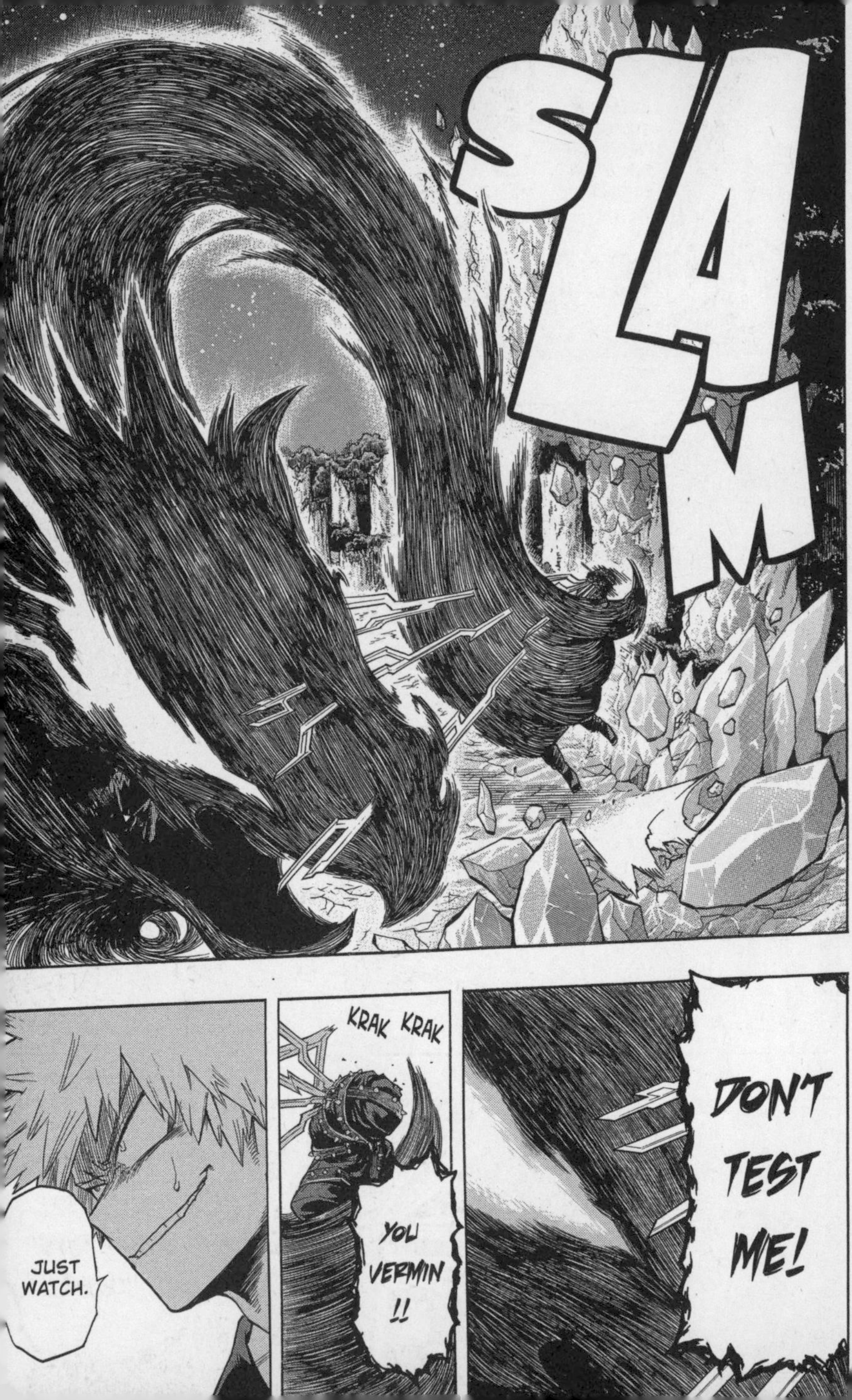
SLAM
DON'T TEST ME!
KRAK KRAK
YOU VERMIN !!
JUST WATCH.

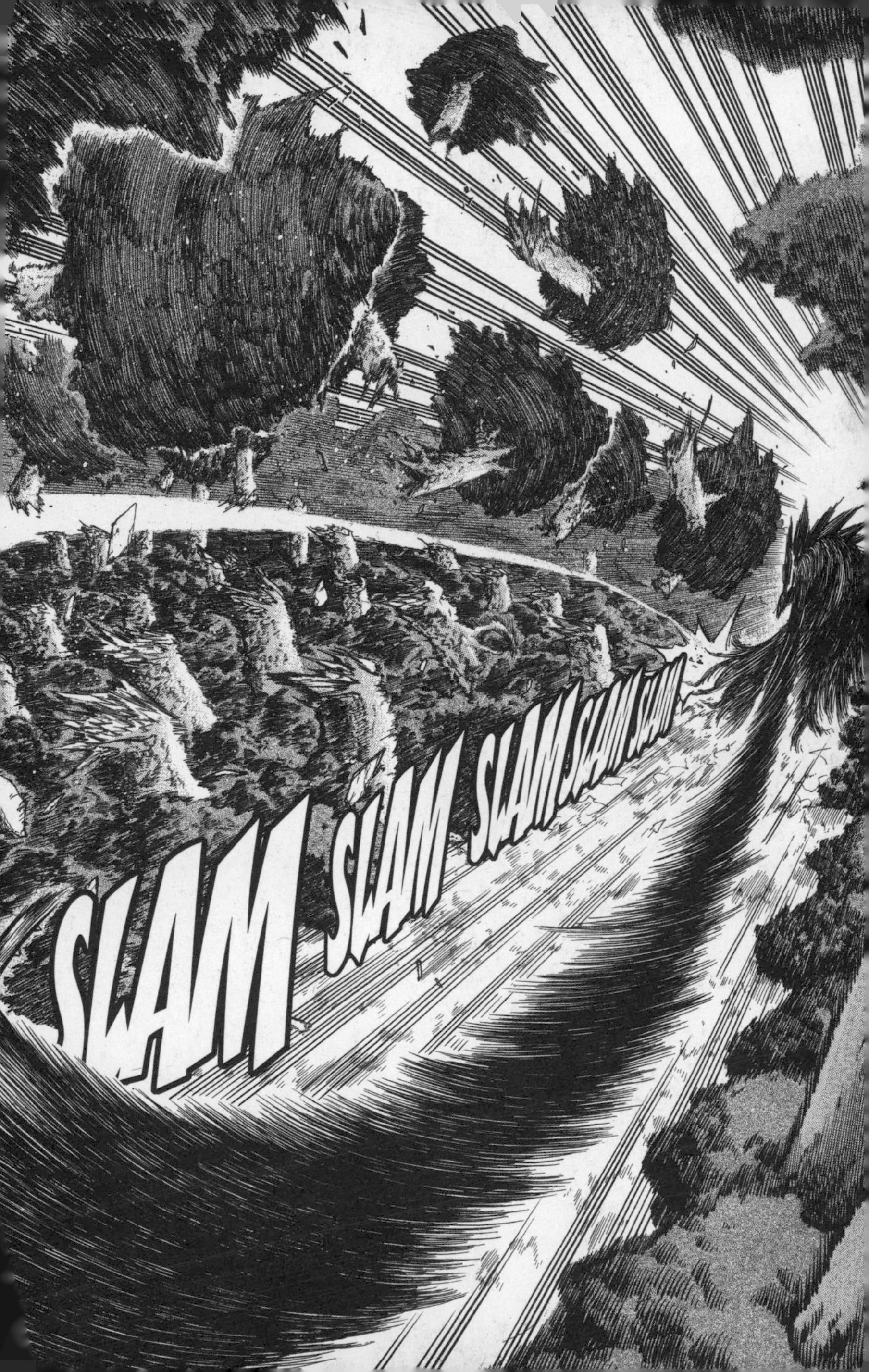
SLAM
SLAM
SLAMSLAMSLAM

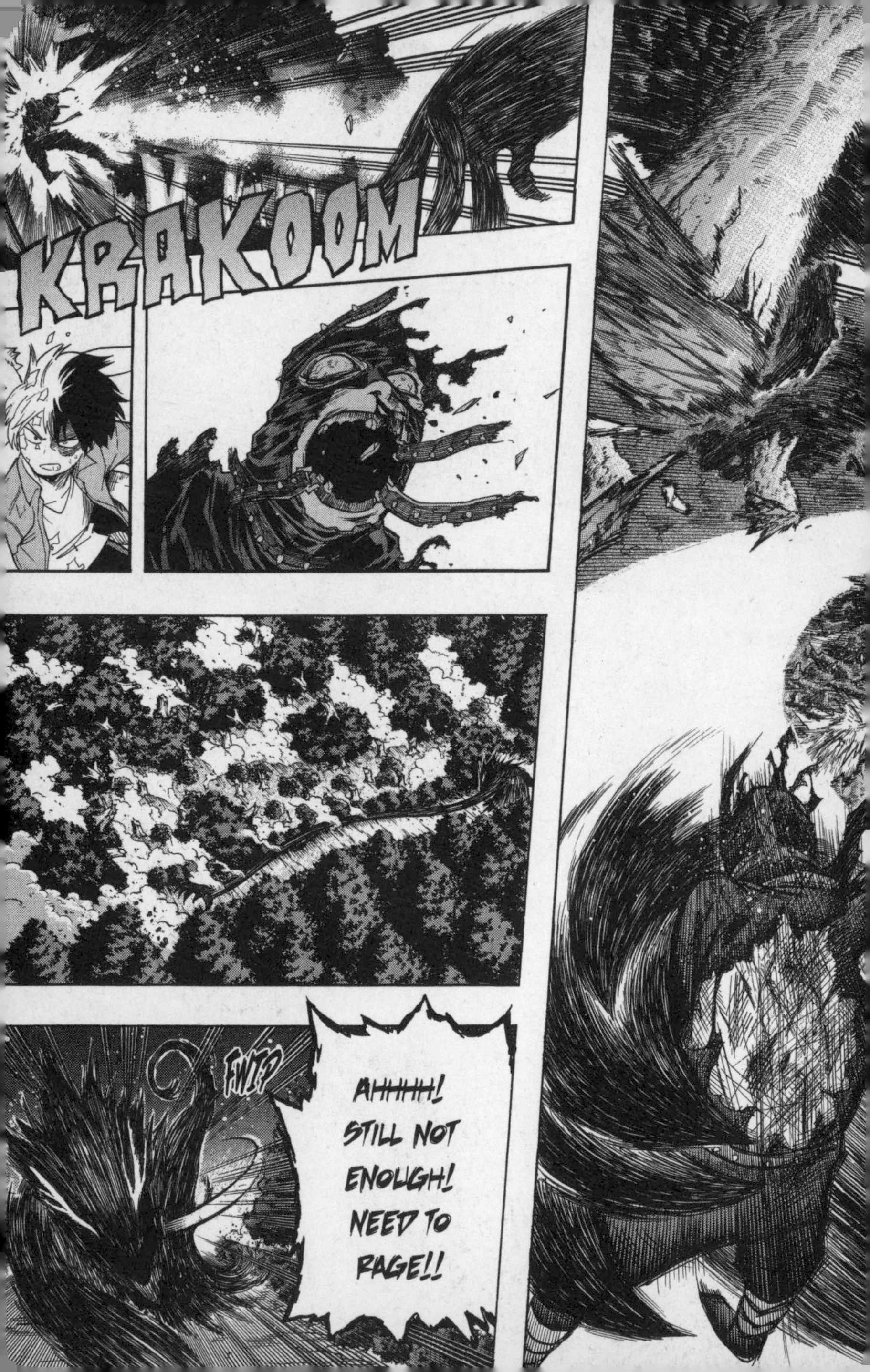
KRAKOOM
FWIP
AHHHH! STILL NOT ENOUGH! NEED TO RAGE!!

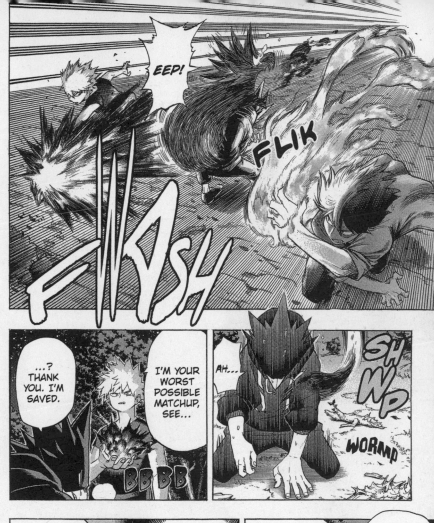

EEP!
FLIK
FWASH
SHWNP
WORMP
AH...
I'M YOUR WORST POSSIBLE MATCHUP, SEE...
BBBBB
...? THANK YOU. I'M SAVED.
WE WERE STRUGGLING JUST TO SURVIVE AGAINST THAT GUY, BUT IN AN INSTANT, YOU...
YOU OKAY, TOKOYAMI? GOOD JOB FOLLOWING MY INSTRUCTIONS.
TOKOYAMI!! DON'T STRUGGLE. JUST GIVE IN TO DARK SHADOW!
SHOJI... I'M SORRY... YOU TOO, MIDORIYA... MY SPIRIT IS STILL LACKING.

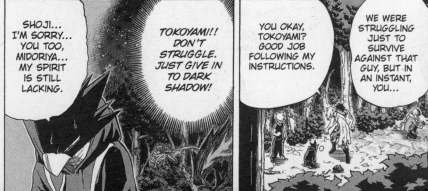

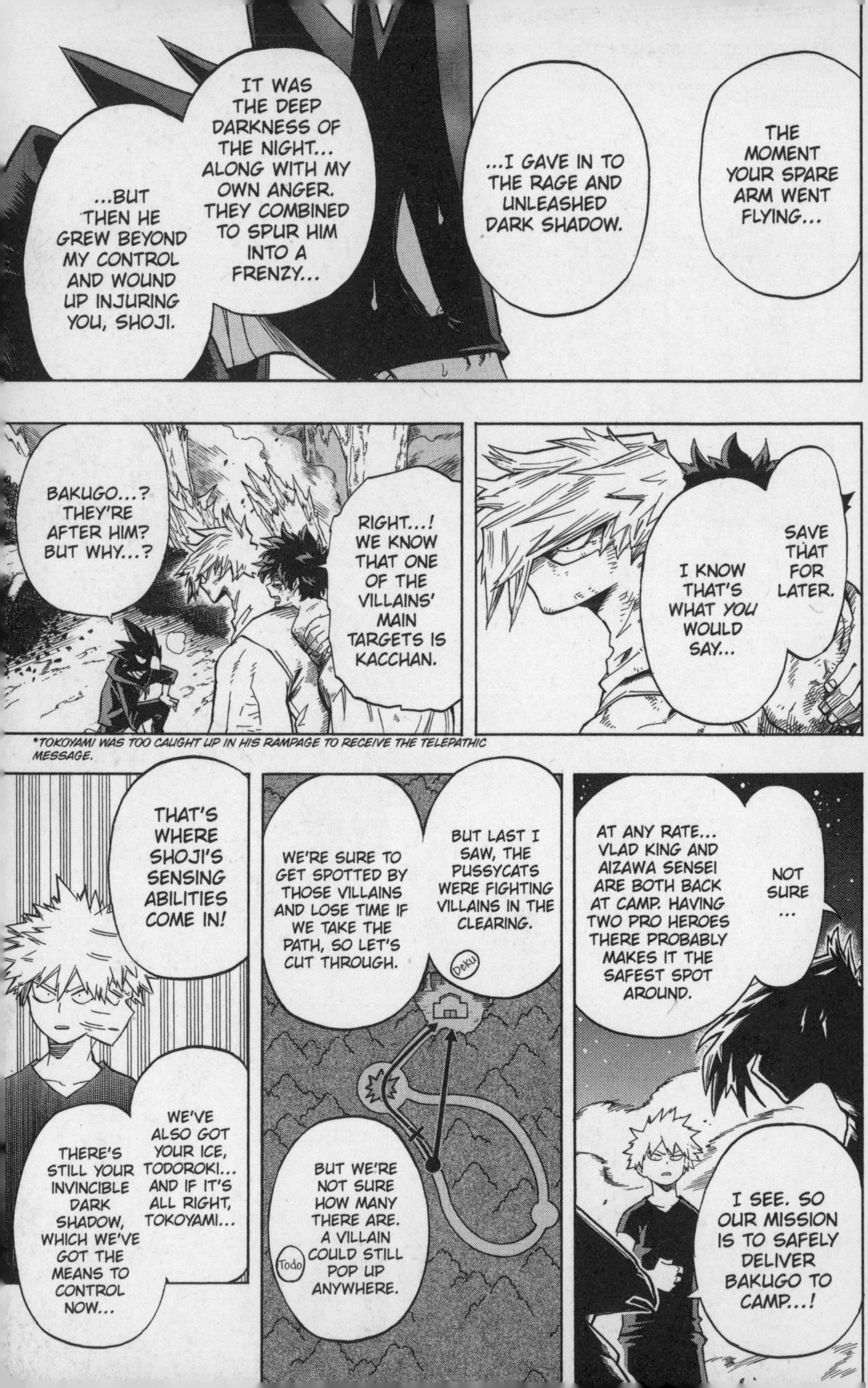
THE MOMENT YOUR SPARE ARM WENT FLYING...
...I GAVE IN TO THE RAGE AND UNLEASHED DARK SHADOW.
IT WAS THE DEEP DARKNESS OF THE NIGHT... ALONG WITH MY OWN ANGER. THEY COMBINED TO SPUR HIM INTO A FRENZY...
...BUT THEN HE GREW BEYOND MY CONTROL AND WOUND UP INJURING YOU, SHOJI.
SAVE THAT FOR LATER.
I KNOW THAT'S WHAT *YOU* WOULD SAY...
RIGHT...! WE KNOW THAT ONE OF THE VILLAINS' MAIN TARGETS IS KACCHAN.
BAKUGO...? THEY'RE AFTER HIM? BUT WHY...?
NOT SURE...
AT ANY RATE... VLAD KING AND AIZAWA SENSEI ARE BOTH BACK AT CAMP. HAVING TWO PRO HEROES THERE PROBABLY MAKES IT THE SAFEST SPOT AROUND.
I SEE. SO OUR MISSION IS TO SAFELY DELIVER BAKUGO TO CAMP...!
BUT LAST I SAW, THE PUSSYCATS WERE FIGHTING VILLAINS IN THE CLEARING.
WE'RE SURE TO GET SPOTTED BY THOSE VILLAINS AND LOSE TIME IF WE TAKE THE PATH, SO LET'S CUT THROUGH.
Deku
BUT WE'RE NOT SURE HOW MANY THERE ARE. A VILLAIN COULD STILL POP UP ANYWHERE.
Todo
THAT'S WHERE SHOJI'S SENSING ABILITIES COME IN!
WE'VE ALSO GOT YOUR ICE, TODOROKI... AND IF IT'S ALL RIGHT, TOKOYAMI...
THERE'S STILL YOUR INVINCIBLE DARK SHADOW, WHICH WE'VE GOT THE MEANS TO CONTROL NOW...

*TOKOYAMI WAS TOO CAUGHT UP IN HIS RAMPAGE TO RECEIVE THE TELEPATHIC MESSAGE.

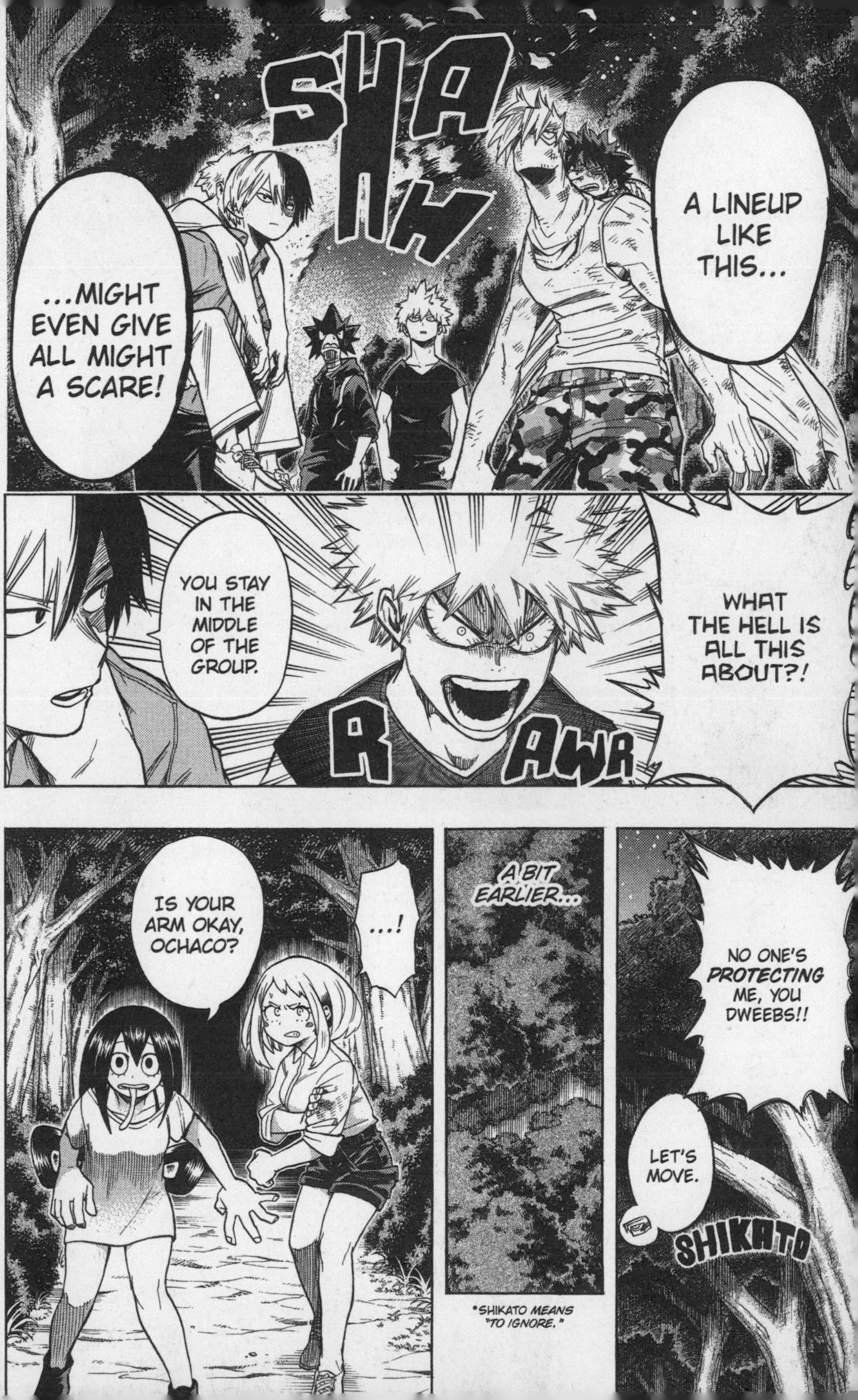
SHAAH
A LINEUP LIKE THIS...
...MIGHT EVEN GIVE ALL MIGHT A SCARE!
WHAT THE HELL IS ALL THIS ABOUT?!
RAWR
YOU STAY IN THE MIDDLE OF THE GROUP.
NO ONE'S *PROTECTING* ME, YOU DWEEBS!!
LET'S MOVE.
SHIKATO
A BIT EARLIER...
...!
IS YOUR ARM OKAY, OCHACO?
*SHIKATO *MEANS* "TO IGNORE."

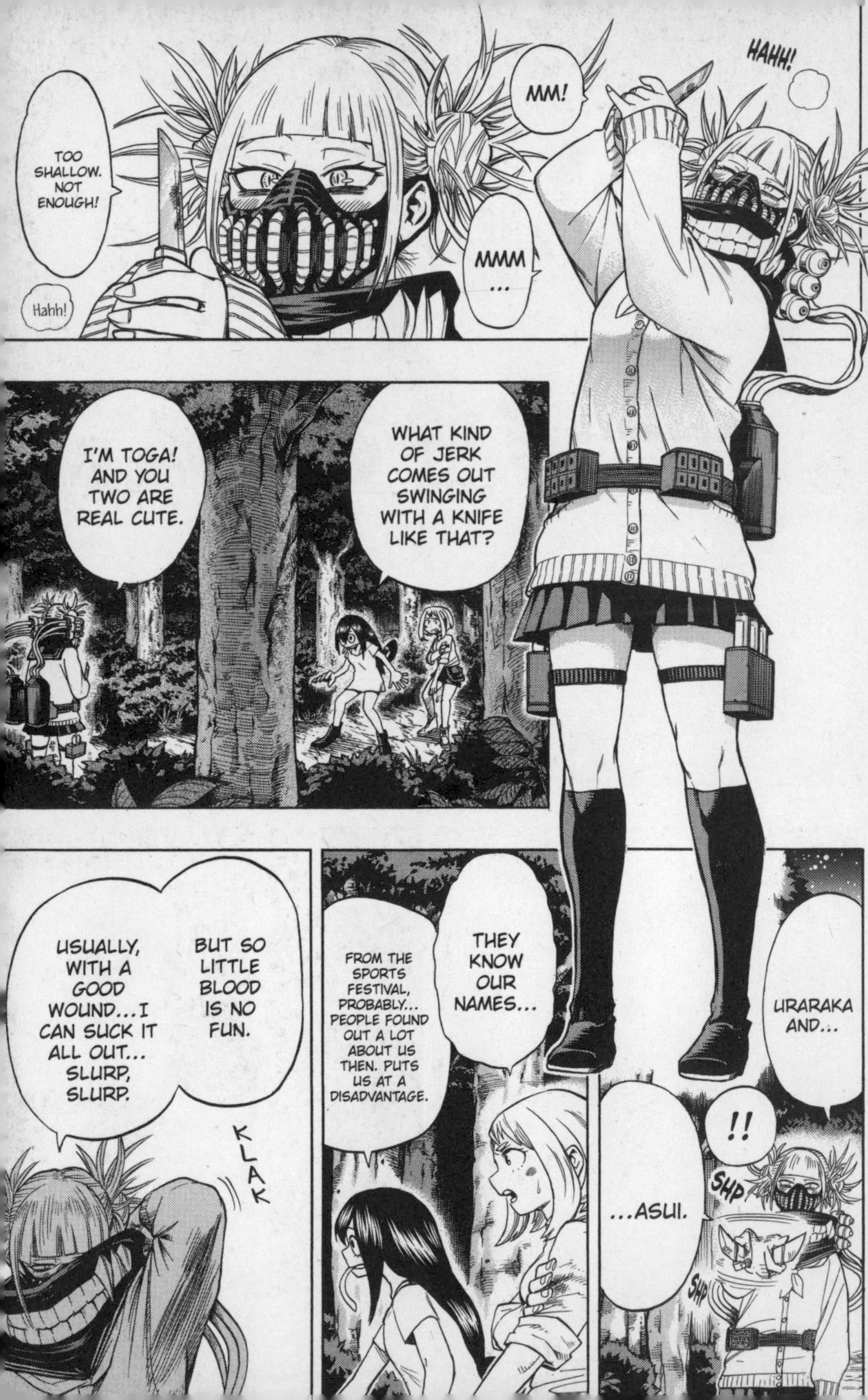
HAHH!
MM!
MMM ...
TOO SHALLOW. NOT ENOUGH!
Hahh!
WHAT KIND OF JERK COMES OUT SWINGING WITH A KNIFE LIKE THAT?
I'M TOGA! AND YOU TWO ARE REAL CUTE.
URARAKA AND...
!!
...ASUI.
SHP
SHP
THEY KNOW OUR NAMES...
FROM THE SPORTS FESTIVAL, PROBABLY... PEOPLE FOUND OUT A LOT ABOUT US THEN. PUTS US AT A DISADVANTAGE.
BUT SO LITTLE BLOOD IS NO FUN.
USUALLY, WITH A GOOD WOUND...I CAN SUCK IT ALL OUT... SLURP, SLURP.
KLAK

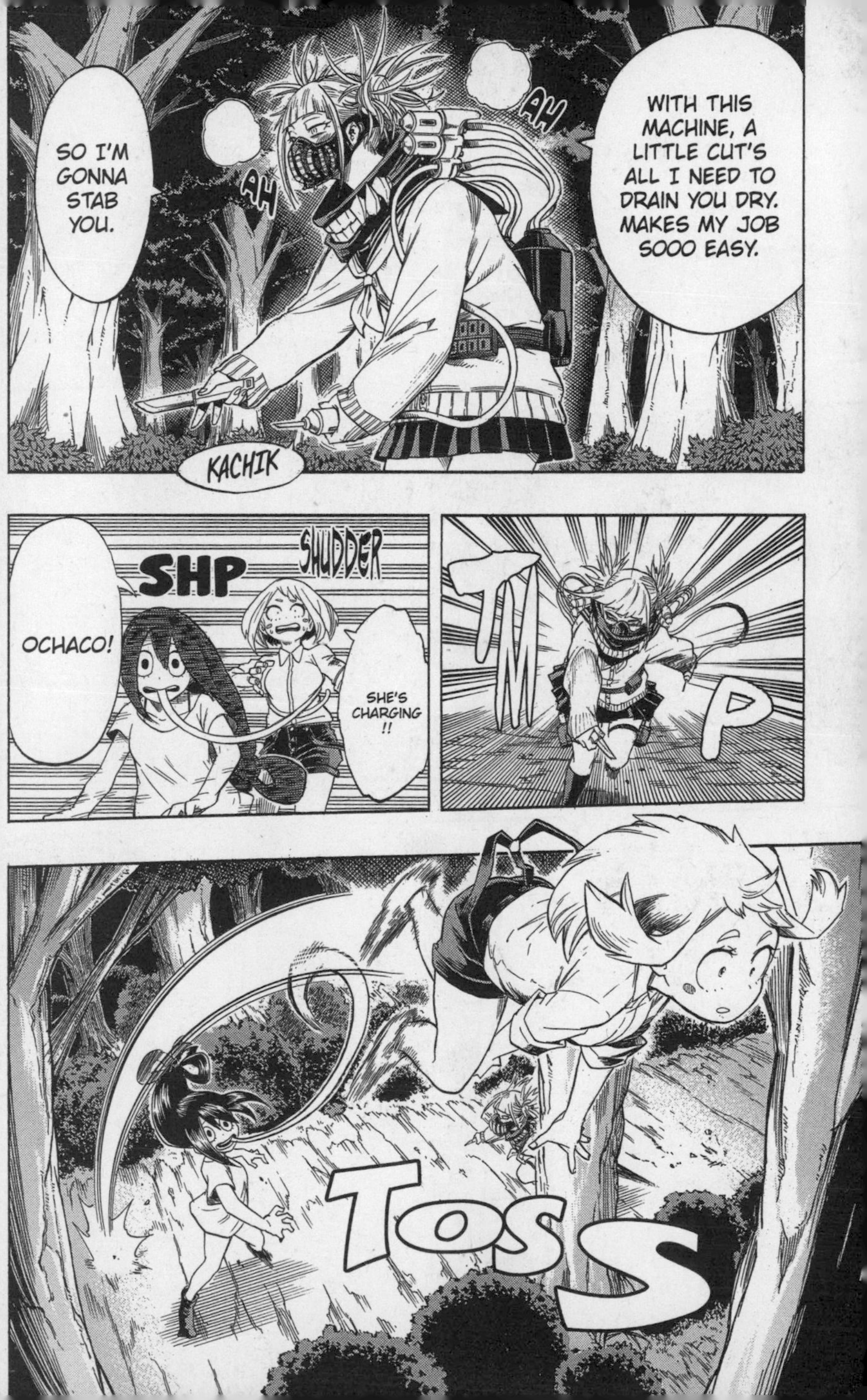
WITH THIS MACHINE, A LITTLE CUT'S ALL I NEED TO DRAIN YOU DRY. MAKES MY JOB SOOO EASY.
AH
AH
SO I'M GONNA STAB YOU.
KACHIK
TMP
SHUDDER
SHE'S CHARGING !!
SHP
OCHACO!
TOSS

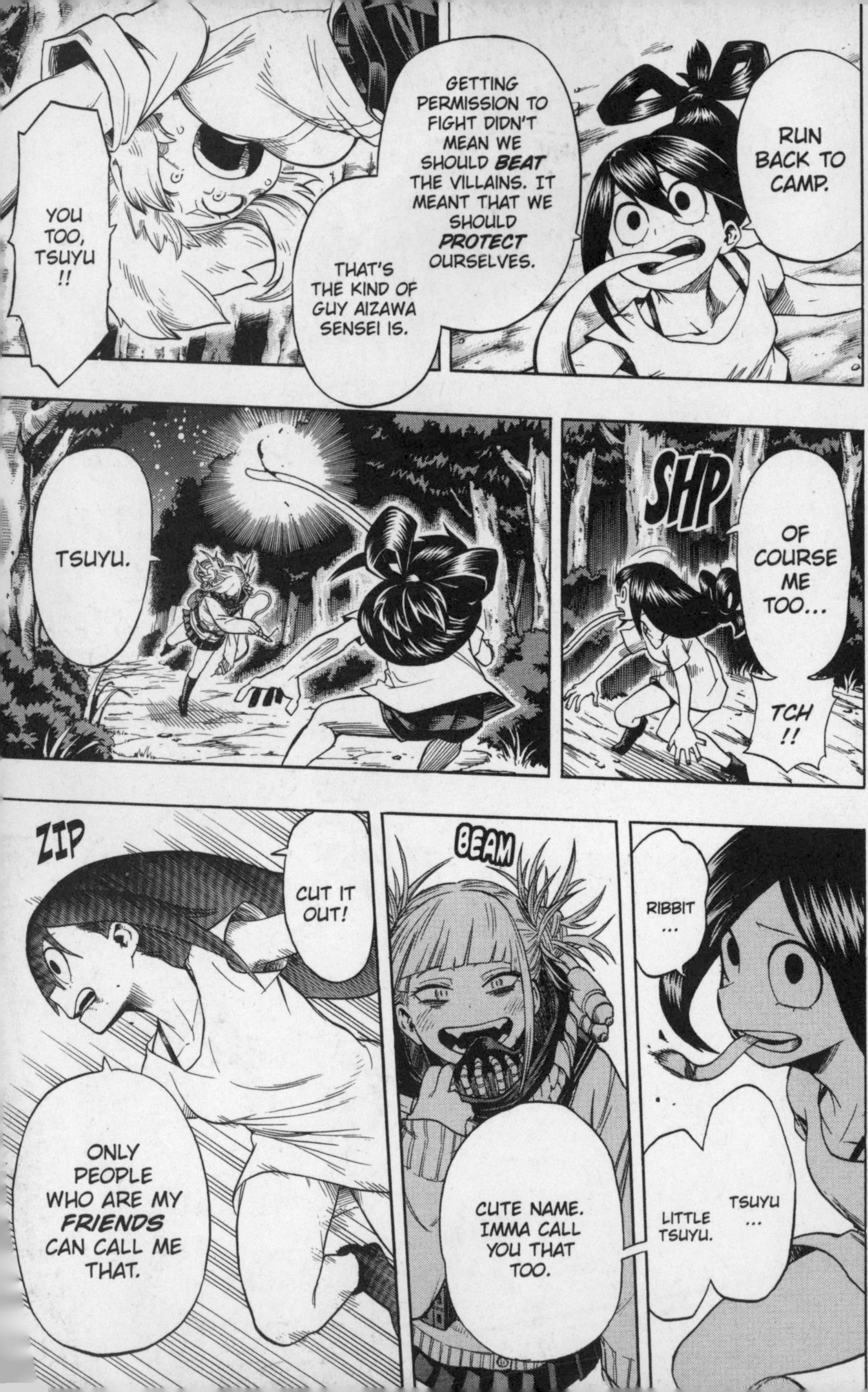
RUN BACK TO CAMP.
GETTING PERMISSION TO FIGHT DIDN'T MEAN WE SHOULD BEAT THE VILLAINS. IT MEANT THAT WE SHOULD PROTECT OURSELVES.
THAT'S THE KIND OF GUY AIZAWA SENSEI IS.
YOU TOO, TSUYU !!
SHP
OF COURSE ME TOO...
TCH !!
TSUYU.
RIBBIT ...
TSUYU ...
LITTLE TSUYU.
BEAM
CUTE NAME. IMMA CALL YOU THAT TOO.
ZIP
CUT IT OUT!
ONLY PEOPLE WHO ARE MY FRIENDS CAN CALL ME THAT.

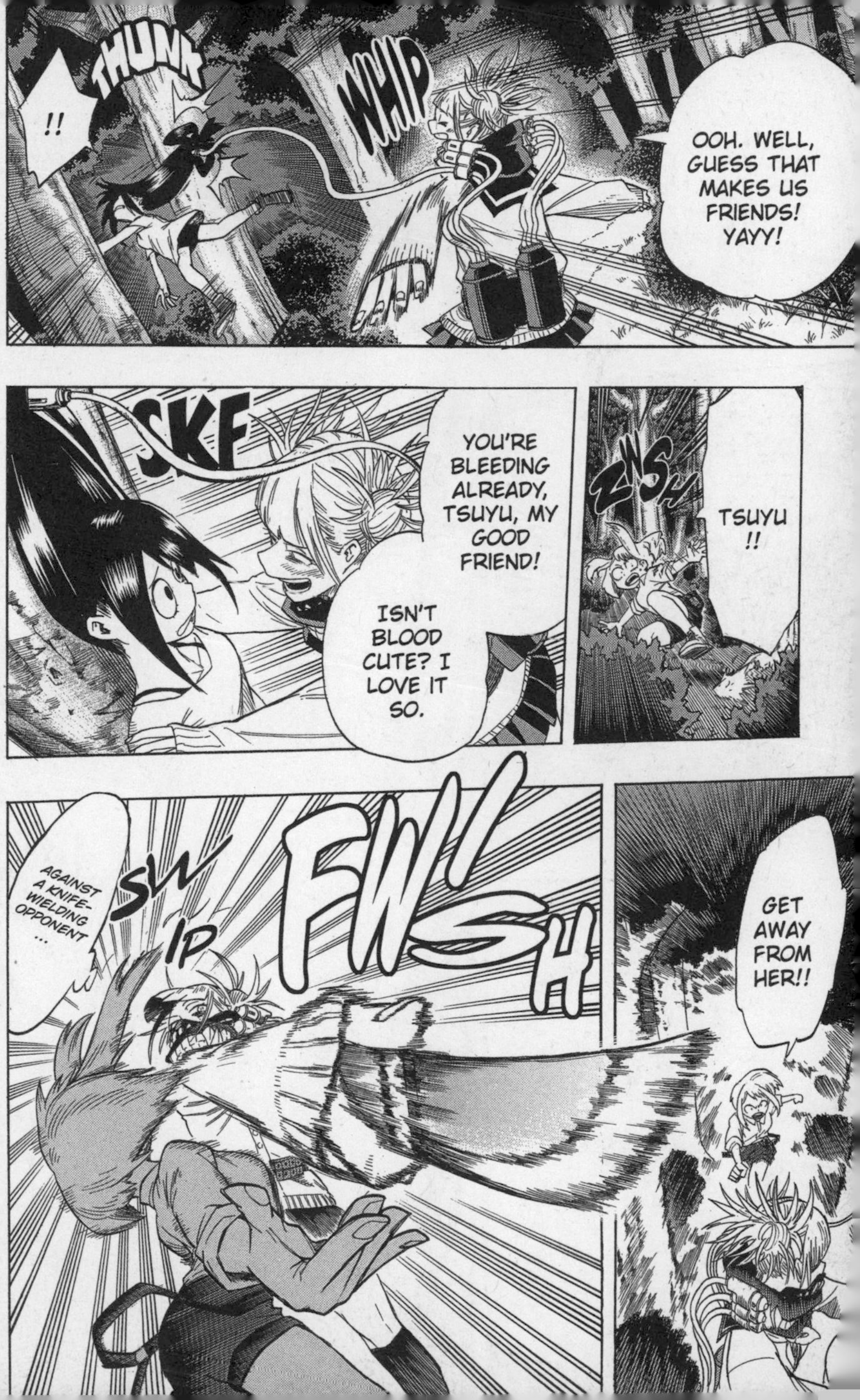
OOH. WELL, GUESS THAT MAKES US FRIENDS! YAYY!
WHIP
THUNK
!!
ZNSH
TSUYU !!
SKF
YOU'RE BLEEDING ALREADY, TSUYU, MY GOOD FRIEND!
ISN'T BLOOD CUTE? I LOVE IT SO.
GET AWAY FROM HER!!
FWSH
SWIP
AGAINST A KNIFE-WIELDING OPPONENT...

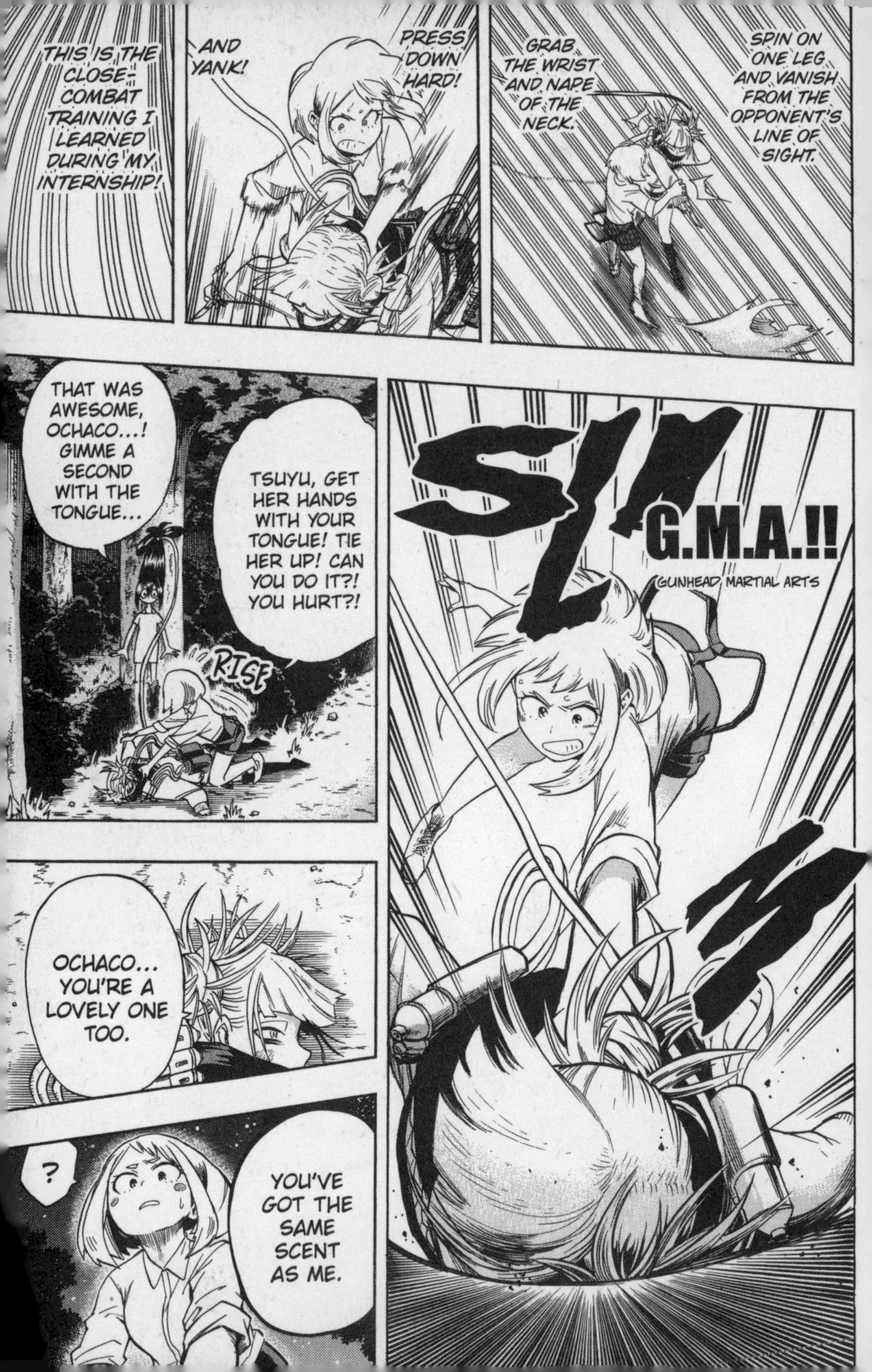
SPIN ON ONE LEG AND VANISH FROM THE OPPONENT'S LINE OF SIGHT.
GRAB THE WRIST AND NAPE OF THE NECK.
PRESS DOWN HARD!
AND YANK!
THIS IS THE CLOSE-COMBAT TRAINING I LEARNED DURING MY INTERNSHIP!
SL
G.M.A.!!
GUNHEAD MARTIAL ARTS
M
TSUYU, GET HER HANDS WITH YOUR TONGUE! TIE HER UP! CAN YOU DO IT?! YOU HURT?!
RISE
THAT WAS AWESOME, OCHACO...! GIMME A SECOND WITH THE TONGUE...
OCHACO... YOU'RE A LOVELY ONE TOO.
YOU'VE GOT THE SAME SCENT AS ME.
?

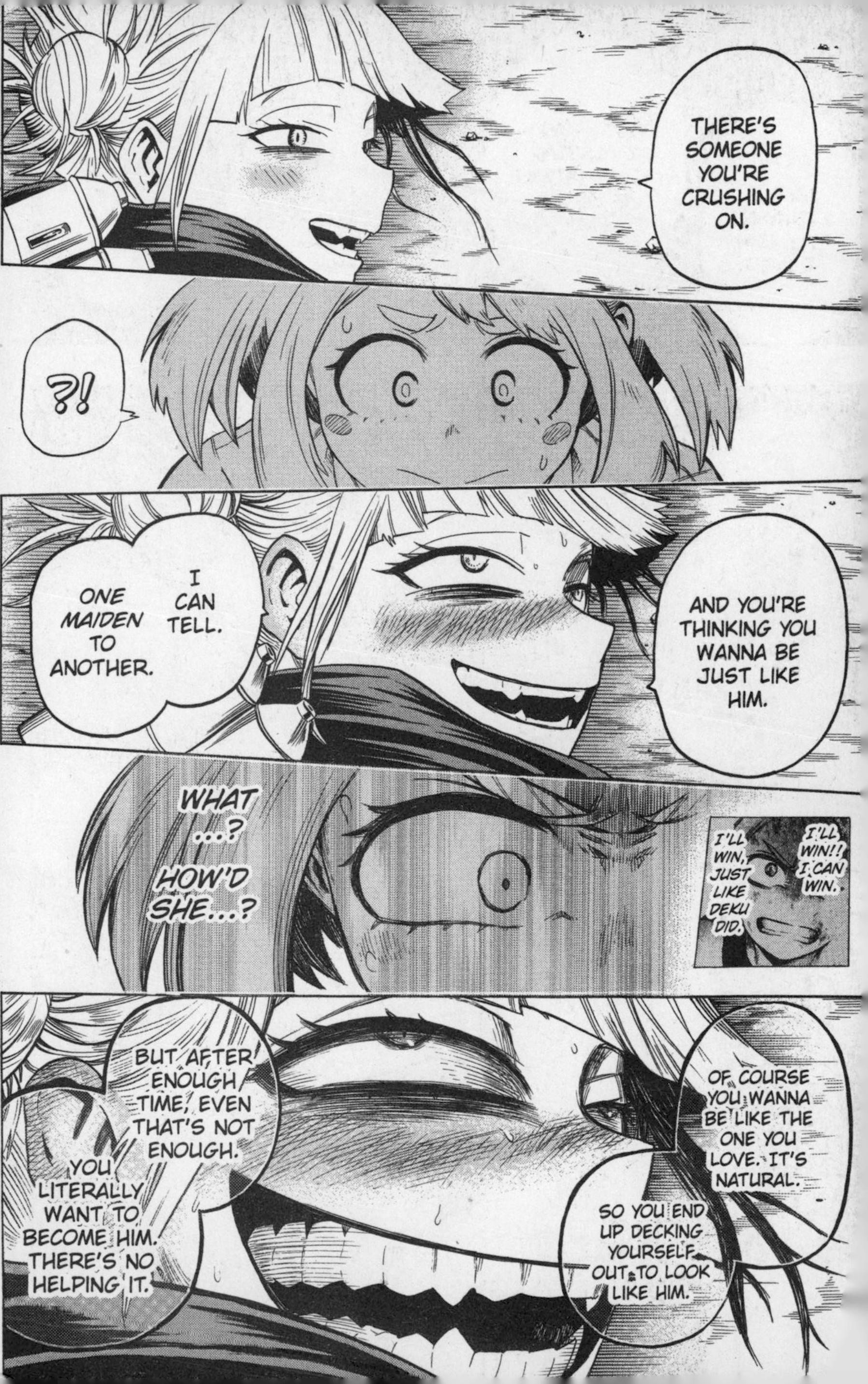
THERE'S SOMEONE YOU'RE CRUSHING ON.
?!
AND YOU'RE THINKING YOU WANNA BE JUST LIKE HIM.
I CAN TELL.
ONE MAIDEN TO ANOTHER.
I'LL WIN!! I CAN WIN.
I'LL WIN, JUST LIKE DEKU DID.
WHAT ...? HOW'D SHE...?
OF COURSE YOU WANNA BE LIKE THE ONE YOU LOVE. IT'S NATURAL.
SO YOU END UP DECKING YOURSELF OUT TO LOOK LIKE HIM.
BUT AFTER ENOUGH TIME, EVEN THAT'S NOT ENOUGH.
YOU LITERALLY WANT TO BECOME HIM. THERE'S NO HELPING IT.

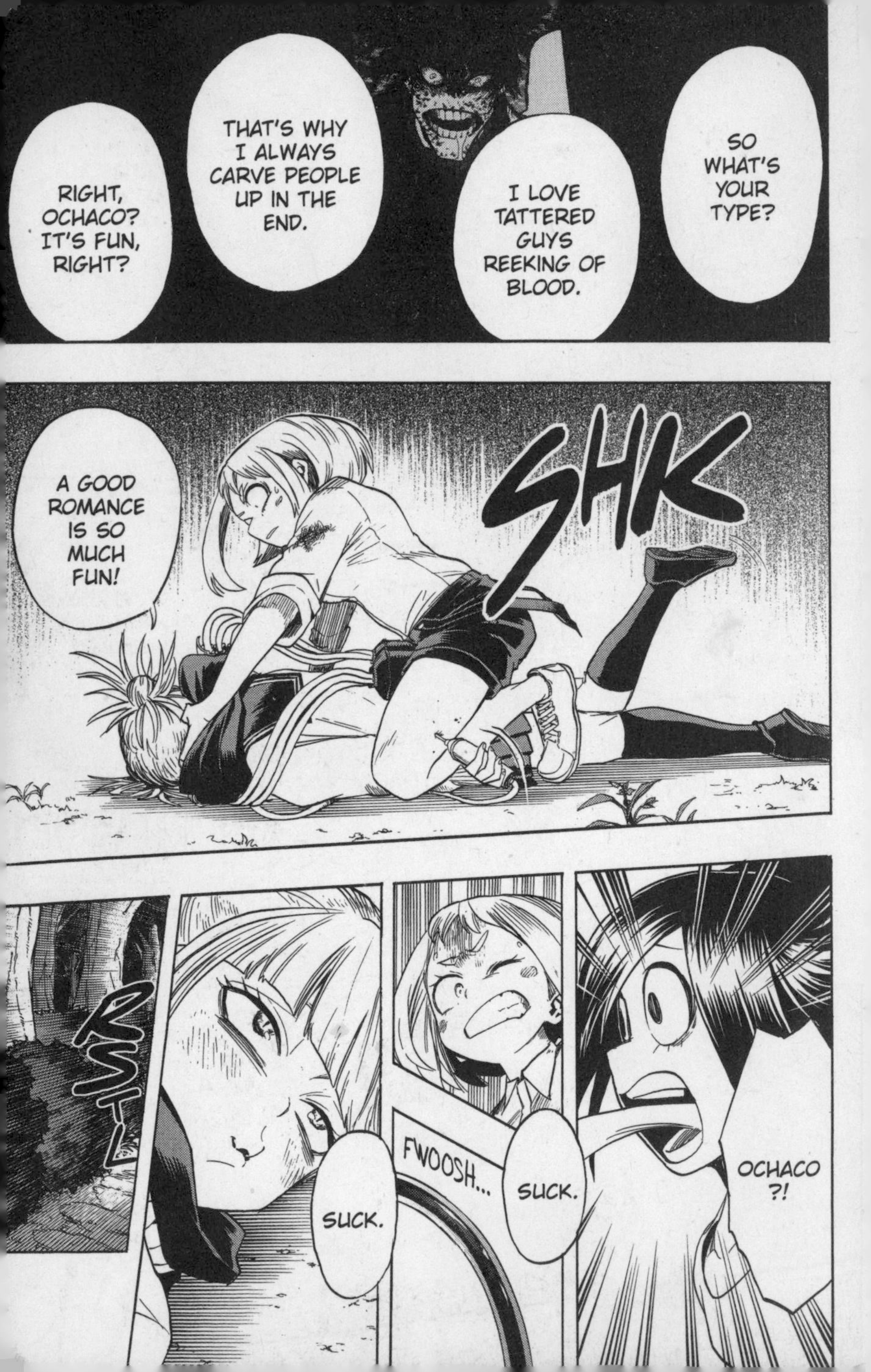
SO WHAT'S YOUR TYPE?
I LOVE TATTERED GUYS REEKING OF BLOOD.
THAT'S WHY I ALWAYS CARVE PEOPLE UP IN THE END.
RIGHT, OCHACO? IT'S FUN, RIGHT?
SHK
A GOOD ROMANCE IS SO MUCH FUN!
OCHACO ?!
SUCK.
FWOOSH...
SUCK.
RSTL

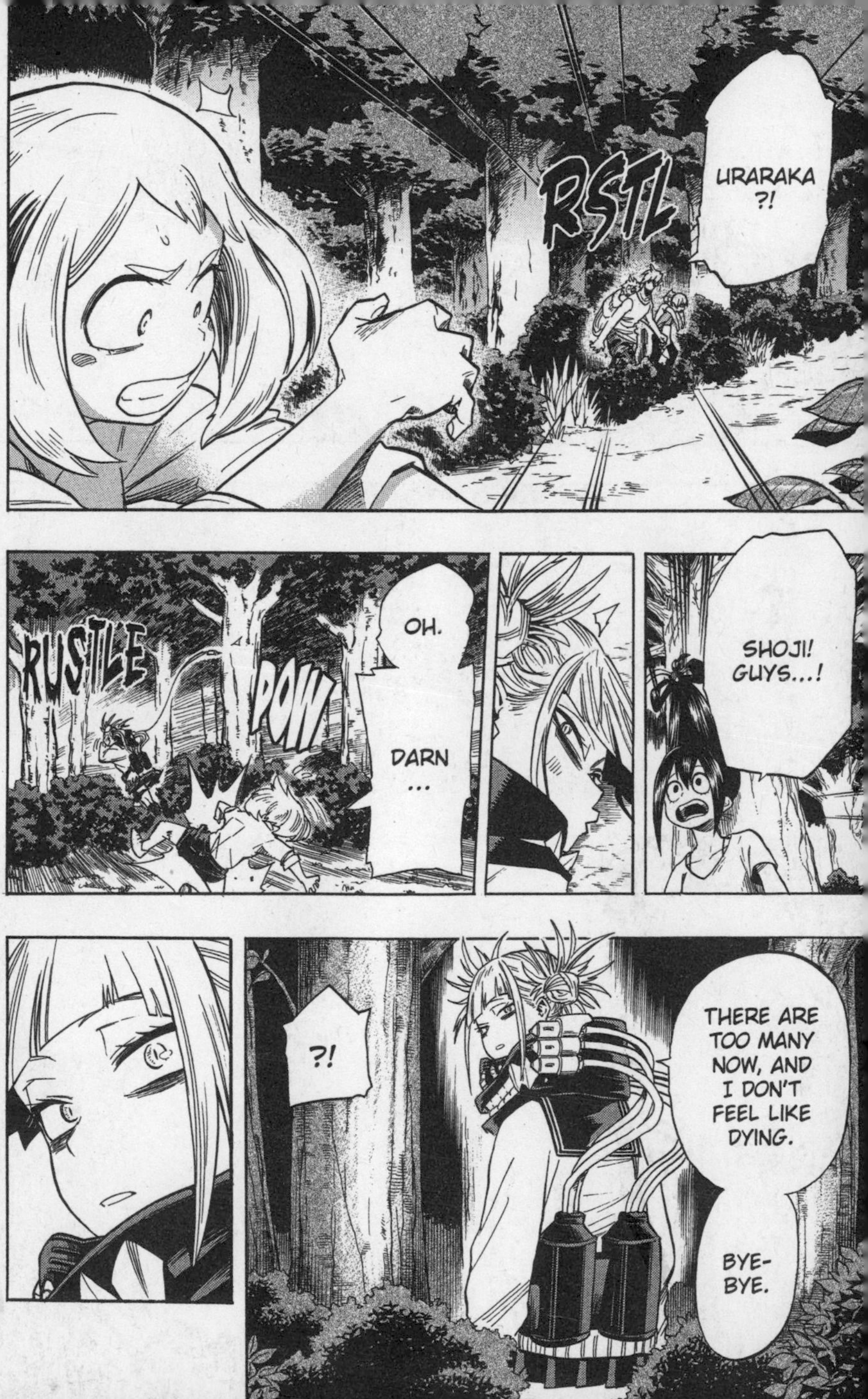
RSTL
URARAKA ?!
SHOJI! GUYS...!
OH.
RUSTLE
POW
DARN ...
THERE ARE TOO MANY NOW, AND I DON'T FEEL LIKE DYING.
BYE-BYE.
?!

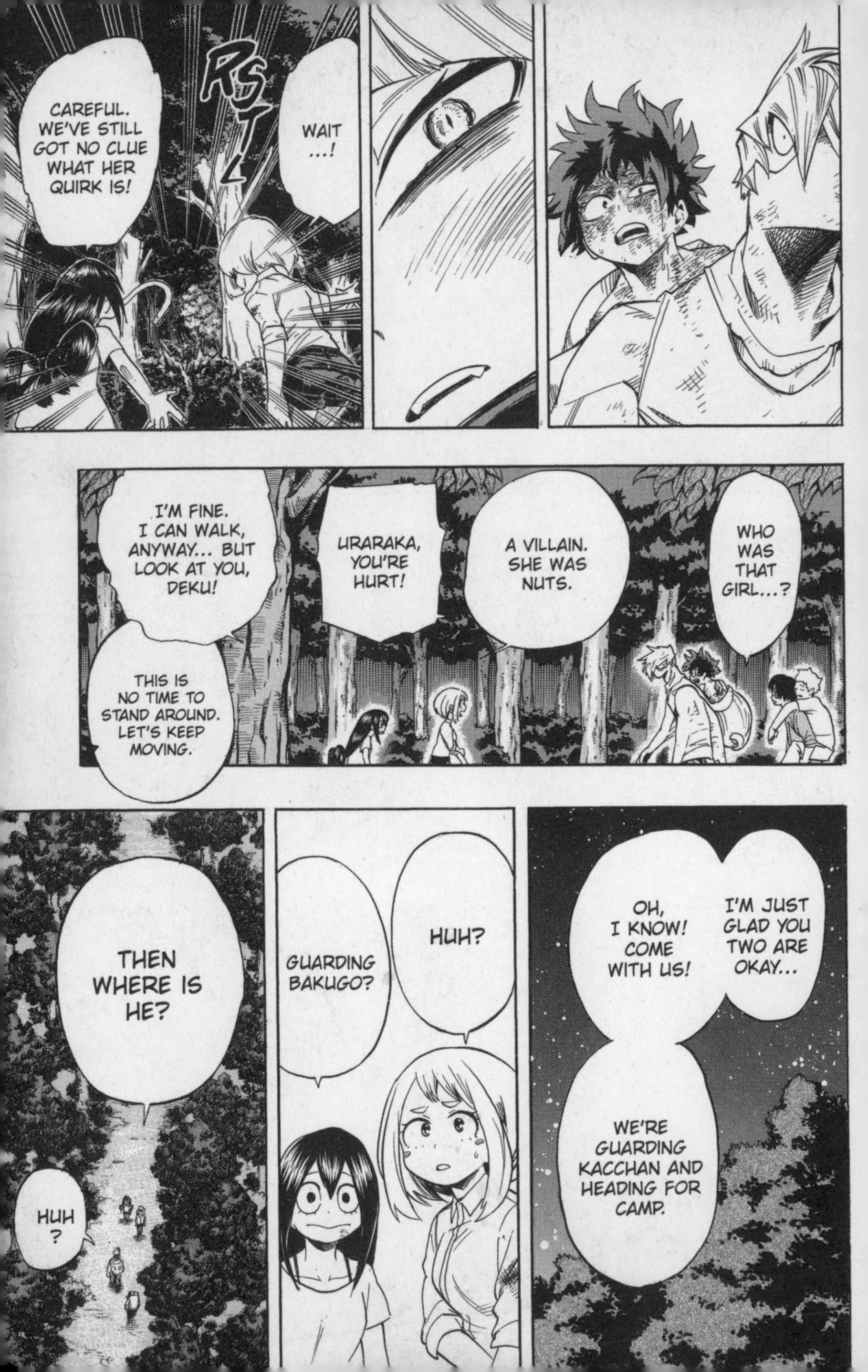
WAIT ...!
RSTL
CAREFUL. WE'VE STILL GOT NO CLUE WHAT HER QUIRK IS!
WHO WAS THAT GIRL...?
A VILLAIN. SHE WAS NUTS.
URARAKA, YOU'RE HURT!
I'M FINE. I CAN WALK, ANYWAY... BUT LOOK AT YOU, DEKU!
THIS IS NO TIME TO STAND AROUND. LET'S KEEP MOVING.
I'M JUST GLAD YOU TWO ARE OKAY...
OH, I KNOW! COME WITH US!
WE'RE GUARDING KACCHAN AND HEADING FOR CAMP.
HUH?
GUARDING BAKUGO?
THEN WHERE IS HE?
HUH ?

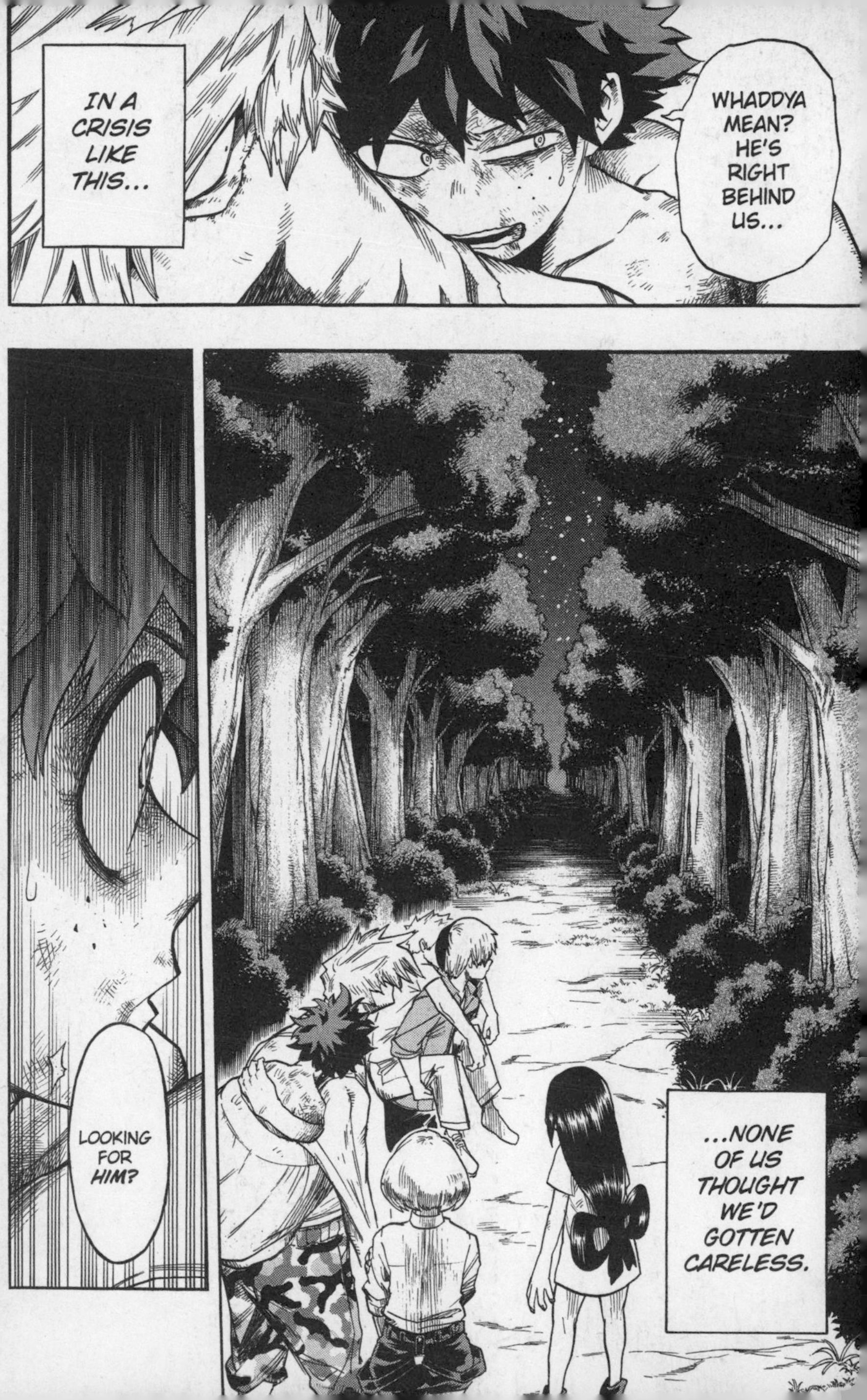
WHADDYA MEAN? HE'S RIGHT BEHIND US...
IN A CRISIS LIKE THIS...
...NONE OF US THOUGHT WE'D GOTTEN CARELESS.
LOOKING FOR HIM?

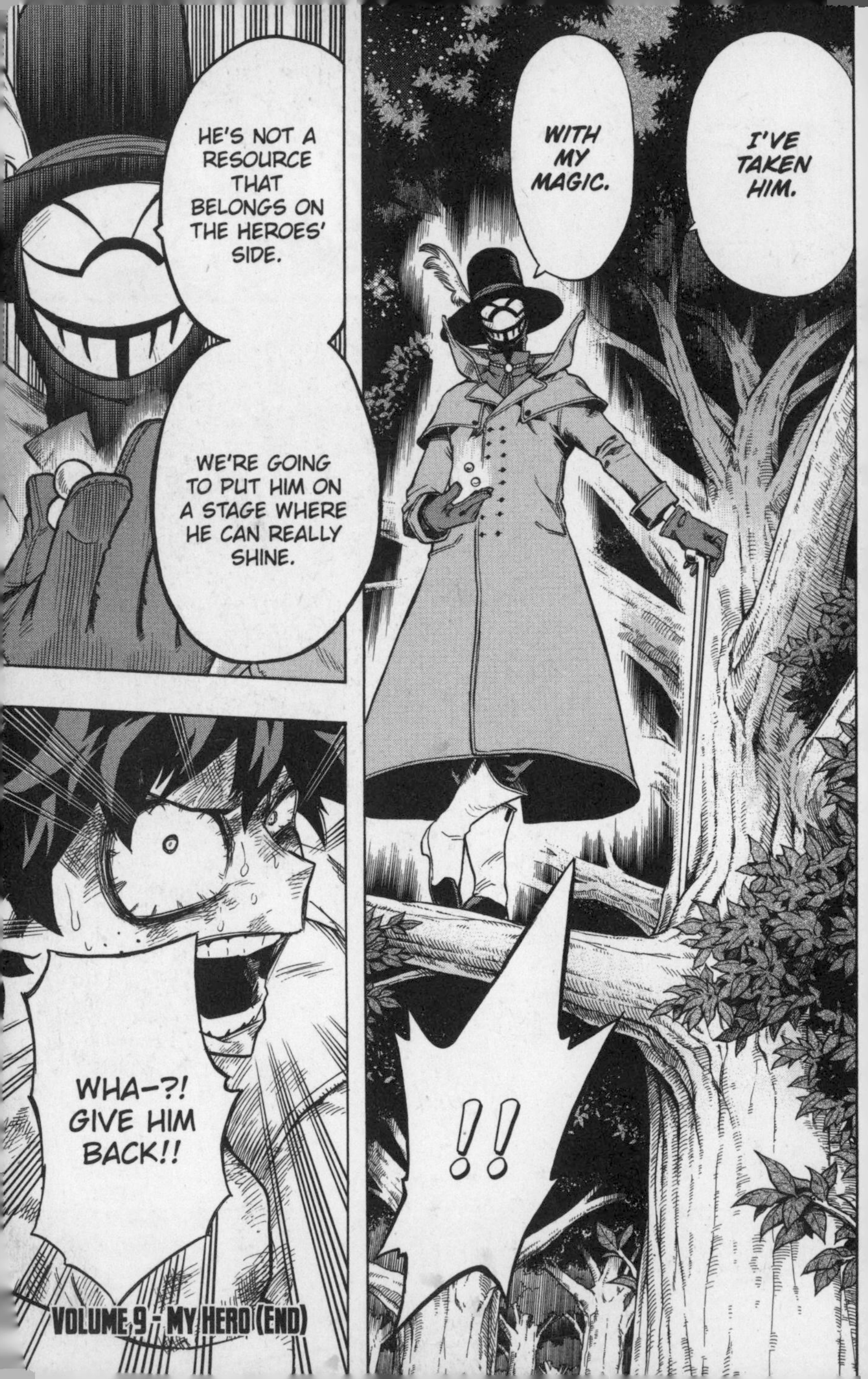
I'VE TAKEN HIM.
WITH MY MAGIC.
!!
HE'S NOT A RESOURCE THAT BELONGS ON THE HEROES' SIDE.
WE'RE GOING TO PUT HIM ON A STAGE WHERE HE CAN REALLY SHINE.
WHA-?! GIVE HIM BACK!!
VOLUME 9 - MY HERO (END)

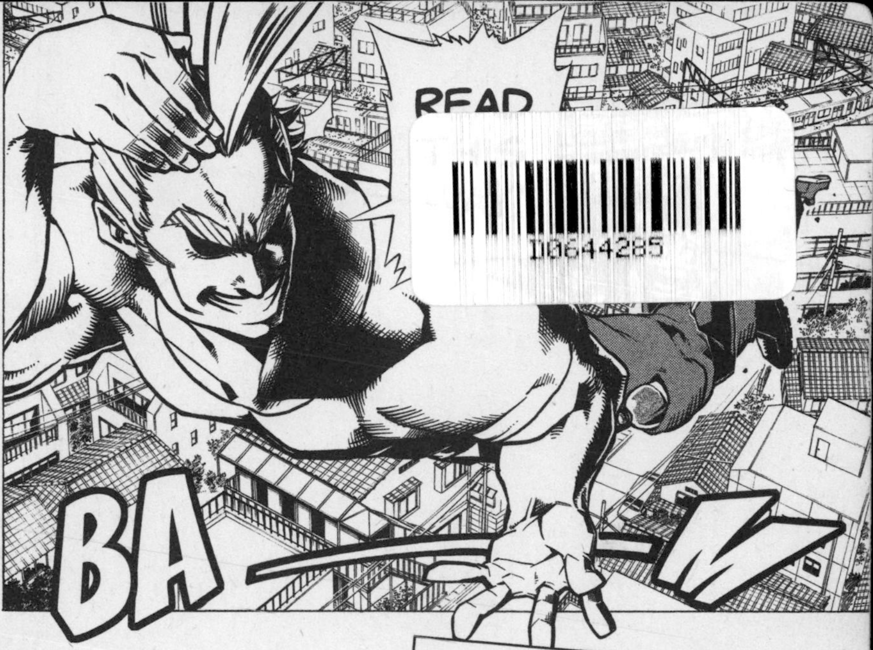
READ
BA—M

MY HERO ACADEMIA

reads from right to left, starting in the upper-right corner. Japanese is read from right to left, meaning that action, sound effects and word-balloon order are completely reversed from English order.

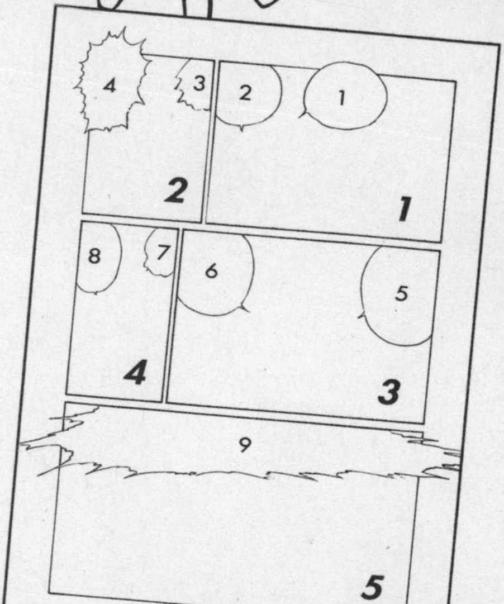
1
2
3
4
5
6
7
8
9
142